Introduction to Discourse Studies

Introduction to
Discourse Studies

Jan Renkema

University of Tilburg

John Benjamins Publishing Company

Amsterdam / Philadelphia

™ The paper used in this publication meets the minimum requirements
of American National Standard for Information Sciences – Permanence
of Paper for Printed Library Materials, ANSI z39.48-1984.

Library of Congress Cataloging-in-Publication Data

Renkema, J.
    Introduction to discourse studies / Jan Renkema.
        p. cm.
    Includes bibliographical references and index.
        1. Discourse analysis. I. Title.

    P302.R458 2004
401'.41-dc22   2004053766
ISBN 90 272 2610 5 (Eur.) / 1 58811 529 1 (US) (Hb; alk. paper)
ISBN 90 272 3221 0 (Eur.) / 1 58811 530 5 (US) (Pb; alk. paper)

John Benjamins Publishing Co. • P.O. Box 36224 • 1020 ME Amsterdam • The Netherlands
John Benjamins North America • P.O. Box 27519 • Philadelphia PA 19118-0519 • USA

Table of Contents

Acknowledgments

This *Introduction to Discourse Studies* is the result of almost twenty-five years of academic and non-academic experience in teaching discourse studies. Guided by the questions and answers of hundreds of students and communication professionals, I have selected and (re)formulated what I consider the key concepts and major issues in discourse studies.

In 1992 I published my first introduction, *Discourse Studies: An Introductory Textbook,* which was reprinted several times and published in four languages. It has been the basis for this book but the enormous number of discourse studies publications and new insights of the past decade that have been incorporated here make this a very different book with over 300 source references and about 500 basic concepts explained. This book touches on various disciplines that previously did not consider discourse, and the broader, dynamic, contexts of discourse in communication science.

At the Tilburg University campus a footbridge connects the library annex e-learning center with the area of the lecture halls. In lecturing I have always considered myself a human bridge between all the books, journals and websites, and the question marks in the students' eyes. And when, in rare moments, these students left my lectures with more insight and more questions, I was grateful to have been a medium for this transfer. I hope that by studying this book and trying to deal with all the questions and assignments students will catch a glimpse of this joy of lecturing. In my opinion this is the best guarantee for a fruitful future in activities concerning discourse.

I would like to thank my colleagues in the Discourse Studies Group at Tilburg University, especially for the opportunity to do research in the USA as a Fulbright fellow. Furthermore, they gave me the chance to be confronted with many student questions abroad while lecturing in different academic cultures, such as at Japanese, South American, South African and German universities. I guess that in past decades I have discussed dozens of the problems brought up in this book with over a hundred colleagues from all over the world. Most of them are mentioned in the bibliography.

There are two people who I would like to thank personally. First, Bertie Kaal at Benjamins Publishers for stimulating me to found a journal on Document Design, which provides me with many new contacts, and for supporting me in "just writing down the notes" of my lectures. Second, Eric Daamen who was of invaluable support in assisting me in reference and index work and all the time-consuming aspects of text production. During this work he became more than only an assistant.

I hope that this course book will help teachers in discourse studies and related or overlapping domains such as communication science, pragmatics, rhetoric, stylistics, conversational analysis and design studies. If they consider this introduction a text-book for their basic courses that can take half of the work out of their hands, then I have done a useful job. Most of all, however, I hope that the bridge I built between the insights in the phenomenon discourse and the students' interest will motivate students to cross it. Perhaps after graduating they will even be stimulated to build a bridge themselves, somewhere between the academic island and the various professional areas where they end up. In any case, I would like to encourage both teachers and students to send me any comments or suggestions that might arise from using this textbook. All contributions are welcome. Please see www.janrenkema.nl for contact information.

Fall 2003, Tilburg University   Jan Renkema

1 Introduction

1.1   A rough definition of discourse studies

Discourse studies is the discipline devoted to the investigation of the relationship between form and function in verbal communication. This short but rough definition is the point of departure for this book. The definition prompts the following questions:

1. What is meant by the relationship between form and function?
2. Is it really necessary to have a separate discipline for the investigation of this relationship?

Answers to these two questions are given in this section. The aim and structure of this book are discussed in the next two sections.

What is meant by the relationship between form and function? Consider the following example of a fragment of verbal communication.

(1)   A: Say, there's a good movie playing tonight.
       B: Actually, I have to study.
       A: Too bad.
       B: Yes, I'm sorry.
       A: Well, I guess I don't need to ask you if you want me to pick you up.

In this example, A's first utterance is in the form of a statement that there is a good movie playing that night. The function of this statement, however, is that of an invitation to B. B knows that A's statement is meant to be an invitation. B could have responded by simply saying, "That's nice" or "I didn't know that." But B responds with a statement in turn expressing a need to study that evening. B's response counts as a refusal of the invitation. A's statement of regret shows that this interpretation is not mere conjecture.

In this fragment the form *statement* has the function of an *invitation* (first utterance of A) and a refusal thereof (first utterance of B). Below is another example: a passage from a statement concerning a newly built office complex and the same passage in a slightly different form.

(2) a.   The new office complex is situated in the old city center. The architectural firm of Wilkinson and Sons designed it.

   b.   The new office complex is situated in the old city center. It was designed by the architectural firm of Wilkinson and Sons.

The active voice is used in the second sentence in (2a): "The firm designed the new office." Whereas in (2b) a passive variant is used: "The new office was designed by the firm." What is the difference in function between these two sentences? In the active form the accent is on the firm that provided the design. In the passive form the office complex is elaborated on. When different forms are used for getting across approximately the same content, they often lead to differences in function. The aim of discourse studies is to provide an explanatory description of the intricate relations between forms of discourse elements and their functions in communication.

The second question is more difficult to answer. Why should there be a separate discipline *discourse studies*? To many researchers the best answer is that the investigation of the relation between form and function requires contributions from different disciplines such as linguistics, literature, rhetoric, stylistics and pragmatics as well as other fields concerned with verbal communication such as communication science, psychology, sociology and philosophy. Discourse phenomena cannot be studied adequately from just one of these perspectives. Because the concepts dealing with these phenomena are taken from many disciplines, a common ground is necessary. Discourse studies is this common ground. It serves as an inter- or multidiscipline that enables different research schools to have the necessary interaction so that specific contributions can be made to research into the relationship between form and function in verbal communication.

1.2   Aim and structure of this book

The aim of this book is to familiarize the prospective student with the most important concepts and the major issues in the field of discourse studies. Knowledge of the basic concepts will serve as a scientific "toolkit" that the student can use in advanced courses in discourse studies. This introduction is also meant as a stepping-stone to further reading in handbooks on different discourse topics and to studying research results in scientific journals on discourse.

This book consists of fifteen chapters spread over four parts. The ordering is inspired by the metaphor of the student who is supposed to be undertaking a scientific journey. After this introductory chapter, Part I provides information about the basic characteristics of this journey through the diverse landscapes of discourse studies. Part II invites students to fill their backpacks with some essential traveling material.

In Part III the different ways of making a scientific journey are presented. In Part IV some specific domains of interest can be chosen.

In Part I, Chapters 2 and 3 provide a general orientation towards the field. The focus is on the last part of the rough definition given earlier: discourse studies is the study of verbal communication. Chapter 2, Communication as action, is the most philosophical chapter in this book. It tries to answer questions like: What is (verbal) communication? What are the principles governing the use of the instrument "language"? What are the strategies that are brought to bear when we communicate? Verbal communication is presented as the performance of acts which must have some relevance for partners involved in it. This chapter stimulates the student to think of what verbal communication is about. Chapter 3, Discourse in communication, focuses on discourse as part of the situation in which people communicate. Discourse is no discourse at all without a sender and a receiver. Therefore, discourse cannot be studied adequately without the discourse situation being taken into account. Within this framework two basic discourse questions are answered: How can discourse best be studied in a perspective in which forms are related to functions in a discourse situation? What makes a string of sentences or a couple of utterances discourse?

In Part II, Chapters 4, 5, 6, 7 and 8 present the basic concepts for studying discourse. Chapter 4, Discourse types, gives an overview of the variety of forms of discourse such as written (a tax form), oral (a doctor–patient conversation), electronic (an e-mail), etc. It also discusses the attempts that have been made so far in putting the main varieties into some sort of model that reflects the essential differences between them. The classic intriguing question behind this modeling is: What exactly is a discourse type? The discussion on constructing a model is followed by the question of how to study new electronic communication situations in which combinations of modes (oral, written and visual) are used. Chapter 5, Structured content, presents the approaches to discourse with respect to the structuring of the message content. How can this structure be described for the different levels of discourse? Three levels are distinguished here: the global structure (the discourse as a whole), the mesostructure (the study of topics and themes) and the local structure (the smallest meaning units). The central question in Chapter 6 is: What are the formal ties that keep the different content elements together? Descending from a global structure, an overview of different knots and links to connect content elements is given. Special attention is paid to techniques of referring back- and forward in discourse and to so-called discourse relations and their markers. Chapter 7, Contextual phenomena, deals with discourse elements from both the production and the perception side, which are directly linked to the context. Examples are the fact that the meaning of "I" depends on the person using it or the possibility of putting some information more into the back- or foreground in order to produce a special effect on readers or listeners. However, the link not only goes from discourse to context, it goes the other way round as well. We always deal with discourse on the basis of knowledge and attitudes that we already have. We are no black boxes. Otherwise we would all give exactly the same rendering after having seen the same movie; nevertheless these renderings do differ in content.

In Chapter 8, Style, the last chapter of this first part, an overview of stylistic variation in discourse is given. After a brief discussion of classical rhetoric, the concepts of style and register are clarified. Special attention is paid to stylistic phenomena that can easily be studied by students and to stylistic research that highlights the different manifestations of seemingly the same messages. Consider, for example, the different renderings of one movie again, now focusing on the differences in formulation.

Part III deals with four central modes of communication. In everyday life we can "just talk" or make conversation intuitively without knowing the outcome, but we can also use language intentionally to give information, to tell a story or to try to convince someone. Chapter 9, Conversation analysis, gives insight into a more sociological way of discourse studies: conversation as a kind of glue between the members of a community or a society. Chapter 10, Informative discourse, focuses on the readability of information and the improvement of documents. In this chapter old methods to measure readability are dealt with, as well as the notion of discourse quality in a more contemporary view. Chapter 11, Narratives, starts with a more literary approach to discourse and illustrates how narratives are studied from three different perspectives: sociolinguistic, psycholinguistic and organizational. Chapter 12, Argumentation and persuasion, starts with approaches to analyzing the validity of reasoning in everyday language and presents a social-psychological framework for studying the way in which discourse can be persuasive. Here the emphasis is on stylistic elements.

In Part IV, Special interests, the three most important domains of discourse studies are presented. In Chapter 13, Discourse and cognition, the focus is on what goes on in our brain during the production and the perception of discourse. Cognitive psychologists have done extensive research into modeling the way we speak and listen or write and read. Several of these models and some highlights of current cognitive approaches are presented here. Chapter 14, Discourse and institution, focuses on the institutional aspects of discourse within the sociological approach. Some key publications are presented, dealing with institutions such as law, health and media. Chapter 15, Discourse and culture, presents the major topics in the study of discourse from a societal point of view. The main question is: Can discourse tell us something about the way in which the producer views the world? This is made more concrete by addressing questions such as: Can discourse analysis reveal something about power relations in society or, for example, the place of women in masculine cultures? These types of questions are of special importance in the study of intercultural communication.

1.3   The presentation of the material

The material in this book has been organized to serve as a first introduction to discourse studies at university level. Inherent in the interdisciplinary nature of the field of discourse studies is the fact that each phenomenon can be looked at from different viewpoints. Moreover, the danger exists of trivializing theoretical concepts, as they are taken out of their disciplinary context. Special attention will therefore be paid to the origins of key concepts in discourse studies.

Inter- or multidisciplinary discourse studies arose during the 1980s. However, it is rooted in classical rhetoric and language philosophy and in classic psychological and sociological studies from both the Anglo-American and the European traditions. It is for that reason that relatively much attention is given to classic or impressive landmarks in the field of discourse studies.

When dealing with the conceptual arsenal, examples of scientific applications are given whenever possible. The research examples chosen are not always the most recent ones. In this book attention is also paid to approaches upon which contemporary developments are based. In the bibliography almost half of the references date from before 1990 as in this introductory textbook the focus is on concepts and approaches that have proved to be soundly based and not just trendy. After studying this book the student will have most of the fundamental apparatus to do his or her job. The index at the end of this book, containing about 500 entries, is a good basis for studying the most important concepts in the field. The index entries only refer to the page on which the concept in question is most elaborately explained. This makes it a concise "guide" to the major concepts in discourse studies.

Obviously, an introductory work cannot delve deeply into discussions about definitions of key concepts or elaborate on issues. For students who wish to study more specific topics, each chapter or section is accompanied by a list of suggested readings. The main aim of this bibliographical information is to incite the reader to study the classic or key publications in the field. Books comprise about 80% of these references. The other 20% consist of what are considered seminal articles. All the references in each chapter's bibliographical information are listed at the end of the book, with reference to the specific section they refer to.

Each chapter ends with questions and assignments. These are meant to stimulate reflection upon and discussion of seemingly unproblematic topics, which it is hoped may encourage students to initiate reasoned articulation of their own astonishment about (mis)communication. The key at the end of this book provides answers to these questions. The assignments can be seen as proposals for students to work on in the library at their own campus. The extent to which the assignments are to be worked out depends on conditions of time and curriculum and on special wishes the lecturer may have. The number of questions and assignments may vary per section, depending, for example, on the length of the section or the nature of the subject that the section deals with.

Questions and assignments

Questions

1.1.1   Explain in your own words what discourse studies is.

1.1.2   Explain in terms of form and function what is going on in the following fragment of dinner conversation.

A: Could you pass the salt?

B: Of course. (B continues eating without passing the salt.)

1.1.3   Describe the differences in form and function between the following two passages:

a.   A general practitioner at our health center closed his practice yesterday after local demonstrations. He was suspected of molesting patients.

b.   A general practitioner at our health center, who was suspected of molesting patients, closed his practice yesterday after local demonstrations.

Assignments

1.1.1   One journal issue on discourse analysis can contain several papers that, according to their authors, all have to do with discourse. Explain how the following subjects could fit the definition of discourse studies that is given in the introductory chapter of this book. This assignment is inspired by a passage in Johnstone (2002).

1.   Descriptive terms used of the accused in the media coverage of a murder trial.

2.   A discussion of differences between English and Japanese.

3.   An analysis of expressions of identity in Athabaskan (Native American) student writing.

4.   A discussion of sonnets by Shakespeare.

5.   A paper about the epitaph of the spiritual master of a sect of Muslims.

6.   A discussion on whether the pronoun I should appear in formal writing.

7.   A study of political debate.

1.1.2   The bibliographical information of this chapter contains a list of the most widely known journals in the field of discourse studies. However, the notion *discourse* frequently occurs in all sorts of journals not specifically linked to discourse studies. Some examples are an article on the communication skills of people with dementia (in the *Journal of Communication Disorder*), one on text comprehension in relation to children's narratives (in the *British Journal of Developmental Psychology*) and research into organizational changes as discourse (in the *Academy of Management Journal*). Select any issue of one of the journals mentioned in the bibliographical information of this chapter or find a journal comparable to the ones mentioned above. Look at the summary of one of the articles and try to determine whether it falls within the definition of discourse studies. Support your opinion.

Bibliographical information

The article *Discourse analysis* by Zellig Harris (1952) is viewed by many as the starting point of discourse studies. Harris was the first to use the term *discourse analysis* in a scientific article. He discussed an advertisement text by analyzing the way in which sentences are linked and the way in which the text correlates with society and culture. A salient detail is the fact that in the first footnote Harris thanks his research assistant, who ended up developing the most influential theory on elements *within* a sentence: Noam Chomsky.

In the decades following the year in which Harris wrote his article, a vast quantity of books and articles on discourse studies has been published. So it is obvious that this textbook is not the only introduction to this field of research. On the contrary, one of the aims of this book is to serve as a reference guide to a qualitative selection of other handbooks and readers. In this first bibliographical overview more general works are mentioned whereas in the following chapters the references are more geared to specific aspects of discourse studies.

Several important introductions to discourse studies were published in the early 1980s. Prominent German-language publications are Kalverkämper (1981), Coseriu (1981), Sowinski (1983) and Scherner (1984). The most widely used English-language publications of that time are De Beaugrande and Dressler (1981), Brown and Yule (1983), Stubbs (1983) and Cook (1989). In the past decade various new introductions were published, which underlines the vitality of the broad field of discourse studies. The most important publications of recent date include the following: Salkie (1995) is a workbook, with exercises to detect various discourse phenomena; Jaworski & Coupland (1999) give a collection of some thirty passages from key publications on discourse studies; Goatly (2000) provides a clear introduction with practical exercises for developing critical awareness of the relationship between text production and consumption; Johnstone (2002) approaches discourse not as a discipline but as a research method, connecting it with six topics that shape it, such as world, audiences, medium and purpose.

There are also introductions to specific parts of the research field and books that indirectly have this function. The most significant ones dating from the 1980s and early 1990s deal with the analysis of conversation (Edmonson, 1981; Henne and Rehbock, 1982; McLaughlin, 1984; Nofsinger, 1991) and with stylistics (McMenamin, 1993). Recent publications emphasize the socio-cultural aspects of discourse studies, for example, Gee (1999), and narratives, for example, Georgakopoulou & Goutsos

(1997) and Toolan (2001). For good publications on discourse analysis in general see Coulthard (1985), Nunan (1987), McCarthy (1991), Mann and Thompson (1992) and Hoey (2001).

In addition to books, numerous journals from various research traditions have been founded in discourse studies. Below are the most widely known titles. Periodicals considered the core journals are marked with an asterisk.

- Applied Cognitive Linguistics
- Cognition
- Cognitive Linguistics
- College Composition and Communication
- Computational Linguistics
- Discourse and Society*
- Discourse Processes*
- Discourse Studies*
- Information and Document Design Journal
- Human Communication Research
- IEEE transactions on professional communication
- Information and Management
- Journal of Business Communication
- Journal of Communication
- Journal of Documentation
- Journal of Language and Social Psychology
- Journal of Pragmatics*
- Journal of Semantics
- Journal of Sociolinguistics
- Language and Cognitive Processes
- Language and Communication
- Pragmatics
- Text
- Written Communication*

Teun van Dijk is viewed by many as the founding father of contemporary discourse studies. He founded a number of journals, including the above-mentioned periodicals *Text*, *Discourse and Society* and *Discourse Studies*. Moreover, he is known for editing two major handbooks in discourse studies, namely *The Handbook of Discourse Analysis* (1985) and *Discourse Studies: A Multidisciplinary Introduction* (1997). Two other noteworthy handbooks dating from the past decade are Schiffrin (1994) and the exhaustive work by Schiffrin, Tannen & Hamilton (2001). A new library on discourse studies should undoubtedly include these four works.

PART I

General orientation

2 Communication as action

2.1 The Organon model

In the last decades, the slogan "Communication is action" has come into fashion, but in fact this view of communication is more than two thousand years old. One of the earliest works on language, Plato's *Cratylus* (a dialogue on the origin of language written in about 390 B.C.), describes speech as a form of action and words as instruments with which actions can be performed.

The German philosopher and psychologist Karl Bühler was referring to this work when he described language as a tool, "Organon", which people use in order to communicate with one another. Bühler's Organon model (1934/1990) has had a major impact on the way language is dealt with in discourse studies. Bühler stated that a sound can only qualify as a linguistic sign if a three-fold relationship exists connecting the sound to a sender, a receiver, and an object that is being referred to. Parallel to this three-pronged relationship, each linguistic sign (S) has three functions simultaneously:

1. A sign functions as a symptom as it says something about a sender, for example, whether the sender is female or male or what the intention of the utterance is.
2. A sign is a symbol because it refers to objects and states of affairs.
3. A sign serves as a signal because a receiver must interpret it or react to what has been said.

This three-part division can be illustrated with any utterance. Below is an example.

(1) Have you heard that strange story about the drunk who decided to play barber and cut off his friend's ear?

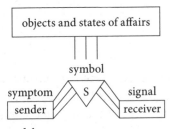

Figure 1. Bühler's Organon model

By asking this question, the speaker indicates that he wants information from the person who is being addressed. By using the word "strange", the speaker is also expressing an opinion. This is the *symptom* aspect. In the utterance a reference is made to a story, a real event. That is the *symbol* aspect. The question is an appeal to a listener. A listener is not expected to just answer "yes" or "no" and change the topic. Something along the line of "No, tell me about it" or "Yes" followed by the listener's own reaction is expected. This is the *signal* aspect.

In this chapter the focus is on the basic assumptions of the Organon model, namely, that language is an instrument with which objectives can be achieved and that this instrument cannot considered to be separate from speakers and listeners, or writers and readers, in performing communicative acts.

Language, and therefore discourse, is a two-way instrument, an instrument for a speaker and a listener or a writer and a reader. Or as the Danish linguistic philosopher Otto Jespersen wrote in the introduction to his *Philosophy of Grammar* (1924):

(2)   The essence of language is human activity – activity on the part of one individual to make himself understood by another, and activity on the part of that other to understand what was in the mind of the first.

If two parties use an instrument for an "activity", then such an activity can only be successful if both parties adhere to general rules or principles and thereby utilize certain strategies. This can be illustrated with a non-linguistic example. If two people want to hang a painting (activity), they use a hammer, nails, and a ladder (instruments), and they have to coordinate their actions. There will have to be some form of cooperation; while one is standing on the ladder, the other can hand the tools to the first, etc. Rules concerning politeness will also have to be followed; while one person is on the ladder, the other should not try to push the first off. One general principle of collective activity is *cooperation* and an often-used strategy to achieve this is *politeness*. This is also true in the case of verbal communication. On the basis of this cooperation principle and guided by so-called politeness strategies the communicators have to perform their communicative acts. But what precisely are those communicative acts? The theory, called *speech act theory*, provides an answer to this question.

2.2   Speech act theory

In speech act theory, language is seen as a form of acting. This theory stems from the school of philosophy that is called *ordinary language philosophy*. The proponents of this school, which flourished in England in the middle of the last century, wanted to analyze philosophical problems by looking at ordinary language and trying to ascertain what insights it could offer into reality. For example, the ethical question of why human activity is judged to be good or bad, demands that the way individuals apologize for bad behavior also be studied. An apology is an act in which a justification is given. By studying how people perform speech acts such as apologizing, promising, ordering, etc., these "philosophers of ordinary language" wished to contribute to the solution of philosophical problems.

Speech act theory has had a strong influence on the field of discourse studies as this theory focuses on the question of what people are doing when they use language. Consider the next example. There is a striking difference between the following two sentences.

(3) It's raining.
(4) I promise that I will give you one hundred dollars tomorrow.

In (3) a statement is made that may or may not be true. As for (4), however, it is not possible to say that it is true or that it is not true. With verbs such as *to promise* (in the first person), not only is something being said; more importantly, something is being done. In (4) an act is being performed through an utterance. By saying "I promise ...", a promise is made. But saying "It's raining" does not make it rain.

The English philosopher John Austin (1976) used the terms *constative* and *performative* to describe this difference. In constatives, such as sentence (3), something is stated about reality; in performatives, such as (4), an act is performed by the utterance itself. Austin was not successful, however, in establishing criteria for describing the difference between these two concepts. It can, after all, be argued that an act is being performed in the case of constative utterances as well; a warning given or a statement being made as in the case of (3).

This led Austin to the conclusion that all expressions of language must be viewed as acts. He distinguished three kinds of action within each utterance. First, there is the *locution*, the physical act of producing an utterance. Second, there is the *illocution*, the act that is committed by producing an utterance: by uttering a promise, a promise is made; by uttering a threat, a threat is made. Third, there is the *perlocution*, the production of an effect through locution and illocution, for example, the execution of an order by the addressee.

Consider another example. In the statement "There is a draft in here", the locution is the production of the utterance. Depending on the situation, the illocution could be a request, an order, a complaint, etc. The perlocution could be that a door or window is closed or that the addressee replies that he is not a servant. It is important to emphasize that the reaction to an illocution, the so-called *uptake* that leads to a perlocution, can differ depending on the situation. Below is an example of four different uptakes of the same utterance.

Table 1.   Various uptakes of the same utterance

Locution of the speaker	Illocution	Uptake by the listener
There's a good movie tonight	Invitation	O.K. let's go
There's a good movie tonight	Advice	O.K. I will go there
There's a good movie tonight	Excuse	Never mind
There's a good movie tonight	Offer	Thank you!

In speech act theory the illocution is the focus of attention. Language philosophers have tried to give an overview of all possible illocutions, from assertives to requests, from promises to exclamations. This, however, proved to be a very difficult task, because it is by no means clear what exactly the characteristic differences between the proposed illocutions are. For example, a promise could be a threat in the locution "I promise, I'll get you!" First, the phenomenon illocution itself has to be studied.

Among the intriguing problems with illocutions, there is one that has drawn special attention, namely, the issue of successful illocutions. It is easy to see that certain minimum requirements must be met for an illocution to be successful. If anyone other than a church leader excommunicates someone, then the act of excommunication has not been executed. If in a casino someone at the roulette table suddenly calls "*Rien ne va plus!*" ("No more bets!" or "Game over!"), this cannot be construed as being the illocution *refusing* if this person is not the dealer.

The philosopher John Searle (1969) formulated four *felicity conditions* that illocutions must meet. These four conditions are illustrated below using the illocution *to promise*.

(5)   Felicity conditions for *to promise* (speech act)
   a.   the propositional content
         In the case of "promising", the act that the speaker commits himself to (the proposition) must be a future act to be carried out by the speaker himself. One cannot make a promise for someone else or promise to do something that has already been done.
   b.   the preparatory condition
         This condition concerns those circumstances that are essential for the uptake of an illocution as the intended illocution. In the case of promising, these circumstances would require that the content of the promise is not a matter of course. Another preparatory condition is that the promise must be advantageous to the addressee; one cannot promise something that is solely disadvantageous.

c. the sincerity condition
    The speaker must honestly be willing to fulfill the promise. Even if he is not
    willing, he can be held to his promise.
d. the essential condition
    This is the condition that separates the illocution in question from other
    illocutions. In the case of "promising", this means, among other things, that
    the speaker takes upon himself the responsibility of carrying out the act
    stated in the content of the promise.

Searle used these felicity conditions to show that the successful exchange of illocutions
is also bound by certain rules. In terms of form and function, this means that a form
can only acquire a valid function given certain conditions.

Another approach is provided by the German sociologist Jürgen Habermas
(1981). According to Habermas, speakers claim that their illocutions are valid. In the
case of the illocution *predicting*, for example, the speaker claims that the statement will
come true in the future. In the case of *congratulating*, the claim to validity is based on
an expression of emotion on the part of the speaker, namely, that the congratulations
are sincere. In the case of *ordering*, the speaker bases the claim to validity on assumed
authority to issue the order.

Habermas based these validity claims on Bühler's Organon model and the three
aspects that can be distinguished in language signs: symbol, symptom and signal (see
Section 2.1). Through the symbol aspect of an utterance, a claim is made as to the truth
of the statement as in the prediction example above. Through the symptom aspect, a
claim is made regarding sincerity; see the congratulation example. Through the signal
aspect, a claim is made regarding legitimacy as in the order example. In Habermas's
view, an illocution is only successful when the addressee acknowledges the claim to
validity. Take the example of a teacher asking a student the following question:

(6) Could you bring me a glass of water?

The student can refuse this request as invalid on the basis of all three aspects.

(7) Dispute of the validity of (6)
     a. symbol aspect: truth. (The content of the statement does not correspond to
         reality.) "How can you request something like that? The nearest faucet is so
         far away that I would never be able to make it back before the end of class."
     b. symptom aspect: sincerity. "No, you don't really want any water. You're just
         trying to make me look bad in front of the other students."
     c. signal aspect: legitimacy. "You can't ask me to do something like that. I'm
         not here to fetch and carry for the teacher!"

Table 2.   Basic illocutions according to Habermas

Aspect of the utterance	Claim to validity	Type of illocution
symbol	truth	constative
symptom	sincerity	expressive
signal	legitimacy	regulative

Using Bühler's three-way division, Habermas defines three main types of illocution: constatives (with a symbol aspect), expressives (with a symptom aspect), and regulatives (with a signal aspect).

The illocutions *claiming* and *describing* are examples of constatives; *promising* and *congratulating* of expressives; *inviting* and *requesting* of regulatives.

2.3   Illocutions in discourse

How does the more philosophical speech act theory in the previous section contribute to the study of discourse? First, it can provide insights into the requirements that a form (the locution) must meet to ensure that the illocution and the intended uptake take place. This illocution serves as a prerequisite for the achievement of the perlocution the speaker or writer has in mind. Second, this theory can serve as a framework for indicating what is required in order to determine the relationship between form and function, between locution, on the one hand, and illocution and perlocution, on the other hand.

There are a number of cases in which the utterance itself, the locution, provides an indication of the intended illocutions. John Searle (1969) calls these indications IFIDs, *illocutionary force indicating devices*. IFIDs include performative verbs, word order, intonation, accent, certain adverbs, and the mode of the verb. If an IFID is present, the utterance is said to have an explicit illocution; in all other cases the utterance is said to have an implicit or indirect illocution. Below are a few examples of explicit illocutions.

(8)   I request that you put out your cigarette.
(9)   He is putting out his cigarette.
(10)   Is he putting out his cigarette?
(11)   Are you going to put that cigarette out or not?
(12)   Would you please put out your cigarette?

In (8) the performative verb "to request" makes the illocutionary intent explicit. The difference in word order between (9) and (10) is indicative of the illocutionary intent, in this case "statement" and "question", respectively. Ascending intonation and an accent on the word "cigarette" can also convey an expression of surprise. In (11) the tag "or not" is indicative of the imperative character of the illocution. In (12) the mode of the verb indicates that this is a request; the adverb "please", depending on the intonation, can make this request either cautious or insistent. It is also possible to convert (12) into an order by placing a special accent on "please" and "cigarette".

It should be noted that IFIDs do not always provide a definitive answer regarding illocutionary intent. The IFID *if… then* in the following two examples would suggest a conditional promise, but in fact only (13) contains a conditional promise.

(13)   If you take the garbage out, I will give you a beer.
(14)   If you keep this up, you will have a nervous break down.

In (14) the IFID is not the only relevant factor; more background information is needed, specifically that a nervous breakdown is dangerous. Otherwise, it is impossible to deduce why (14) is generally seen as a warning. If so much additional information is needed to determine the function of explicit language utterances, then it should be clear that this is even more difficult in the case of implicit or indirect utterances. See the example in Table 1 of Section 2.2 again, "There is a good movie tonight", which could function as an indirect invitation or excuse.

Much knowledge is needed to link the right illocution to a locution. Consider the next example in the form of an interrogative.

(15)   Can you stop by in a minute?

Why is this interrogative generally interpreted as a request? A request can be identified by the following felicity conditions:

(16)   Felicity conditions for requests
    a.   the propositional content
        The content must refer to a future act, X, which is to be carried out by the addressee.
    b.   the preparatory condition
        1.   The addressee is capable of executing X and the speaker believes that the addressee is capable of doing it.
        2.   It is obvious to both conversational participants that the addressee will not perform the act without being asked.
    c.   the sincerity condition
        The speaker actually wants the addressee to do what has been requested.
    d.   the essential condition
        The utterance serves as an attempt to persuade the addressee to execute X.

On the basis of rules in this definition, it can be said that the interrogative given in (15) possesses the illocutionary intent of a request. This does not, however, explain why this interrogative must be interpreted as an order when it is uttered by a supervisor to a subordinate. In this case the illocution is far from self-explanatory. For correct interpretation, knowledge of the discourse situation and knowledge of the relation between the participants are required. However, that is not all. Something like knowledge of the world is necessary as well. Compare the following examples.

(17)   This panther has brownish-yellow spots.
(18)   Your left eye has brownish-yellow spots.

Both cases can be viewed as simple statements, but (18) can also be intended as a warning if a situation is being described which could be viewed as dangerous. It could, on the other hand, also be seen as a sign of affection. So, an illocution, a simple form, can in many cases only be interpreted, have a function, when different kinds of knowledge are used. When a form can have so many different functions, how can people communicate at all? If the interpretation of a locution depends on so many different factors – linguistic cues, knowledge of the discourse situation, knowledge of the world – could it be that in the exchange of illocutions more is involved to guide our interpretation procedures and to prevent us from miscommunication? Yes, was the answer of another famous philosopher.

2.4   The cooperative principle

An utterance often conveys more than the literal meaning of the words uttered. The following example is from the classic article *Logic and Conversation* (1975) by the logician and philosopher Herbert Grice.

(19)   Suppose that A and B are talking about a mutual friend, C, who is now working in a bank. A asks B how C is getting on in his job, and B replies, "Oh quite well, I think; he likes his colleagues and he hasn't been to prison yet."

The form of this utterance does not say everything about the meaning and, therefore, the function. A can derive from B's remark that B does not hold a high opinion of C. In fact, B has basically said that C is a potential criminal. Yet, this cannot be derived from the literal meaning of B's words. Why then can A draw these conclusions? Because A can assume that there is some relevance to B's, at first glance, superfluous addition concerning prison. The only reason B would add that remark is if B meant to imply that C is a potential criminal.

Grice called this derivation *conversational implicature*. In fact, it is the meaning that an addressee has to deduct from the locution, considering the context of the utterance. By using the term *implicature*, Grice wanted to emphasize that it is not a logical implication such as the if-then relationship expressed by the formula "A→B". The addition of the word *conversational* denotes that the derivations being dealt with are an essential part of the information-transfer process in conversations.

A speaker can only get such a meaning – in example (19) that C is a potential criminal – across if the listener cooperates. To capture this notion, Grice formulated a general principle of language use, the *cooperative principle*:

(20)   The cooperative principle
       Make your conversational contribution such as is required, at the stage at which
       it occurs, by the accepted purpose or direction of the speech exchange in which
       you are engaged.

Grice distinguished four categories within this general principle. He formulated these in basic rules or maxims. In two categories he also introduced supermaxims.

(21)   Grice's maxims
       I   Maxims of quantity
             1.   Make your contribution as informative as is required (for the current
                  purposes of the exchange).
             2.   Do not make your contribution more informative than is required.
       II   Maxims of quality
             Supermaxim: Try to make your contribution one that is true.
             Maxims: 1.   Do not say what you believe to be false.
                         2.   Do not say that for which you lack adequate evidence.
       III   Maxim of relevance
             1.   Be relevant.
       IV   Maxims of manner
             Supermaxim: Be perspicuous
             Maxims: 1.   Avoid obscurity of expression.
                         2.   Avoid ambiguity.
                         3.   Be brief (avoid unnecessary prolixity).
                         4.   Be orderly.

The maxims of the cooperative principle can be used to describe how participants in a conversation derive implicatures. Grice gives the following example. A is standing by an obviously immobilized car and is approached by B. The following exchange takes place:

(22) A: I am out of petrol.

  B: There is a garage round the corner.

A can deduce from B's reaction that B means that there is a garage around the corner that is open and sells gasoline. B, however, has not mentioned these facts. A can only make these assumptions if he assumes that B is acting in accordance with the cooperative principle and is adhering to the maxim of relevance.

In discourse studies the cooperative principle and its maxims are often referred to as they provide a lucid description of how listeners (and readers) can distill information from an utterance even though that information has not been mentioned outright. This is of importance to research on the relationship between form and function.

Grice did, however, have a number of additional comments concerning the cooperative principle. First, the maxims are only valid for language use that is meant to be informative. This excludes, for example, such categories as debating and small talk. Second, there are, from the esthetic or social point of view, other possible maxims. Grice suggests the maxim "Be polite". Third, another principle is at work here. Consider the quantity maxim. An overabundance of information does not necessarily mean that it is this maxim that is being violated, since it can also be seen as a waste of time and energy and thus as a violation of some efficiency principle.

In addition the Gricean maxims have been criticized for several reasons. Some maxims are rather vague. For example, how can it be determined which information is required (first maxim of quantity)? The four maxims have been presented as being of equal importance, but there are situations in which the maxim of quality is more important than the maxim of manner, and vice versa. Nevertheless, Grice's cooperative principle has had a great impact on discussions in the field of discourse studies. This is probably because Grice showed with everyday examples that communication, which seems to enroll without rules, is organized by basic rules.

2.5 Relevance theory

In the literature on Grice's maxims special attention is given to the maxim of relevance. One reasons for this is that it is unclear how it can be determined whether a contribution to a conversation is relevant or not. A number of suggestions have been made in the direction of a clear description of relevance. It has, however, proved to be exceedingly difficult to determine exactly when the maxim of relevance has been violated. Regard the following example of a question and a number of possible answers:

(23)　A:　Where's my box of chocolates?

　　　　B:　a.　Where are the snows of yesteryear?

　　　　　　b.　I was feeling hungry.

　　　　　　c.　I've got a train to catch.

　　　　　　d.　Where's your diet sheet?

　　　　　　e.　The children were in your room this morning.

Speaker A could react with surprise and ask why speaker B is suddenly quoting a line of poetry, in the case of answer (a), or with "I was talking about chocolates and now you're talking about the children", in the case of answer (e). At first sight, it seems that B is not acting within the constraints of the maxim of relevance. However, if A assumes that B is adhering to the maxim of relevance, then any reaction B gives could be construed as being relevant.

(24)　a.　B is not just quoting poetry; B is not really asking a question. B, by reacting the way he does, is simply making clear that the chocolates, like the snows of the past, have gradually disappeared and that there is no good answer to A's question.

　　　　b.　B is making clear that he has eaten A's chocolates.

　　　　c.　B does not want to answer the question because he is in a hurry. Or, B is evading the question with an excuse; he knows more than he is letting on.

　　　　d.　B is postponing giving an answer; first he wants to know whether or not A should be eating chocolate.

　　　　e.　B is suggesting that the children ate the chocolates. Or, B is suggesting that the children know where the chocolates are.

Obviously, numerous other possible reactions for B are conceivable. The main point is that every reaction can be construed as being relevant. It is, of course, possible to imagine contributions to conversations that would, at first sight, appear to be irrelevant, but these usually end up sounding like excerpts from a comedy routine.

(25)　A:　Would you care to dance?

　　　　B:　I'd love to. Do you know anyone else who would like to?

(26)　A:　(teacher) You should have been here at nine o'clock.

　　　　B:　(student) Why? Did something happen?

However, even in these examples, B's reaction could be interpreted as being relevant if in (25) A is a waiter or if in (26) school does not start until 9:30. The problem now is that it can be fairly objectively established when or whether the maxims of quality, quantity and manner are violated, but it seems quite impossible to determine when an utterance no longer counts as relevant. This makes it unclear what the value of the maxim of relevance is.

The omnipresence of relevance in communication has led to the Relevance Theory of Dan Sperber and Deirdre Wilson (1995). They took a different starting point, and made the relevance concept the cornerstone of their view of communication while abandoning the other three maxims. That is to say, they turned the disadvantage of the vagueness of relevance to the benefit of a clearer theory of what we mean by "understanding each other".

A good start to getting their point is to realize that language in use is characterized by what is called *indeterminacy* or *underspecification*. We have already seen that the example in Section 2.2, "There is a good movie tonight", can be vague or ambiguous if one does not take into account the discourse situation. This can be seen as a form of underspecification. But even when the discourse situation is known and the locution is clear, the locution is often underspecified. A good example is this notice often found on the door of a lecture hall:

(27)   Doors must be locked and windows closed when leaving this room.

This locution can bear the meaning that a student must lock up whenever he leaves class for, say a toilet break, but obviously no student will interpret the utterance in that way. Almost anyone will understand that the notice only applies or is relevant when at the end of the day the last lecture has ended and people leave the room without returning. None of this extra information is included in the thus underspecified notice, and still this missing information is filled in and as a result the utterance is understood correctly.

Sperber and Wilson argue that such ambiguities are dissolved in the right context on the basis of the relevance concept. While an addressee interprets the meaning of an utterance such as in (27), he assumes that it makes sense, that it is relevant and that it forms a coherent whole. The addressee only selects the relevant features of the context and recognizes whatever the addresser communicates as relevant. But how does that work, attaching relevance to contributions such as the movie example or example (27)?

First, it is important to recognize an utterance as an act of "ostensive communication", i.e., an act of making something manifest to the addressee and helping the addressee to understand the meaning of this. Second, communication must not be seen as just getting the thoughts of the speaker into the mind of the addressee but as a means of enlarging mutual "cognitive environments". The cognitive environment is a set of facts perceptible in reality or inferable from knowledge about reality. Hearers and readers make sense of (a piece of) discourse, they interpret the connections between utterances as meaningful, drawing conclusions based on their background knowledge of the world: they use their cognitive environment and, as a result of interpreting the utterance, their cognitive environment is enlarged.

If an addresser knows or at least can assess the cognitive environment of an addressee by an act of ostensive communication, then he knows what kind of assumptions the addressee will actually make in reaction to an utterance. In the case of (27) the addresser knows that the cognitive environment of an addressee in a lecture hall will be something like: when I leave class for a toilet break, other people will stay there, I will return in a few minutes and continue listening to the lecturer. The addresser will assess the addressee's reaction to the utterance as something like: there is no need to lock up and close the windows because of what I know about the situation. And thus the addresser knows that a notice as in (27) will suffice in the given situation and will only be judged as relevant in the right context: at the end of the day when the lecture hall is definitively left.

The theory of Sperber and Wilson added two important notions to studying the way people understand each other: explicature and degree of relevance. These notions can be clarified in discussing the following passage from a "ticket buying interaction", which is taken from Cutting (2002).

(28) A: Well there's a shuttle service sixty euros one-way. When do you want to go?
      B: At the weekend.
      A: What weekend?
      B: Next weekend. How does that work? You just turn up for the shuttle service?
      A: That might be cheaper. Then that's fifty.

The participants have to interpret the verbal acts of the other as attempts to change their mutual cognitive environment. This ostensive communication is the input for the explicature, which is the enrichment of the underdetermined locution or the formulation of the intended explicit content. It is like filling in missing words. Sperber and Wilson consider this explicature a necessary stage before making a conversational implicature.

This explicature, this specification of underspecified utterances, is ruled by the principle of relevance. Only that information is filled in that is relevant to the communication situation. In this conversation, B assumes that A will understand "At the weekend" to mean "Next weekend". B assumes that this underspecification is relevant enough. However, since A is going to sell a ticket, he needs to verify if this is true. A's last answer, "That might be cheaper. Then that's fifty", is not a complete answer. If A had wanted to be more explicit, he could have said: "If you purchase a ticket now, you have booked a seat, which costs 60 euros. If you buy the ticket when you turn up, it costs 50 euros." A, however, presumes B to be able to infer all of this and fill in the missing words.

Through this explicature it can be made reasonable that not all utterances are equally relevant and that not all utterances are equally successful. Utterances cannot be divided into relevant or irrelevant utterances. There is a degree of relevance. This degree of relevance of an utterance is determined by two factors: contextual effects and processing efforts. Contextual effects concern the way new information can interact with what is already known, i.e., everything that contributes to the addressee's representation of the world. Processing effort pertains to the effort of decoding linguistic information and the effort of accessing information in the context to link the new information to. The degree of relevance can then be described as follows: the greater the contextual effect and the less effort it takes to create that effect, the greater the relevance is. So, in this example the utterance by B "At the weekend" has low relevance, because the information cannot be linked to what is already known, as can be seen by A's reaction. The processing effort can only be successful when the exact weekend is known. And in this context the last utterance by A has a high degree of relevance. The new information "cheaper" and "fifty" can easily be linked to information that is already given in A's first utterance.

So much for a more philosophical-inspired theory about the foundations of communication. This theory has influenced the analysis of discourse mainly through the concept of underspecification and the focus on the relation between discourse and the situation.

2.6   Politeness theory

Notions such as cooperation and relevance are mainly valid for informative language use. Language users are not, however, always interested in the effective transfer of information or relevance of an utterance. In the following examples the speaker wants the addressee to close the door.

(29)   a.   Close the door.
       b.   There's a draft.
       c.   Would you close the door?
       d.   Would you be so kind as to close the door?

According to the maxims of the cooperative principle, (29a) is sufficient. Language is, however, often used more indirectly, as in (29b). Sometimes certain politeness forms such as in (29c) and (29d) are applied as well.

An important source of inspiration in the study of politeness phenomena is the work done by Erving Goffman (1956). This social psychologist introduced the concept of *face*. By this he meant the image that a person projects in his social contacts with

...ers. Face has the meaning as in the saying "to lose face". In Goffman's opinion, every ...rticipant in the social process has the need to be appreciated by others and the need ...be free and not interfered with. Goffman calls the need to be appreciated "positive ...ce" and the need to not be disturbed "negative face".

Goffman wanted social interaction, which includes verbal communication, to be studied from the perspective that participants are striving for stability in their relationships with others. Participants in conversations should, therefore, not violate one another's face. Refusing a request or reproaching someone is an action that can form a threat to the other's positive or negative face. In the case of these "face threatening acts" (FTAS), something is needed which will reduce the violation of face to a minimum and, therefore, preserve stability as much as possible. This can be achieved by using "face work techniques". Examples are broad circumspect formulations of refusals, which make it clear that the request made is impossible to grant.

How does politeness fit into this approach? Politeness prevents or repairs the damage caused by FTAS. The greater the threat to stability, the more politeness, face work technique, is necessary. Just as there are two types of face, there are two types of politeness. Face work that is aimed at positive face is called "solidarity politeness"; this kind of politeness is, for example, achieved by giving compliments. Face work that deals with negative face is known as "respect politeness", and can be achieved by not infringing another's "domain" in the communication. Below are a few examples. When a personnel manager has to turn down a job applicant who should not have applied in the first place owing to lack of education, this is an FTA that threatens the positive face of the applicant, and that of the manager. For this reason the personnel manager will be more apt to write (30b) than (30a).

(30) a.   We do not understand why you bothered to apply.
      b.   We have some doubts concerning your prior education.

In the following interaction between an instructor and a student at the end of a tutoring session, the second variant is more polite as it is less damaging to the instructor's face and that of the student.

(31) A: I've tried to explain this as clearly as possible. Now I have to leave as I have another appointment. I hope that the homework will be easier next time.
      B: a.   I still don't understand the material.
          b.   If problems should arise, is it all right if I stop by tomorrow?

Inspired by Goffman's work, Penelope Brown and Stephen Levinson (1978) developed a theory on the relationship between the intensity of the threat to face and linguistically realized politeness. The intensity of the threat to face is expressed by a weight (W) that is linked to an FTA. This weight is the sum of three social parameters: (a) the *rate* of imposition, which is the "absolute weight" of a particular act in a specific culture; (b) the social *distance* between the speaker and the person addressed; (c) the *power* that the person being spoken to has over the speaker. The term *absolute weight* refers to the fact that, for example, the request "May I borrow your car?" is in a category other than "May I borrow your pen?" The request to borrow a car is of course not quite such a great demand if the person requesting the car is the car owner's brother. This illustrates that the factors *distance* and *power* influence the ultimate weight.

The ultimate weight of an FTA can be expressed by a value according to the formula:

(32) Intensity of threat to face

$$W(\text{FTA}) = R + D + P$$

Weight of Face Threatening Act = Rate of imposition + social Distance + Power

Brown and Levinson did not indicate how values are to be assigned to R (rate of imposition), D (social distance), and P (power). But it should be clear that the value for P is different in the following examples.

(33) a. Excuse me, sir, would it be all right if I close the window?
      b. Mind me closing the window?

Utterance (33a) is more likely to be said by an employee to his boss, while in the same situation, (33b) might be said by the boss to the employee. In these examples parameters R and D have the same values.

In their research on linguistically realized politeness, Brown and Levinson investigated a number of languages. Their analyses indicate that there are many ways of committing an FTA with a given weight. All of these variants can, according to Brown and Levinson, be reduced to five strategies:

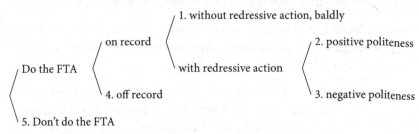

Figure 2.   Possible strategies for doing FTAS

The fifth strategy is implemented when the risk of speaking is too great, when, for instance, an individual does not risk answering an impertinent and face-threatening question and simply remains silent. "Off record" means that the FTA is not recognizable as such. An example of this is the (33c) variant of the request that is made in (33).

(33)   c.   I'm just so cold.

When the addressee replies "Then close the window", the speaker can still maintain that a request has not been made. "Redressive action" refers to an action that is meant to improve the stability between conversational partners and is, therefore, an action that minimizes or prevents a loss of face.

Below are examples of different strategies for asking a person for a hundred dollars.

(34)   a.   Hey, lend me a hundred dollars. (baldly)
       b.   Hey, friend, could you lend me a hundred bucks?
            (positive polite)
       c.   I'm sorry I have to ask, but could you lend me a hundred dollars?
            (negative polite)
       d.   Oh no, I'm out of cash! I forgot to go to the bank today. (off record)

The strategies are numbered according to their degree of politeness. (Strategy 5 is, from this point on, left out of consideration.) If the W of an FTA is high, the speaker will choose a strategy with a higher number. This explains why grave accusations or inconvenient requests are often formulated indirectly (strategy 4).

The Goffman approach and Brown and Levinson's theory provide an adequate research framework for determining gradations of politeness and for analyzing indirect language. The following question is an example of an indirect request:

(35)   Are you doing anything special tonight?

The form of this utterance makes it clear that this is an inquiry about an individual's planned activities. This question can, however, also be an invitation on the part of the speaker to the addressee to go out together.

How can a question in this form have an entirely different function? According to Levinson (1983), the answer is that in some cases speakers first make a pre-request in order to find out whether they will get a positive response to their request. Levinson describes this in an underlying structure consisting of four positions. Below are an example and the underlying structure.

(36)   A: (1)   Are you doing anything special tonight?
       B: (2)   No, not really. Why?
       A: (3)   Well, I wanted to ask if you would like to go out to dinner with me.
       B: (4)   I'd love to.

(37) The underlying structure of (36):
     (1) Pre-request
     (2) "Go ahead" reaction
     (3) Request
     (4) Consent

Goffman's work on face offers an explanation for the pre-request phenomenon. If B had given an evasive answer to the pre-request, then that would have eliminated the necessity of making the main request, preventing the loss of face of both participants. A does not have to deal with a refusal and B does not have to refuse the request in a direct manner; after the pre-request, B can claim to be extremely busy which will soften the blow of the refusal.

Indirect requests have certain similarities with pre-requests in that both are attempts to ascertain whether or not there are grounds for refusing a direct request. Consider the following example. A customer walks into a shoe store and asks:

(38) Do you sell jogging shoes?

This question is actually a preliminary check to see if the sales clerk will be able to give an affirmative response to a request to see an assortment of jogging shoes. In Levinson's (1983) opinion, indirect requests can be viewed as pre-requests in an underlying structure consisting of four positions.

(39) A: (1) Do you sell jogging shoes?
     B: (2) Yes.
     A: (3) Would you show me some, please?
     B: (4) I'll go get them for you.

In many cases the reaction to a pre-request is the same as to the direct request.

(40) A: (1) Do you sell jogging shoes?
     B: (4) Yes, I'll show you some.
     A: Thank you.

This reduction can be explained with the politeness strategy. It ensures that the customer does not lose face; the customer is no longer obliged to formulate a direct request.

Questions and assignments

Questions

2.1.1   Use the Organon model to distinguish the functions in the following utterance:
This is quite an interesting model!

2.2.1   Formulate a possible illocution and a possible perlocution for the following utterances:
a.   It's raining.
b.   Here comes a dog.

2.2.2   Using the following sentence, indicate what is wrong with the propositional felicity condition for *promise* as stated in Section 2.2:
I promise you that someone will come tomorrow.

2.2.3   Using the illocutions flatter and lie, show that problems arise if an illocution is only considered successful when the addressee understands which illocution is meant.

2.2.4   Classify the following illocutions using Habermas's basic types:
invite, presume, defy, offer condolences, request, describe, acquit, guarantee, order.

2.3.1   What kind of knowledge is required to deduce from the following statement that a threat and not a promise is implied?
I promise you that you will get a whipping if you do that again!

2.3.2   Give an example of an utterance which, depending on the situation, can have the illocutionary force order, request, warn, and complain.

2.3.3   Indicate which elements of the following utterances are the reason for the assignment of an illocutionary force.
a.   I am warning you, there's a bull coming towards you.
b.   There's a bull coming towards you.

2.4.1   Using the term *conversational implicature*, explain why A can deduce from B's remark what time it is.
A: What time is it?
B: Well, the mail's arrived.

2.4.2   Provide arguments that would support the statement that not all of Grice's maxims are equally important.

2.4.3   Argue for or against the following line of reasoning from Leech (1983:15,16).

"... of Grice's two Maxims of Quality (which I call submaxims), the second seems to be a predictable extension of the first:

Maxim 1: Do not say what you believe to be false.

Maxim 2: Do not say that for which you lack adequate evidence.

If we say something for which we lack evidence, we do not know whether what we say is true or false. Therefore Maxim 2 simply says 'Do not put yourself in a position where you risk breaking Maxim 1'; and both can be summarized in the precept 'Avoid telling untruths'."

2.4.4   Which maxims of the cooperative principle are being violated in the following dialogues? Indicate which conversational implicatures this leads to.

a.   A: Are we going to eat soon? I'm hungry.
      B: In a minute. I just have to fry the liver.
      A: Suddenly, I've lost my appetite.

b.   A: Mrs. Johnson is an old witch.
      B: It's wonderful weather for this time of year, don't you think?

2.4.5   Explain how deliberate violations, or "floutings" as Grice calls them, of the cooperative principle as in (a) and (b) can still bear meaning. Also explain when such deliberate violations do lead, for example, to lying, by discussing some conditions that must be met for flouting to render the appropriate or intended effect. (This question is inspired by an example in Cook 1989.)

a.   I love it when you sing out of key all the time.

b.   My cell phone's battery runs dead every five minutes.

2.5.1   Is B's reaction a counter-example to the proposition that every utterance can be relevant in a conversation?

A: (waiter) Can I get you something to drink?
B: (customer) Naturally, everybody drinks.

2.5.2   Recall example (27) from Section 2.5. Now try to explain in your own words how the relevance principle works by applying it to the following example: a notice often found in the London Underground (subway).

"Dogs must be carried on escalator."

2.6.1   Use the terms face and face work techniques to explain the misunderstanding in the following dialogue.

A: Are you going to do anything with those old chairs?
B: No, you can have them.
A: Oh, no, that's not what I meant.

2.6.2   In the following dialogue, is B being positively or negatively polite? (B thinks the dress is ugly.)

   A: So, what do you think of my new dress?

   B: Well, it's risqué, that's for sure.

2.6.3   Rank the following statements from "extremely polite" to "less polite" using Brown and Levinson's theory. Indicate which strategy has been used.

   a.   Do you agree to pay half of the bill thirty days before delivery?

   b.   Thirty days before delivery you will receive a bill for half of the order.

   c.   You have to pay half of the bill before delivery.

   d.   Though we do not like to make this demand, it is this company's policy that half of the bill be paid thirty days before delivery.

2.6.4   Explain why B does not answer with "Yes", but immediately makes an offer in the following dialogue.

   A: Do you have ice cream?

   B: Do you want chocolate topping?

Assignments

2.5.1   In Section 2.5 it is argued that language is often/always underspecified. Consider the example "Thank you for observing no smoking". Try to explain why language is often underspecified. Think, for example, of the economy principle, which applies in most human behavior.

2.5.2   Mikhail Bakhtin was a famous Russian philosopher and language theorist at the beginning of the last century (see also Section 4.2). In *The Bakhtin Reader* by Morris (1994:26–37) the following quote from Volosinov (a friend's name under which Bakhtin wrote) is included:

   "To understand another person's utterance means to orient oneself with respect to it, to find the proper place for it in the corresponding context. For each word of the utterance that we are in process of understanding, we, as it were, lay down a set of our own answering words. The greater their number and weight, the deeper and more substantial our understanding will be."

   Try to point out the differences and/or similarities between Volosinov's reasoning and the view on relevance of Sperber and Wilson, as presented in Section 2.5 of this chapter.

Bibliographical information

2.1   For Plato's view on language as a form of action, the reader is referred to the Fowler edition (1977), Part IV, pp. 19–23. The view that language is an activity can also be found in other works, for example, the German linguist and philosopher Wegener (1885) and the English linguist Gardiner (1969, 2nd edition), who dedicated his work to Wegener. Gardiner also stressed the cooperative aspect in language use.

Bühler developed his vision in publications at the beginning of the last century. A more elaborate explanation of his views is given in his opus *Sprachtheorie* (1934). A translation of this work appeared in 1990.

The work done by Jespersen has also been influential. His major work, dating from 1924, has been reprinted many times, the most recent being in 1992.

2.2   Austin first presented his ideas in a series of William James Lectures at Harvard University in 1955. The lectures were published posthumously by Urmson and Sbisà and titled *How to Do Things With Words*. See Austin (1976).

The most influential philosopher in the area of speech act theory was John Searle. An oft-quoted publication of his is *Speech Acts* (1969).

Habermas presented his ideas in his major work *Theorie des Kommunikativen Handelns* (1981). In this work he also criticizes Searle. The classification of illocutions is not dealt with further in this introduction, as this problem is not in the mainstream of contemporary discourse studies.

2.3   The example of felicity conditions for requests was taken from Searle (1969). For a good panorama of what is being done in contemporary speech act theory, see Vanderveken and Kubo (2001). This collection of papers is more oriented towards illocutionary logic than to "classical" speech act theory. It should be mentioned that this is not a beginners' book.

2.4   Grice was mainly interested in natural language. He wanted to prove that a natural language was as precise as a logical language, provided an extra set of rules governing natural language is taken into account. By stating this, he took issue with those philosophers who claimed that natural language was too imprecise for scientific purposes. Grice, like Austin (see 2.2), presented his proposals in a William James Lectures series at Harvard University in 1967, twelve years after Austin. A summary of these lectures was published in 1975.

2.5   The standard work on relevance is Sperber and Wilson (1995). Carston (2002) provides a thorough and comprehensive panorama of the relevance debate up until now. Example (26) is taken from Smith and Wilson (1979); (28) and (29) from Leech (1983). Example (31) is taken from Grundy (2000). Blakemore (1992) gives an introduction to pragmatics that is based on Relevance Theory.

2.6   Goffman based his concept of *face* on his research into ritual elements in social interaction, that is, those standardized acts with which individuals express respect or deference for each other or objects. Goffman first presented his ideas in *The Presentation of Self in Everyday Life* (1956). A good way of getting acquainted with his ideas is to read Goffman (1967). One of his last publications dates from 1981.

Leech approaches politeness phenomena in an entirely different manner. In Leech (1983) the politeness principle is proposed to be separate from the cooperative principle, complete with accompanying maxims such as the maxims of tact and modesty. Since, however, the number of maxims is greatly expanded and violation of the maxims does not lead to implicatures such as occurs with the cooperative principle, the theory has not gained a large following.

For more on Brown and Levinson's theory, the reader is referred to their 1990 publication that reports on research done on politeness phenomena in a number of languages. The proposal on the analysis of indirect requests is from Levinson (1983).

3 Discourse in communication

The pragmatic perspective

In the previous chapter communication has been presented as action, more precisely as the combined action of speakers and listeners, or writers and readers, in which they exchange illocutions, following the principle of cooperation and the relevance maxim and obeying politeness strategies. If anything has become clear, then it must be that the verbal part of communication, discourse, cannot be studied without taking into account the context in which the communicative acts take place. Only in this way can the relation between the form and the function of discourse be clarified.

A good framework for studying discourse in the form-function approach is pragmatics. Pragmatics, literally "the study of acts", is itself part of a philosophical approach to the phenomenon *sign*, specifically the question of how signs, and therefore also linguistic signs, function. This is known as semiotics. Two names associated with semiotics are those of the American philosophers Charles Peirce and Charles Morris. Peirce's ideas, first published at the beginning of the previous century, were elaborated by Morris and gained prominence in the 1960s. For a good insight into the status of the pragmatic perspective in discourse studies some information about semiotics in general is needed.

The central concept in semiotics is the notion of sign. A sign, according to Peirce, cannot be seen independently of its object and its interpretant. A sign, in the form of a representamen, let's say the word *castle*, stands for its object. A sign can only be a sign if it is addressed to somebody, and creates an "idea" in the mind of the addressee; this is called the interpretant. In other words, a sign is "nothing" without its function, referring to an object and creating an idea. This three-part approach calls to mind a similar approach in the Organon model (see Section 2.1), but there is more. Peirce distinguished three types of signs. A sign can be an icon, which means that the sign resembles some object, e.g., a picture of a castle on a billboard, the picture of a man on a toilet door or an emoticon in e-mail. A sign can be an index, which means that it directs attention to the object. For example, a weathercock is an index of the direction of the wind, the phone ringing is an index of someone who wants to talk to you and an arrow on a crossroads can be an index to a castle. The third sign is the symbol. A symbol is associated with an object by "rule". For example, we have learned that a building with battlements, a drawbridge and towers is called a castle. A symbol represents its object and determines its interpretant on the basis of conventions. Most words are symbols.

It is important to note that many signs are mixed signs. Peirce himself gives the example of a man walking with a child and pointing into the sky, saying, "Look, there is a balloon." The pointing arm is an index and is as such essential for understanding the symbol. If the child then asks, "What is a balloon?", the father can answer by using an icon: "O, that is something like a big soap bubble." In comparison with the Organon model, the sign philosophy in semiotics is much richer, stimulating us to think about what the symbols that we use in discourse precisely are. Figure 1 and Table 1 summarize the aspects of a sign and its three categories.

Elaborating on Peirce, the philosopher Morris (1938) distinguished three areas in the field of semiotics: 1. syntax, the relationship between signs within a sign system; 2. semantics, the relationship between signs and the objects they refer to; 3. pragmatics, the relationship between signs and the people who use them. Pragmatics is concerned with such questions as why an individual uses a specific sign, which circumstances call for the use of a specific sign and how we interpret signs. Pragmatics, in other words, deals with questions about how signs function. Applied to discourse, the pragmatic approach deals with the question of how discourse is produced and interpreted in context, in specific situations. With the study of production and perception we find ourselves in the area of cognitive studies (see Chapter 13). When the focus is on discourse in context, in specific situations we are in the research area of language and institutions (see Chapter 14) and language and culture (see Chapter 15).

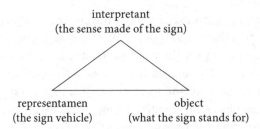

Figure 1.   Peirce's semiotic triangle

Table 1.   Three categories of signs

Icon	Index	Symbol
a likeness to some object (natural or by convention)	a causal connection to the object	a conventionally stipulated relation (most words)

It is important to note that in discourse studies pragmatics is mostly not considered a separate branch of linguistics in the way that phonetics, syntax and semantics are. Should this be the case, however, pragmatics is often used as a kind of wastebasket term for the study of linguistic phenomena that cannot be described at "lower levels" in linguistics. On the contrary, pragmatics in discourse studies means a pragmatic view of all levels of communication through the use of symbols, thus also syntactic and semantic aspects. Compare the sentences in the following two examples.

(1)   Mary went to Ann because she wanted coffee.
(2)   Mary got angry with Ann because she was not at home.

How can it be explained that "she" in (1) can refer to Mary and Ann, but in (2) usually only to Ann? To explain this difference in grammatical reference we need a rule about language use like "If there are two possible antecedents then the pronoun is normally used to refer to the subject, unless the state of affairs represented gives an overruling cue for the other referent". Now consider a semantic example. The word "just" can have the meaning "a short time ago". But there is a difference between the following sentences.

(3)   I just came from the toilet.
(4)   I just had my holidays in India.

Both sentences refer to the past, but the action described in (3) is usually nearer to the present than the action in (4). From a pragmatic perspective it is interesting to study the manner in which rather fixed meanings can vary in language use.

In discourse studies the pragmatic approach has become very important, since discourse is not just an abstract combination of syntax and semantics, possibly combined with phonetics in spoken discourse. In the pragmatic approach the focus is on language in use in specific situations. What are the regularities, what are the rules that pragmatics wants to detect in language use?

3.2   Rules for symbolic interaction

Pragmatics is about the social rules for the interchange of symbols. These rules differ from rules in physics or logic, for example. An example of a physical rule is the law of gravity; this rule exists independently of humans. An example of a logical rule is that if A is bigger than B, and B is bigger than C, we can draw the conclusion that A is bigger than C. By contrast, a social rule is not logical and exists only because people exhibit some regularity in behavior, in this case verbal behavior.

Social rules have six characteristics, which are important for studying language in use. These characteristics can be illustrated by the following fragment of conversation.

(5)   A: How are you doing?
      B: Fine. And you?

The rules by which A and B act are (1) *acquired* and (2) *usually not applied consciously*. A language user has to learn how to react to a question about his health. The fact that rules are acquired implies that they are learnable and that it is possible to act according to these rules. Nevertheless, most of the time a language user will not be aware of these rules.

Furthermore, social rules are (3) *communal*. They are not private rules, but are acted upon by groups of people. This means that specific expectations exist about verbal behavior. On the basis of a communal rule for reacting to an enquiry about someone's health, A is allowed to expect B to react in a certain manner.

The fourth characteristic is based on the third. Rules are (4) *a framework for understanding and judging an illocution* in terms of (in)consequence, implications and appropriateness. In certain circumstances B can interpret A's question as an attempt to start a conversation. In this case A may interpret the tenor of B's counter-question as a notification that B wants to have a conversation as well. If B were to start a conversation with C immediately after his utterance to A, A would judge this as inconsequent or inappropriate.

The last two characteristics are important as well. Rules (5) *can be violated* and rules are (6) *liable to change*. The fact that rules can be violated is proved by B's possible reaction of starting a conversation with C. The rule "answer B's counter-question only by saying 'fine'" can change in the sense that the person addressed is expected to provide something more than just a formal answer, for example: "Well, actually quite fine these days" or "Well, not so good, to be honest".

In relation to the above-mentioned characteristics of social rules, an often-used pair of concepts must be broached, namely *descriptive* and *prescriptive*. These concepts are of help in explaining the nature of rules, and in clarifying the difference between a rule and a norm.

By using rules it is possible to describe how language is used, but the same rules can also indicate how language must be used, for example, that a greeting has to be answered with a counter-greeting. As long as one purely describes, it is a matter of descriptive rules. If one prescribes or dictates, it is a matter of prescriptive rules. From a discourse-analytical point of view, rules are descriptive. However, rules are prescriptive for a language user that wants to know how to use language. One rule can thus be viewed from both a descriptive and a prescriptive perspective.

Norms vs. rules

What sets rules apart from norms? Norms always concern the question of how one should behave. They are guidelines with an ethic aspect. Norms are the values that one uses when answering questions about what is (morally) right or wrong: for example, to eat meat or not, or to use foreign words in your own language or not. A language user can interpret norms for language use as prescriptive. The concept of norm has to be clearly discerned from the concept of rule, since the latter does not always imply a guideline.

The previous paragraph discussed the distinction between rules and norms. But what is the difference between rules and maxims (discussed in Section 2.4)? Rules can be represented in the form "If X then Y". An example is the rule that if one is greeted, one responds with a counter-greeting. The if-sentence indicates the situation in which the rule applies. Such a situation serves as the demarcation of a rule's reach. Other restraints can be an enumeration of terms or conditions under which a rule is valid. For example, the illocution *to promise* implies the rule that the speaker commits himself to do what he has promised.

There are also general rules without a condition in an if-sentence, for example, this rule in language use: "Avoid ambiguity". Such a general rule is called a maxim or a ground rule. Another example would be "Avoid unnecessary prolixity". When several of these maxims can be attached to one underlying concept, one speaks of a principle, in this case for example, the efficiency principle. On the basis of maxims of ambiguity and prolixity, which can be attached to this principle, language use in certain situations can be described by means of rules.

The difference between rules on the one hand and maxims on the other can be summarized as follows. Maxims are assumed to always be valid, whereas rules only apply in specific situations or are valid for specific illocutions.

Now that the aspects of signs, the different types of signs and rules for the exchange of symbols have been dealt with, we take a closer look in Section 3 at how signs are combined into messages between sender and receiver.

3.3   Messages between sender and receiver

In layman's terms, a discourse is 1. a set of connected meaningful sentences or utterances (the form) by which a sender 2. communicates a message to a receiver (the function). This popular approach to discourse as a coherent series of symbols is, however, not useful for scholarly purposes. Two problems arise. First, it is not clear whether or not a text qualifies as a set of coherent meaningful sentences. Second, the terms *sender* and *receiver* may obstruct one's view of what senders and receivers are actually doing as participants in communicating the meaning of series of symbols. With regard to these two problems, consider the following example, an experimental poem.

(6) Ota
     Ota ota ota
     Boo
     Ota ota
     Ota ota ota boo
     Oo Oo
     Oo Oo ota ota ota

Does this (anglicized) poem by Dutch poet Jan Hanlo given in (6) qualify as a meaningful set of coherent utterances? With some imagination, it is possible for a reader to argue that the poem is somehow coherent, for example, as a composition of aural effects or as a satire on traditional poetic conventions. The attribution of coherence is, therefore, partially dependent on the disposition of the receiver. So, perhaps it is better to define discourse as a set of utterances that can be conceived of as meaningful or relevant.

The use of the terms sender and receiver presupposes that there is an information package that has to be transmitted from one person to another. In fact, this view of the participants in discourse stems from a view of communication that is inspired and influenced by the invention of the telephone at the beginning of the last century. It is known as the general communication model, which originates from Claude Shannon and Warren Weaver (1949). For a better understanding of this concept of discourse, a short explanation is required.

This diagram is to be read as follows. In the *information source* a message is selected. This can consist of written or spoken words, images, music, etc. The *transmit-*

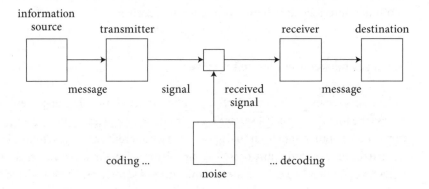

Figure 2. Shannon and Weaver's general communication model

ter encodes the message in a signal that is sent through the communication channel to the *receiver*. The receiver translates the signal into a message – decodes it – and transmits this message to the *destination*. In communication, the message can undergo changes caused by *noise*; this is called "interference".

The general communication model has often been applied to discourse. The speaker/writer then is the information source. (What a speaker/writer has in mind can of course be based on other sources of information.) The message is coded into words. This is then transported through a communication channel, voice, paper or screen, to the receiver. The receiver decodes the message, after which the message arrives at the final destination, the reader's mind.

This communication model is appealingly uncomplicated, but the process of communication is, in fact, much more complex. There are two major objections that can be put forward. First, nothing can be said about illocutionary force in the sender-message-receiver approach. The message "I'll come tomorrow" can be a promise, a statement, or a threat. If the communication is to be successful, the receiver must not only understand that the "I" in the sentence will be present on the day following the message, but also understand what kind of speech act is being committed. The same holds true for indirect language use. An utterance like "Are you doing anything special tonight?" can, in certain situations, be seen as an invitation. It is left to the receiver to deduce this from the message.

Second, the model does not take into account the discourse situation in which the communication originated. The situation does, however, play a role in the interpretation of a message. Consider the following sentence:

(7)   Pete told John that he was sick.

The sentence can mean that Pete is sick, but it can also mean that John is sick. In practice this ambiguity rarely leads to difficulties because the situation usually makes it fairly obvious which meaning is intended. In the sender-message-receiver approach no description can be given of how the process of decoding determines the applicable interpretation, because the situation is not taken into account.

In short, discourse is more than a message from sender to receiver. In fact, sender and receiver are metaphors that obfuscate what is really going on in communication. Specific illocutions have to be linked to the message depending on the situation in which discourse takes place. The illocutions have been dealt with in Section 2.4. How the sender-receiver metaphor obfuscates what is really going on in communication is very insightfully demonstrated in a study by the psycholinguist Herbert Clark (1996), *Using Language*. Pursuing old ideas of, for example, Jespersen (see Section 2.1), that language is a human activity on the part of at least two individuals, Clark compares language in use with a business transaction, paddling together in a canoe, playing cards or performing music in an orchestra. Communication is a form of social action, of joint action.

Clark's common ground

A central notion in Clark's study is common ground. The joint activity is undertaken to accumulate the common ground of the participants. With common ground is meant the sum of the joint and mutual knowledge, beliefs and suppositions of the participants. This view is perhaps easier to understand by considering the Latin roots of the verb to communicate: the meaning "to make common". In Clark's view this means that communication as a joint activity adds information to the common ground of the participants (and not "senders" and "receivers"). In dealing with all kinds of everyday conversations Clark showed that discourse cannot be studied without taking into account this common ground. According to him common ground divides into three types, as shown in Table 2.

Applied to the joint action of a client and a clerk in a drugstore, these three types of common ground can be filled in as follows. The initial common ground pertains to the fact that both the client and the clerk presuppose the standard procedures in their culture for exchanging money for goods. They also presuppose that they both speak the same language and that the client has enough money, etc. The current state of affairs is different from the initial state of affairs, and visible to the client and the clerk. After the client has, for example, placed two items on the counter and said "I'd like these two things", it is clear to both him and the clerk that one is the server, the other the current customer, that the client refers to the items on the counter, that the clerk has to ring them up on the cash register, etc. When the clerk then, for example, says "Here's your change", both he and the client presuppose a sequence of public events so far: the client has caught the clerk's attention, he has specified the items to be bought, the clerk has rung them up, the client has given money and the clerk has returned the change. With his focus on common ground Clark stresses the importance of studying communication on the basis of what participants verbally exchange in a real situation.

Table 2.   Representations of common ground

	Type of common ground	Explanation
1.	Initial common ground	The set of background facts, assumptions and beliefs the participants presupposed when they entered the joint activity.
2.	Current state of the joint activity	What the participants presuppose to be the state of the activity at the moment.
3.	Public events so far	The events the participants presuppose have occurred in public leading up to the current state.

3.4   The discourse situation

In the discussion on illocutions, it was noted that these could be seen as functions of certain forms. The form "announcement" can function as order, request, etc. Obviously, this does not adequately describe the term *function*. Function here means the objective and effect in a given situation. For instance:

(8) A: Do you smoke?
     B: Well, if you've got a cigarette.

The function of A's utterance could be that A wants to make B feel at ease by using the question form for the illocution *to offer*. A's objective has a specific effect: B makes it clear that the illocution is understood, and counters with, as a perlocution, a suggestion which makes it clear that A's objective has been achieved. The interpretation of possible objectives and effects, however, can be strongly influenced by the situation in which the utterance takes place. If, for example, the question "Do you smoke?" is asked by a physician, it does not function as a means of starting a conversation, but as a medical question.

The situation in which discourse is produced and processed can be analyzed and defined using a large number of factors that can have an influence on possible objectives and effects of discourse. Such a description is available for the speaking situation. It was developed by the anthropologist Dell Hymes (1972) who, on the basis of ethnographic research, summed up the components of the "speech event". Hymes distinguished sixteen components, which he grouped using the word SPEAKING as an acronym. In the following outline the components are italicized.

(9) Hymes's SPEAKING model

S	*Setting*	Time, place, and other physical conditions surrounding the speech act.
	Scene	The psychological counterpart to setting. What is meant here is that a setting can be changed, for example, from formal to informal, by the participants.
P	Participants	The *Speaker* or Sender, the *Addresser*, the *Hearer*, Receiver or Audience, and the *Addressee*.
E	Ends	The *Purpose – outcomes* and *Purpose – goals*.
A	Act Sequences	The *Form* and the *Content* of the message.
K	*Keys*	The tone of the conversation, for example, serious or mocking.
I	Instrumentalities	The *Channels*; written, telegraph, etc., and the *Forms of Speech*; dialect, standard language, etc.
N	Norms	The *Norms of Interaction*, e.g., interruption and *Norms of Interpretation*, for example, how a listener's suddenly looking away must be interpreted.
G	*Genres*	Fairy tale, advertisement, etc.

This model became popular largely because of the handy grouping using the letters SPEAKING. It is unclear, however, what the influence of the different components is. Moreover, the outline is not complete. Background knowledge shared by the speaker and the listener, and possible differences in background knowledge, can influence discourse. The same holds true for posture or attitude.

Though the model is fairly general, by using it, the factors comprising the discourse situation can be clarified. Moreover, the differences between two comparable situations can be highlighted. For example, take on the one hand the discourse situation in a classroom where a student and a teacher have a conversation and on the other hand the situation in which the same student talks with his roommate in the dormitory. By using a few letters from the model, possible differences can be explained.

The discourse situations can be defined using elements from the components S, P and N: from *setting* the place of occurrence, and the *scene*, the psychological occurrence, from the *participants* their societal role, and from *norms* those that are bound by place. It is obvious that this student finds himself in two different settings: in a classroom and in a student dorm. The scene is different as well under the influence of the different roles that the participants take: the student-teacher conversation will be more formal than the student-student conversation in the dorm. This student has to act according to varying norms as well, when talking with a teacher or with a fellow student.

The remaining factors comprising the SPEAKING model clarify the discourse situation as well. These factors deal with the relationship between function and form as mentioned earlier. For example, the student-teacher conversation will be of a different genre than the conversation between the student and his roommate: at school he asks a question, at home he tells a joke. And perhaps the student uses dialect when he is at home, whereas he will probably use standard language in a conversation with his teacher. The student's conversations will serve different ends too. In class the purpose is to have a question answered; in the dorm the goal is to amuse his roommate.

A very important point to remember is that discourse is not only a part of the situation, but can change the situation or even create a context as well. The way in which discourse can change the situation can also be observed in the classroom example. Suppose that one of the students knows the teacher as a neighbor and wants to let him know that last night's party, which the teacher organized, was too noisy. This changes the situation in a classroom from a student-to-teacher conversation into a neighbor-to-neighbor conversation.

An example of discourse creating a context is the opening sentence of a conversation. This activates a mental mapping for both speaker and listener. If two strangers are sitting on a park bench, a context is created when one asks the other "Could you perhaps tell me the time?" or "I think it'll be raining soon". Both persons have an idea of the situation that enrolls and about the way it may evolve.

A last, terminological, question concerns the following. The term *context* is often used instead of situation or discourse situation. This term can, however, cause some confusion as the word *context* is also used to denote the piece of discourse surrounding an element in discourse, for example, the context of a word, a sentence, or a paragraph. For this reason the word *context* is often qualified: the "verbal context" or "textual environment" as opposed to the "social context" or "pragmatic context". The social context is often divided into the context of situation and the context of culture. The word *cotext* can also be used to denote verbal context, thereby distinguishing it from *context* in the sense of discourse situation.

3.5   The socio-semiotic approach

So far in this chapter we have seen that discourse cannot be studied adequately without taking into account the addresser and addressee who use discourse for all the purposes communication can be used for (Section 3.1). We have also established that the main aim of studying discourse can be formulated as to detect the rules that underlie this "symbolic interaction" (Section 3.2). Within this approach two related aspects are very important. First, an addressee is not just a receiver of the message; in fact receivers are active, cooperating participants in the communication (Section 3.3). Second, discourse is always situated in a social context and in a specific situation (Section 3.4). The most important question in discourse studies as an (inter)discipline has not yet been posed: Which theory or approach offers a good general framework for analyzing all the different aspects of discourse? The best candidate seems to be the so-called socio-semiotic approach.

functional grammar

The founding father and mother of the socio-semiotic approach are the linguists Michael Halliday (1978) and Ruqaiya Hasan. Their approach is generally labeled as *functional grammar*, because it focuses on the function of discourse in context. It is also called *systemic functional linguistics*, because it studies the functions in a systematic whole. However, the term *socio-semiotic* seems more precise as it explains the roots in semiotics (see Section 3.1) and the sociological focus. With the prefix *socio* the social context is meant, in which the context of culture and the context of situation can be distinguished. With *semiotic* the act of conveying meaning with symbols, in our case in discourse, is meant. The central claim in this approach is: Every (piece of) discourse has to be studied in its social context, in the culture and situation in which it appears.

Halliday and Hasan (1985) describe three aspects of social context: field, tenor and mode. These concepts make it possible to interpret the social context of a discourse, the environment in which meanings are exchanged.

1. *Field*

The field of discourse refers to what is happening and to the nature of the social action that is taking place. More specifically, it answers questions about what the participants are engaged in, in which the language figures as some essential component. In general it is the gist of what the discourse is about. The field refers to all different kinds of social actions, from doing the dishes to a parliamentary debate. Field is mostly restricted to institutional settings like lectures, visits to a doctor, etc.

2. *Tenor*

The tenor of discourse refers to who is taking part, to the nature of the participants, to their statuses and roles. It says something about the kinds of role relationship that exist between the participants. It explicates both the types of speech role that participants assume in dialogue and the whole cluster of socially significant relationships in which they are involved.

Tenor can be analyzed using categories such as power and social distance, which have already been addressed in Section 2.3 on politeness strategies. Tenor also refers to affect, the degree of emotional charge in the relationship between the participants, the attitudes and emotions that play a role in communication. Compare a more objective discussion between judges and a discussion at a protest meeting.

3. Mode

The mode of discourse refers to what part the language plays and the participants' expectations about what language can do for them in that situation. It is about the symbolic organization of the text, its status, and its function in the context, including the channel (spoken, written or a combination of the two) and the rhetorical mode. Finally, it says something about what the text achieves in terms persuasive, expository, and didactic categories, and the like. In discourse studies the mode aspect is central. The most important questions are: "What is the organization of the discourse?", "What is its function in context?" and "What is achieved by discourse?"

The three aspects of the social context outlined above correlate with three aspects of the discourse: ideational, interpersonal and textual meaning. Meaning connects discourse to the context. Simply stated, this is the reference using symbols to elements in the context. Hence the connection between discourse and context be situated on the semantic level of semiotics.

Table 3 gives an overview of the correlation between the three aspects of the social context and the three aspects of the discourse.

Table 3.   Key concepts in functional grammar

Situation components of context	Discourse aspects of meaning
Field	Ideational meaning
Tenor	Interpersonal meaning
Mode	Textual meaning

From the discourse point of view of discourse, the ideational meaning of a discourse corresponds to the field. It is the content of a discourse as it refers to what is going on in a particular situation or a specific topic. The ideational meaning must be given as an answer to the question: What is this discourse about?

The interpersonal meaning of a discourse corresponds with the tenor of context, and can be detected by analyzing how participants in the discourse are related to the content or ideational meaning and how they use language to act. For example, the use of a command can reveal that the person has the power to give a command. Or an adjective such as *horrible* reveals an affectual aspect of a person who uses this word.

Finally, the textual meaning corresponds to the mode of the context. The textual meaning is the organization of the content elements in a larger structure, e.g., the perspective in which a topic is dealt with, and the techniques of putting some information in a prominent place or the combining of sentences.

A last point to be mentioned is the way discourse is embedded in the different levels of social context and the correspondence with discourse characteristics. Halliday and Hasan distinguished two levels in social context: the context of culture and the context of situation. Up till now neither the different types of discourse nor the different styles or registers in which discourse occurs have been discussed. But with this division of context into two levels, the phenomena of different types and styles have a well-defined place within this socio-semiotic approach. The notion of cultural context is linked to discourse type and the notion of situational context to style. In this view cultural aspects have given discourse types such as a news story or an instruction their form. And the way in which language can differ in style – informal, bureaucratic, persuasive, etc. – is dictated by the situation in which a discourse takes place. In the next part of this book, the first chapter (Chapter 4) is about types, the cultural context, while the last chapter (Chapter 8) is about style and register, the situational context. The intermediate chapters deal with the mode aspects of discourse.

3.6   What makes discourse discourse?

Discourse has many different manifestations in many different situations, from chat to deed of purchase, from sermon to shopping list. These manifestations are so different that one may wonder if the term *discourse* is perhaps too vague to span all differences. What is actually meant by discourse?

What all different kinds of discourse have in common can be indicated with reference to the etymology of *discourse*. The word stems from the Medieval Latin word "*discurrere*", which means "to circulate". Literally, it means "to run to and fro" or "to run on", like a person who gives a speech and runs on about a topic. A discourse is something that runs from one person to another. By the way, the shopping list can only do that by "running back" to the person who made this list. The etymology of the related word *text* can also be useful for clarifying the nature of discourse. The word *text* has the same roots as *textile*: the Latin verb "*texere*", which means "to weave". Woven in a text, in a discourse, are the different meaning units in a bigger whole. The textile metaphor we know from such expressions as "to lose the thread of communication" or "to tie up loose ends" in finishing a plea or argument, and "to spin a yarn" (dishing up an incredible story) exemplifies this.

Of course, this etymological approach is not enough for the study of the essentials of discourse. What makes a sequence of sentences or utterances a discourse? The following fragment is, in any case, not a normal discourse.

(10) John wants to visit his girlfriend. Mr. Smith lives in a small village nearby. The vacuum cleaner didn't work. The barber down the street couldn't help. The last paper had been sold. It is going to be a long dull talk.

This fragment seems to have come into existence by a number of unrelated sentences being placed in random order. But if some words are changed, a piece of discourse is the result.

(11) John wants to visit his girlfriend. Mary lives in a small village nearby. The car wouldn't start. The garage down the street couldn't help. The last bus had already left. It is going to be a long hot walk.

The example illustrates that the existence of connections between sentences is an important characteristic of discourse. The term *connection* is, however, somewhat vague. Robert de Beaugrande (1981), one of the grand old men in discourse studies, has formulated seven criteria for textuality, that is, criteria that a sequence of sentences must meet in order to qualify as a discourse.

a. *Cohesion* is the connection that results when the interpretation of a textual element is dependent on another element in the text. Consider the following example.

(12) The store no longer sold porcelain figurines. It used to, the man behind the counter said, but they didn't sell very well. Since the business had switched to plastic, sales were doing a lot better.

The interpretation of "It" is dependent on that of "store" just as "they" is dependent on that of "porcelain figurines". The meaning of "used to" is dependent on "sold porcelain figurines". The word "plastic" can only be completely interpreted in relation to "(porcelain) figurines". Cohesion refers to the connection that exists between elements in the text.

b. *Coherence* is the connection that is brought about by something outside the text. This "something" is usually knowledge which a listener or reader is assumed to have. The following example is not problematic in terms of cohesion even though the sentences hardly seem to be connected.

(13) The procedure is actually quite simple. First you arrange things into different groups. Of course, one pile may be sufficient depending on how much there is

to do. If you have to go somewhere else due to lack of facilities, that is the next step, otherwise you are pretty well set.

It is important not to overdo things. That is, it is better to do too few things at once than too many. In the short run this may not seem important, but complications can easily arise. A mistake can be expensive as well.

At first the whole procedure will seem complicated. Soon, however, it will become just another facet of life. It is difficult to foresee any end to the necessity for this task in the immediate future, but then one never can tell.

After the procedure is completed, one arranges the materials into different groups again. Then they can be put into their appropriate places. Eventually they will be used once more and the whole cycle will then have to be repeated. However, that is part of life.

This seemingly disjointed passage becomes coherent when certain knowledge of the world, i.e., knowledge of washing clothes, is applied to the text. The text then becomes easy to interpret.

c. *Intentionality* means that writers and speakers must have the conscious intention of achieving specific goals with their message, for instance, conveying information or arguing an opinion. According to this criterion, the sequence of words in the experimental poem *Ota Boo* in Section 3.3 can only be called a discourse after an authorial intention has been assigned to it. When no intention is assigned, the word sequence becomes the equivalent of a page of random words not unlike the penmanship practice of elementary school pupils.

d. *Acceptability* requires that a sequence of sentences be acceptable to the intended audience in order to qualify as a text. Consider the claim "This book is mine. Don't you see my name is in it?" This example has a somewhat skewed internal logic and is therefore unacceptable to many people.

e. *Informativeness* is necessary in discourse. A discourse must contain new information. If a reader knows everything contained in a discourse, then it does not qualify. Likewise, if a reader does not understand what is in a discourse, it also does not qualify as a discourse.

f. *Situationality* is essential to textuality. So, it is important to consider the situation in which the discourse has been produced and dealt with (see Section 3.4).

g. *Intertextuality* means that a sequence of sentences is related by form or meaning to other sequences of sentences. This chapter is a discourse because it is related to the other chapters of this book. And this book is a discourse because it is a member of the group of textbooks. An example of intertextuality where the two sequences are related by meaning is a news bulletin on a topic that has previously been dealt with in a news program.

Criteria *c, d*, and *e* are somewhat subjective. Recognition of intentionality, acceptability and informativeness are observer-dependent. It is conceivable that within the boundaries of the situationality criterion, the following example can be seen as an acceptable and informative fragment of discourse:

(14) Shakespeare wrote more than 20 plays. Will you have dinner with me tonight?

This non-discourse might at first seem to be the last line of a newspaper article followed by the first line of an entirely unrelated article. Yet it is possible to think of a situation in which these two sentences could form part of a discourse, for example, the situation in which the speaker has wagered a dinner as to the number of plays that Shakespeare wrote.

Not all criteria are considered equally important in discourse studies. *Intertextuality* is mainly dealt with in the field of discourse typology. *Situationality* and the subjective characteristics *intentionality* and *informativeness* are of secondary importance. They do play a role in research into textual functions where function is defined as the goal (*intentionality*) and the effect (primarily the transfer of information) in a specific situation. The criterion *acceptability* only occurs in normative approaches to discourse studies, for example, in the investigation into the question: What is a good discourse? In discourse studies most attention has been paid to the first criteria of *cohesion* and *coherence*, sometimes taken together as *connectivity*. Cohesion is usually defined as the connectivity that is literally detectable in discourse, e.g., by synonyms and pronominal words such as *she, it*, etc. Coherence is the connectivity that can be inferred from the discourse by the reader or listener, e.g., we can place the word *therefore* or *thereafter* between the following sentences in order to explicate the relation we have inferred: "She had a child. She married".

Questions and assignments

Questions

3.1.1 In the preface to his *Principles of Pragmatics* (1983:x) Geoffrey Leech approached pragmatics in the following manner:

> "But my approach to pragmatics is by way of the thesis that communication is problem-solving. A speaker, *qua* communicator, has to solve the problem: 'Given that I want to bring about such-and-such a result in the hearer's consciousness, what is the best way to accomplish this aim by using language?'"

Indicate the similarities and differences between the pragmatic approach to discourse in Section 3.1 and Leech's approach.

3.2.1 Is a grammatical rule descriptive or prescriptive? Support your answer.

3.3.1 Comment on the proposition "A text is a collection of connected utterances" on the basis of the following "texts". Do they, in your opinion, count as texts? Example (a) is a graffiti text and example (b) is a notice on a shop door.
   a.   In the springtime this building blossoms.
   b.   Closed

3.3.2 The etymology of the words *text* and *textile* goes back to the same Latin verb, "*texere*", which means "to weave" or "to join together". Define *text* using words that also describe characteristics of textiles.

3.3.3 Use examples to illustrate that the causes of non-comprehensibility of texts can be localized in the various components of the general communication model.

3.4.1 A suspect appears in court and reacts to a question posed by the judge in the following way:
   A: You are John Smith?
   B: I've been asked that three times already during the investigations. You should know by now.
   Explain in terms of objectives and situation what is going wrong in this communication.

3.4.2 By using the letters S, E, N and G from the SPEAKING model, point out the differences between the discourse situations in which a doctor and a nurse find themselves when they are working together at the hospital and when they go for drinks at a local bar after work.

3.5.1 Give examples of the three types of meaning (ideational, interpersonal and textual) in example (1) in Section 1.1.

3.6.1   In the following examples the word "run" has different meanings. Does the determination of the correct meaning have to do with cohesion or coherence?

a.   I'm going to wind up these old clocks I found in the attic, but I don't know if they will run or not.

b.   A number of lesser-known candidates were promised government funding, but I don't know if they will run or not.

3.6.2   Explain whether or not the coherence criterion is valid in example (a) in question 3.3.1.

3.6.3   Use the cooperative principle and the maxim of relevance to illustrate that the informativeness criterion (see Section 3.6) is also applicable in situations in which ostensibly no new information is being given. An example is the situation in which A and B both know that John is asleep and they also both know that the other knows this, but A still says to B: "John is sleeping."

Assignments

3.1.1   Compare the three functions that Bühler assigns to a linguistic sign (see Section 2.1) with the three-part approach to a sign of Peirce. Comment on the similarities as well as on possible differences between these two perspectives.

3.4.1   Explain how discourse can create or modify a situation by using an example you have constructed yourself.

3.4.2   Johnstone (2002) mentions six aspects of the shaping of discourse. Each of the categories corresponds to one way in which contexts shape discourse and discourse shapes contexts. The list is given below. Give examples of how discourse shapes and is shaped for each of these six ways.

1.   Discourse is shaped by the world, and discourse shapes the world.

2.   Discourse is shaped by language, and discourse shapes language.

3.   Discourse is shaped by participants, and discourse shapes participants.

4.   Discourse is shaped by prior discourse, and discourse shapes the possibility for future discourse.

5.   Discourse is shaped by its medium, and discourse shapes the possibility of its medium.

6.   Discourse is shaped by purpose, and discourse shapes possible purposes.

3.5.1   In Section 3.5, the explanation of the notion *mode* contains a sentence ending with the words "and the like". Try to fill in, in your own words, what "and the like" can mean in this context.

3.5.2   Take a print advertisement from a newspaper or magazine and analyze the depicted verbal and visual codes by using the triad field, tenor and mode.

3.6.1   In Section 3.6 it was explained what it is that makes discourse discourse. Now consider the following "game" that is inspired by a research method discussed in Johnson-Laird (1983). With a group
of four to five people, have the first person write down a sentence on a piece of paper. Let the next
person read this sentence and then add a sentence. Then fold the paper so that only the second
person's sentence is visible to the third person. Now the third person adds a sentence. Repeat this
procedure until everyone has read the predecessor's answer and contributed a sentence. Discuss
to what extent the produced discourse qualifies as discourse, given the definition in Chapter 1
and the criteria in Section 3.6. Is the previous contribution always used or is it rationally "thrown
away"? Repeat the assignment, but instead of one sentence per person let everyone now write
down three or more sentences. Does this influence your judgment of the qualification of the discourse as discourse?

3.6.2   In this chapter, it was explained what it is that makes discourse discourse. However, there are
almost as many definitions as there are textbooks. Below are a few examples from noteworthy
publications by other authors. Try to point out the differences between these various views on
discourse.

From Stubbs (1983:1):

"Discourse is language above the sentence or above the clause."

From Brown and Yule (1983:1):

"The analysis of discourse is, necessarily, the analysis of language in use."

From Tannen (1988:xi):

"That mysterious moving face that creeps in between the words and between the lines,
sparking ideas, images and emotions that are not contained in any words one at a time – the
face that makes words into discourse."

From Fairclough (1992:28):

"'Discourse' is for me more than just language use: it is language use, whether speech or
writing, seen as a type of social practice."

Bibliographical information

3.1   There are a number of different approaches and definitions in pragmatics. Though notions of pragmatics have altered during the past decades, the publication by Watzlawick, Beavin and Jackson
(1967) may still be regarded as an outstanding contribution to the field. It is written in a magnificent and clear style, dealing with a great number of empirical studies, illustrated with examples
from everyday life as well as from the academic domain.

Good introductions to pragmatics are Green (1989) and the outstanding overview provided
by Levinson (1983). Of more recent date is the work by Mey (2001). Though more concise than the
latter publication, Grundy's (2000) work is very useful, offering splendid exercises and questions.
For a succinct and accessible introduction, illustrated with comments, lively examples and exercises, see Peccei (1999). See also Cutting (2002).

A landmark publication is the acclaimed *Handbook of Pragmatics* by Verschueren, Östman
and Blommaert (1995), spanning the multiple and diverse approaches to pragmatics and exploring
in depth important and central issues in pragmatics. An online version of the *Handbook of Pragmatics* became available in 2003 (see www.benjamins.com/online). See also Verschueren (1999) for
a comprehensive and accessible introduction to pragmatics.

A still very good introduction to semiotics is that by Tejara (1988).

3.2   A good overview of the extensive literature on rules is given by Vanneste (1980). Still one of the
best publications on the study of rules and norms is the more philosophical approach in Bartsch
(1987).

3.3   The general communication model was developed by the American mathematician Claude Shannon, who published an article in 1948 entitled *The Mathematical Theory of Communication*. This
article was reprinted with the addition of an introduction by the scientific advisor Warren Weaver.
See Shannon and Weaver (1949).

In discourse studies different terms are used for written and spoken communication and the
actors. The *message* with a *sender* and a *receiver* can be a *text* or a *document* with a *writer* and a
reader or a *conversation* or an *interaction* with *participants* (a *speaker* and a *listener* or an *addressee*
or a *recipient*). In this book the term *discourse* is used as the general term.

3.4   For the SPEAKING model, see Hymes (1972). The attraction of mnemonical letter classification is
strikingly illustrated by the French adaptation of this proposal. After regrouping, Hymes arrives at
PARLANT, which stands for: *participants, actes, raison (resultat), locale, agents, normes, ton, types*. See
also Vanneste (1980) where the situation is described with the SITUE model: "*scène, instrumentalités,
thème, usagers, effet*".

The concepts *situation* and *context* are defined in the literature in a number of different ways
ranging from the very broad to the more precise. See, among others, Van Dijk (1977), De Beau-

grande (1981) and Brown and Yule (1983), which distinguishes between *discourse context* and *context of situation*.

For further study see the articles collected by Auer and Luzion (1992), and Duranti and Goodwin (1992), which provide insight into the central issues concerning the relation between language and context.

3.5   The socio-semiotic approach originates from Halliday and Hassan. The three key publications on this matter are Halliday (1978) and (1994), and Halliday and Hassan (1985). Table 3 is based on Halliday and Hassan (1985). Many other discourse analysts, mainly from the UK and Australia, work in this framework. See, for example, Kress (1989) and Martin (1992). A good introduction to the systemic functional approach in discourse analysis is Martin and Rose (2002), which is based on Martin (1992).

3.6   Examples (10) and (11) were taken from Den Uyl (1983), example (13) from Bransford and Johnson (1973).

The seven criteria for textuality were formulated by De Beaugrande (1981) with the claim that a text is non-communicative if the criteria do not apply to it. The concept of *intertextuality* is also important in French discourse theory. For an introductory publication in this area, see Macdonell (1986). In the literature many different definitions are provided for the concepts *cohesion* and *coherence*. A distinction between syntax and semantics (for cohesion) on the one hand and pragmatics (for coherence) on the other hand is often made. Sometimes the term *connectivity* or *connectedness* is used for both terms.

PART II

Backpacking for a scientific journey

4 Discourse types

4.1 The variety of functions and forms

Discourse has many different functions. Therefore, it is not surprising that discourse has many different forms as well. Following the three functions of language given in the Organon model (see Section 2.1) we can distinguish three main discourse types. If the symbol aspect of language, the reference to reality, is predominant, then the function is the transmission of information. If the accent is on the symptom aspect, then the function is expression, e.g., in a story or in poetry. When the signal aspect is accentuated, then the function is persuasion, for example, in an argumentative text. In schematic form this becomes:

Table 1. The Organon model as a starting point

Organon model	Functions	Types
symbol	information	informative discourse
symptom	expression	narrative discourse
signal	persuasion	argumentative discourse

However, this threefold division is much too simple to serve as a basic scheme for covering all the varieties of discourse. Moreover, the functions seldom occur in their pure forms. A writer can tell a story in order to persuade people about a certain issue. This three-part division says something about aspects of language that can play a role simultaneously. A more critical objection, however, is that many more functions are possible. For instance, language can be used to conceal information, to give instructions or to instill a feeling of camaraderie. One of the most influential scholars in linguistics and literary sciences, Roman Jakobson, who was educated at Russian universities, distinguished in a famous "closing statement" at a conference on "Style in Language" (1960) six functions that can also occur in combination. He based his distinctions on an extended version of the communication model discussed in Section 3.3. Below are the functions presented within his communication model.

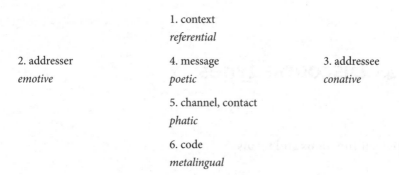

Figure 1. Functions according to Jakobson

A message is sent from the addresser to the addressee. This message refers to something in the world, the context, and is transported using a code, e.g., symbols, via a channel, between the participants in the communication. The channel consists of a physical and a psychological connection, hence, the two words *channel* and *contact*. The most important function is the one at the top, i.e., the reference to something in the world, the referential function. Its pendant in the Organon model is the symbol aspect. Two other functions are linked with the participants. The emotive or expressive function expresses the attitude of the addresser. The conative function is the orientation towards the addressee, e.g., giving a command or an instruction. These two functions related to the participants are more or less the same as the functions related to symptom and signal in the Organon model.

The fourth function in this scheme is language used in focus on the message itself. It is called the poetic function because the most pure form of this function is poetry. However, the poetic function is also apparent in everyday language, not only in puns in ads but also when someone argues that "John and Margeritha" sounds nicer than "Margeritha and John". Language is not only used for giving information. Language is also used for checking the channel or making contact. This is called *phatic communion*, the fifth function. Examples of this are "Hello, you are still there?" and – in a context where both participants know that they will have to wait for a long time – "I guess we will have a long wait?" Sometimes the language focuses on the code itself, for example, "I don't follow you" or "Am I understood?" This is called the metalinguistic or glossing function.

So much for this functional approach to varieties in discourse. Note that more functions can be distinguished, for example giving explanations in a course book like this one or making addressees shudder by telling a horror story. Nevertheless, Jakobson's six-part division is generally considered a good framework for discussing the variety of (mixed) functions of discourse.

Another way to map the variety of discourse is starting with all the different types and forms themselves, from telephone calls to telephone bills, from hypertext to chat, from interrogations to lectures. The names of these various kinds of discourse suggest that there is a difference between a scientific article and an essay, between a sermon and a political speech, etc. Especially intriguing is the fact that language users can distinguish between different kinds of discourse: "This is not a business letter, it's a personal one." People can recognize mistakes in classification: "This is called a fairy tale, but in fact it is a saga." Changes in the character of discourse can be observed as well: "At this point the news bulletin took on the character of an editorial." People also have opinions about the suitability of given kinds of discourse for specific types of messages: "That's not the kind of remark you want to put into the minutes." And, finally, discourse types can be parodied: a story can be molded into the form of an explorer's diary or a civil service letter. It would appear that people have certain intuitions regarding discourse types. In order to ascertain what these intuitions are based on, it is necessary to have a system of discourse classification within which discourse characteristics can be related to kinds of discourse.

Many attempts have been made to design a classification system. Three approaches can be distinguished in the classification of the variety of discourse. In the first approach a discourse typology is based on the relation between the discourse situation and general discourse characteristics. In the second approach abstract forms are the basis for distinguishing general discourse types to which different kinds of discourse can be assigned. In the third approach specific lexical and syntactic characteristics are related to communicative functions. Below are representative and more or less classic examples of these three approaches.

In the classification of oral discourse by Hugo Steger et al. (1974), the point of departure is the discourse situation. On the basis of sociological analysis, six discourse situations are distinguished, each with a distinctive discourse type: 1. presentation; 2. message; 3. report; 4. public debate; 5. conversation; 6. interview. The double quotation marks denote the fact that these are not everyday designations but abstract discourse types. The discourse situations can be distinguished on the basis of a large number of characteristics. Some examples are given in Figure 2.

For oral discourse the main division is into monologue as opposed to dialogue. This is the first factor in Steger's approach. In this case the criterion is the existence or absence of interaction. Dialogue or interactive discourse is divided according to the division *symmetrical–asymmetrical*. In this system this characteristic is called *rank*. *Unequal* means that the conversational participants do not have the same rights, for instance, in the case of an interrogation or a class discussion where the judge and the teacher, respectively, determine who gets to say what. An example of an equal discourse is a conversation between two friends.

	presentation	message	report	public debate	conversation	interview
Number of Speakers — One Speaker	+	+	+			
Multiple Speakers				+	+	+
Rank — Equal				+	+	
Unequal	+	+	+			+
Theme fixation — Theme predetermined	+	+	+	+		+
Theme not predetermined					+	
Method of Theme Treatment — Descriptive		+	+			
Argumentative	+			+		+
Associative					+	

Figure 2. Classification by Steger et al. (1974)

In the case of a concrete discourse it is necessary to first determine the main type, and then determine the factors in the discourse situation on the basis of which this kind of discourse distinguishes itself from related kinds of discourse. For example, a doctor–patient talk can be categorized as an *interview*. But an interrogation is also a form of interview. Using this model as a point of departure, it is possible to investigate which factor in the discourse situation can best be used to describe the difference, for example, the role of the participants and the goals of the interview.

Egon Werlich's discourse typology (1982) refers to the second approach: from abstract forms to discourse types. Werlich distinguishes five basic or ideal forms that are fundamental to discourse types. He argues for the choice of these five basic forms by referring to studies on innate categorization possibilities in human thinking. The basic forms are given in the first column of Table 2 below.

Werlich relates these basic forms to specific sentence structures. The characteristic type of sentence for the *instructive*, for example, is the imperative. The *narrative* requires a certain type of informative sentence which has a verb in the past tense and indications of time and place, as in the sentence: "The passengers arrived in New York in the middle of the night."

The five basic forms are each divided into two methods of presentation: subjective (the writer's perception) and objective (which can be verified by readers). Here too, discourse characteristics are named. The passive voice is, in Werlich's opinion, a

Table 2.   Werlich's discourse typology (1982)

Basic Forms	Subjective	Objective
(1) Descriptive	impressionistic description	technical description
(2) Narrative	report	news story
(3) Explanatory	essay	explication
(4) Argumentative	comment	argumentation
(5) Instructive	instructions	directions, rules, regulations and statutes

characteristic of objective presentation, while the active voice is typical of subjective discourse types. The discourse types determined in this way must then be further subdivided in terms of the *channel*, for example, the oral channel as opposed to the written channel. After this subdivision, a specification can be given of kinds of discourse. Then, as Werlich observes, it will become clear that a specific discourse can contain a number of different basic forms, for example, a story that opens with an impressionistic description. An important point of discussion in Werlich's approach is the status of the five basic forms. The existence of innate categorization possibilities is difficult to prove. For this reason, attempts have been made to make divisions on the basis of other criteria.

In the first approach the line went from discourse situations to general discourse characteristics. In the second approach the line went from general forms to discourse types. The third approach relates the co-occurrence of linguistic features to communicative functions. In Biber's typology (1989) a restricted set of text prototypes is distinguished on the basis of five sets of lexical and grammatical features. Biber analyzed about 500 texts by looking at the way in which seventy linguistic features co-occurred. The linguistic features had a wide range, from the tense of verbs to lexical classes (nouns, prepositions, modals, etc.), from passivization to the use of specific words. After statistical analysis he found that there were five clusters of features. These five dimensions were labeled as follows.

(1)   The five dimensions of Biber (1989)
   1.   Involved versus informational production
   2.   Narrative versus non-narrative concerns
   3.   Elaborated versus situation-dependent reference
   4.   Overt expression of persuasion
   5.   Abstract versus non-abstract style

In dimension 1 are, on the one hand interactive and affective discourse types, like conversations and personal letters, and, on the other hand highly informative texts, like editorials and academic prose. The types are characterized by the presence or absence of a set of features. In dimension 2, narrative texts – with, among other features, many past-tense verbs and third-person pronouns – are distinguished from non-narrative texts. Dimension 3 sets the highly explicit context-independent texts, like official documents, apart from all other discourse types. Dimension 4 characterizes all text with persuasive elements, such as ads and politicians' speeches. Dimension 5, with features like passives, characterizes the abstract and formal style.

On the basis of these five dimensions Biber distinguished eight text prototypes such as "intimate personal interaction", "imaginative narrative" and "situated reportage". With his statistical analysis of the co-occurrence of linguistic features and the linking to communicative functions Biber showed that general concepts like *narrative form*, *explanatory form*, *expository form* and *interactive discourse* in other models are much too vague. According to Biber there is no single expository form. There are, for example, big differences in linguistic features between (abstract) scientific expository texts and the so-called "learned expository" in "literate prose" with a more active style. Moreover, in interactive discourse there proved to be a big difference between the linguistic features of "intimate interaction" (the more phatic communion) with a low informational load and the characteristics of the more informational interactions as in telephone conversations between business associates.

The three typologies mentioned here have not been fully developed into a typology of all possible discourse types. In contemporary discourse studies, few attempts at an all-encompassing classification can be found. In the last few decades much attention has been paid to the differences between spoken and written communication and the dialogic aspects of written discourse; see Section 4.2. Notwithstanding the fact that discourse studies is mainly restricted to everyday discourse, the poetic function of language manifests itself frequently in "prosaic" discourse. So, more information about the poetic function is needed to understand the practice of discourse analysis; see Section 4.3. The most recent mode in discourse is the computer screen. Some characteristics of electronic discourse are dealt with in a special section; see Section 4.4. After these three sections, the problem of type and genre are dealt with again, but now from a new perspective on ordering the variety of discourse; see Section 4.5. Chapter 4 concludes with a section about a topic that has been a focus in discourse studies in recent years and that will probably shed new light on the factor *mode* in variety. It is the phenomenon of *multimodality*, which means that communication is increasingly being realized in different modes simultaneously; see Section 4.6.

4.2   Written language and verbal interaction

The term *discourse* is used for all forms of oral and written communication. There are, however, important differences between oral and written discourse. According to Wallace Chafe (1982), two factors explain the differences between written discourse and verbal interaction: 1. Writing takes longer than speaking; 2. Writers do not have contact with readers. The first factor is responsible for what Chafe calls "integration" in written language as opposed to the "fragmentation" that supposedly takes place in verbal interaction. This integration is achieved through, among other things, the use of subordinate conjunctions. These subordinate conjunctions occur more often in written language than they do in verbal interaction. The second factor is responsible for the detachment from the reading public in written language as opposed to the involvement that is present with verbal interaction. Speakers and listeners are more involved in communication than writers and readers. This expresses itself, according to Chafe, in references to the participants in the conversation and comments on the topic of conversation. That the involvement in written language is not as great is made clear, among other things, by the more frequent use of the passive voice in which the person who is acting remains in the background.

The difference can also be described in terms of *situation*. Verbal interaction is part of a shared situation that includes both speakers and listeners. In such a situation, information is also passed along through means other than language, such as posture, intonation, hand gestures, etc. Moreover, speakers can quickly react to nonverbal reactions on the part of listeners. A written discourse, on the other hand, is not part of a shared situation existing between writers and readers.

This difference obviously has far-reaching consequences. Yet, there are a large number of discourse studies issues in which this difference hardly plays a role at all. In both forms of verbal communication, phenomena can be studied that are related to the cooperative principle, politeness strategies, cohesion and coherence, stylistic variation, etc. It is for this reason that *addressee* or *receiver* can be used to denote both readers and listeners, and *producer* can be used for both speakers and writers.

One similarity between text and dialogue that is often overlooked is that, although writers cannot process an addressee's reactions, they can anticipate probable reactions and write the text accordingly. The following illustrates this phenomenon.

(2) 1. Discourse studies is not a separate science. 2. It can be seen from the discourse studies publications that have appeared up until the present that there are no common targets or goals that can be formulated from the various research topics. 3. This is the least that can be expected from researchers wishing to do work in a new field of research. 4. There are researchers who see in the concept "breakdown in communication" a binding element, but even in this approach the theoretical underpinnings are at best rudimentary.

This passage can be seen as a dialogue in which the contributions made by the conversational partner have been omitted. The relationship between the sentences can be made apparent by interjecting questions.

(3) 1.   Discourse studies is not a separate science.
     1a. How does the author reach this conclusion?
     2.   It can be seen from the discourse studies publications that have appeared up until the present that there are no common targets or goals that can be formulated from the various research topics.
     2a. Is this really an argument?
     3.   This is the least that can be expected from researchers wishing to do work in a new field of research.
     3a. There are other criteria for a separate science, aren't there?
     4.   There are researchers who see in the concept "breakdown in communication" a binding element, but even in this approach the theoretical underpinnings are at best rudimentary.

This example of dialogue aspects in discourse shows that written communication can also be studied from the perspective of a situation in which verbal interaction takes place. The scholar who gave a big impulse to this view of (written) discourse as dialogic interaction was the Russian philosopher and literary theorist Mikhail Bakhtin. He developed his ideas in the 1920s, but only after the translation of his work into English, more than half a century later, did his ideas become influential. A central idea in his work is that language in use cannot be considered a set of words with abstract meanings as described in dictionaries, but that the meaning of words is actualized in discourse owing to the interaction of the participants. In other words, for all utterances only some potential meanings can be given with reference to dictionaries, but it is the particular situation that determines which meaning is actualized. Utterances like "That is a nice house" can have different meanings, but the situation actualizes the specific meaning of admiration, irony or desire to buy it, etc. So, if you consider language to be an abstract system of structures and meaning, it will not bring you far in discourse studies.

The right way of studying discourse, according to Bakhtin (1981) and many other researchers, is to view discourse as inherently dialogic. Also in written discourse utterances are responses to other utterances, for example, questions provoked or expected by readers. And for discourse containing references to different persons, for example, a novel with quotations from different persons, Bakhtin coined the music metaphor "polyphony". This "multivoicedness" is an important factor in many types of discourse, for example, a news story in which the journalist reports the viewpoints of different actors, or in a judicial report describing statements made by different witnesses.

It is precisely this dialogic and sometimes polyphonic aspect of discourse that provides an argument to study written language and verbal interaction in the single discipline of discourse studies. The issues that specifically apply to verbal interaction are dealt with in Chapter 9. In the other chapters, both text and talk are under consideration unless otherwise stated.

4.3   Everyday and literary language

In principle the term *discourse* is not used to distinguish between everyday and literary language. Of course, there are important distinctions. Literary language does, after all, serve a very different purpose than, for example, informative language. Literary elements, however, can also be found in everyday language. But what makes a kind of language use literary?

An important difference between everyday and literary language can be demonstrated by way of the following statement by Jakobson, who was introduced in Section 4.1 on functions of communication. He was one of the first researchers to pay attention to the poetic function in communication. This is his famous, but difficult statement about the poetic function.

(4)   The poetic function projects the principle of equivalence from the axis of selection into the axis of combination.

For a better understanding of the terms *selection* and *combination*, two important aspects of language, the syntagmatic and the paradigmatic aspect, need to be discussed. These terms can best be explained using the concepts *horizontal* and *vertical*. The syntagmatic or horizontal aspect has to do with syntax, the combination of words in a sentence. The way these combinations are made is governed by fixed rules. The combinations possible in everyday language can be described using rules of grammar, for example, the rule that a verb like *to go* cannot be followed by a direct object. Sentence (5a) is not English, sentence (5b) is.

(5)   a.   John went the school.
      b.   John went to school.

The paradigmatic aspect is the vertical aspect as in "paradigm" in the sense of a list of verb forms: I walk, you walk, he walks, etc. Instead of John in (5b), a word can be substituted from a whole list of other words such as *the man* or *the girl*. The same holds true for the words that follow "John" in the sentence. In this way it is possible to generate a sentence like: "Pete drove to the beach."

In everyday language the paradigmatic selection process is simply a matter of choosing words that are categorically equivalent. "Equivalent" in this case means that the elements must have something in common. *John* can be replaced by *Pete* but not by *is* or *two*. The commonality can consist of both words being the same kind of word, or of both words possessing the same meaning element, in this case a person doing something.

The syntagmatic element involves the horizontal combination axis, while the paradigmatic element involves the vertical selection axis. Jakobson's remark implies that in poetic language the syntagmatic axis is somehow special and that this special quality has to do with the choice based on equivalence along the paradigmatic axis. It might be said that in poetic language, the syntagmatic axis is of lesser importance than the paradigmatic axis because the syntagmatic axis is influenced by the paradigmatic one.

Consider the following example. When an individual wishes to make it clear that he would rather take the car instead of the train, he has a number of possibilities, including those in (6):

(6)   a.   Give me the car any day.
      b.   Driving is nice.
      c.   It's great to be behind the wheel.
      d.   Alive when I drive.

Example (6d) is by far the most poetic. The influence of equivalence from the paradigmatic selection axis on the horizontal combination axis is obvious in the first and the last word. In everyday language the equivalence is limited to one position on the combination axis; in (6a) and (6b), another word may be chosen for "car" or "nice". In poetic language, equivalence manifests itself in multiple positions. In the example above, the words "alive" and "drive" are equivalent because they rhyme. This type of equivalence is called *projection*. Equivalence is obviously not just a question of rhyme. Jakobson also mentions the repeated use of the same grammatical construction and makes special note of the parallelism phenomenon, for example, the repetition of the same patterns in different lines of poetry. This kind of repetition does not have to be contained in a single text. A sentence can also have a poetic function on the basis of intertextuality, for example, because the structure of that sentence is reminiscent of the structure of a sentence from another kind of discourse. This is the case in the following example taken from an advertisement.

(7)   Quiet type seeks acquaintance with provocative sweatshirt.

The structure of this sentence bears a distinct resemblance to the type of phrase often seen in personal advertisements. This form of parallelism is, in Jakobson's view, responsible for the poetic character of such a sentence.

Jakobson's statement explains clearly the difference between language with a focus on the encoded message and other types of language use. Insight into this poetic function is important for discourse studies because this function often occurs in nonliterary discourse, for example, in advertising texts, graffiti, flyers and newspaper headlines. Also stylistic techniques such as pleonasm (e.g., "a round circle"), metaphor or personification (e.g., "the wind howls") cannot be studied adequately without reference to this poetic function.

4.4   Electronic discourse

Since the 1970s a new mode of communication has emerged. It is called electronic discourse, "netspeak", web communication, computer-mediated communication or e-language. The impact of this communication mode is considered as big as the impact of the telephone and television was. Hence, many researchers and professionals expect that this new communication channel, and especially the Internet, will change our communication patterns.

Just as spoken and written language are cover terms for different discourse types, computer-mediated discourse also refers to different discourse types. A distinction currently used is that between synchronous communication and asynchronous communication of which the most common discourse types are presented in Table 3.

Table 3.   Discourse types in computer-mediated communication

Type	Example
synchronous	chat groups, instant messaging, MUDs (multi-user dimensions, e.g. for recreation and education)
asynchronous	e-mail, discussion lists, websites

In the field of discourse studies computer-mediated discourse prompts at least three questions: 1. What is the place of this communication between written and spoken discourse? 2. What is really new in this newest mode of communication? 3. What is the influence of the channel of communication on discourse? In this section the first trials and attempts to answer these questions are dealt with.

a. *Written speech or spoken writing?*
Computer-mediated communication has the immediateness of spoken language and the permanence of written communication. A chat in a chat group is like a face-to-face chat or conversation, but typing is slower than speaking. An e-mail looks like a letter when one writes it, but there seems to be more informality in e-mail contact just like in a message left on an answering machine. Is the new mode of communication a perfect mix that can be labeled as "textual conversation", "talking in writing", "written speech" or "spoken writing"?

In Section 4.2 it was argued that the distinction between writing and speaking is not as clear as it seems. The same holds true for the varieties of electronic discourse. Remarkable in electronic communication is the possibility of interaction, originally prevailing in oral communication, and the possibility of browsing and skipping, originally prevailing in written documents, or scrolling (as in a roll of parchment). The interaction, however, is not the same as in verbal interaction where speakers can interrupt each other. In chat groups the reactions of participants appearing after a remark might have been composed before that remark appeared. With hyperlinks the readers of a website are only given the possibility of using the click options of the website design, so the interactivity is controlled by the design. And the browsing possibility (screen by screen) is completely different from browsing in a newspaper or a book where the reader has many more opportunities to explore the outline, and can skip whole passages or parts of it and never get lost. It seems safe to conclude that computer-mediated communication only partially combines some aspects of spoken and written communication: the interactivity, and the browsing and skipping facilities. In that respect, the question about its place between written and spoken communication seems to be formulated incorrectly. Computer-mediated communication cannot be characterized in terms of spoken language or writing.

b. *What is new in netspeak?*
In many studies on Internet language it is tacitly presupposed that the new medium *computer* has a huge influence on the discourse produced using that medium, just as the once-new traffic media *car* and *train* have changed our modes of transportation. However, whether this comparison is justified is questionable. Has the medium *telephone* changed our conversation? One of the most interesting attempts to describe the

aspect "new" in computer-mediated discourse is offered by the linguist and stylistician Crystal (2001) who wrote the book *Language of the Internet*. He uses the framework of Grice's maxims (see Section 2.4) to describe some characteristics of netspeak.

The first maxim of quantity says: "Make your contribution as informative as is required." But on the Internet one can abstain from communicating by lurking in a chat group, e.g., without making any contribution. And junk mail and the need for spam filters prove that on electronic highways many non-informative messages are transported. Of course this is a flouting, a violation of the maxim. The question, however, is whether spam is a different flouting of the quantity maxim than unsolicited advertising brochures in written communication.

The second maxim of quality says: "Try to make your contribution one that is true." However, if you read a contribution to a chat group you are not sure whether the participants are who they claim to be, or whether what they are saying is true. In face-to-face conversation this uncertainty is normally not so high or at least it can more easily be diminished during the interaction.

The third maxim of relevance says: "Be relevant." But many contributions in chat groups or personal websites seem to have the function of so-called *phatic communion* (see Section 4.1) only indicating "I am here as a possible partner in a virtual community". And browsing the web using a search engine may result in many irrelevant hits.

The fourth maxim of manner says: "Be perspicuous." Advice on clear writing based on this maxim, such as "Be brief" or "Be orderly", also apply to electronic discourse. But in spite of many navigation techniques the degree of disorder in electronic documents seems much higher than in written documents.

In computer-mediated communication there are many floutings of the Gricean maxims, but it remains unclear whether these floutings constitute a new mode of verbal interaction or, for example, a principle other than the cooperative principle, which is the base of these four maxims.

c. *Electronic language use*
It is plausible that the use of language in computer-mediated discourse is influenced by the medium, just as the style of a telegram was once influenced by the telegraph. The influence of the medium can be detected on three levels: 1. graphics, 2. formulation and 3. structure. These levels are dealt with in the remainder of this section.

In electronic discourse we can only make use of the ascii characters on our keyboard. This explains why these characters are used to mimic face-to-face interaction with facial expression and physical action through emoticons, such as the smiley :-) or a wink ;-) or laughing <gg>. Repetition is also used to express emotions: "helllooo". The need to stimulate the speed of spoken language can be seen in abbreviations or acronyms like "bbfn" ("bye-bye for now") often in combination with literal "character pronunciation" as in "u2" ("you too") and "icq" ("I seek you").

A more essential difference with oral or written communication would be a stylistic difference in wording or syntax. A representative example of research in this area is the study of oral and written aspects in computer conferencing by Yates (1996). He compared large corpora of spoken, written and computer communication, and analyzed language use according to two of the three aspects of the socio-semiotic approach (see Section 3.5): field and tenor. In field, i.e., what it is in discourse that participants are engaged in, he counted the use of modal verbs like *must, may* and *should*, indicating how the participants relate to the actions described in the discourse. In tenor, the relationship between the participants, he counted the use of pronouns in the first and second persons. Table 4 shows the results.

Electronic discourse differs significantly from speech and writing in the use of modal verbs. This could indicate that the field of computer-mediated communication differs from the fields of speech and writing, presumably because it contains more informal discussions in which the use of modals is more appropriate. As for pronouns, electronic discourse is more like speech than writing. An explanation could be that participants in writing are not as salient as in the other two modes of communication.

A very restrictive condition of computer-mediated discourse is that only one screen at a time is available to produce and understand a message. This phenomenon has led to an extensive use of a device we previously knew only from scientific books, i.e., referring to other information with a number or other link to footnotes or endnotes. Moreover, the demand for extracting information from large databases on the basis of individual needs and preferences, such as in reference books, alphabetic lists or tables and schemas, has prompted further development of non-linear structure, as, for example, in menu-based telephone systems ("If you would like information about X, press 3 ...").

The number referring to a note or a special question-answer pattern in programmed phone conversation is called a link or hyperlink in electronic discourse. This linking is the main structural characteristic of hypertext and is the focus of much research into the design of computer-mediated discourse. Hypertext is electronic discourse in which pieces of information are linked through references, mostly leading

Table 4.   Some differences between speaking, writing and electronic discourse

	speech	writing	electronic discourse
modal verbs (permillage)	14.5	13.7	18.3
"I" and "you" (percentage of pronouns)	58	27	64

towards the information referred to. This link – usually a highlighted word or phrase, or an icon – may just be an annotation like a pop-up link explaining a difficult term. But hyperlinks can also refer to sections and subsections (like headings in a book) or to other information on topics and subtopics related to the message outside the webpage. Research into the structure of hypertexts includes questions like: How does the "departure and arrival information" on the linking labels affect the usability of a website? Where on the screen are hyperlinks preferred? How to give information about a linking path to prevent the reader from getting lost? From a discourse perspective this research is very important because the non-linear structure of many electronic discourse types seems to be the characteristic in which computer-mediated communication differs mostly from spoken or written communication.

4.5   Conventionalized forms for conventionalized occasions

The attempts to describe the different functions of language use, discussed in Section 4.1, proved not to be comprehensive enough to catch the parameters of functional variety. Moreover, the development of classification models prompted questions about what precisely the characteristics of the different discourse types are. For some main types the differences seemed to be clear, see the sections 4.2 and 4.3, but an accurate description of the different genres proved to be an unfeasible goal.

The difficulties in describing discourse types led to another approach to genres, which was again inspired by the Russian philosopher of literature, Bakhtin, who was already introduced in the discussion about the dialogical aspect of written discourse in Section 4.2. Important in Bakhtin's work is the focus on discourse use in specific situations. In situations that are more or less the same, the discourse will have more or less the same characteristics. In situations such as cross-examining suspects, presenting acquired knowledge in an educational situation or commenting on news facts, specialized forms of discourse will emerge which can fulfill the demands of the participants. In the aforementioned situations these forms would be interrogations, doctoral theses and editorials. And precisely knowledge of how to practice these conventionalized forms of discourse gives the opportunity to fully participate in a specific communicative situation.

The most important approach to genres as conventionalized forms was developed by Swales (1990). His characterizations of genres can be summarized as follows:

(8) Genre, as defined by Swales (summary)
A genre is a class of communicative events with shared recognizable communicative purposes. These purposes give rise to exploitable constraints concerning content and form.

A communicative event is an event in which discourse plays an indispensable role, for example, a lecture as opposed to driving a car (which can be done almost without discourse). Genres are not defined on the basis of similarity in lexical and grammatical features or intended audience or channel. Genres are primarily conceived of as communicative vehicles for achieving purposes. These purposes are shared by and recognizable to the participants in the communicative event. Were they not, then only a participant's private purposes would be at issue, and private purposes alone are not strong enough to shape the discourse in structure and style.

Given the shared purposes, there are restrictions on content and form. Swales gives the example of the positive letter and the rejection letter after a job interview. The purposes of these two genres dictate the content, the structure and the style of the discourse. A positive letter will have an enthusiastic and inviting style; the negative letter will have a more formal style and be focused on ending the contact. These constraints, however, are exploitable. Expert genre writers can be very creative in dealing with these constraints. Hence, there is a difference between a standard rejection letter and one with more quality in which, for example, some personal statements are made about the career opportunities of the rejected applicant. On the other hand, these constraints have to be learned before they can be exploited. Swales gives a nice example: an opening sentence by a Ph.D. student in aquaculture who has trouble writing a research article.

(9) In aquaculture, the relations among nutrients, stocking rate, water quality and weather are complex.

Why does this sentence not fit into the genre of a scientific article? This sentence better suits a textbook, as the specialized readers of a journal about aquaculture already know that the relations are complex. In adding that knowledge to the formulation the sentence is made more suitable as an opening sentence.

(10) In aquaculture, the relations among nutrients, stocking rate, water quality and weather are known to be complex.

This reformulation can only be made if one knows the impact of the shared purposes of the genre "research article" on the style of discourse. How can this genre theory be made applicable to the analysis of the variety of discourse? In Bhatia (1993) this theory is demonstrated in an analyzing technique in which the shared purposes of a genre are reformulated in moves that must be recognizable in the discourse. Below is an example of the analysis of a research article abstract. The purpose of an abstract is to indicate the content of a paper in advance. Why does the following passage count as an abstract?

(11)   This paper sets out to examine two findings reported in the literature: one, that during the one-word stage a child's word productions are highly phonetically variable, and two, that the one-word stage is qualitatively distinct from subsequent phonological development. The complete set of word forms produced by a child at the one-word stage were collected and analyzed both cross-sectionally (month by month) and longitudinally (looking for changes over time). It was found that the data showed very little variability, and that phonological development during the period studied was qualitatively continuous with subsequent development. It is suggested that phonologically principled development of this child's first words is related to his late onset of speech.

An abstract is characterized by the purpose of providing concise information on the four aspects of research that it describes: 1. What the author did; 2. How the author did it; 3. What the author found; 4. What the author concluded. Answers to these four questions are given using the following four moves.

(12)   Four moves in a research article abstract
    1.   Introducing the purpose: This move gives a precise indication of the author's intention, thesis or hypothesis that formed the basis of the research being reported. It may also include the goals or objectives of research or the problem that the author tackled.
    2.   Describing the methodology: In this move the author gives a good indication of the experimental design, including information on the data, procedures or method used and, if necessary, the scope of the research being reported.
    3.   Summarizing the results: This is an important aspect of abstracts where the author mentions his observations and findings and also suggests solutions to the problem, if any, posed in the first move.
    4.   Presenting the conclusions: This move is meant to interpret results and draw inferences. It typically includes some indication of the implications and applications of the present findings.

When the four moves are applied to the abstract given in example (11), it can be seen that the first sentence introduces the purpose, that the second sentence describes the methodology, and that the third sentence summarizes the results. The last sentence presents the conclusions. Figure 3 provides a schematic overview.

This paper sets out to examine two findings reported in the literature: one, that during the one-word stage a child's word productions are highly phonetically variable, and two, that the one-word stage is qualitatively distinct from subsequent phonological development.   1

The complete set of word forms produced by a child at the one-word stage were collected and analysed both cross-sectionally (month by month) and longitudinally (looking for changes over time).   2

It was found that the data showed very little variability, and that phonological development during the period studied was qualitatively continuous with subsequent development.   3

It is suggested that phonologically principled development of this child's first words is related to his late onset of speech.   4

Figure 3. The four moves in (11)

In the genre theory dealt with in this section, the focus is on conventions in form in recurring situations. In this view, discourse types can best be characterized by considering them as a series of moves to reach communicative goals. In the last section of this chapter the focus is on the modes that are used in reaching a goal.

4.6 Multimodality

This chapter started with the various functions of language use: giving information, persuading an addressee, making contact, etc. These functions, however, seldom occur in a pure form. Mostly they are merged, for example, in a TV program that mixes information with entertainment, "infotainment", or when a company tries to sell more products by "just" giving information about something new, the "infomercial". The channels, which are used are also mixed. We watch television and simultaneously we read the subtitles and hear the sounds. This mix of modes, which is nearly always present in communication is called multimodality. In discourse studies the simultaneous use of modes was neglected a long time. The study of the discourse itself, be it spoken or written, uncovered more than enough interesting problems. But the last few decades saw so much mixture of modes, especially the visualization of communication, that multimodality has become an important factor in discourse studies.

One aspect of multimodality which has received special attention in discourse studies is the co-deployment of the visual element in written discourse: a text with a diagram, a picture, etc. There is old folklore wisdom in the saying "A picture is worth more than a thousands words." Below is a well-known example from Bransford and

Johnson (1973). Many people who read the following passage have trouble under-standing what it is about. They cannot "make a picture" out of this.

(13)   If the balloons popped the sound wouldn't be able to carry since everything
        would be too far away from the correct floor. A closed window would also
        prevent the sound from carrying, since most buildings tend to be well insulated.
        Since the whole operation depends on a steady flow of electricity, a break in
        the middle of the wire would also cause problems. Of course, the fellow could
        shout, but the human voice is not loud enough to carry that far. An additional
        problem is that a string could break on the instrument. Then there could be no
        accompaniment to the message. It is clear that the best situation would involve
        less distance. Then there would be fewer potential problems. With face-to-face
        contact, the least number of things could go wrong.

It is better for this passage, with signs at the symbolic level, to be vizualized, thus pre-sented at an iconic level. Then, words are even superfluous (see Figure 4).

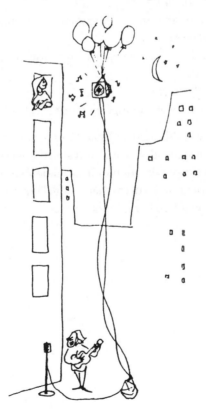

Figure 4. Picturalization of (13)

Sometimes it is clear how a picture, a schema or a diagram can replace a text, but it is far from clear how visual elements can add to verbal information. In discourse studies some analysis schemes have been presented for research into illustrated discourse. A scheme that is suitable to start with is the GeM model of Judy Delin and John Bateman (2002). GeM stands for *genre* and *multimodality*. The aim of this model is to provide data on different genres using combinations of text, layout, graphics, pictures and diagrams. In this model, multimodal documents are analyzed on five levels of structure that define the possibilities for electronic or paper documents.

(14) The GeM model
1. *Content structure*
    The raw data out of which the document is constructed.
2. *Rhetorical structure*
    The way the content is "argued", the audience-focused relations between content elements.
3. *Layout structure*
    The nature, appearance and position of communicative elements on paper
4. *Navigation structure*
    The ways the intended mode(s) of consumption of the document is/are supported.
5. *Linguistic structure*
    The structure of the language used to realize the layout elements.

The main advantage of this model is that it can be used for analyzing both textual and visual meaning. Subsequently it can motivate and question some of the choices that have been made in the presentation of information on a page. How does this scheme for analysis work? The authors of the GeM model present, among others, the following example: a page from a bird book (Figure 5).

Gannet   *Sula bassana*
Family SULIDAE.   Gannets   No. 27

This great bird has the magnificent wings and flight of a giant Gull, and a wing-span of nearly 6 ft.   It can sight a fish from a great height while on the wing and will drop like an arrow into the water after its prey.   The plumage is white with a tinge of buff on the head and neck, and dark brown, almost black, wing-tips.   Immatures are first dusky all over, later piebald or white sprinkled with dark spots.
Haunt The coast and sea, and at breeding time rocky isles and stacks, chiefly on the north and west of the British Isles.
Nest Of seaweed and tufts of grass or thrift; on the rocky ledge of a stack or island in a great colony with others.
Eggs 1, nearly white, chalky.   April or May.
Food Fish.
Notes Short and harsh.
Length 36 or 37 in (91 or 94 cm)
Status Resident

Figure 5.   Gannet, *The Observer Book of Birds* (1972:22)

The content structure, the "gannet content", can be organized into topic segments as illustrated in Figure 6. The hierarchical representation shows the relations between the content parts, without distinguishing linguistically and graphically presented information. The hierarchical structure does not account for why which information is placed where in the page shown in Figure 5. Moreover, the content hierarchy does not explain why some of the information is presented in one way and some in another, but it questions whether this was the right decision.

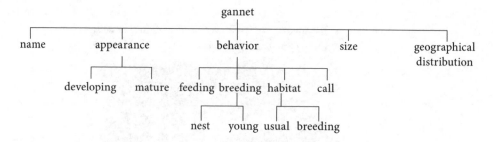

Figure 6. Hierarchical representation of content of the gannet page

The rhetorical structure pertains to the way in which the content is argued and the various segments are interrelated textually, see Figure 7. At the highest level, the content is divided into the picture and the text. The major part of the text is organized into text segments that provide other facts about the gannet: wings and wingspans in the first sentence, fishing behavior in the second, followed by a segment on plumage, etc. Specific text segments at lower levels further specify the concept of *gannet*. The title information serves as a preparation to the main content.

The layout structure is characterized by a division in three zones: the title information, the gannet illustration and the text below. Typeface and spacing in the title

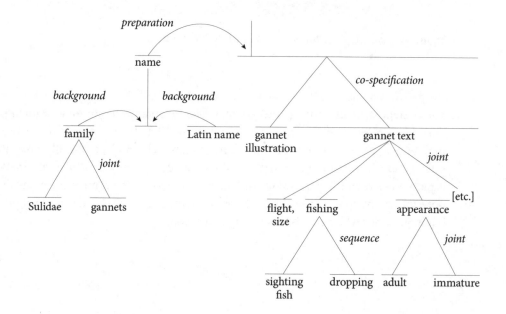

Figure 7. Rhetorical structure of the gannet page

information vary. The bird's name in English at the top left in bold print signifies that it is the most important part of the title information and serves as a starting point for reading. However, it remains unclear why, for example, "Sulidae" is in small caps and the English and Latin family names are illogically placed. The picture of the gannet has a central place. The two textual components that follow both have a different alignment and font size. The split of comparable information across these two different modes of presentation seems arbitrary.

At the navigation level it can be seen that the bird entry number "No. 27" has to do with the internal structure of the bird book and has nothing to do with gannets. It is not necessary to place this information within the block that is meant for gannet-related title information. Moreover, because the entry number is not sufficiently distinguished (typographically) from other unrelated information, it fails to stand out as a usable navigation element.

Interestingly, the linguistic structure is the last of the five structure levels. In the main textual section complete clauses are used, while the labeled list is in telegraphic style. These two types of linguistic structure evoke different expectations related to these typographic conventions. The main body text is somewhat involved, as the author evaluates the gannet rather than presenting it factually, e.g., the bird is described as "this great bird" having "magnificent wings" and it will "drop like an arrow". Language use and typography clearly go together, as the author refrains from lively descriptions and complete sentences in the labeled list.

According to Delin and Bateman the GeM model makes it possible to detect the motivation for some of the choices that have been made in rendering information on a page through analysis at different levels of structure. Using the GeM model makes it possible to uncover slippage between various levels of a multimodal document, and enables an adaptation of typography and imagery to content and rhetorical structure. Finally it may give insight into why, in some cases, a designer has made a decision that is clearly a compromise.

Questions and assignments

Questions

4.1.1   Which of Werlich's basic forms can occur in an informative discourse?

4.1.2   Using the Steger model, in which category would you place the following kinds of discourse?
sermon, radio news bulletin, oral exam

4.2.1   Describe some of the important differences between verbal interaction and written discourse using the following examples taken from a newspaper article on the attempted bribery of a drug dealer. The newspaper article is given in (a) and the reproduction of the conversation mentioned in (a) is given in (b).
Indicate to what extent the differences named by Chafe apply in this case.

a.   Drug dealer S.E. (...) gave extensive testimony of his contacts with Revenue Service employee M.V. S.E. had received an income tax assessment notice which had led to a lien being put on his house. When he went on to talk about the 80,000 euros he owed, V. appeared willing to lower the amount to 30,000 euros. In a later conversation V. offered to lower S.E.'s tax debt by another 13,000 euros if S.E. would provide incriminating testimony against the Happy Family, a youth center. S.E. had a later discussion in his car with V. concerning this issue. The dealer taped this conversation.
S.E. testified that V. told him that his statements had to correspond with two depositions that the Revenue Service had provided on the Happy Family. S.E. stated that his impression was that the Revenue Service was attempting to "nail" the Happy Family in this way. V. did not say exactly what he wanted from S.E., but the conversation led S.E. to believe he was to confirm previously given testimony. This testimony dealt with the magnitude of drug sales taking place at the Happy Family, an issue that had led the Revenue Service to start procedures against the youth center.

b.   S.E.: Listen, I want to make sure that if I pay the 17,000 euros I'll be rid of it after I testify.
V.: That can be arranged, believe me. And I want, see with you, with regard to that, I will declare in the presence of ... (name unintelligible, ed.) who is there, I hope it's not someone else then you can always start civil procedures against the Revenue Service, then you can say if I declare it in front of both of you, then I will give you some legal leverage which would make me pretty uh ... and besides that I, you could verify it yourself, just call Mr. B, no problem, and then you'll hear exactly what the agreement is. There won't be any manipulating, that's not my style. I want us to be able to look each other straight in the eye and if it's worth it to us, we'll pay for it. You shouldn't have to deal with it after the fact. With regard to that, there is one condition and that condition is that the statement is concrete, that we can do

something with it and there are, just between you and me, two others which have to do with the Happy Family and we know a lot about that.

4.3.1   Using Jakobson's statement, explain the poetic function of "Life is a disaster in spite of your master's" (read on a banner during a students' protest).

4.4.1   What does *interactive* mean in a conversation and in a hypertext or chat group? Explain the differences.

4.4.2   Is there any difference between lurking in a chat group and eavesdropping in a face-to-face conversation?

4.4.3   In a study by Davis and Brewer (1997) it was shown that in chat group contributions participants relied on private verbs (e.g., *think*, *feel*, *know*). Private verbs are those where the activity cannot be publicly observed; they contrast with the public verbs such as *say* and *tell*. Explain this result and why it is in line with results mentioned in Section 4.4 on the use of personal pronouns.

4.5.1   Which characteristics of social rules that were mentioned in Section 3.2 are important in the notion of genre rules in Swales's definition of genre?

4.6.1   Consider example (13) and the illustration in Figure 4. Name three elements that the text in (13) adds to the visual presentation in Figure 4.

Assignments

4.1.1   A large number of attempts to design a discourse classification system are reminiscent of literary scientific research done in the area of genre theory. In this theory the four genres "fairy tale", "myth", "saga", and "legend" were distinguished according to the two factors "religious" and "historical". Look up in the literature what is said about these four genres and try to define them. Give an example of each genre (book or story title). Then point out the differences through a classification by scoring the genres (+ or –) on the factors "religious" and "historical".

4.2.1   See Bakhtin's view of written discourse in Section 2.4 (dialogic interaction): the meaning of the words is actualized in discourse owing to the interaction of the participants. In which way does this approach differ from the Latin expression "*verba valent usu*", which means "words get their meaning in their use"?

4.3.1   Take an advertisement text and try to analyze which stylistic or literary techniques (such as pleonasm, metaphor and personification) were used in writing this text.

4.4.1 Try to explain why an e-mail message often lacks an opening but almost always has an ending.

4.4.2 Verify in handbooks or on websites on clear writing what sort of advice is given on clear language use in computer-mediated communication that does not apply to written or oral language use.

4.5.1 Take the summary or abstract mentioned in assignment 1.1.2 of Chapter 1, and determine whether or not it complies with the four moves that are mentioned in Section 4.5.

4.6.1 Take a text of your choice and analyze it according to the levels of the GeM model.

Bibliographical information

4.1   Jakobson (1960) borrowed the term *phatic communion* from the anthropologist Malinowski (1930), who observed the phenomenon among a "primitive" people in the 1920s.

Jakobson sparked the discussion about functions. Publications of historical importance in this field are those by Steger (1974) and Werlich (1982). For more information on classification that includes the situation as a criterion, see Dimter (1981). Nowadays, the work of Biber (1989) is the most cited work.

4.2   Bakhtin developed his ideas in the period directly after the Communist Revolution. Because of conflicts with official Soviet literary dogma, Bakhtin is supposed to have also published under the real names of other people. See, for example, Morris (1994) for a collection of articles by Bakhtin, Medvedev and Voloshinov. The latter two are friends under whose name Bakhtin wrote. See further Wales (1988) for an introduction to Bakhtin.

The suggestion that a discourse can be seen as "half a dialogue" can also be found in Roulet (1984). See further Nystrand (1986), which gives much attention to anticipating readers' expectations and attending to their needs. A good starting point for further research is Van Kuppevelt (1995).

4.3   The definition of poetic language can be found in Jakobson (1960). This definition has prompted much discussion in the field of literary science. For a critique, see Werth (1976).

4.4   One of the first publications on computer-mediated discourse is Jones (1995), who focuses on news-groups. Rouet, Levonen and Dillon (1996) present empirical research into the cognitive processes involved in using hypertext. See also Herring (1996) for a collection of scholarly discussions from cross-cultural viewpoints that examine electronic discourse. A good introduction to the analysis of MUDs is Cherny (1999).

Consult Crystal (2001) when starting with the main issues and problems concerning electronic discourse. Pemberton and Shurville (2000) is a varied collection of articles on language use in computer-based media. It provides a good overview of the various research questions on, for example, language structure, hypertext links and interaction.

For the study of websites, Nielsen (1999) is an essential publication. For a more practically orientated book, see Price and Price (2002). On the Internet, also see the *Journal of Computer-Mediated Communication*, which has been online since 1995.

4.5   Besides Biber (see Section 4.1), Swales (1990) is now influential. Bhatia (1993) builds on this range of thought. Example (11) and (12) and Figure 3 are taken from his work.

4.6   A good introduction to multimodality is Kress and Van Leeuwen (2001). The most recent overview of articles on multimodality is provided by Ventola, Charles and Kaltenbacher (2004). For further study see also Glenberg (2002). Figure 4 is taken from Bransford and Johnson (1973: 394). Figures 5, 6 and 7 are taken from Delin and Bateman (2002). In addition to the five levels mentioned in this section, the GeM model also includes three constraints, which are not dealt with here, because of their specificity.

5 Structured content

5.1 Propositions

The building blocks for discourse are (written) sentences or (spoken) utterances. Within these smallest units of discourse it is possible to convey about the same content in a number of different ways. A well-known example is the similarity between a sentence in the active voice and one in the passive voice. The following sentences have some content elements in common.

(1) This butcher sells only steak.
(2) Only steak is sold by this butcher.

For certain types of discourse analysis, it is convenient to disregard differences in formulation with approximately the same meaning. Differences in formulation are of less importance when the focus is on the information itself and not on the discourse situation. It is likewise convenient to disregard other aspects, e.g., the writer's attitude concerning the sentence. This aspect plays a role in the following examples.

(3) If only this butcher sold steak!
(4) This butcher only sells steak?

Sentence (3) expresses a wish while in (4) incredulity or surprise is expressed.

The four sentences show important differences, but they are also similar in a number of ways. They all refer to a butcher and selling steak. This common element is referred to as a proposition. The proposition can be described as the meaning of a simple assertive sentence. The addition of the word *simple* makes it clear that a sentence can contain more than one proposition. *Assertive* signifies that it is irrelevant whether the sentence is a question, a wish, an exclamation, etc. There are four propositions in the following exclamation.

(5) What a pity that the poor boy can't cope with the horrible truth!
   1. It is a pity that x.
   2. The boy can't cope with the truth.
   3. The boy is poor.
   4. The truth is horrible.

In a propositional analysis the situation in which the sentences are uttered and the writer's or speaker's attitude as well as the forms in which they occur are disregarded.

The concept *proposition* is taken from the fields of philosophy and logic. There it has a well-defined meaning. In discourse studies proposition is used in a more general sense, to denote the minimal unit of meaning. What does such a unit of meaning look like? A proposition has a verb, the predicate, as its core and one or more arguments that relate to it. Below is an example of a proposition, (6a), which is the basis of a sentence, (6).

(6)   John finally bought a present for mother.

   a.   to buy ((John)$_{\text{subject}}$(present)$_{\text{object}}$(mother)$_{\text{indirect object}}$)

The predicate is the verb *to buy*. It is accompanied by three arguments in a relationship which is represented above in grammatical terms. The tense (in this case, the past tense of the verb *to buy*) and the modal aspect ("finally") are not taken into account. One advantage of this method of notation is that it immediately becomes clear that the following sentences have the same propositional structure.

(7)   For mother, John bought nothing.
(8)   Could John have bought anything for mother?

A proposition consists of a predicate and one or more arguments. Below is an example of a propositional analysis of a text fragment.

(9)   Paper
      If you were to begin to enumerate the various uses of paper, you would find
      the list almost without end. Yet, there was a time when this familiar item was
      a precious rarity, when the sheet of paper you now toss into the wastebasket
      without thinking would have been purchased at a great price and carefully
      preserved.

The propositional analysis is given below. The elements in the propositions are not to be equated with the words in the text as they can be phrased in different ways. It is for this reason that the propositions are printed in small capitals. The numbers in the propositions refer to the propositions which precede or follow. The first proposition given here contains the condition for the second; this condition functions as a predicate. Note that the third proposition is, through the second proposition, embedded in the first, etc.

(10)   Propositional analysis of (9)

1.	(CONDITION, 2)
2.	(ENUMERATE, 3)
3.	(USES, PAPER)
4.	(VARIOUS, 3)
5.	(FIND, 6)
6.	(WITHOUT END, 3)
7.	(ALMOST, 6)
8.	(6, CONTRAST, 9)
9.	(RARITY, PAPER)
10.	(9, TIME: PAST)
11.	(FAMILIAR, PAPER)
12.	(PRECIOUS, 11)
13.	(PURCHASE, PAPER)
14.	(13, PRICE)
15.	(14, GREAT)
16.	(PRESERVE, 15)
17.	(16, MANNER: CAREFULLY)
18.	(17, CONTRAST, 21)
19.	(TOSS, PAPER)
20.	(19, PLACE: WASTEBASKET)
21.	(19, TIME: NOW)
22.	(19, MANNER: WITHOUT THINKING)

As can be seen in this analysis, the propositions do not consist of predicates and arguments with well-defined meaning relations. Usually, there are two elements. One can be seen as the subject, for example, *paper* in proposition [3]. The other can be a predicative element, *enumerate* in [2] and *purchase* in [13], but also a noun that functions as an object as in [3] *uses* in conjunction with *paper*. Such designations as place and time in [20] and [21] are also predicates. Sometimes, a proposition has a logical subject-predicate structure as in [6]. In [18], however, a three-part division can be made. In this analysis, compound propositions also occur, for example, [16] in which [15] – and through [15], [14] and [13] – is also incorporated.

A propositional analysis can best be described as a list of minimal meaning units showing which ones are directly related. The relation of these units with propositions as a subject-predicate or a predicate-argument structure remains somewhat vague. It should also be mentioned that there are hardly any criteria which could be given to test the accuracy of the analysis. In the analysis of the first sentence, for example, propositions [3] and [6] could be mentioned first because they hold a central position. The others refer to these two propositions. [2] and [3] could also be combined using the predicate *enumerate* and the argument *uses of paper*. This example is meant to illustrate how a propositional analysis works in practice.

In discourse studies, the focus is mainly on the relations between propositions. Take, for example, the first part of the second sentence ([8]–[12]): "Yet, there was a time when this familiar item was a precious rarity." The relation between these propositions can be illustrated in a diagram as shown in Figure 1 below, where [12] is the most embedded proposition.

This type of analysis is important for measuring the difficulty of discourse or for gaining insight into the process of discourse understanding. Examples of hypotheses for which this analysis is necessary are: The more embedded propositions there are, the more difficult the discourse will be. A proposition at the lower level 4 is not as easy to remember as one at level 3. For a given group of readers, there can be no more than three propositions at level 2.

So much for propositions, which can be linked endlessly to build a discourse. In discourse analysis it is useful to consider a level between the microlevel of propositions and the macrolevel of the discourse as a whole: a mesolevel of topics, which encompass series of propositions that are linked together.

5.2   Topics

A topic or a theme is what a discourse, a discourse fragment or a sentence is about. It is the shortest summary of a discourse, the main proposition of a paragraph or what is commented on in a sentence. The term *topic* is usually defined as the "aboutness" of a unit of discourse. The vagueness of the definition makes awareness of the distinctions important.

A distinction has to be made between a discourse topic and a sentence topic, i.e., the topic dealt with in a discourse or a sentence, respectively. Below are two examples.

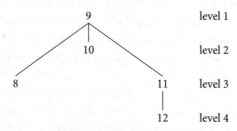

Figure 1.   The relation between propositions

(11) The New York Yankees won.
(12) A: Did you see the Yankees-Sox game yesterday?
      B: Yeah, who would have thought that the Yankees would win!

When normal intonation is used, sentence (11) is about the New York Yankees; therefore, the New York Yankees is the sentence topic. What is stated about the topic is called the comment. In fragment (12) the Yankees-Sox game is the topic of conversation, and therefore the discourse topic, with B's remark serving as the comment.

The concepts *topic* and *comment* often lead to confusion as the distinction between these and related concepts remains unclear. First, among those other concepts is the concept set *theme–rheme*. A theme is what is "under discussion" in a given situation; often it is the subject of a sentence. The rheme is what is said about the theme; usually this is the predicate of a sentence. In (11) the theme–rheme distinction runs parallel to the topic-comment division, but this is not necessarily always true. As the theme–rheme concepts are more or less synonymous with the subject and the predicate, these terms are used less frequently. A sentence topic is not necessarily the subject of the sentence; see A's utterance in (12) where the topic is the object.

Second, there is the concept set *given–new* (see also Section 7.2). As the topic is what is dealt with in the sentence and is, therefore, usually known, *topic* and *given* are often used interchangeably. Yet, there is a distinction. Below is an example; pay careful attention to B's utterance.

(13) (A, B, and C are participants in a meeting)
      A: Shall we discuss the minutes now?
      B: I didn't receive a copy.
      C: Mine is unreadable.

In B's utterance, "I" is the topic and the comment is that a copy has not been received. In the comment there is, however, a word which owing to the question about A's "minutes" is already given: the word "copy". The new element in the comment is that it has not been received.

Third, there is the concept set *foreground–background* information (see also Section 7.2). Since the topic is what the sentence is about, it usually does not contain the most important information in a sentence. Often the topic is more in the background. But this is not always the case, as can be seen in the following example. In B's utterance the element about the neighbor can be seen as the topic, even though this information is in the foreground.

(14) A: I had coffee at Mary's yesterday.
      B: Say, did you hear that her neighbor wants to get a divorce?

The concept *topic* thus deals with something which is discussed in a sentence or discourse. And that "something" can alternatively be defined as background, foreground, given, new, etc. Below is one more example to clarify this somewhat elusive distinction.

(15)   A: Was there any news today?
         B: Yes, there has been another flood in Bangladesh.

The discourse topic here is "news". In B's utterance the sentence topic is that there is news, and the comment is that there has been a flood in Bangladesh. The theme is "flood" and the rheme that it took place in Bangladesh. Depending on the intonation, "flood" or "Bangladesh" can be given or new. The word "another" is also more foregrounded than "flood" or "Bangladesh".

Although there are no unequivocal criteria for determining the topic of a sentence, some tendencies can be given. A topic is: 1. more likely to be *definite* than *indefinite*; 2. sooner pronoun than noun; 3. sooner subject than object. In the following example all three tendencies can be seen.

(16)   The blonde woman saw a man cross the street. She immediately started walking faster.

Because "blonde woman" is definite and in the subject position, it can sooner claim the topic status. The topicality is strengthened by the pronoun "she" in the sentence which follows. That these are only tendencies is proven by the following example.

(17)   The blonde woman saw a man cross the street. The man looked scared.

In this case, "man" appears likely to have topic status. "Man" is, however, indefinite in the first sentence and does not return as a pronoun. There also appears to be a tendency in the order: first the topic and then the comment. But this is only a slight tendency.

For the analysis of the sentence topic, certain tendencies can be indicated. For the analysis of the discourse topic, only intuitions apply. It is usually possible to come to a consensus as to what the topic of a given discourse fragment is. It is more difficult to determine where a subtopic begins or if there is, in fact, topic continuity, topic shift or topic digression. In example (14), for instance, topic shift takes place. This shift results in a subtopic if the conversation eventually returns to drinking coffee at Mary's. It has proven quite difficult to generate adequate criteria for topic shifts.

Within a (sub)topic, topic digression can take place if a sidetrack is taken. An example of this would be if the conversation in (14) were to turn to the special way in which the coffee was made at Mary's. However, as in the case of topic shifts, it is difficult to formulate criteria for digressions. The same is also true for topic continuity. Look at the following examples.

(18) a. The Prime Minister stepped off the plane. Journalists immediately
          surrounded him.
      b. The Prime Minister stepped off the plane. He was immediately surrounded
          by journalists.

In (18b) there is topic continuity. "The Prime Minister" remains the subject in the following sentence in the form of a pronoun. In (18a) there would appear to be a topic
shift, as the following sentence starts with another subject. But it would depend on how
the discourse went after these two sentences.

Intuitions about subtopics and topic shifts have proven to be quite intersubjective.
This was shown in an experiment by the British linguist, Eugene Winter (1976). He
rearranged the sentences in a text and had students attempt to put them back in the
correct order, that is, arrange them so that they linked up topically. Winter also asked
the students to mark the ends of paragraphs, that is, mark where new subtopics com-
menced. This experiment is repeated in the last assignment of this chapter.

Aside from this consensus of intuitions, another pattern can be pointed out in
discourse. It has to do with the relationship between the degree of topicality and the
amount of "language material". Talmy Givón (1989) has called this relationship the
code quantity principle. According to this principle, a topic is defined as that which is
predictable or accessible.

(19) Givón's code quantity principle
      The less predictable or accessible a referent is, the more phonological material
      will be used to code it.

Compare the following examples.

(20) a. He watched how the gas station attendant hooked up the hose.
      b. The man watched how the gas station attendant hooked up the hose.
      c. The man behind the wheel watched how the gas station attendant hooked
          up the hose.

If a "man behind the wheel" and a "gas station attendant" are both characters in a story,
and the first man possesses topic status through "he", then the topic status is lowered
as more phonological material is used. The code quantity principle would appear to
provide a good basis for topic analysis.

5.3   Macrostructures

Readers are generally able to give a summary of the topics they have just read. Below is an example of a short story and two possible summaries.

(21)   Pete decided to go on a skiing vacation that year. Up until then he had only gone hiking in the mountains in the summertime, but he had decided that he wanted to learn how to ski and the winter mountain air might be beneficial to his health. He went to a travel agency to get information so that he could choose a destination. Utah seemed the most attractive. Once he had made his choice he went back to the travel agency to book the flight and reserve a room at a hotel that he had found in one of the folders. Naturally, he also needed skis, poles, and boots, but since he did not have the money to buy them, he decided to rent them when he got there. In order to avoid the seasonal rush, he decided to go after the New Year. When the big day finally arrived, he was taken to the airport by his father so that he would not have to deal with his luggage on his own. He took the night flight. He was actually able to sleep on the plane. The following morning Pete arrived, well rested, at his destination. It was snowing. The hotel was right next to the ski resort. The view of the mountains was beautiful. He immediately felt right at home.

   a.   Pete wanted to go skiing in Utah that winter. He made the necessary arrangements. He went by plane. He liked the hotel in the mountains.
   b.   Pete went skiing. He really liked it.

How do readers manage to arrive at these types of summaries? This can only be explained by assuming that a discourse has a structure of meaning that makes clear what does and what does not belong to the core of the content, or the gist of the discourse. Teun van Dijk (1980) introduced the term *macrostructure* to denote this structure of meaning. This term is the opposite of *microstructure*. The term *microstructure* denotes the relations between sentences and sentence segments; these can be represented with the help of propositions; see Section 5.1.

   A macrostructure is the global meaning of discourse. Thus, the macrostructure (21a) or (21b) can be attributed to text (21). Below is an explanation of how macrostructures are formed using three *macrorules*.

a. *Deletion rule*

This rule eliminates those propositions that are not relevant for the interpretation of other propositions in discourse. Take the following example, which contains three propositions.

(22)   A girl in a yellow dress passed by.
   1.   A girl passed by.
   2.   She was wearing a dress.
   3.   The dress was yellow.

By using the deletion rule, propositions [2] and [3] can be eliminated, leaving only [1] as a proposition. The deletion rule is a negative formulation: eliminate irrelevant propositions. When formulated positively, it is a selection rule: select those propositions that are necessary for the interpretation of other propositions. The deletion rule can be split into a weak and a strong variant. The weak deletion rule eliminates irrelevant propositions; the strong deletion rule only eliminates propositions that are relevant at the microlevel but not at the macrolevel. Below is an example.

(23)   John is sick. He will not be going to the meeting.

At the microlevel the proposition "John is sick" is relevant for the interpretation of the sentence which follows. If, however, the text does not continue with the theme of John's illness, then this proposition is irrelevant at the macrolevel.

b. *Generalization rule*

Using this rule a series of specific propositions are converted into a more general proposition. Here is an example.

(24)   Mary was drawing a picture. Sally was skipping rope and Daniel was building something with Lego blocks.
   1.   The children were playing.

This rule does not just eliminate irrelevant details. Rather, specific predicates and arguments in a series of propositions are replaced by more general terms so that one proposition may suffice.

c. *Construction rule*

By means of this rule one proposition can be constructed from a number of propositions. See the following example and the *macroproposition* that was constructed from it.

(25)   John went to the station. He bought a ticket, started running when he saw what time it was, and was forced to conclude that his watch was wrong when he reached the platform.
1.   John missed the train.

The difference between this rule and the generalization rule is that the propositions on the basis of which a general proposition can be constructed do not all have to be contained in discourse. In (25) neither "train" nor "missed" are mentioned. Yet, on the basis of general knowledge, it is possible to construct a proposition from this incomplete description.

How do these macrorules work in determining the global meaning structure of discourse? Below are a text fragment and a simplified version of a short example of macroanalysis.

(26)   1.   A tall slim blonde in a white summer frock walking just ahead of him caught Ken Holland's eye.
2.   He studied her, watching her gentle undulations as she walked.
3.   He quickly shifted his eyes.
4.   He hadn't looked at a woman like this since he had first met Ann.
5.   What's the matter with me? he asked himself.
6.   I'm getting as bad as Parker.
7.   He looked again at the blonde.
8.   An evening out with her, he thought, would be sensational.
9.   What the eye doesn't see, Parker was always saying, the heart doesn't grieve about.
10.   That was true.
11.   Ann would never know.
12.   After all, other married men did it.
13.   Why shouldn't he?
14.   But when the girl crossed the road and he lost sight of her, he jerked his mind back with an effort to the letter he had received that morning from Ann.
15.   She had been away now for five weeks, and she wrote to say that her mother was no better, and she had no idea when she was coming back.

The deletion rule and the generalization rule apply to [1]. The information about clothing can be eliminated. The description of the blonde can be generalized to "an attractive woman". The message about "walking" is, at the microlevel, relevant for the interpretation of [2], and can, therefore, not be eliminated according to the weak variant of the deletion rule. It is, however, possible to eliminate "walk" and "undulations" by applying the strong deletion rule and the generalization "an attractive woman". The way in which the woman walks is of secondary importance. The following discourse elements can be generalized to "looking at": "caught Ken Holland's eye" [1], "studied" and "watching" [2], "shifted his eyes" [3], "looked" [4], and "looked again" [7]. On the basis of [3], [4], [5] and [6], it can be deduced that Ken Holland feels guilty because he, a married man, wants to date another woman. Sentences [9] through [13], which provide, as it were, the argumentation, can be generalized into "There is no reason not to go out with another woman." The generalization can possibly be eliminated when it has become clear that the argumentation is irrelevant for the rest of the story. Sentences [14] through [15] are linked to [1] and [2] and provide information about the main character. On the basis of this information, it can be construed that Ken Holland is unhappy. This information is not in the text, but can be deduced using presupposed knowledge of the married man's psyche. After this analysis, van Dijk arrives at the following macrostructure.

(27) 1. Ken Holland is looking at a beautiful girl in the street (from [1], [2], [7] and [8] by generalization).
      2. He has a guilty conscience about that because he is married (from [3], [4], [5] and [6] by construction).
      3. He is frustrated because his wife is absent (from [14], [15] by construction).

Clearly, this is not the only possible macrostructure. The text about Ken Holland can also be summarized as follows.

(28) A man shortchanged two women.

Macrorules are not rules that can be used in order to trace *the* meaning structure of discourse. The rules only describe the procedures with which *a* meaning structure can be assigned.

5.4   Superstructures

In many cases discourse contains not only a meaning structure, but also a kind of prefab structure to present a structured content: a *superstructure*. A good example is a letter of application. This type of letter usually has a specific form: an introduction to the application, which is followed by an argumentative segment or sales pitch and, in conclusion, perhaps a reference to the curriculum vitae or references. Within such a discourse schema, the content can vary. For this formal structure, Van Dijk introduced the term *superstructure*. Superstructures are conventionalized schemas that provide the global form for the macrostructural content of a discourse. In other words, macrostructures deal with the content and superstructures with the form. The

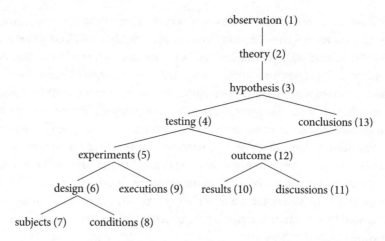

Figure 2. Superstructure of a scientific article reporting on experimental research

term *superstructure* also illustrates the fact that the discourse form stands above the content in some sense. When a letter of application is being written, an existing discourse form can be used with a specific content. The addressee of the letter can then easily determine where to find specific information.

Superstructures are also used for other types of discourse. The superstructure of a scientific article in which experimental research is reported on could look like Figure 2 above.

As an illustration, a fake investigation is described that has the concept *superstructure* as its topic. Newspaper articles often have a structure that can be represented approximately like this: First, there is a *headline* (sometimes accompanied by a subtitle), which serves as a short summary. Following this is a *lead*: bold print containing the basic gist of the news item. Then comes the news article itself, the *flat text*, which is the detailed report of the news item. This is, of course, not a complete description. Furthermore, these rules do not apply to editorials. For simplicity's sake, however, it is assumed that the following observation (1) is correct; news bulletins have a superstructure with a *heading*, a *lead*, and a *flat text*.

An interesting question is to what degree the superstructure influences the assimilation of the text. Or, to phrase the question in a more limited fashion: Is more or less information acquired from the flat text when there is no lead? On the basis of a theory (2) on text comprehensibility, it can be assumed that a reader will gain more information from a text if it is clear beforehand what the text is about. The following hypothesis (3) can be derived from this theory: More information can be deduced from news articles that have a *lead* than from those that do not. This hypothesis can be tested (4) experimentally (5). For example, readers are given news articles with or without *leads* and are asked questions about the text after they have read it in order to determine the degree of information assimilation. The set-up of the experiment (6), information on the subjects (7), and the conditions (8) will have to be included in the report. If, for example, it were to become clear that some subjects possessed a good deal of prior knowledge concerning the topic of the news article, the results would be less reliable. It must also be reported how the experiment was performed (9), whether the subjects were given equal amounts of time, etc. The results (10), in this case the differences between the answers to the questions, are discussed (11) with the outcome (12) leading to a conclusion (13), in which it is stated whether or not the hypothesis has been confirmed. The components mentioned in the above schema do not have to occur in exactly the order described here. This superstructure or a variation on it can, however, be found in many research reports.

One question that has frequently been investigated is whether a study text is easier to learn if the text itself provides clues about the macrostructure or superstructure. These clues are called *advance organizers*. An organizer can be a title or a subtitle that indicates the content, but it can also be an introductory paragraph in which the structure of the text is explained. Actually, every text fragment that describes the text that follows is an advance organizer. Numerous experiments have made it clear that in certain circumstances advance organizers can aid the learning process, for instance, when a student has very little prior knowledge of the topic. For this reason, many textbooks contain introductory sections that explain the content (macrostructure) and construction (superstructure) of the text.

Questions and assignments

Questions

5.1.1 Do a propositional analysis of the following discourse fragment, taken from Kintsch and Vipond (1979).

> A great black and yellow V-2 rocket forty-six feet long stood in a New Mexico desert. Empty, it weighed five tons. For fuel it carried eight tons of alcohol and liquid oxygen.
>
> Everything was ready. Scientists and generals withdrew to some distance and crouched behind earth mounds. Two red flares rose as a signal to fire the rocket.

5.1.2 Give a schematic overview of the relations between the propositions in the first four sentences in discourse fragment (26).

5.2.1 Analyze the following fragment (from the opening segment of this book) in terms of discourse topic and topic shift. What is the topic in A's first utterance and what is the comment? Demonstrate that a sentence topic does not always have to be given.

A: Say, there's a good movie playing tonight.

B: Actually, I have to study.

A: Too bad.

B: Yes, I'm sorry.

A: Well, I guess I don't need to ask you if you want me to pick you up.

5.2.2 Demonstrate, using your own examples, that a topic does not have to be definite, subject or pronoun. Show also that the topic does not need to precede the comment.

5.2.3 In the following text the sentences have been rearranged. Arrange them by topic and indicate where topic shift takes place. The text is from an experiment by Eugene Winter which is reported by Michael Hoey (1983).

1. In England, however, the tungsten-tipped spikes would tear the thin tarmac surfaces of our roads to pieces as soon as the protective layer of snow or ice melted.

2. Road maintenance crews try to reduce the danger of skidding by scattering sand upon the road surfaces.

3. We therefore have to settle for the method described above as the lesser of two evils.

4. Their spikes grip the icy surfaces and enable the motorist to corner safely where non-spiked tires would be disastrous.

5. Its main drawback is that if there are fresh snowfalls the whole process has to be repeated, and if the snowfalls continue, it becomes increasingly ineffective in providing some kind of grip for tires.

6. These tires prevent most skidding and are effective in the extreme weather conditions as long as the roads are regularly cleared of loose snow.
7. Such a measure is generally adequate for our very brief snowfalls.
8. Whenever there is snow in England, some of the country roads may have black ice.
9. In Norway, where there may be snow and ice for nearly seven months of the year, the law requires that all cars be fitted with special steel spiked tires.
10. Motorists coming suddenly upon stretches of black ice may find themselves skidding off the road.

5.3.1 Which macrorules have been used to convert discourse fragment (a) into summary (b)?
a. Mother was singing while she did the dishes. Father was busy vacuuming the floor.
b. The parents were cleaning the house.

5.4.1 Is a superstructure a necessary characteristic of discourse? Discuss.

5.4.2 Is the table of contents of a book an advance organizer? Explain.

Assignments

5.1.1 Have subjects read a short paper or story. Ask them to retell it half an hour later. Which propositions do they omit and how do they apply the generalization and construction rules?

5.2.1 Take a text and delete the paragraph boundaries. Have ten subjects divide the text into paragraphs again. See if there is agreement and try to explain the differences by using the terms *topic* and *subtopic*.

5.3.1 Ask a few people to summarize the story in (26). Which macropropositions, see for example (28), does this yield?

5.4.1 Look up a scientific article in your library and examine whether or not it complies with the superstructure given in Figure 2.

Bibliographical information

5.1   The examples of the propositional analysis of discourse fragments were taken from the dissertation by Baten (1981). For additional examples, see Kintsch (1998).

5.2   The term *topic* is, according to Brown and Yule (1983), "the most frequently used unexplained term in the analysis of discourse." Consult this source for further information. Example (28) on topic continuity was also taken from this volume.

The *theme–rheme* concept set originated in the Prague school. This school, which flourished primarily in the 1930s, included a number of linguists whose main interest was the communicative function of word order differences. See, for example, Firbas (1992). Much of the literature on thematics is scattered over different disciplines (literature, psychology, linguistics and cognitive science). Louwerse and Van der Peer (2002) have edited a detailed collection to provide a coherent overview.

5.3   For further study, see Van Dijk (1980). The examples given here were for the most part taken from this publication. The Ken Holland passage is an excerpt from *Tiger by the Tail* by James Hadley Chase (1966).

5.4   For further study, see Van Dijk (1980). The term *advance organizer* was introduced by Ausubel (1960). An overview of the research is given in Mayer (1979). For further study, see Jonassen (1982) in which six functions of advance organizers are defined. See also Polanyi and Van den Berg (1996), who demonstrate a framework for helping to identify and resolve complex issues in the structure and interpretation of discourse.

6 Discourse connections

6.1 Cohesion

The most salient phenomenon of discourse is the fact that sentences or utterances are linked together. For this "connectedness", this "texture", two concepts are used: *cohesion*, referring to the connections which have their manifestation in the discourse itself, and *coherence*, referring to the connections which can be made by the reader or listener based on knowledge outside the discourse. In a sentence like "Mary got pregnant and she married" the fact that *she* refers to *Mary* is an example of cohesion, and the interpretation that her pregnancy was the reason for her to marry is an example of coherence (see Section 6.3).

This first section deals with the connections evident in the discourse, with cohesion. Michael Halliday and Ruquaiya Hassan (1976), who were already introduced in Section 3.6, were the first to analyze this kind of discourse connection. They distinguished five types of cohesion.

a. *Substitution*
Substitution is the replacement of a word(group) or sentence segment by a "dummy" word. The reader or listener can fill in the correct element based on the preceding. Three frequently occurring types of substitution are that of a noun (1), of a verb (2) and of a clause (3).

(1) These biscuits are stale. Get some fresh *ones*.
(2) A: Have you called the doctor?
     B: I haven't *done* it yet, but I will *do* it.
     A: Though actually, I think you should *do* it.
(3) A: Are they still arguing in there?
     B: No, *it* just seems so.

b. *Ellipsis*
Ellipsis is the omission of a word or part of a sentence. Ellipsis is closely related to substitution, and can be described as "substitution by zero". The division that is normally used is nominal, verbal and clausal ellipsis.

(4)   These biscuits are stale. Those are fresh.

(5)   He participated in the debate, but you didn't.

(6)   Who wants to go shopping? You?

c. *Reference*

Reference concerns the relation between a discourse element and a preceding or following element. Reference deals with a semantic relationship whereas substitution and
ellipsis deal with the relationship between grammatical units: words, sentence parts
and clauses. In the case of reference, the meaning of a dummy word can be determined
by what is imparted before or after the occurrence of the dummy word. In general, the
dummy word is a pronoun.

(7)   I see John is here. *He* hasn't changed a bit.

(8)   *She* certainly has changed. No, behind John. I mean Karin.

But reference can also be achieved by other means, for instance, by the use of a definite
article or an adverb, as in the following examples:

(9)   A man crossed the street. Nobody saw what happened. Suddenly *the* man was
      lying there and calling for help.

(10)   We grew up in the 1960s. We were idealistic *then*.

d. *Conjunction*

Conjunction is the relationship which indicates how the subsequent sentence or clause
should be linked to the preceding or the following (parts of the) sentence. This is usually achieved by the use of conjunctions (also known as connectives). The following are
examples of three frequently occurring relationships; addition, temporality, causality.
The relationship can be hypotactic (as in the a-examples, which combine a main clause
with a subordinate clause or phrase) or paratactic (as in the b-examples, which have
two main clauses).

addition

(11)   a.   *Besides* being mean, he is also hateful.

       b.   He no longer goes to school *and* is planning to look for a job.

temporality

(12)   a.   *After* the car had been repaired, we were able to continue our journey.

       b.   The car was repaired. *Afterwards* we were able to continue our journey.

causality

(13)   a.   He is not going to school today *because* he is sick.

       b.   Ann got a beautiful job last year *and* now she is rich.

e. *Lexical cohesion*

Lexical cohesion refers to the links between the content words (nouns, verbs, adjectives, adverbs) which are used in subsequent segments of discourse. Two types of lexical cohesion can be distinguished: reiteration and collocation.

Reiteration includes not only repetition but also synonymy. Reiteration can also occur through the use of a word that is systematically linked to a previous one, for example, *young* and *old*. In general, reiteration is divided into the five following types.

1. repetition (often involving reference)

(14)   A *conference* will be held on national environmental policy. At this *conference* the issue of salination will play an important role.

2. synonymy (often involving reference)

(15)   A *conference* will be held on national environmental policy. This *environmental symposium* will be primarily a conference dealing with water.

3. hyponymy/hyperonymy (e.g., the relation of *flower* to *tulip* and vice versa, subordination and superordination)

(16)   We were in town today shopping for *furniture*. We saw a lovely *table*.
(17)   Did you see the wooden *igloos* in this new town? Oh, they build even stranger *houses* here.

4. meronymy (part vs. whole)

(18)   At its six-month checkup, the *brakes* had to be repaired. In general, however, the *car* was in good condition.

5. antonymy (e.g., *white* vs. *black*)

(19)   The *old* movies just don't do it any more. The *new* ones are more appealing.

Collocation, the second type of lexical cohesion, deals with the relationship between words on the basis of the fact that these often occur in the same surroundings. Some examples are *sheep* and *wool, congress* and *politician* or *college* and *study*.

(20)   *Red Cross* helicopters were in the air continuously. The *blood bank* will soon be desperately in need of *donors*.
(21)   The hedgehog *scurried* across the road. Its *speed* surprised me.

In the five main types of cohesion (substitution, ellipsis, reference, conjunction and lexical cohesion), the interpretation of a discourse element is dependent on another element that can be pointed out in discourse. In (21), for instance, the correct interpretation of the word "speed" is only possible by reading the preceding sentence within which the word "scurried" is of primary importance.

6.2   Referential elements

A special type of referential cohesion results from the use of pronouns.

(22)   John said that *he* was not going to school.
(23)   When *he* came in John tripped over the blocks.

Back-referential pronouns, such as the pronoun in (22), are called anaphora. The term is derived from a Greek word which means "to lift up" or "to bring back". Forward-referential pronouns, such as the one in (23), are called cataphora: *cata-* is the opposite of *ana-*. In the examples mentioned here, "he" can also refer to another person. Then it is called an *exophor* or a deictic element.

Anaphoric relations are not only found when personal pronouns are used. See the proverb in the following example.

(24)   If John is not going to school, then I won't *do* it either.

The research into anaphora is focused on the following question: How are anaphora interpreted and which factors play a role in the interpretation process? Compare the following discourse fragments.

(25)   Mary said nothing to Sally. She would not understand the first thing about it.
(26)   Mary told Sally everything. She could not keep her mouth shut.

In (25) "she" can only refer to "Sally". In (26) both references are grammatically possible. While in (27), "she" can only refer to "Sally".

(27)   Mary told Sally everything. She could not keep her mouth shut and Mary really told her off for doing it.

An interesting phenomenon can be observed in the following sentences.

(28)   Julius left. He was sick.
(29)   He was sick. Julius left.
(30)   He was sick. That's why Julius left.

In (28) "he" can refer to Julius. In (29) it is much more plausible that "he" refers to someone other than Julius while, in (30) "he" can be interpreted as referring forward to "Julius". These differences can be explained by assuming an interpretation principle suggested by Peter Bosch (1983).

(31) Principle of natural sequential aboutness
      Unless there is some reason to assume the contrary, each following sentence is
      assumed to say something about objects introduced in previous sentences.

On the basis of this principle, according to Bosch (1983), the "he" in (29) cannot
be interpreted as Julius. The fact of Julius leaving says nothing about the preceding
sentence: "He was sick." In (30), on the other hand, the word "that" indicates that
something is going to be said which is linked to the preceding sentence. This indication is reinforced by the reader's knowledge that one consequence of "being sick" is
found in the words which follow, that is, that sickness can be a reason for leaving. It
is for this reason that the sentence about Julius can be linked to the preceding sentence. This interpretation is, therefore, very much dependent on the reader's general
knowledge. This can also be seen in the following example, in which the relation is
the same as in (30).

(32) He screamed. That is why Julius left.

As someone's screaming is not usually a reason for that same person's leaving, it can
be assumed on the basis of the interpretation principle that the second sentence does
not say anything about the person in the first sentence. Thus, the "he" in (32) cannot
be interpreted as referring to "Julius".

Experimental research has determined which factors play a role in the interpretation of anaphora. In an experiment conducted by Susan Ehrlich (1980), subjects were
given sentences of the following type.

(33) Steve blamed Frank because he spilled the coffee.
(34) Jane blamed Bill because he spilled the coffee.

The time it took for the subjects to determine which name was the antecedent for the
anaphor "he" was measured. Most of the subjects determined that "he" in sentence (33)
referred to Frank. This decision did not require grammatical knowledge but general
knowledge. Spilling coffee is clumsy and inconvenient and is, therefore, a reason for
blame. If Steve is blaming Frank, then it is most likely the latter who spilled the coffee. The use of general knowledge is a pragmatic factor. In (34) this knowledge is not
necessary for the interpretation of "he". Knowledge of grammar makes it clear that "he",
being a male-gender pronoun, can only refer to Bill.

If pragmatic factors always play a role in the interpretation of anaphora, then the
subjects would have spent equal amounts of time in determining the antecedent for
both sentence (33) and (34). If, however, readers first apply their grammatical knowledge and only then their general knowledge, if necessary, then the interpretation of
(33) will take less time than that of (34). After all, in the case of (34) grammatical

knowledge is sufficient. The experiment did indeed prove that the interpretation of (34) took less time than that of (33). This led to the conclusion that pragmatic factors only play a role when grammatical clues are lacking.

6.3   Coherence

If propositions are the building blocks of discourse, then discourse relations are the cement between the blocks. Below are some examples from the many different kinds of discourse relations that exist. We are looking at the relation between the two sentences in each discourse fragment.

(35) a.   The government has taken emergency measures. They will become effective next year.

(36) a.   The president will probably run for reelection next year. This was announced yesterday by the White House press secretary.

(37) a.   The president was not available for comment. At that particular moment he was receiving his Chinese counterpart.

In (35a) the follow-up sentence elaborates on one constituent, "measures." In (36a) the second sentence encapsulates the first sentence. In (37b) the situation is different: the follow-up provides an explanation for the content of the first sentence.

The relations in (35a) and (36a) add very little to the meaning of the sentences. In (37a), however, a meaning element is added. This can be seen if the sentences are rewritten as one single sentence. Only in (37b) will a meaning-laden conjunction be necessary.

(35) b.   The government has taken emergency measures which will become effective next year.

(36) b.   The White House press secretary announced yesterday that the president will run for reelection next year.

(37) b.   The president was not available for comment as he was receiving his Chinese counterpart at that particular moment.

Research into discourse relations has concentrated on those links between sentences which bear meaning. This is not the case in examples (35a) and (36a). This discourse does not contain a meaningful link between the main sentences and the adjectival subordinate clause (35a) and the object complement (36a). The link in example (37a), however, does have its own meaning: *reason*.

In the research done into (meaning-bearing) discourse relations, two basic types are distinguished: the additive relation and the causal relation. The additive relation can be traced back to a conjunction and as such is related to various types of coordination. Among the coordinating relations are those which can be represented by words such as *and* (conjunction or addition), *but* (contrast), *or* (disjunction), or an equivalent of these words. Below is an example of a contrast relation.

(38)   John bought a present for his mother. (But) he forgot to take it with him.

A causal relation can be traced back to an implication, and is as such related to subordination. The most important causal relations are the seven types distinguished in traditional grammar:

(39)   cause
       John did not go to school. He was sick.

(40)   reason
       John did not come with us. He hates parties.

(41)   means
       Would you mind opening the door? Here is the key.

(42)   consequence
       John is sick. He is not going to school.

(43)   purpose
       The instructions should be printed in capital letters. It is hoped that in this way, difficulties in reading them will be avoided.

(44)   condition
       You can get a job this summer. But first you have to pass your exams.

(45)   concession
       He was rich. Yet he never gave anything to charity.

These discourse relations can be distinguished as follows. A cause indicates a consequence that is outside the domain of volition. A reason always indicates that a volitional aspect is present. A means is a deliberate utilization of a cause in order to achieve a volitional consequence. A purpose is a volitional consequence. A condition is a necessary or possible cause or reason for a possible consequence. A concession is a cause or reason for which the expected consequence fails to occur, or the yielding of a point.

Discourse relations can be grouped or classified according to specific characteristics which they share. One of these characteristics is the *semantic-pragmatic* dimension. The literature includes various definitions of these terms. The following are fairly common. Semantic relations connect segments on the basis of their propositional content, the locutions of the segment, linking the situations that are referred to in the propositions. Pragmatic relations connect segments on the basis of their illocutions.

A good example of a semantic relation is (40). A hearer can interpret John's hating parties as a reason, without having to deal with the illocutions of the segments. It is the two situations in the consecutive sentences that are related: the situation "hating parties" in the last sentence is a reason for the situation "not coming along" in the first sentence. An example of a pragmatic relation can be seen in the following sequence.

(46)   I'll get the groceries. I have to go shopping anyway.

In this example, the relation does not pertain to the two situations in both sentences, but to the illocutions. After all, "going shopping" in the last sentence is not necessarily a reason for "getting the groceries" in the first sentence as far as its propositional content is concerned. If this were the case, then anyone who was ever to go shopping would also get the groceries.

It is, however, sometimes difficult to draw a precise boundary between the semantic and pragmatic relations. For example, is the relation in (45) semantic or pragmatic? The relation is a semantic one in a world where it is very unconventional for someone who is rich not to make donations to charity. But the relation is pragmatic when the speaker has the apparent intention of making an accusation.

A special subset of pragmatic relations is rhetorical relations. These are the relations with which speakers or writers apparently have the intention of bringing about a change in opinion, position or behavior of readers or listeners. Usually the five following rhetorical relations are distinguished.

(47)   evidence
       No single measure has had an effect. The traffic jams are still as bad as ever.

(48)   conclusion
       The window is open. There must have been a burglar.

(49)   justification
       Now I am throwing in the towel. I've tried it ten times.

(50)   solution
       No single measure has had an effect. With this proposal our goals will be achieved.

(51)   motivation
       Do you want to know more? Send us a stamped self-addressed envelope.

Other types of pragmatic relations are distinguished in the literature as well, for example the following by Eve Sweetser (1990): epistemic, speech act and metalinguistic relations. Epistemic relations are pragmatic relations, expressing a writer or speaker's conclusion based on a causal relation in reality. An example is (52), which shows that the writer or speaker's knowledge that the "he" has drunk a lot produces the conclusion about the headache. The connection then does not lie in the external reality, but in the mental domain of the speaker.

(52)   He must have a headache. He has drunk too much.

In a speech act relation the speech act is motivated by reference to a situation constituting the reason for it, for example: "What are you doing tonight, because there is a good movie on". Metalinguistic relations refer to discourse itself, for example: "In conclusion I would like to remark ..."

In this section various sorts of discourse relations have been presented. Section 6.4 introduces a notable theory on how to analyze these relations, while in Section 6.5 some problems and research topics concerning discourse relations are dealt with.

6.4   Rhetorical Structure Theory

In the past two decades several attempts have been made to create a method for the analysis of discourse and discourse relations between text segments. One of the best-known proposals is the Rhetorical Structure Theory (RST) by William Mann and Sandra Thompson. This theory, developed in the 1980s, considers a discourse to be a hierarchical organization of text segments.

An RST analysis starts by dividing a text into minimal units, such as independent clauses. Then the connection between these units is labeled by choosing a relation name. Mann and Thompson propose a set of over 20 relations. They distinguish subject matter relations and presentational relations, a division that roughly corresponds to the semantic-pragmatic dichotomy. A schematic overview of this classification is given below.

(53)   Classification of RST relations
        Subject matter relations
        Elaboration, Circumstance, Solutionhood, Volitional cause, Volitional result,
        Non-volitional cause, Non-volitional result, Purpose, Condition, Otherwise,
        Interpretation, Evaluation, Restatement, Summary, Sequence, Contrast
        Presentational
        Motivation, Antithesis, Background, Enablement, Evidence, Justification,
        Concession

Mostly, the units in a relation are either nucleus or satellite. This means that one member of the pair, the nucleus, is more essential to the writer's purpose, while the supporting element is the satellite. A pair consisting of a nucleus and a satellite unit is called a span. Spans can be linked to other units or spans, so that the text as a whole is connected together into a hierarchic structure. The largest span created in this manner encompasses the whole text.

Below is an example of a text and the corresponding RST diagram. The text is divided into six units, beginning with the title, indicated by numbers which have been added.

(54) 1. Leading indicators
2. Steep declines in capital spending commitments and building permits, along with a drop in the money stock pushed the leading composite down for the fifth time in the past 11 months to a level 0.5% below its high a year ago.
3. Such a decline is highly unusual at this stage in an expansion;
4. for example, in the three most recent expansions, the leaders were rising, on average, at about a 7% clip at comparable phases in the cycle.
5. While not signaling an outright recession,
6. the current protracted sluggishness of the leading indicators appears consistent with our prognosis of sluggish real GNP growth over the next few quarters.

Unit 4, which refers to previous expansions, forms evidence for unit 3, which states that the present declines are unusual. Units 3 and 4 together are a span that elaborates the "steep declines" that are mentioned in unit 2. Units 5 and 6 interpret the span that is formed by units 2–4. Unit 5 provides limits on the degree of interpretation, while

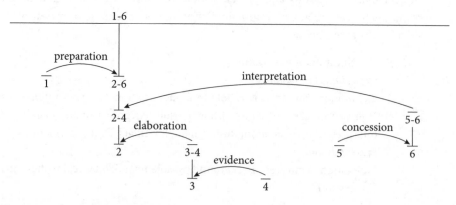

Figure 1. RST analysis of text (54)

unit 6 provides the interpretation. Finally, unit 1 is a title that prepares the reader for what is to come. Note, though, that the preparation relation was not included in the original classification.

6.5   Discourse relation research

Up until now, RST has remained one of the best-known and widely applied methods for discourse analysis. However, being the center of attention, it has also been the subject of debate and critique in the past few decades. In the discussion seven topics can be distinguished that are dealt with in this section. One major criticism is the fact that the set of relations in RST is purely descriptive, not doing justice to the differences between specific relations, but throwing them all on two heaps. To this date, no agreement has been reached on exactly which relations and categories should be distinguished. As a result, there is no generally acknowledged standard set of relations.

As often as not, a set of relations is presented without further structuring. There is no order in the classification. Sanders et al. (1992) have argued that a set of discourse relations must not only be descriptively adequate, but also be psychologically plausible. In their view, the latter does not apply to, for example, RST, as the relations that Mann and Thompson distinguish are all on the same level. However, some relations (e.g., volitional cause and evidence) are more similar than others (e.g., volitional cause and contrast). Sanders et al. propose a classification based on the assumption that discourse relations are ordered in the human mind by four fundamental ordering principles which they call "primitives":

(55)   Sanders et al.'s four primitives
   1.   Basic operation: Each relation has a *causal* or an *additive* component.
   2.   Source of coherence: Each relation is coherent on *semantic* or *pragmatic* grounds.
   3.   Order of segments: This distinction only applies to causal relations. These have a *basic order* when the antecedent (e.g., cause) is to the left of the consequence (e.g., result) and a *non-basic order* when the antecedent is to the right of the consequence.
   4.   Polarity: A relation is *positive* when the basic operation connects the content of two text segments as given and *negative* when it connects the content of one of the segments with the negation of the content of the other.

The four primitives can be combined in order to obtain twelve classes of discourse relations. The set of relations can then be organized in terms of its own "meaning characteristics": when a relation contains causality, it belongs to a different group than a relation that is not causal. The cause-consequence relation, for example, is defined as Basic Operation = Causal, Source of Coherence = Semantic, Order = Non-Basic, Polarity = Positive. An example of this is (56).

(56)   Last week it rained a lot in Scotland, because there was low pressure over Ireland.

A third point of attention is the definition of discourse relations, i.e., the assignment of the "correct" relation label. Owing to the vagueness of the description, it cannot be unequivocally determined which relations are applicable in an analysis. Consider the following example.

(57)   Sue is corporate president. You should take this to her.

Is this a reason relation or a conclusion? If the accent is put on the first sentence, are the relations of motivation or justification also possible? If so, a third problem arises: relations are applicable that in, for example, RST belong to two separate categories of relations, in this case subject matter (e.g., reason) and presentational (e.g., motivation). The view that perhaps two (or more) relations can hold at the same time is known as the Multi-Level Hypothesis (MLH). In essence it argues that discourse relations can exist on more than one level simultaneously, thus on both a semantic and a pragmatic level.

Two fervent supporters of MLH are Moore and Pollack (1992). They claim that the interpretation of discourse requires the co-existence of so-called informational and intentional relations. Informational relations, corresponding to semantic relations, pertain to the relation between information in two consecutive text segments. Intentional relations correspond to pragmatic relations. They concern the notion that texts are meant to realize changes in a reader's mental state. Moore and Pollack use the following example to prove that two relations exist at the same time. According to them, a volitional cause as well as an evidence relation applies between the two text segments: the first sentence can be both a volitional cause and evidence for the action in the second sentence.

(58)   The president supports big business. He's sure to veto House Bill 1711.

A fifth important issue in discourse relation research is the nucleus-satellite division. If there is an asymmetry between the parts of a relation, e.g., if one member of the pair is more essential to the writer's purpose, then the most important element is the nucleus. In (58), for example, the first sentence would be the satellite in case of a volitional cause or evidence relation. In additive relations such as (59), there can be two nuclei, but not necessarily. The context decides which one is the nucleus. If in the case of (59) the topic in the context is forgetfulness, then the second sentence is the nucleus. If the topic is the fact that John loves cooking, then the first sentence is the nucleus.

(59)   John prepared a pie for his parents. (But) he forgot to put it in the oven.

Sixth, there is the order of the parts. In (60), for example, the condition comes after the statement, but the reverse order is also possible, as in (61), where the concession precedes the statement. This raises some intriguing questions. Is there a marked and unmarked order of parts? And if so, under what conditions will an unmarked order appear?

(60)   You can go to that party this Saturday. But first you have to clean up your room.
(61)   He liked taking care of his sister's kids. Yet he and his wife never had children themselves.

A last issue worth mentioning is the division into explicit and implicit relations. This depends on the presence or absence of a conjunction. In the examples given above, such as (59), it is clear that the use of conjunctions is optional. Moreover, a conjunction can indicate more than one relation. Look again at example (60), in which the word *but*, indicating a coordinating contrast relation, marks a conditional relation. The question is under which conditions the use of conjunctions can enhance comprehensibility.

Questions and assignments

Questions

6.1.1   Using your own examples, show that substitution and ellipsis deal with grammatical relationships while reference deals with semantic relationships.

6.1.2   Using your own examples, show that the conjunction *and* can express relationships other than addition.

6.1.3   Which cohesion phenomena are contained in the following excerpt from Alice in Wonderland? For an extensive analysis, see Halliday and Hasan (1976: 340).

> (1) The last word ended in a long bleat, so like a sheep that Alice quite started. (2) She looked at the Queen, who seemed to have suddenly wrapped herself up in wool. (3) Alice rubbed her eyes, and looked again. (4) She couldn't make out what had happened at all. (5) Was she in a shop? (6) And was that really – was it really a *sheep* that was sitting on the other side of the counter? (7) Rub as she would, she could make nothing more of it ...

6.2.1   Are the words in italics in the following discourse fragment (taken from Kallmeyer, 1980) anaphora or cataphora?

> As for your second question: to *that* (1) I only wish to say *this much* (2): this party finds the proposals adequate and satisfactory. *Therein* (3) lies a possibility for alleviating the situation. *That* (4) is why I am sure Parliament will ratify this bill. I would like to add *one thing* (5): we are of the opinion that *this* (6) is only a first step. *This* (7) has always been our standpoint; *that* (8) will not change. And finally, to get back to your third question, *the following* (9): discussions are still going on. *That* (10) is why I cannot say anything concrete at this time. In my view *it* (11) is possible that the committee will deal with this issue when it next meets. In any case, *that* (12) is what I will propose; if I am correct, *what* (13) will happen is that your suggestions will be taken into account. *In this way* (14) it will be possible for the bill to be presented to Parliament before the summer recess.

6.2.2   Try to explain why anaphorical language use occurs much more often than cataphorical language use.

6.2.3   In which sentence is the anaphor "he" more difficult to interpret and why?
   a.   John told Pete that he would have to quit.
   b.   John told Pete that he should stop complaining.

6.3.1   The following four sentences (taken from Michael Hoey, 1983) can be placed in 24 different sequences:

a.   I was on sentry duty.

b.   I saw the enemy approaching.

c.   I opened fire.

d.   I beat off the attack.

Below are three examples using subordinating, coordinating and other linking constituents.

a.   I beat off the attack *by* opening fire. *Then* I saw the enemy *while* I was on sentry duty.

b.   I saw the enemy approaching *because* I was on sentry duty. *But* I opened fire *and* I beat off the attack.

c.   Seeing the enemy approach was for me *cause* to open fire. *In this way* I beat off the attack. *At that time* I was on sentry duty.

Provide three additional examples of your own.

6.3.2   Designate the relation(s) between the two sentences in each of the examples below.

a.   In the memo, possibilities for retraining and extra training were dealt with. Knowledge of its contents will improve your chances of employment elsewhere in this company.

b.   Many employees in our department are not motivated to go to night school. As the employees' representative on the board I would like to stress the importance of continuing education.

c.   Noise pollution has not decreased. This is because the insulation factor of the soundproofing was lower than was expected.

d.   Study the plans at your leisure. Then it will become clear that all the specifications have been followed to the letter.

e.   The government has presented a number of new measures. They will become effective next year.

f.   The new plans can be executed. The board of directors has allocated a large sum of money for just this purpose.

6.3.3   Determine whether the relations in examples 38–45 and 56 are implicit or explicit, and which parts are nuclei and which are satellites. Determine which words are needed or need to be left out in order to change the order of the parts.

6.4.1   Give an RST analysis of the following text taken from Mann and Thompson (1988:253).

1.   Farmington police had to help control traffic recently

2.   when hundreds of people lined up to be among the first applying for jobs at the yet-to-open Marriott hotel.

3.   The hotel's help-wanted announcement – for 300 openings – was a rare opportunity for many unemployed.

4. The people waiting in line carried a message, a refutation, of the claim that jobless could be employed if only they showed enough moxie.

5. Every rule has exceptions,

6. but the tragic and too common tableaux of hundreds or even thousands of people snake-lining up for any task with a paycheck illustrates a lack of jobs,

7. not laziness.

6.5.1 Categorize the following types of discourse relations according to the semantic-pragmatic distinction:

epistemic, informational, intentional, metalinguistic, presentational, speech act, subject matter.

6.5.2 Analyze the relations in the following three examples according to the four primitives provided by Sanders et al. (1992).

a. Because there is a low-pressure area over Ireland, bad weather is coming our way.

b. Nests or dead birds may clog up chimneys. Therefore, have your chimney checked once a year and swept when necessary.

c. The consumption of mineral water has been advocated strongly over the last few years in the Netherlands, but the results of an investigation in Germany on the composition of bottled water were not so good.

6.5.3 Provide a context sentence that causes a change in the nucleus-satellite structure in the volitional cause relation between the following two clauses.

a. Mary buys her husband flowers every week

b. because he cooks so deliciously for her.

Assignments

6.1.1 Use a search engine on the Internet to collect passages in which the Red Cross/Crescent occurs and try to give a description through collocations. Compare the description with an encyclopedic description of the Red Cross/Crescent.

6.2.1 In this book the distinction between syntax, semantics and pragmatics (e.g., syntactic, semantic and pragmatic relations) has been explained, for example, in Chapters 3 and 6. Di Blas and Paolini (2003) mention the existence of syntactic, semantic and pragmatic anaphora. Within this threefold distinction, the notions semantic and pragmatic correspond, respectively, with, for example, synonyms and collocation or dictionaries and encyclopedia. Try to comment on these parallels.

6.3.1   Look up various definitions of the concession relation in the literature and try to indicate why you have a preference for one specific definition.

6.4.1   In Section 6.4 it was mentioned that the preparation relation in (54) is not included in the original classification by Mann and Thompson. Would you classify this relation as subject matter (semantic) or as presentational (pragmatic)? Provide arguments for your choice.

6.4.2   In an experiment conducted by the Discourse Studies Group at Tilburg University the following discourse fragments were presented to respondents with the question: "Is the relation between the two sentences semantic or pragmatic?" The results showed that text (a) was considered to be semantic, while text (b) was judged to be pragmatic. Try to explain this outcome.
   a.   Enroll for the exam in good time. Then you won't risk a fine.
   b.   Go for a swim every day. Then you will feel healthy again.

6.5.1   Provide arguments for or against the Multi-Level Hypothesis as explained using example (58).

Bibliographical information

6.1   The discussion of cohesion is based on the standard work by Halliday and Hasan (1976) in which the different types of cohesion are defined more precisely. The definition in Section 3.6, as well as a number of examples, was also taken from Halliday and Hasan. For more on lexical cohesion, see Kress (1989).

6.2   The distinction between anaphora and cataphora is taken from Bühler (see the 1990 edition). See Halliday and Hasan (1976) for the term *exophor*. Easy entry to the literature on anaphora is offered in Bosch (1983) and Fox (1987). An overview of experimental research is given by Sanford and Garrod (1981). For a language-processing approach to referential elements and coherence, see Chapter 18 in Jurafsky and Martin (2000).

6.3   A landmark publication on discourse relations that is still worth reading is Grimes (1975). Though relatively old, a quality collection of papers on discourse relations is Haiman and Thompson (1988). For a publication on the position of adverbial clauses in spoken language from a discourse perspective, see Ford (1993). Longacre (1996) is a must for a good basis in cohesion phenomena. Examples of research into connectives are given in Couper-Kuhlen and Kortmann (2000).

6.4   The key publication on Rhetorical Structure Theory is Mann and Thompson (1988). Example (19) is taken from Mann and Thompson (2001).

6.5   For various viewpoints on the issue of the classification of discourse relations, the reader is referred to Hovy and Scott (1993) and Knott (1993). Example (55) was taken from Knott and Sanders (1998). The concept of intentionality in discourse was introduced by Grosz and Sidner (1986). See Rambow (1993) and Moser and Moore (1996) for further publications on this issue. The latter also touches upon the nucleus-satellite distinction in relation to intentionality. For a good contribution to the discussion on overlapping discourse relations, see Ford (1986). For a critical analysis of Moore and Pollack's approach, see Sanders and Spooren (1999). Many good papers on discourse relation research are found in Sanders, Schilperoord and Spooren (2001).

7 Contextual phenomena

7.1 Deixis

In the study of the relation between discourse and context six concepts are used frequently. The first is deixis, the phenomenon in which the dependency of discourse on the situation is most striking. The word deixis, which is derived from the Greek word meaning "to show" or "to indicate", is used to denote those elements in a language which refer directly to the discourse situation. Deictic words are words with a reference point that is speaker- or writer-dependent and is determined by the speaker's or writer's position in space and time. See the following example.

(1)   I am now standing on the roof.

The word "I" refers to the person uttering the sentence. The time which "now" denotes is dependent on the moment the statement is uttered. This situation dependency does not occur with words such as "roof"; the meaning of this word remains more or less constant in different situations.

The research into deixis was inspired by Karl Bühler (1934/1990), who also developed the Organon model (see Section 2.1). Bühler was one of the first to map out deictic phenomena. He distinguished two fields in language: the deictic field (*das Zeigfeld*) and the symbolic field (*das Symbolfeld*). Words such as *roof, run, nice*, etc., belong to the symbolic field. These words – called *Nennwörter* by Bühler – have a more or less constant meaning, independent of the situation.

Bühler compared the words in the deictic field to signs on a footpath that direct walkers to their destination. The word *I* points out the speaker and the word *you* the listener. Likewise, *there* points to a specific place and *yesterday* to a specific time. Bühler distinguishes person, place, and time deixis in contrast to mental or phantasmatic deixis. This latter form refers to a mental or fantasy field. The phantasmatic form of deixis (*Deixis am Phantasma*) can be seen in novels in which the first-person narrator does not necessarily have to refer to the author. It can also occur in quotes.

(2)   Pete said: "I'll do something about it tomorrow!"

The deictic field of the quote is different from that of "Pete said". Three time fields play a role here: a. the time at which the speaker uttered the sentence; b. the time at which Pete said what is being quoted; c. the moment "I" refers to.

At the center of the deictic field, which Bühler calls the *Origo*, are the words *I*, *here*, and *now*. Deictic words are generally focused from the speaker's perspective. In other words, deixis is egocentric, with an I-here-now Origo in person, place and time deixis.

a. *Person deixis*

Deixis to person is realized using personal pronouns. The speaker as first person, *I*, directs the utterance to the listener as second person, *you*, and could be talking about a third person, *he* or *she*. In many languages person deixis can also contain other meaning elements, for example, the gender of the third person. The manner in which the second person is addressed can, in some languages, also provide an insight into the relationship between the first and the second person. This phenomenon is often called social deixis. The best-known example of this is Japanese, which has an elaborate system of politeness forms called "honorifics". The choice of a specific form of address is determined by, among other things, the gender and social status of the addressee.

An interesting phenomenon in this regard takes place with the deixis of the first person plural, *we*. This word can mean the group as a whole:

(3)   Do we have time for that? (when the utterance is being directed at the group in general)

This is the inclusive *we*. The word *we* can also be used to denote a segment of a group excluding the other members of the group: the exclusive *we*.

(4)   Do we have time for that? (when you ask someone else for advice)

Oddly enough, the exclusive *we* can also be used to denote precisely that excluded group.

(5)   Do we have time for that? (asked by a mother who sees her children taking out a new toy two minutes before bedtime)

b. *Place deixis*

The following is an example of place deixis.

(6)   Left of Mr. A sits Mrs. B.

This statement is initially interpreted from the speaker's viewpoint and not from Mr. A's. If a statement like this is made to an audience from a stage, the reference point will be mentioned in order to avoid confusion, e.g., "For me left, but for you right of Mr.

A." In place deixis a speaker can refer to something that is in the vicinity or further away: *this, these* as opposed to *that, those*. Place deixis can be realized not only by the use of demonstrative pronouns, but also by the use of adverbs of place: *here* and *there*. In other languages there are more subtle distinctions. Latin possesses, in addition to the words *hic*, which means "that which is close to the speaker" and *iste*, which means "that which is close to the listener", the word *ille* which means "that which is neither close to the speaker nor the listener".

An interesting phenomenon in place deixis is the ambiguity that arises because reference can take place from different spatial positions. The following sentence can have at least two meanings.

(7) Mary is standing in front of the car.
    a. Mary is standing between the car and the speaker.
    b. Mary is standing in front of the car's front end.

If (7) has the meaning of (7a), the place-bound deixis is related to the speaker; if it has the meaning of (7b), it is related to the car. This is the difference between speaker-oriented and object-oriented deixis.

c. *Time deixis*

Deixis to time would seem to be a simple form of deixis. The language resources are the adjectives of time in the sequence "... yesterday ... now ... tomorrow ..." and the verb tenses. The verbs, however, sometimes also have another function besides referring to a specific time. See the following examples.

(8) I had been walking there. (past perfect progressive)
(9) I have been walking there. (present perfect progressive)

The past perfect and the present perfect (whether progressive or not) both refer to events or actions that started somewhere in the past. One of the main differences is that the present perfect always indicates that either the event or the time frame in which it takes place is still going on, which cannot be said of the past perfect. Time deixis is often accompanied by other meaning elements and is, therefore, difficult to isolate.

7.2 Staging

Words in discourse follow each other in a linear fashion. This does not mean, however, that the information in discourse is presented linearly. The information is presented in line with the importance it is supposed to have in a given context. Compare the following examples.

(10)   a.   John is sick.
     b.   Jóhn is sick.

In both sentences, information is provided about John. Yet there is a difference. In (10a) the aspect of sickness is in the foreground, while in (10b) the fact that it is John who is sick is in the foreground. What is foreground information in (10a) is background information in (10b). Below is another example.

(11)   a.   Every year I go on vacation to Aruba for two weeks.
     b.   Every year I go to Aruba on vacation for two weeks.
     c.   For two weeks every year I go on vacation to Aruba.
     d.   I go on vacation to Aruba for two weeks every year.

Using normal intonation, "Aruba" will be slightly accented in sentence (11a). In (11b), the important element is that the activity in question is a vacation; the information given on the destination and the time spent there is background information. In (11c), "two weeks" is foreground information and in (11d) "every year" is in the foreground.

The phenomenon of foreground and background information is called, using a theater metaphor, *staging*. Speakers and writers can present their information in such a way that some elements will be in the foreground while others remain in the background. The theater metaphor can, however, be misleading on one point. The relationship between foreground and background in discourse can be much more complex than that on a stage.

The head–tail principle is a good starting point for analyzing the presentation of information. The more to the left (head) or right (tail) the information is presented, the more important, prominent and in the foreground it becomes. This is illustrated by the following two sentences.

(11)   e.   Every year I go to Aruba for two weeks on vacation.
     f.   Aruba is where I go on vacation for two weeks every year.

In (11e), "on vacation" is more in the foreground than it is in (11b), where it is in the middle position. In (11f), "Aruba" is more in the foreground. The front positioning can be accentuated by a so-called cleft construction in which a sentence of the form "x does y at z" is given the structure "z is where x does y". Two different methods of staging can be observed in the following examples. Following the neutral order in (12a), there is a topicalization in (12b) and another cleft construction in (12c):

(12)   a.   I asked her to marry me in the middle of an autumn storm.
     b.   In the middle of an autumn storm I asked her to marry me.
     c.   It was in the middle of an autumn storm that I asked her to marry me.

The head–tail principle is also at work in paragraphs and longer passages of text. Compare the following passages.

(13) a. I am against an expensive overseas vacation. We have already spent so much money on special things this year. And after all, there are so many fun things we can do in our own country.

b. We have already spent so much money on special things this year. And after all, there are so many fun things we can do in our own country. That is why I am against an expensive overseas vacation.

c. We have already spent so much money on special things this year. That is why I am against an expensive overseas vacation. And after all, there are so many fun things we can do in our own country.

The most important message in this passage is the opposition to an expensive overseas vacation. This message must, therefore, hold a prominent position; in (13a) it is at the beginning, the head, and in (13b) at the end, the tail. The middle position is the least conspicuous; thus (13c) seems to be less cohesive than (13a) or (13b).

On the basis of the head–tail principle, it can also be deduced why sentences sometimes appear not to link up very well. Compare the following passages.

(14) a. The health department, in a report on cattle neglect, states that more and more farmers these days are confronted with financial and infrastructural problems, while in the past cattle maltreatment was usually caused by lack of food and expertise. The problems cannot, however, be blamed solely on the failing EU policy of recent years.

b. The health department, in a report on cattle neglect, states that while in the past cattle maltreatment was usually caused by lack of food and expertise, more and more farmers these days are confronted with financial and infrastructural problems. The problems cannot, however, be blamed solely on the failing EU policy of recent years.

The sentences in (14b) are linked together better than those in (14a). In (14a) the elements "in the past" and "lack of food and expertise" are towards the end of the sentence and will, therefore, attract more attention. The reader may thus expect that the following sentence will continue dealing with these elements. This is, however, not the case. In (14b) the element "problems" at the end of the sentence attracts more attention than in (14a). The following sentence continues dealing with this. This tail-head linking is why (14b) can be judged as more coherent than (14a).

An intriguing problem is the question to what degree the main-subordinate clause distinction reflects the foreground–background relationship, and to what extent the head or tail position of the clause is of influence. Compare the following examples.

(15) a. It was already dark when our hero awoke.
      b. Our hero awoke after it had already become dark.

It appears that the information in the main clause is more foregrounded than that in the subordinate clause. Assuming that discourse proceeds with the foregrounded element, it can be expected that (15a) will proceed to deal with the element "dark", while (15b) would center on the element "awoke". Consider these final examples.

(16) a. The 34-year-old soldier, who had been arrested three times before for extortion and fraud, has been sentenced to ten years' imprisonment for taking an army colonel hostage. The court believed that the soldier was not personally responsible for the death of the colonel. The colonel was actually killed by a marksman's shot.
      b. The 34-year-old soldier, who was sentenced to ten years' imprisonment for taking an army colonel hostage, had been arrested three times before for extortion and fraud. The court believed that the soldier was not personally responsible for the death of the colonel. The colonel was actually killed by a marksman's shot.

Passage (16b) seems to be inferior to (16a). One possible explanation is that the continuation in (16b) deals with the backgrounded information from the relative subordinate clause in the first sentence rather than the foregrounded information about "extortion and fraud".

7.3   Perspectivization

Information can be presented from a number of different perspectives. Compare the following examples.

(17) a. There was a man at the bar. The door opened. A woman and a child came in.
      b. There was a man at the bar. The door opened. A woman and a child walked inside.
      c. There was a man at the bar. He looked up when the door opened. A woman came in, followed by a child.
      d. A woman opened the door for the child. He walked in and saw a man sitting at the bar.

In (17a) the narrator is present inside the bar. In (17b) the narrator is apparently not inside the bar, otherwise the sentence would not have read "walked inside". The narrator could, for example, be looking through a window into the bar in a position from which he can see the man at the bar but not the people outside the door. In (17c) the story is told from the man's perspective and in (17d) from that of the child.

The term *perspective* is used to describe these different points of view. The comparison to cinematic art is often made by defining perspective as the camera position. In discourse studies three approaches are of importance: firstly, the more sociologically-inspired research into the ideological perspective or *vision*; secondly, the more literary-oriented research into the narrator's perspective or *focalization*; thirdly, the syntactically-oriented research into the speaker's attitude, which is called *empathy*.

a. *Vision*
Information can be presented from an ideological perspective: a system of norms and values pertaining to social relations. This explains why two newspapers reporting on the same event can produce different reports. The following examples are the opening sentences from a conservative right-wing daily and a leftist daily dealing with a large peace demonstration in the Netherlands. Try to determine which is which.

(18)   With 400,000 demonstrators participating, double that of the organizers' highest estimates, the peace demonstration in Amsterdam has already been labeled an important political event.

(19)   The fears on the part of thousands of Dutchmen that the peace demonstration in Amsterdam would culminate in an aggressive anti-America orgy were not fulfilled.

Most readers will instantly recognize the progressive (18) and the conservative (19) ideological perspectives. The central question in the research on vision is how an ideology affects language use. Below is an example of experimental research that has been done in this framework.

As part of a refresher course, a group of journalists were asked to write a news story based on a fictitious event: a schoolteacher who was on the verge of being fired from her job at a Christian school for becoming pregnant out of wedlock. Afterwards, the journalists, who were not aware of the research goals, were given a questionnaire that asked their personal views concerning the issue. One question, for example, asked if firing the teacher was justified. By setting the investigation up in this manner, it was possible to ascertain that these personal views determined the way in which a given event was reported. Below is an example of differences in reporting. The material that the journalists were given included the transcript of a telephone conversation with the teacher. At a certain point in the conversation the teacher answered the question "Do they want to get rid of you?" as follows:

(20)   Yes, well, I find it difficult to comment on this, yeah, well, I don't think it is
        wise, with the dismissal and the atmosphere at school where everyone is turned
        against me.

This answer was worked into the articles in different ways. Compare the following
accounts.

(21)   The teacher has decided to wait and see what happens: "I find it difficult to
        comment on this. With the dismissal and the atmosphere at school where
        everyone is turned against me."
(22)   The central figure in this controversy has no idea why she is being dismissed.

The first account was given by a reporter who, according to the questionnaire, was on
the teacher's side. The hesitation in (20) is interpreted in a positive manner as being
a wait-and-see attitude. The second account was given by a journalist whose position
was neutral. The teacher is, nevertheless, portrayed in a more negative fashion. In (21)
the teacher is hesitant whereas in (22), it is stated that she really does not know why
she is being fired. On the basis of the analytical model developed in this investigation,
it was possible to show that even journalists who say that their position concerning a
given issue is neutral also report in a subjective manner.

b. *Focalization*

An entirely different approach is provided by perspective analysis which incorporates
narrative theory. The central idea is that the narrator could be someone other than
the individual who has witnessed or is witnessing an event. This is clear in (17c) and
(17d). The person who is telling the story is not the man looking at the door or the
child who sees the man. Following the French literary theoretician Gérard Genette, the
term *focalization* is used to describe this. This relationship can be signaled in discourse
through verbs of observation (*to see, to hear, to notice*, etc.). In focalization, there is a
subject and an object, an observer and something that is being observed. The subject
of the focalization is called the focalizer. This could be a narrator who is observing
everything from an external viewpoint as in (17a) and (17b); in this case the subject
is called an external focalizer. It could, however, also be a character in the story itself,
as in (17c) and (17d); these are called character-bound focalizers. Below are further
examples. The verbs of observation have been italicized.

(23)   a.   Pete gave a start when he *heard* the man coming up the stairs.
        b.   Mary *felt* that Pete was startled when he *heard* the man coming up the stairs.

In (23a), there is a character-bound focalizer and in (23b) Pete is embedded in Mary's
object of focalization as a focalizer. Focalization analysis helps determine from which
observation point a story is being told and if, for example, a change of perspective has

taken place. It also helps to determine how tension is built up in the story. Below is a more elaborate version of the first story.

(24)   There was a man at the bar. He looked despondent. He was mumbling something about "murdering his great love and his only future."
The door opened. A woman and a little boy entered. The boy gazed at the customer at the bar. Suddenly he felt the woman's hand in front of his eyes. Through her fingers he could see ...

From the verbs of observation used, it can be deduced that at first there is an external focalizer. A change takes place when the child appears on the scene, at which point the story continues from the child's perspective. The tension in this story is established by the fact that the reader, thanks to the external focalizer, knows more than the woman and the child, namely, the threat of murder.

c. *Empathy*
Empathy in discourse studies is used to describe the degree to which a speaker identifies with a person or object which is part of an event or condition that is described in a sentence. The term was introduced by Susumu Kuno (1987). He showed that empathy is expressed in the syntactic structure of a sentence. Some examples:

(25)   a.   John hit Mary.
        b.   John hit his wife.
        c.   Mary's husband hit her.

In (25a), the empathy is almost equally divided. In (25b), however, more empathy is directed towards John than Mary. One indication of this is that "John" is in the subject position; another is that Mary is labeled as John's wife. In (25c), the speaker identifies more with Mary than with her husband. Kuno concluded that if a possessive noun phrase, such as "Mary's husband", is used, the empathy will be closer to the referent of the possessive (Mary). He also stated that two conflicting empathies cannot occur in one sentence. This would explain why the following sentence sounds odd.

(25)   d.   Mary's husband hit his wife.

In the subject position, the speaker expresses empathy with Mary according to the rule of the possessive noun phrase. In the object position, empathy is expressed for John as Mary is referred to as "his wife". Kuno also showed that there are restrictions on changing empathy. Compare the following examples.

(26)   a.   Mary had quite an experience last night. She insulted an important guest.
        b.   Mary had quite an experience last night. An important guest was insulted by her.

Example (26b) is not as good as (26a), a fact which can be explained as follows. The empathy in the first sentence is with Mary. In the second sentence of (26a), the empathy remains with Mary due to the "she" in subject position. In (26b), on the other hand, a new character is introduced in subject position in the second sentence and becomes the focus of empathy as a result. With this example and scores of others, Kuno showed that the empathy of the speaker is evident in the sentential structure.

7.4   Given–new management

So far we have seen that three factors play an important role in presenting information. First, there are direct links with the situation via deixis to person, place and time (7.1). In the discourse situation some elements can come to the foreground while others remain in the background (7.2). The information can also be described from certain perspectives (7.3). In order to determine which perspectives, the following questions have to be answered. From which ideological viewpoint is the issue presented (vision)? Whose viewpoint is being communicated (focalization)? Which character does the speaker identify with the most (empathy)?

There is a fourth important variable in the presentation of information: the knowledge on the part of readers or listeners that is assumed by the speaker or writer. Research on the use of definite and indefinite articles provides a good introduction to the research being done into given and new information.

The psycholinguist Charles Osgood (1971) did the following experiment with his students. He asked them to describe simple observations. He used the following objects: an orange ring, a black ball, a red cup and a green cup. With these objects, he gave demonstrations which can be described as follows.

(27)   Osgood's demonstrations
1.   There is an orange ring on the table.
2.   Someone is holding a black ball in his hand.
3.   There is a black ball on the table.
4.   Someone is holding a red cup in his hand.
5.   There is a green cup on the table.

Osgood asked his students to describe, as simply as possible in one sentence, what they observed. The demonstrations [1], [3] and [5] are equal in the sense that they all deal with an object on the table. Yet, the descriptions proved to be different. Below are a few examples.

(28) There is an orange ring lying on the table.

(29) The black ball is on the table.

In descriptions of demonstration [1], as in (28), the word "ring" has no definite article. Demonstration [3], which followed a demonstration in which a black ball had been shown, led to a good number of descriptions containing definite articles, as in (29). The same held true for the final demonstration in which students were shown a green cup after having been shown a red cup. With this relatively simple experiment, Osgood showed that a definite article is used when knowledge of the objects involved is presumed.

However, the distinction given–new is less clear-cut than it seems. It has been suggested that new information is information which cannot be ascertained from the preceding discourse. The following example shows how problematic this definition is.

(30) Your fáther did it.

The new element here is "father". But this element can in part be seen as given, as the speaker can assume that the concept *father* is in the listener's consciousness. For this reason, it has been suggested that the listener's consciousness be incorporated into the definition of given and new. Wallace Chafe (1976) provided the following definition: "Given (or old) information is that knowledge which the speaker assumes to be in the consciousness of the addressee at the time of the utterance. So-called new information is what the speaker assumes he is introducing into the addressee's consciousness by what he says."

Within this approach, even finer distinctions are necessary; there are a number of gradations between given and new. Ellen Prince (1981) suggested the following distinctions.

(31) Prince's given–new taxonomy

New	Inferable	Evoked
brand new		situational
unused		textual

An example of *brand new* is "an orange ring" in (28). An example of *unused* is (30): the concept of father is known but not yet activated. In the following examples the *inferable* elements have been italicized.

(32) My whole suitcase was searched by them. Luckily, it didn't occur to them to open the *tube of toothpaste*.

(33) I was approaching the intersection at high speed. *The traffic light* was green.

In (32) the element "tube of toothpaste" is somewhere between new and given. It has not been mentioned before, but it can be inferred from prior knowledge people have concerning the contents of travelers' luggage. Approximately the same is true for (33). "The traffic light" is neither given nor new but can be inferred on the basis of "intersection".

The evoked elements are given. This is possible because of the discourse situation. If in (33) the first-person narrator is already telling the story, then the "I" is situationally evoked. Textually evoked refers to those elements that have already been mentioned in the discourse. Below are two further examples.

(34)   It has been said that a good deal of hashish is used there. But while I was there nobody smoked a *joint*.

(35)   There was a young couple walking in front of me. While walking, *he* put his arm around *her*.

For those students who find Prince's five-part division too finely-meshed, there is always Chafe's three-part division: active, semi-active and inactive. A concept, according to Chafe, can be active (given or evoked) or inactive (brand new or unused) in the listener's consciousness. A concept is semi-active (inferable) when it is quickly activated on the basis of all available knowledge. It is clear that, regardless of which analysis is applied, a simple binary distinction between given and new will not suffice.

7.5   Presuppositions

Examples were given in 7.4 that indicate that listeners and readers can sometimes infer information from the discourse. In fact, this is a more general characteristic of discourse: more can be derived from discourse than is explicitly stated. Consider the example below.

(36)   It took John seven years to complete his studies.

The following information can be derived from this sentence.

(36)   a.   There is a person named John.
       b.   John was a student.
       c.   John was not a brilliant student.

The information that there is an individual named John is not stated explicitly in (36), but can be derived from the fact that a person is mentioned who is called by that name. The fact that John was a student is likewise not stated explicitly, but this can be derived from the statement that he took seven years to finish his studies. Depending on the concrete situation, more information could be derived. Sentence (36) could contain (36c) as implicit information if it had just been stated that the program John was in usually takes four years to complete.

A special type of implicit information is called *presupposition*, meaning "to assume beforehand", a term which originated in the philosophy of logic. Information which is explicitly stated is referred to as a *claim* or an *assertion*. The example above makes it clear that all kinds of information can be derived from a sentence. The term *presupposition* is reserved for the implicit information which must be true for the sentence in question to be itself true or false. A sentence such as "I have stopped smoking" can only be true or false if the person saying it in fact used to smoke. The presupposition of this sentence is thus "I used to smoke." Put another way: a presupposition is the only type of information that is unaffected by denial of the original sentence. Look at the following examples.

(37)   John is (not) opening the window.
     a.   The window is closed.
(38)   Democracy must (not) be restored in Surinam.
     a.   Surinam was once a democracy.

The a-sentences given here are presuppositions because they are also true if (37) and (38) are denied. Of course, the whole sentence has to be denied, and not just one or more constituents, for its presuppositions to be maintained. Note that a negative sentence can be denied; the result is then a positive sentence. In a more formal notation, the presupposition is written out as follows.

(39)   B is a presupposition of A if and only if $(A \rightarrow B)$ *and* $(\neg A \rightarrow B)$

The symbol $\rightarrow$ is the implication sign for "if-then" and the symbol $\neg$ is the symbol for negation. The definition given in (39) is known as the negation test.

A presupposition is thus the implicit information that must be true for the sentence to be either true or false and which is not affected by a negation. The implicit information can be derived from different elements in a sentence. In (37) and (38) it is derived from the meaning of the words. In (37), use of the verb "to open" suggests the window is now closed, and in (38) the word "restored" can lead to the conclusion that at one point or another there was a democracy in Surinam.

Presuppositions can be prompted by the words themselves or by the sentence structure:

(40)   Carl has the flu again.
     a.   Carl has had the flu before.

(41)   Carl is a better linguist than Pete.
    a.   Pete is a linguist.

Presupposition (40a) can be derived from the word "again". In (41) the comparison implies that Pete has the same profession as Carl.

Emphasis also plays an important role in deriving presuppositions. Sometimes the emphasis is already clear owing to the syntactical structure as in *cleft constructions*, for example, one in which "x is doing y" is given the structure "it is x who is doing y" (see also Section 7.2). This puts extra emphasis on x, as in the following example.

(42)   It was Pete who pointed out the problem to me.
    a.   Somebody pointed out the problem to me.

In the following sentence there are four possibilities, depending on which word receives extra stress.

(43)   Pete sells paintings to museums.
    a.   (*Pete*) Pete, and no one else.
    b.   (*sells*) Pete does not give them away.
    c.   (*paintings*) Pete does not sell sculptures.
    d.   (*museums*) Pete does not sell paintings to individuals.

Similarly, a certain presupposition can be prompted by a specific emphasis in (41) and (42). If in (41) "linguist" is stressed, then this implies (41b) below. If in (42) "pointed out" is heavily stressed, then (42b) is a more obvious presupposition than (42a). Presuppositions can, therefore, be prompted not only by lexical and syntactical elements but also by intonation phenomena.

(41)   b.   Carl is in other areas inferior to Pete.
(42)   b.   I solved the problem myself.

One of the best-known sentences in presupposition research was originally used in an article published at the beginning of the last century by the philosopher Bertrand Russell. The sentence reads as follows.

(44)   The king of France is bald.

This sentence has the following existential presupposition, that is, a presupposition which can be derived from a proper name or a nominal constituent containing a definite article (see also example 36a).

(44)   a.   There is one and only one king of France.

Following the definition of presupposition, there is an opposite claim with the same presupposition.

(45)   The king of France is not bald.

In the case of (45), the same presupposition, (44a), is presumed to be true. These sentences pose a difficult problem for philosophers and logicians. If it is assumed that either a claim or its negation is true, so either (44) or (45) must be true, and if it is also assumed that (44a) can be derived from (44) or (45), then a presupposition can be deduced which is logical but untrue: France is, after all, a republic.

Although Russell suggested a way of getting around this problem, the solution remained unsatisfactory. A half-century later the issue became a topic in presupposition research. In 1950 the philosopher Peter Strawson provided a pragmatic analysis, the gist of which is the following: sentences can only be true or false if their presuppositions are met (i.e., are true). Only in the situation before the French Revolution was (44a) true; thereafter it was no longer true. So, only before the French Revolution were the presuppositions of either (44) or (45) met and could they have a truth value (be either true or false).

The debate between Russell and Strawson played an important role in launching the research into presuppositions. If the situation in which an utterance takes place is taken into account, then the research becomes far more complex. And yet, this extension is a natural one. A strict approach using the results of the negation test is only a partial mapping-out of the information implicit in an utterance. From sentence (46), for example, much more can be deduced than just the existential presupposition (46a).

(46)   Go to the student advisor.
  a.   There is a student advisor.

Since (46) is an order, it can be deduced that the speaker is in a position to give orders to the addressee. The problem is, however, that much unspoken information can be derived from language in use. A presupposition can even be instantly denied. Example (45) has (44a) as a presupposition. Language in use, on the other hand, is not hampered by the conclusion that there is a king of France. The following utterance is acceptable, at least for some language users.

(47)   The king of France is not bald; there is no king of France.

When discourse is looked at in a specific situation, it is not just the implicit information derived from the negation test, the presupposition, that is available; other implicit information is also derivable from a given sentence. The term for this is *inference*.

7.6   Inferences

Inference is the collective term for all possible implicit information which can be derived from a discourse. The term *inference* (from the Latin "*inferre*" meaning "to carry in") is used to denote the phenomenon that discourse summons up knowledge or information which can be used to understand the information. The most significant cases of this, besides presupposition, are *entailment, conventional implicature, conversational implicature*, and *connotation*. Below is an example of each.

Entailment is a term taken from logic. If A is greater than B and B is greater than C, then it can be concluded that A is greater than C. In discourse studies the term can be used more broadly. Look at the following example.

(48)   Pete bought oranges.
    a.   Pete bought fruit.

Example (48a) is an entailment of (48). The difference between an entailment and a presupposition is clear here. The entailment does not have to be true if the claim is denied. Understanding entailments is often necessary in order to make connections. The inference that oranges are in the category of fruit is necessary if discourse continues as follows.

(48)   b.   Pete bought oranges. Unfortunately, he completely forgot that he had bought them. After several weeks his cupboard started to smell of spoiled fruit.

The term *conventional implicature* was coined by Grice (see Section 2.4). Grice gave the following example.

(49)   He is an Englishman; he is therefore brave.

From the word "therefore" one can, through the fixed meaning or by convention, derive the conclusion that Englishmen are brave. Grice calls this type of implicature "conventional" in order to distinguish it from *conversational implicature* (see also Section 2.4). An example of the latter is given in the following conversation.

(50)   A: Did you already buy fruit?
    B: The oranges are already in the refrigerator.

On the basis of Grice's second maxim of quantity (Do not make your contribution more informative than is required.), it would have sufficed for B to answer "Yes". A can assume that B is complying with the cooperative principle and can, therefore, also assume that B has a reason for providing what at first appears to be extraneous information. Depending on the situation, B can implicitly communicate one of the following.

(50) a. I'll decide what kind of fruit is bought.
      b. You know that I buy oranges every week.
      c. I have done even more than you requested; I have already put the fruit in
          the refrigerator.

An example of connotation is provided by the following story, which causes problems
for many readers.

(51) A father and a son are sitting in a car. They are in a serious accident. The father
      is killed on impact and the son is taken to the hospital in critical condition. As
      the victim is wheeled into the operating room, the surgeon exclaims; "Oh no, I
      can't operate. That's my son!"

The profession of surgeon, at least in some western cultures, evokes the image of a man.
This association makes the story puzzling. The same is true of the story about the two
Indians, one of whom is the son of the other while the other is not his father. When
readers derive from the word "surgeon" or "Indian" that the individual is a male, this
is an inference on the basis of a culturally-determined association or connotation.

The term *inference* covers quite a broad area of meaning. A number of attempts
have been made in the literature to develop a classification system. The two main distinctions made are those between "necessary" and "possible" and between "forward"
and "backward". Compare the following examples.

(52) No longer able to control his anger, the husband threw the delicate porcelain
      vase against the wall. It cost him over one hundred dollars to replace the vase.
(53) No longer able to control his anger, the husband threw the delicate porcelain
      vase against the wall. He had been feeling angry for weeks, but had refused to
      seek help.

To understand (52) properly, it is necessary to make the inference that the vase has
been broken. In (53) this inference is not necessary. If the inference that the vase has
been broken takes place in the second sentence of (52), it is called a backward inference or bridging inference. If in (53) the inference concerning the broken vase is
already drawn in the first sentence, then it is called forward inference or elaborative
inference.

To what extent are inferences really made during the reading process? One of
the best-known experiments carried out to answer this question was done by Susan
Haviland and Herbert Clark (1974). They had subjects read fragments of discourse
such as the following:

(54) a. Herb took the picnic supplies from the car. The beer was warm.
      b. Herb took the beer from the car. The beer was warm.

The sentences were shown on a screen and the subjects were to press a button when they had finished reading the sentence. This made it possible to measure reading time. If an inference is made, it is logical to assume that it will take time. In (54a) an inference is necessary, namely, that beer was included in the picnic supplies. The results showed that the time taken to read the second sentence in (54a) was longer than the time needed to read the second sentence in (54b). It could be argued that this has more to do with word repetition, which occurs in (54b) and not in (54a), than with inference. This explanation was, however, ruled out in another experiment in which fragments such as the following, in the context of a picnic, were used:

(54)　c.　Herb was especially fond of beer. The beer was warm.

In this fragment an inference is also made, namely, that Herb got some beer. As in the earlier experiment, the result was that the second sentence in (54c) took longer to read than the second sentence in (54b). Inferences are indeed made during the process of listening and reading.

Questions and assignments

Questions

7.1.1 Provide examples which show that the deictical elements *I* or *me* and *you* can also be used anaphorically and cataphorically.

7.1.2 Point out the deictical elements in the following sentences.
    a.   The phone of John is ringing.
    b.   I've got six of them.
    c.   There is no such thing as ghosts.
    d.   Pete is sitting in the garden.

7.1.3 According to an estimation by the language philosopher Yehoshua Bar-Hillel (1954), deictical elements occur in nine out of ten language utterances. Bar-Hillel cited the following thought experiment.
    A logician, Tom Brown, makes the New Year's resolution not to use sentences which contain deictical elements. He notifies his wife of the experiment and decides upon awakening on New's Year Day that he would like breakfast in bed.
What sentence could he use to make his wish clear to his wife without using deictical elements?

7.2.1 Give a counterexample for the idea that main-subordinate clause structure mirrors the relationship between foreground and background information.

7.3.1 Is there an external focalizer or a character-bound focalizer in the second sentence in the following example? Provide arguments.
    A man was sitting at the bar looking despondent. The door opened with a sad groan. A woman and a child came in.

7.3.2 Use Kuno's empathy approach to explain why the following sentence is flawed.
His brother was hit by John.

7.4.1 Describe the difference between the following sentences.
    a.   I was driving down the highway. Suddenly the car began to weave.
    b.   I was driving down the highway. Suddenly a car began to weave.
What are "the car" and "a car" called in Prince's five-part division?

7.4.2 Determine which types of cohesion (see Section 6.1) qualify as evoked elements and which as inferable.

7.5.1   Which inferences in example (36a–c) can be defined as presuppositions?

7.5.2   Is B answering the claim or the presupposition in the following exchanges?
    A: I've had enough of that racket from next door.
    B: Well, then do something about it.
    A: I've had enough of that racket from next door.
    B: Are the neighbors making that much noise?

7.5.3   How does B react to the presupposition in the following exchanges?
    A: Democracy must be restored in Surinam.
    B: But there has never been any democracy in Surinam.
    A: Do you still drink a lot?
    B1: No, I've cut down.
    B2: I've never been a heavy drinker.

7.6.1   Indicate if an inference is necessary or possible in the following sentences and if the inference is forwards or backwards. Also determine what kind of knowledge is necessary in order to draw the inference.
    a.   His views are quite conservative, but all in all he's a nice guy.
    b.   The neighbors are having a party tonight. It's going to be a short night's sleep.
    c.   A rather interesting experiment was done by S. Mehlam. Her hypothesis was the following.
    d.   He opened the door and immediately sensed that someone else had been in the room. Suddenly he felt cold breath on his neck. He stood still, paralyzed with fear. For a short while all was deathly silent. It was only after a few minutes that he noticed that he was standing in a draft.

7.6.2   Make a prediction about the difference in reading time for the last sentence in the following fragments, assuming that when the name "John" is first encountered, the forward-directed inference is made that John is a schoolboy. (The sentences were taken from Sanford and Garrod, 1981).
    a.   John was on his way to school. The bus trundled slowly along the road. Last week he had trouble controlling class.
    b.   The teacher was on his way to school. The bus trundled slowly along the road. Last week he had trouble controlling class.

Assignments

7.1.1   Consider the sentence "To the left of Mr. A is Mrs. B". In terms of deixis, this description can be of two types (Levelt, 1982). It is ego-oriented if A is to the left of B from the speaker's point of view. The description is pattern-oriented when B is to the left of A from A's point of view. This distinction can also be construed as speaker or object oriented. Now consider the following diagram.

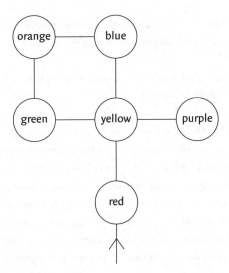

Now try to describe the diagram pictured above in such a way that a person who has not seen the figure would be able to duplicate it. Compare your description with the two types given in (a) and (b). Explain whether you have given an ego-oriented (speaker) or pattern-oriented (object) description.

a. 1. In the middle, to begin, a grey nodal point.
    2. From there upward, a red nodal point.
    3. Then to the left, a pink nodal point from red.
    4. Then from pink again to the left a blue nodal point.
    5. Then back again to red.
    6. Then from red to the right a yellow nodal point.
    7. And from yellow again to the right a green nodal point.

b. 1. I start at crossing point gray.
    2. Go straight on to red.
    3. Go left to pink.
    4. Go straight on to blue.
    5. Turn around to go back to pink.
    6. Go back, straight on to red.
    7. Straight on to yellow.
    8. Straight on to green.

7.2.1 Take an essay that has been judged as incoherent and use the head–tail principle to analyze the presentation of information.

7.3.1 Apply the three notions of vision, focalization and empathy to the discourse of a tennis match.

7.3.2   Collect news items on the same topic from two ideologically different newspapers and attempt to ascertain whether or not the ideological perspective is expressed in language use and, if so, how.

7.4.1   Apply Prince's given–new taxonomy to the nouns in fragment (d) in question 7.6.1. Try to criticize the arrangement of the text.

7.5.1   Indicate to what extent reactions are being given to the presuppositions of the disputed statement in the following excerpt (taken from a letter to the editor printed in a newspaper).

> In a column in a previous issue of this paper my attention was drawn to the following statement by a well-known lesbian professor: "Naturally a woman with an I.Q. of 120 is homosexual." This statement is not only nonsensical and insulting but also dangerous. On the surface it would seem to say: an intelligent woman is inevitably homosexual. Therefore all heterosexual women are stupid. It also suggests that no stupid women are homosexual. (...) The claim that women with an I.Q. of 120 are homosexual in fact would suggest that all middle-class women are homosexual and that marriages in this social class will soon be a thing of the past. In the working class the possibility of a woman being heterosexual would seemingly still be present. In short: a woman's sexual preference depends on the "type" of woman she is.

7.6.1   In Vonk and Noordman (1990) the following was mentioned as a characteristic of necessary and possible inferences:

> A denial of a necessary inference leads to an inconsistency in discourse; a denial of a possible inference does not.

Determine on the basis of this criterion if presuppositions and entailments are necessary or possible inferences.

Bibliographical information

7.1   Bühler (1990, newest edition) is a good introductory publication on deixis. The deixis phenomenon is also known as "egocentria particulars" or "indexical signs" or "indexical expressions";
see Bar-Hillel (1954). A deictic element is also called an *exophor*, since it refers from within the
discourse to something outside the discourse. In that respect, it fits in with such terms as *anaphor*
and *cataphor* (see Section 6.2).

    See Levinson (1983) for a more detailed overview of English language studies on deixis. For
deixis in narratives, see Duchan et al. (1995). See also Levelt (1989).

7.2   A good starting point for research on staging is Brown and Yule (1983).

7.3   An overview of the research into perspective is given in Graumann and Kallmeyer (2002). For
more on focalization, see Bal (1985). For more on empathy research, see Kuno (1987). The ideological perspective plays a role chiefly in media research. See, for example, Fowler (1991). The
experimental research mentioned in this section is from Renkema (1984).

7.4   The development of the given–new theory can be traced through the following articles: Chafe
(1976) and Prince (1981 & 1997). The research that is mentioned in this section can be found in
Osgood (1971). For other research, see Clark and Haviland (1977). See also Brown and Yule (1983)
in which Prince's five-part division is elaborated on.

7.5   For a more detailed introduction to presupposition research, see Levinson (1983). Example (47) is
taken from Wilson (1975).

7.6   A good introduction to cognitively inspired research on inferences is provided in Noordman and
Vonk (1992). A collection of articles that gives a good overview is Graesser and Bower (1990). A
key article in the history of research on inferences is Haviland and Clark (1974). Examples (19)
and (20) are taken from Sanford (1990).

8 Style

8.1 Form, content and situation

It is possible to say approximately the same thing in any number of different ways. The word *style* is used to denote these "different ways". This word is derived from the Latin word *stilus* which means *pen*. The form of letters is influenced by the way in which a pen (feather quill) is cut, yet it is possible to write the same letters with different pens; the letters only differ in their style. When we examine the use of the word "pen" in the expression "His pen is dipped in blood", we can see that "how to write" also means "how to formulate".

The concept of style stems from old, classical rhetoric, the theory and practice of effective language use that can persuade a public in a special situation, e.g., to reduce a suspect's sentence or to gain support for going to war. Stylistics has a history of about 2,500 years. The Greek philosopher Aristotle (4th century B.C.) says in his famous *Rhetorica* that an orator has to use a style, a form for his material, which is appropriate and also "unaccustomed" by using metaphors, for example. And the Latin rhetorician Quintilianus (1st century A.D.) presented in his *De Institutione Oratoria* four "virtues of style": correctness, perspicuity, appropriateness and ornamentation. Nowadays, questions concerning correctness are mainly dealt with in writing education. The perspicuity of a text is now studied in the cognitive approach to discourse, how people understand information. The other two characteristics of style still play an important role in stylistic research. In fact, the tension between the appropriateness (to the situation) and the elegant deviation or ornamentation (to draw attention) still lies at the heart of discussions about good style.

The starting point for stylistic research is that the same content can be expressed in different forms. A well-known example is the following. When an individual wishes to tell about a man he had seen acting strangely on the bus that morning and who he had met again, coincidentally, that afternoon, there is an infinite number of ways to do so. Below are just two of the ways it may be done (see Raymond Queneau, 1947/1981):

(1) How tightly packed in we were on that bus platform! And how stupid and ridiculous that young man looked! And what was he doing? Well, if he wasn't actually trying to pick a quarrel with a chap who – so he claimed! the young fop!

– kept on pushing him! And then he didn't find anything better to do than to rush off and grab a seat which had become free! Instead of leaving it for a lady! Two hours after, guess whom I met in front of the gare Saint-Lazare! The same fancypants! Being given some sartorial advice! By a friend! You'd never believe it!

(2)   I was not displeased with my attire this day. I was inaugurating a new, rather sprightly hat, and an overcoat of which I thought most highly. Met X in front of the gare Saint-Lazare who tried to spoil my pleasure by trying to prove that this overcoat is cut too low at the lapels and that I ought to have an extra button on it. At least he didn't dare attack my headgear.

A bit earlier I had roundly told off a vulgar type who was purposely ill-treating me every time anyone went by getting off or on. This happened in one of those unspeakably foul omnibi which fill up with hoi polloi precisely at those times when I have to consent to use them.

Many differences can be pointed out between the two stories above. In (1) the accent is on the storyteller's surprise at meeting the same person again, while in (2) the focus is on the protagonist's experiences. Furthermore, in (2) a departure is made from chronological order. There are also differences in sentence structure and word choice. Still, the two stories have the same basic content. However, it proves to be very difficult to describe the differences in vocabulary, grammar and discourse structure. And, even more important is the question to what extent these differences can be seen as stylistic variation, i.e., variation that can be linked to appropriateness and ornamentation.

In discourse studies the concept of style is mainly studied with a focus on appropriateness, and not with a focus on the more literary ornamentation. Stylistics is more or less restricted to prose stylistics, to everyday use of language. Within this domain appropriateness is mainly related to the situational context. This narrow use of the concept *style* is covered by the term *register*, in the sense of a church organ's registers that can make the same piece of music (the content) have various different sound "colors" (the forms). Register is the stylistic variation that can be explained with the situation, or more precisely, with the sixteen factors of the SPEAKING model, introduced in Section 3.4. The influence of these situational factors is also evident in the terms used to denote different stylistic variations: telegram style (the *channel* factor), city hall style (the *setting* factor), and court ruling style (the *genre* factor), etc. In many studies the terms style and register are used without any distinction, but in cases where not only the formulation but also the relation between language use and situation is meant, the term register is to be preferred.

In the study of style and register the starting point is not only that some content can have different formulations but also that these different formulations highlight different aspects of the possible meaning that has to be conveyed. So in the example below there must be (slight) differences in meaning as a result of the formulation.

(3) a.   John does not go to school, because Mary is ill.
     b.   Because Mary is ill, John does not go to school.
     c.   Mary is ill. So, John does not go to school.
     d.   John does not go to school. Mary is ill.

Following the theme-rheme distinction (see Section 5.2), in formulation (3a) the rheme is the illness of Mary, and in (3b) the fact that John does not go to school. The theme-rheme distinction presupposes what is called the left-right principle. This means that new information (the rheme) is mostly placed at the end of an utterance if there are no other reasons to put some information in focus, for example, by intonation in "Not Mary, but Jóhn does not go to school." So formulations (3a) and (3b) differ in focus on what the speaker wants to convey as kernel information. The first two formulations contain a clause and a subclause, a subordination, and the last two formulations have two full sentences, a coordination. Connecting or not connecting full sentences with connectives like "because" and "so" can highlight the salience of the relation. In (3c) the conclusion is more salient than in (3b) because of the use of "so", and in (3d) the explanation is a more independent proposition.

From a stylistic viewpoint there is no free variation in formulation. Each formulation has its own "stylistic" meaning. The assumption that there is a one-on-one relation between form and meaning is known as Humboldt's principle. This influential nineteenth-century German philosopher coined this principle in his research into linguistic change. To give a simple example, if a language adopts the word *bar* as well as the word *pub* (with more or less the same meaning), a difference in meaning will develop. Another example would be that if the same propositional content can be expressed in different ways, say in an active and a passive form, there must be a difference in meaning. Following Humboldt's principle every language has a tendency against homonymy, one form with different meanings, like *bank* (of a river) and *bank* (money) and synonymy, different forms with one meaning, like *liberty* and *freedom*. Humboldt's principle forms the basis of much stylistic analysis: at first sight different formulations may appear equivalent, but application of the principle will enable us to recognize subtle shades of meaning and shifts in focus.

8.2   Views on style

One of the most challenging problems in stylistics is the problem of defining style. A description of all the differences between the two stories at the beginning of this chapter does not guarantee that the style has been mapped out. In the literature on stylistics a great deal of attention has been given to the definition of style. The numerous views on style can be divided into three categories, corresponding to the Organon model's division into symbol, symptom and signal (see Section 2.1).

First, when the symbol aspect of language (the reference to reality) is central, style can be seen as a possible form for a specific content. Second, from the angle of the symptom aspect of expression (from the perspective of the writer or speaker), style can be seen as the choice of specific forms. Third, from the angle of the signal aspect of persuasion (the perspective of the reader or listener), language can be seen as a deviation from a given expectation. Every interpretation, when viewed more closely, poses problems.

a. *Style as a possible form for a specific content*
When dealing with style as a possible form for a specific content, the question arises whether it is possible to alter the form of language without changing the content. At the word level, the main question is: Do true synonyms really exist? Do the words *dad*, *father*, and *my old man* have the same meaning? In part they do, namely, the procreator of a child. The answer to the question whether or not synonyms have the same meaning depends on the definition assigned to the word *meaning*. If the definition of meaning also includes a reference to the class of people who use certain words, for example, the fact that predominantly young children use the word *daddy* to denote their fathers, then there are no true synonyms and the conclusion must be drawn that the form does change the content at least partially.

A similar argument holds true for differences in sentence composition. (See the remarks on the difference between the active and the passive voice in Section 1.1.) The research into stylistic variation presupposes that the texts to be compared have something in common. This "something" may be called basic content, as in the two stories in the preceding section. In that case, however, the basic content in question is no more than "meeting on a bus". The propositional content of these stories is rather different. In discourse studies "that which remained unchanged" can be defined in a number of ways. It is generally used to refer to propositional content. The focus when texts are compared is then on differences in formulation. The phrase can, however, also be used to denote basic content, for example, sequences of events such as in the stories by Queneau given above. Sometimes, from a more pragmatic viewpoint, a more abstract definition is given. In this case it is assumed that only illocutionary force remains the same. Within this definition different basic contents can be used, for example, to utter the same threat. The interpretation of style as a possible form for a specific content proves, therefore, to be too vague.

b. *Style as a choice of specific patterns*

To see style as choice patterns, one takes the point of view of the writer or speaker, who has a number of different possibilities in phrasing what he would like to say. Here is a well-known example. If A and B are together in a room and A wants B to close an open window, then A can make this clear in a number of ways.

(4) a. Could you perhaps close the window?
     b. Hey, can't that window be closed?
     c. The window's open.
     d. Close the window!
     e. You should be careful about drafts, the way you're feeling.
     f. I'm not paying to heat the outdoors.

When dealing with style as choice, it is necessary to know what choices writers or speakers have or had at their disposal. Some choices are partially determined by the situation. Perhaps A and B in the example above do not have a relationship in which orders would be appropriate. The style-as-choice approach is, however, suitable for determining in which way the situation limits choice, for example, which factors in the situation might contribute to (4a) being preferable to (4b) in some cases.

c. *Style as a deviation from expectations*

In a third view, style is seen as a deviation from expectations. Owing to long-term exposure to certain routine patterns, readers and listeners develop expectations about the way in which a specific content can be given form, and about the choice of certain forms. When readers make a stylistic judgment about a given form of language use, it is apparently because the form deviates from what they are used to.

Take the genre "State of the Union address", which is reasonably well-known. Because the genre is familiar, people have developed expectations concerning the language in such a speech. Here are three possible introductory sentences.

(5) a. In recent years our country has truly been put to the test. Many have lost their jobs. Thousands of young people were unable to find employment.
     b. Our country has not had it easy in recent years. Among adults, but especially among young people, unemployment is high.
     c. These last years have been tough, really tough. So many have lost their jobs! So many young people were never able to get one!

It is very likely that the style used in (5a) will be characterized as somewhat formal and that readers will evaluate the wording in (5b) as too informal for a State of the Union address. Words like *lively* will probably be found applicable to the style used in (5c). Formulation (5a) will in all likelihood be judged as the most suitable.

One problem with the style-as-deviation approach is that readers' expectations can be quite divergent. It has been suggested that a norm for language use be set and that every deviation from that norm be viewed as a stylistic characteristic. In order to do this, however, it is obvious that normal language must be characterized first. For this reason it has been suggested that related texts be used as a point of comparison, as a norm. In the stylistic analysis of, for instance, civil service style, the differences between civil service documents and murder mystery novels are not at issue, but the differences between these documents and editorials or informational leaflets are.

These three views of style can be recognized in current research, in which a great deal of attention is paid to the problem of describing differences between texts and measuring the effect of stylistic devices on the attitude of the reader.

8.3   Stylistic analysis

The concept *style* in itself is an evaluative concept, as we can see in expressions like "That guy has style!" Style normally means "good style". This can explain why stylistics has a long tradition in a more qualitative and normative approach dealing with issues like: "How to produce a good text" or "How to avoid a 'complex', a 'rigid', a 'harsh' or an 'informal' style". Apart from this approach, attempts have been made to connect the rather vague stylistic qualifications, like the ones given in the previous sentence, to patterns in formulation. These two approaches are dealt with in this section.

a. *The normative approach*
In many languages style guides have been published in an educational setting in which the style virtue "perspicuitas", referred to in Section 8.1, plays a central role. These handbooks on clear or effective writing provide many hints and tips on how to produce a good text. One of the famous examples for the English language is the booklet *The Elements of Style* by Strunk and White (2000), originally published in 1918, and still influential at the end of the last century. This guide to writing in a satisfactory style concludes with 21 suggestions, a few of which are given below.

> (6)   Some cautionary hints concerning good style
>   1.   Place yourself in the background.
>   2.   Write in a way that comes naturally.
>   3.   Work from a suitable design.
>   4.   Write nouns and verbs.
>   (…)
>   19.   Do not take shortcuts at the cost of clarity.

20. Avoid foreign languages.
21. Prefer the standard to the offbeat.

Suggestions like these cause different problems for a discourse studies perspective. Let us look at the three most important ones. First, it is seldom clear how these suggestions can be implemented in producing discourse. What kind of stylistic devices must a writer avoid or use in order to place himself in the background? What is natural writing? Second, must these suggestions always be followed? In some cases, the use of a more unconventional style (see suggestion 21) or using foreign words (number 20) can be more effective in reaching your goals. And third, it is by no means clear that acting upon a piece of advice results in a better text. Is it really true that, whatever the circumstances, nouns and verbs should be preferred to adjectives and adverbs (suggestion 4)?

Anyway, hints on using a good style still play an important role in educational settings and organizations' corporate style guides. Their merits are that writers are focused on elements in discourse that before were neglected. Moreover, they provide a good starting point for criticizing the way in which content is molded into a form. Just one example of this language criticism will suffice in this section: the deceptive metaphor, like the following remark from Section 3.3.

(7)   Discourse is more than a message from sender to receiver. In fact, sender and receiver are metaphors that obfuscate what is really going on in communication.

First some information about this figure of speech, which was already mentioned as a stylistic device by Aristotle. The metaphor is a form of figurative language in which an object or concept is denoted using another object or concept. This assignment of one object or concept to another takes place on the basis of certain similarities between the two. Since the "base" of a mountain resembles the "base" of a human in some way, we can speak of the "foot" of a mountain. When human behavior begins to resemble that of a certain animal, the name of the animal is given to that individual: for example, a "sly fox". In everyday language many metaphors occur that are no longer considered to be figures of speech. These are called petrified or dead metaphors. When the metaphor suggests a similarity that is non-existent, it is called a deceptive metaphor.

A general suggestion in normative stylistics is to use figures of speech – like metaphor, personification, irony, etc. – with a certain restraint, and that if they are applied, they must enlighten some aspects of the content. Example (7) is a formulation that can be criticized with regard to perspicuity. When a discourse is characterized as a message from sender to receiver, then a similarity is suggested between a receiver and a listener, reader or addressee. In this telephone metaphor the suggestion is made that a listener picks up signals in a passive way. Nothing could be further from the truth. A listener or reader is obliged to take an active part in the communication process. For more on this, see the observations on coherence in Section 3.6.

b. *The objective approach*

In stylistic analysis there is a long tradition of describing differences in formulation patterns. In these descriptions mostly impressionistic and evaluative adjectives are used, which prompt critics to draw comparisons with tasting wines or advertising cars. Stylistic evaluations of someone's writing style, such as "colorless", "lucid" or "objective" may seem to have a fixed meaning, but it is often unclear what is meant by these characterizations. A striking example is cited in *Grammar as Style* by Tufte (1971). High-school teachers of English were asked to characterize the style of the novel *In Cold Blood* by Capote. The adjectives ranged the whole alphabet and many of them contradicted others. Here are some characteristics.

(8)   Style-labels for Capote's *In Cold Blood* (by Tufte, 1971)
      alliterative, blunt, chiseled, discerning, elaborate, forceful, general, harsh,
      impressionistic, literary, meditative, natural, omniscient, prosaic, rambling,
      stylized, thoughtful, unconventional, vivid, wordy

Even if people agree about the characteristics of, for example, the language of bureaucracy, so-called officialese, it is unclear to what elements of style they must be linked. In different cultures government language is said to be difficult, impersonal and traditional. But it is unclear whether the difficulty is caused by the content, sentence length, sentence complexity or jargon, and whether, for example, a passive form always has to be labeled as impersonal. Actually, even more important is the argument that an official document has to be somewhat traditional, in accordance with the authority of the governmental institution that produced it.

This more qualitative approach in style analysis has inspired much stylistic research in discourse studies in attempts to detect in what stylistic elements documents may differ. If an objective description can be produced of the stylistic phenomena of certain documents, then there is a base for research into the link with stylistic labels given by readers and the effect of the message on the reader. In Table 1 below some elements are listed which have been featured in stylistic research.

It is remarkable that the concept of style is not confined to composition and formulation; choices in content and peculiarities in usage are sometimes considered stylistic phenomena as well. The analysis of spelling errors, for example, is important in what is called forensic stylistics, a branch of stylistics that is used to find additional proof in detecting the authorship of documents that play a role in legal cases (blackmail, etc.). In analyzing composition and formulation, the focus is on the elements that are

Table 1. Some elements in stylistic research

Level	Feature
Content	number and sort of topics, propositional density, number of elaborations
Discourse structure	paragraph length, introduction, conclusion, rhetorical relations, argument structure
Syntax	sentence length, variation in sentence length, sentence-initial structure, number of relative clauses, sub- and coordination, passive voice, cleft constructions, nominalizations
Lexicon	word length, lexical diversity (type-token ratio), frequencies and ratios of various parts of speech (adverbs, qualifiers, function words, etc.), hapax legomena (words occurring only once), impersonal constructions, figures of speech
Usage	frequencies of characters, punctuation marks, spelling errors

countable, for example, the type-token ratio (TTR) as an indicator of lexical richness. This ratio is the number of different words (the types) divided by the number of words in a text (the tokens). The TTR of the previous sentence is 0.71 because words like *the* and *words* were used more than once (in total there are 15 types and 21 tokens). This TTR can be an indicator of the difficulty of a text; more types can make a text more difficult. Another ratio is the noun-verb ratio. If it could be proved that some documents, e.g., bureaucratic documents, have a more nominal style, for example, than newspaper articles or novels (with a more verbal style), then this could be an explanation of style labels for officialese like "dull", "abstract" or "dry".

Of course, an analysis on the basis of these quantitative elements cannot produce a full-fledged description of the style. And many style elements shirk quantitative analysis. How to measure the strength of a good metaphor, for example? The style of a document is as difficult to describe as the character of a person. An old French saying expresses this perfectly: "*Le style est l'homme même*" ("Style is the man himself").

8.4   Examples of stylistic research

In this section four examples of stylistic research are provided. The first example, Carroll (1960), is important as it is the first attempt to describe all possible characteristics that could be of importance stylistically. The next, Sandell (1977), is the first to embed style analysis in the main purpose of rhetoric: persuasion. From research of the last few decades, concerning many stylistic phenomena, two topics were selected: the rhetorical question, Howard (1990), and intensifiers, Hamilton et al. (1990).

Carroll (1960) provided a description of linguistic characteristics that may be responsible for the way prose styles are judged. He based his work on 150 passages, each containing over 300 words, culled from many different types of discourse: newspaper articles, letters, essays, scientific articles, etc. These passages were investigated with attention to 39 characteristics including sentence length, number of subordinate clauses, percentage of verbs and the number of personal pronouns. In addition, experts were asked to give their opinion of the texts. The experts were told to mark on an answer sheet what they thought of the texts: personal-impersonal, hard-easy, serious-humorous, etc. In total there were 29 opposites. This yielded 68 x 150 pieces of information: 39 characteristics and 29 expert answers for each of the 150 passages. Statistical treatment of this large amount of information brought to light a number of relationships between characteristics of discourse and the way that discourse is judged. There appeared to be, among other things, a relationship between the judgments "aloof", "complex", and "deep" and the discourse characteristics "few numerals", and "few adjectives". A link was also discovered between the judgment "emotional" and the discourse characteristic "lots of adjectives". Carroll did, however, remark that this did not prove that the characteristics described were responsible for the differences in style. In this study relatively superficial characteristics were dealt with as the first step towards a stylistic analysis.

Is there a specific style for discourse that is intended to persuade? One of the first researchers who attempted to answer this question was Sandell (1977). He investigated different types of texts: a type of text that is definitively persuasive, advertisements, and a text that altogether lacks persuasive elements, the short foreign-news item. Passages were selected from newspapers and analyzed with attention to, among other things, word length, ellipsis, and alliteration. The advertisements contained significantly higher numbers of adjectives and intensifiers (for example, a superlative or words like *never* and *always*). The average length of the words was also shorter and ellipsis occurred more frequently. It was concluded on the basis of a statistical analysis that the primary characteristic of advertisements is that they contain a large number of adjectives. Sandell explained this by pointing out that for the description of a product it is these adjectives that have an evaluative value and, therefore, influence consumer attitudes. Sandell pointed out that his research was based on a small random selection of advertisements and news reports and that the persuasive effect of other factors cannot be ignored. Among other things, Sandell mentioned the factor *domain*. Advertisements can deal with topics that are entirely different from those in newspaper articles and may for this reason alone be persuasive.

Many different stylistic elements have been investigated in the research into persuasive style. Here are two representative examples. Sometimes a claim is more convincing when it is formulated as a rhetorical question. If a lawyer wants a client acquitted, the summation is more likely to end with (9b) than with (9a).

(9) a. The defendant did not intend to hurt his neighbor. He was always a very peaceable man.

b. The defendant did not intend to hurt his neighbor. Was he not always a very peaceable man?

Research on the use of rhetorical questions such as in (9b) has shown that this type of question invites the answer intended by the questioner. On the question of why this is true, opinions vary. It could be that rhetorical questions are often used when strong arguments are presented and that they therefore become associated with forceful arguments. From the use of rhetorical questions receivers infer that the arguments are strong. If this is true, rhetorical questions will increase the persuasiveness of a message regardless of argument strength. Another opinion is that a rhetorical question elicits a judgment from the receivers. In order to back their judgment, receivers will pay more attention to the arguments presented. If the arguments are strong, they will pass a more positive judgment than will receivers who heard the statement rather than the rhetorical question (in the example, (9a)) and were not stimulated to pay attention to the arguments. If the arguments are weak, the opposite will hold. Receivers who hear the rhetorical question will then pass a more negative judgment than will receivers who heard the statement.

Research by Howard (1990) supports the latter explanation. Howard investigated the consequences of asking rhetorical questions before presenting the arguments. Again, the rhetorical questions evoked a judgment, but this judgment was not founded on the arguments. After hearing the rhetorical questions, receivers were no longer influenced by arguments. They had passed their judgment and kept to it. This would seem to prove that rhetorical questions following the arguments can increase their persuasiveness, whereas rhetorical questions preceding the argument can annihilate the persuasive power of a message.

In the following example, it is made clear how language intensity can be of influence. Which of the following styles is more convincing, the one used in (10a) or that in (10b)? Each of the two following paragraphs is the concluding segment of an address calling for the legalization of the sale of heroin.

(10) a. Legalizing the sale of heroin provides society with several advantages.
It would discourage crime by making heroin relatively inexpensive and
available to addicts. It would help in the fight against organized crime by
taking away an important source of the underworld's income. Finally, it
would nearly eliminate police corruption related to heroin trafficking by
moving the sale of heroin outside their jurisdiction. Legalizing heroin
would also be advantageous to the user. It would gradually reduce the
number of heroin-related injuries due to disease and overdose. In addition,
users would be able to better afford other health-related products.

b. Legalizing the sale of heroin provides society with several clear advantages.
It would deter crime by making heroin relatively inexpensive and available
to addicts. It would help in the fight against organized crime by taking away
an important source of the underworld's income. Finally, it would virtually
eliminate police corruption related to heroin trafficking by moving the
sale of heroin outside their jurisdiction. Legalizing heroin would also be
advantageous to the user. It would sharply reduce the number of heroin-
related deaths due to disease and overdose. In addition, users would be able
to better afford other health-related products.

These texts were used in experiments done by Hamilton et al. (1990). Three factors
were investigated: language intensity, source credibility and gender. To test the effect
of language intensity, the language was intensified in the b-version compared to the
a-version. The word "clear" was placed in front of "advantages". The word "discourage" was replaced by "deter", "nearly" by "virtually", etc. To test the effect of source
credibility, the author in one case was said to be an Assistant Director of the Drug
Enforcement Agency with degrees from Berkeley and Stanford, and in the other
case the author was said to be a former addict. To test the effect of gender, the name
of the author was varied simply by using either the name *John* or the name *Joan*.
Before the subjects were shown the texts, they were asked their views concerning
the legalization of heroin.

The experiments showed that intensifiers had a positive influence on attitude
change. There did not, however, appear to be a direct link between language intensity
and attitude change. The text was perceived as being clearer due to the intensive use of
language, and this clarity facilitated a change in attitude. In this investigation, the large
extent to which other factors outside language use are influential also became clear.
Intensifiers had a positive effect if the source was seen as reliable; the same language
was completely unconvincing if the source was felt to be unreliable. Other examples
of research on convincing people using stylistic devices are dealt with in Chapter 12
on argumentation and persuasion.

Questions and assignments

Questions

8.1.1   Which of Grice's maxims (see Section 2.4) are of particular importance to stylistic research? What other maxims could be formulated from a stylistic perspective?

8.1.2   Which factors from the SPEAKING model (see Section 3.4) are of importance in the following types of language?
emotional style, formal style, legalese, officialese, persuasive language, social workers' jargon, stock exchange language.

8.2.1   Describe, using parameters P and D from politeness theory (see Section 2.6), when which of the utterances (4a) and (4b) would be appropriate.

8.2.2   If style can be seen as a variation in form of approximately the same content, what in (4e) and (4f) in Section 8.2 is that same content?

8.3.1   Metaphoric language is usually not suitable for providing precise descriptions. Consider the term *text grammar* which is often used in discourse studies. Explain why this term is a metaphor, and try to point out why it is deceptive in this case.

8.3.2   What is the type-token ratio of the first three sentences of this chapter?

8.4.1   Should a speaker use rhetorical questions if he wants his audience to think about his arguments?

8.4.2   Should a speaker use intensifiers if he wants his audience to think about his arguments?

Assignments

8.1.1   In Section 8.1 it is argued that free variation in language has a function (Humboldt's principle). Compare this with free variation in nature, which has no function (the form and color of the human eye or the form of one type of tree). Try to formulate arguments against Humboldt's principle, one outside linguistics (e.g., free variation in nature) and one within linguistics (e.g., by looking at homonyms and synonyms).

8.2.1   Collect a few definitions of the concept of style, describe the differences and try to categorize them according to the three approaches to style mentioned in this section.

8.3.1   Form a group with some fellow students. All members are to provide a text they have written themselves. Provide normative as well as objective stylistic criticism of each other's texts.

8.4.1   Write an advertising text without using adjectives.

Bibliographical information

8.1   Stylistics has a rich history, particularly in the fields of rhetoric and literary theory. Aristotle mentions the two style requirements *appropriateness* and *unaccustomedness* in Book 3, Chapter 1. Quintilianus mentions the style virtues in books 8 and 11 of his work *The Orator's Education*. A good and accessible publication on these and other classical rhetoric works is that by Kennedy (1994). Lanham (1991) is handy for a first introduction to rhetoric.

Reid (1956) introduced the term *register*. Central figures in contemporary register research are Biber and Conrad (2001). The literature mentioned in their article provides a very good overview. A good starting point for further study of register is Ghadessy (1993). Urszula Clark (1996) provides a practical introduction to stylistic analysis with exercise material and good explanations requiring no prior knowledge of the necessary grammatical terminology.

It is only in later interpretations of Von Humboldt's (1836) work that he is credited with having introduced a principle. Von Humboldt himself, however, never spoke of a principle.

The examples of the Queneau (1947/1981) story variations are translations by Barbara Wright.

8.2   A good English-language survey concerning definition problems is provided in Enkvist (1973).

8.3   Table 1 is inspired by overviews in the publication by McMenamin (1993), which is a good introduction to stylistic analysis. Another good starting point for style analysis is Crystal and Davy (1969).

A fine overview of research on metaphors is provided by Ortony (1993). See Section 13.6 for the cognitive approach to metaphors.

8.4   Weber (1996) gives a good overview of the field of stylistics in the last four decades of the last century, also touching upon recent developments in critical and cognitive stylistics. Semino and Culpeper (2002) provide a starting point for a study of more literary stylistics. This collection of articles shows how literary analysis can be embedded in a more cognitively oriented study of language production and comprehension.

PART III

Special modes of communication

9 Conversation analysis

9.1 Transcription systems

The study of verbal interaction requires a method of written representation, a transcription system, as the regular spelling conventions are not sufficient for transcription. Intonation, for instance, can only be partially reproduced using punctuation and stress marks. Furthermore, it is important to know exactly who said what when. It is also important to be able to register silence. For this reason, various transcription systems have been developed. The two most prominent systems are score notation and dramaturgical notation.

Score notation was inspired by the written representation of music. A conversation is recorded like tones on music staves, with a line reserved for each participant in the conversation, as in (1) below.

(1) 1. R: ⌜ Peter, well he almost never eats anything   *never* he's never hungry
                                                (0.2)
         J: ⌞   That is surprising
     2. R: ⌜   Strange, isn't it?
         J: ⌞ You wouldn't say that by looking at him.   Yes. Not
     3. R: ⌜   No, but he/who don't eat very little
         J: | that he's fat but   Those muscles must be coming
             ⌞   ((laughs))
     4. R: ⌜   Very, very, strange.
         J: ⌞ from somewhere.

With score notation it is possible to indicate when each participant is speaking, where overlap takes place, and where silent periods are located. A silence can be indicated by seconds denoted between brackets. Comments that are necessary for understanding the conversation can be provided between double brackets. The numbers placed in front of the scoring bars are meant to simplify reference. Usually, a length of time per number of bars is defined in order to denote the length of the entire conversation.

Score notation was developed by the German discourse researchers Konrad Ehlich and Jochem Rehbein (see, for example, Ehlich's 1993 publication). They called their system a "*Halb interpretatieve Arbeitstranskription*" (abbreviated to HIAT). The first part of the name indicates that transcription also entails interpretation. When, for example, a participant in a conversation stops speaking for a moment and then later continues, his words can be registered as one turn or as two different turns with a pause in between them. By using the term "*Arbeitstranskription*", Ehlich and Rehbein made it clear that it is not possible to use the HIAT system to produce a definite transcription in one attempt. Only by listening to a recording of a conversation again and again is it possible to get a precise transcription.

Dramaturgical notation was developed by Gail Jefferson (see, for example, her 1978 publication), one of the pioneers of conversation analysis. This form of notation is based on the written representation of stage discourse. Utterances are ordered one under another according to the order of participation. Whenever possible individual acts are represented on single lines. Below is the same discourse used in fragment (1) in dramaturgical notation:

(2) 1. R: Peter, well he almost ne:ver eats a:nything
     2.   (0.2)
     3.   ne:::ver (.) ⎡ He's never hungry ⎤
     4. J: ⎣ That i:s surprising ⎦
     5.   You wouldn't say that by loo:king at him=
     6. R: =*Strange*: isn't it?=
     7. J: =Yes:: Not that he's fa:t (.) bu:t
     8.   (.)
     9. R: No but he/ ⎡ who don't eat (.) vE::ry little ⎤
   10.   ((laughs)) ⎢
   11. J: ⎣ Those muscles must be coming ⎦
         from so::mewhere
   12. R: Ve:ry/ve:ry stra:nge

Overlap is denoted by a separate symbol, square brackets. The meanings of the other symbols are presented below.

(3) Symbols in dramaturgical notation

==	-	no interruption		xx	-	stress point
		(at the beginning		XX	-	uttered loudly
		and the end of a line)		?	-	tone rises
/	-	word correction		(.)	-	short pause
x:	-	extension		(0.2)	-	0.2 second pause

In both transcription systems only verbal elements are recorded. Posture and mimicry of the conversational participants are not dealt with although they can influence the course of an interaction. For this reason, video recordings are also used. Of the two systems, dramaturgical notation is the most commonly used. It is important to realize that any method of transcription is more or less subjective, not only in the encoding of pauses and prosody, but also in the interpretation of non-verbal aspects and in the presentation of, for example, half an utterance as a full turn in a conversation.

9.2   The turn-taking model

At first glance, most conversational activities seem rather chaotic. One phenomenon, however, seems to be constant: verbal interaction is realized by turn-taking. But even this turn-taking can be quite varied. In conversations, there is no limit to the length of a turn. A turn can vary in length from a single word to a complete story. There are also no rules for determining the order of turns among conversational participants. Likewise, there are no rules concerning the number of turns a participant can take or the possible content of a turn.

Despite the enormous number of variations possible, it is rare for silences to result from participants not knowing whose turn it is. A closer look at conversations shows that exactly simultaneous turn-taking also seldom occurs. In conversations there is a clear tendency to speak in orderly turns with only one speaker speaking at any given moment. This tendency is described in the turn-taking model developed by Harvey Sacks, Emanuel Schegloff and Gail Jefferson (1974). The model consists of two components: the turn-construction component and the turn-taking component. In the first component a turn is constructed, built up of syntactical units: sentences, sentence fragments, or words. The first point at which an assignment of turns can take place is at the end of the first unit. This point is called the transition-relevance place, a possible point of turn transferal. As soon as such a point is reached, i.e., at the end of every syntactical unit, the turn-taking component becomes applicable. This component consists of four rules.

(4)   The rules for turn-taking

    1.   For any turn, at the initial transition-relevance place of an initial turn-constructional unit:

        a.   If the turn-so-far is so constructed as to involve the use of a 'current speaker selects next' technique, then the participant thus selected has the right and is obliged to take the next turn to speak; no others have such rights or obligations, and transfer occurs at that place.

        b.   If the turn-so-far is so constructed as not to involve the use of a 'current speaker selects next' technique, then self-selection for the next speakership may, but need not, be instituted. The person who first starts at that moment acquires the right to a turn, and transfer occurs at that place.

   c. If the turn-so-far is so constructed as not to involve the use of a 'current speaker selects next' technique, then the current speaker may, but need not continue, unless another self-selects.

2. If, at the initial transition-relevance place of an initial turn-constructional unit, neither 1a nor 1b has operated, and, following the provision of 1c, the current speaker has continued, then the rule-set (a) to (c) re-applies at the next transition-relevance place, and recursively at each ensuing transition-relevance place, until transfer is effected.

The following example illustrates how this turn-taking model works.

(5)

1. A: ⌈   well (eh) pretty bad actually 'cause I'd really learned
      B: │ how did the exam go yesterday?
      C: ⌊

2. A: ⌈ the stuff you know but when I was sitting in that lecture hall (eh) I just couldn't come
      B: │
      C: ⌊

3. A: ⌈ up with the answers (1.4) and well (eh)   (1.1) yeah, I was
      B: │   you got a blackout
      C: ⌊

4. A: ⌈ trying to concentrate, but could only think of not coming up with proper answers
      B: │
      C: ⌊

5. A: ⌈
      B: │ well, you shouldn't worry about it too much now
      C: ⌊   yeah   no, indeed

In (5.1) Speaker B chooses A as the subsequent speaker according to rule 1a. Speaker A continues until, after a moment of silence, B takes a turn in (5.3) following rule 1b or rule 1c. After the silence that then follows, rule 1c becomes applicable.

    A number of objections have been raised against this model. First of all, in the analysis of conversations it is often impossible to say which rule applies. Take the following example:

(6) A: Andy just paid me back my fifty bucks.
        B: Great. You guys wanta go out for pizza?
        C: Hey A. Can you loan me ten dollars?

In this phase of the conversation, it is not clear whether C is reacting to A's words or is ignoring B and is just taking a turn. In other words, it is not possible to ascertain if C is getting a turn according to rule 1a (current speaker chooses subsequent speaker) or rule 1b (a conversational participant takes a turn when no subsequent speaker is chosen). Determining which rule is applicable has turned out to be more difficult than the model suggested.

Secondly, it is assumed in the model that conversational participants can recognize a construction unit. This may be true for questions and answers, but in many utterances it is unclear where the possible points of turn assignment are. Moreover, it is possible for a speaker to neutralize these points by beginning a turn with a remark such as: "There are two points that I would like to make clear ..." Formally speaking, the rules for turn assignment become effective at the end of the first point. The content, however, indicates that this point does not demarcate the end of the turn.

Thirdly, conversations do not consist solely of turns but include remarks irrelevant to the flow of the conversation such as: "Would you like something to drink?", "Can I have a handkerchief?", etc. Moreover, conversational participants who do not "have the floor" often voice their involvement with such utterances as *hm, really?, well, well,* etc. This type of utterance is classified as *back-channel behavior* or *collateral communication*. The turn-taking model does not make clear how the distinction is made between turns, on the one hand, and ancillary remarks or back-channel behavior that does not trigger the rules of assignment, on the other.

The turn-taking model prompts thought on the question of what exactly a turn is. Is back-channel behavior, the *hm* made by speakers or the *um* by which listeners indicate a wish to speak, also a turn? If it is appropriate to speak of a turn when a participant takes the floor, then these minimal reactions will not qualify as turns. Instead, another's turn is supported by listener reactions such as "How about that?", "You can say that again" or similar utterances. The speaker can, after such a reaction, simply continue with his turn. If, however, the turn application *um* is seen as a complete turn, then the rules of the turn-taking model do not always apply. Interestingly, a silence can also be seen as a turn. Participants can, by remaining silent, answer a question or agree to a request.

Obviously, it is too simplistic to speak only of a turn when participants become the main speaker, but it is equally wrong to view every utterance, no matter how minimal, as a turn. One solution is to view back-channel behavior as a pre-turn with which participants make it clear that they want a turn, just as the so-called *inbreathe* indicates that participants want to say something. That a silence can sometimes also constitute a turn can be explained by the assumption that positions can be filled by a verbal reaction, or a "null" verbal reaction.

9.3   Sequential organization

A conversational sequence is a systematic succession of turns. In the analysis of sequences the focus has been primarily on the *adjacency pair*. This term refers to the phenomenon that, in a conversation, one utterance has a role in determining the subsequent utterance or at least in raising expectations concerning its contents. Below is an example of the adjacency pair "question-answer".

(7)   A: How do you like college?
      B: (0.3) Well, what can I say?

Schegloff (1977) points out that in an adjacency pair, the second utterance is "conditionally relevant". This means that if there is an adjacency pair consisting of parts A and B, and part A has been uttered, then part B is expected. And, when B has been uttered, then it is viewed by the participants as being relevant to A. B is therefore relevant on the condition that A has been uttered. If B does not occur, then this is not random but a significant or "observable" absence and conclusions can be drawn from this. Both possibilities can be seen in the following example.

(8)   A: Would you like to go and ... uh ... get some coffee?
      B: (2.0)
      A: Or aren't you in the mood?
      B: (1.5) What do you mean?

A's first utterance creates expectations of a reaction. Questions are, after all, usually followed by an answer. It is for this reason that B's silence is not viewed by A as being random. A's second utterance is a reaction to an observably absent answer. B's second utterance is conditionally relevant to this reaction by A. A's question makes B's utterance relevant, that is, interpretable as an answer in the form of a request for more precise information.

In fact, the designation *adjacency pair* is not totally correct. The parts of a pair are often not adjacent. In the following example, the opening question and the answer to this question are separated by another question-and-answer pair.

(9)   A: Can you tell me how to get to the mall?
      B: Do you see that big neon sign?
      A: Yes.
      B: You have to make a left turn there.

The adjacency pair is an important building block in conversation. Besides the adjacency pair, a three-part sequence also often occurs. Below are some examples.

(10) A: Well, Paul, can you come up and find Australia on the map?
      B: That's here, I guess.
      A: Indeed, you are right.

(11) A: How about having a drink downtown?
      B: Yes, good idea!
      A: O.K., there is a taxi.

In in-class interaction, such as in (10), the teacher often asks a question and comments on the answer given by the pupil. This three-part sequence is called a question-answer-evaluation chain. And if someone proposes something as in (11), the positive reaction is usually followed by a suggestion for further action. This sequence is called the offer-agreement-affirmation chain.

An answer to a question is often followed by a comment as in the following example.

(12) A: Can you tell me how to get to the mall?
      B: Turn right at the third light.
      A: Terrific, thank you.

Research on the systematic sequencing of turns concentrated on the beginnings and the ends of conversations. This approach started with a study by Schegloff and Sacks (1973) in which the techniques used by participants to reach a point at which the conversation can be closed were inventoried. In every conversation there is a point at which the conclusion of one turn no longer leads to a subsequent turn and the silence that follows cannot be interpreted as the silence of one of the participants. Schegloff and Sacks analyzed a large number of telephone conversations and found that many of the conversations ended with the following closing pair.

(13) A: Okay?
      B: Alright.

Should B not want to end the conversation, then the possibility exists for B to continue after A's utterance. However, if B fills in the second part of the closing pair with an affirmation of the first part, then the conversation is essentially over (except possibly for mutual greetings). What is interesting is that a pair like the one above can also occur in the middle of a conversation. Speaker A can, following B's reaction, continue with a new topic. Apparently, changing phrases such as "okay" only serve to end a conversation if there is nothing left to discuss.

How do conversational participants know that there is nothing left to discuss? When reviewing their material, Schegloff and Sacks found that topics were usually ended with words such as *good*, *okay*, and *well*, pronounced with a declining intonation after which the speaker started a new topic. Their analysis showed that these types of topic closing are also used as a way of suggesting the end of a conversation. Below is an example taken from Schegloff and Sacks' material in which the word "okay" occurs three times. The first "okay" is a topic closing and thereby a possible pre-announcement of a conversation closing. The second "okay" serves as an announcement or declaration of intent to end the conversation. The third "okay" serves as a sign of agreement with this closing.

> (14)   A: ... and uh, uh, we're gonna see if we can't uh tie in our plans a little better.
> B: Okay / / fine
> A: Alright?
> B: Right.
> A: Okay boy,
> B: Okay
> A: Bye / / bye
> B: G'night.

Obviously, multiple functions can be combined in one "okay". In the following excerpt it can be seen that "okay" serves as both a topic closing and as a declaration of intent to close the conversation.

> (15)   (A has called to invite B, but has been told B is going out to dinner.)
> A: Yeah. Well get on your clothes and get out and collect some of that free food and we'll make it some other time Judy then.
> B: Okay then Jack.
> A: Bye bye.
> B: Bye bye.

Schegloff and Sacks's analysis shows that analyzing a number of turns containing "okay" is insufficient to make it clear why a double "okay" exchange can be followed by a closing in the form of a greeting and return of the greeting. For the analysis of a turn or a pair of turns, it is necessary to look at the context within which it occurs.

9.4   Discourse markers

In the study of written discourse the focus of many researchers is on connectives, which link the various segments; see Section 6.2 and 6.3. In the study of spoken discourse many analysts focus on discourse markers or pragmatic particles, such as *okay* in the last example of the previous section. Discourse markers have as their main functions marking something in the structure and indicating some aspects of attitude. Below are some examples (the italicized words).

(16) A: I think I will stay home. I feel *like* I ran half a marathon.
     B: *And* yesterday you said you would come!

(17) A: *But* I told you not to open the door, not for anybody!
     B: *Well*, I do have my own will, *y'know*.

(18) A: *So*, in the end you have decided to join us *then*.
     B: *After all*, I had to be here *anyway*.

Discourse markers that are used: connectives (like *and*), adverbials (like *anyway*), interjections (like *well*), prepositional phrases (like *after all*) and lexical phrases (like *y'know*). As with most important concepts, definitions of discourse markers given in the literature vary, depending on the theoretical approach. However, most describe discourse markers as signaling devices outside the propositional content, indicating the expressive function of a piece of discourse. The expressive function denotes the attitude of the speaker toward the locution (see Section 4.1). The piece of discourse can be, for example, a turn in a conversation or a topic. Because discourse markers are not a part of the propositional content, they are mostly found at the beginning or the end of an utterance. Discourse markers are usually distinguished from connectives in that connectives assign all kinds of semantic and pragmatic functions to paragraphs, clauses and subclauses, while discourse markers only indicate the attitude of a speaker (or possibly a writer), mostly marking a turn or a topic.

The two markers in example (16) illustrate the attitude approach combined with the function of a turn. The discourse marker *like* indicates looseness. The speaker expresses that the degree of exhaustion does not have to be taken precisely as it is formulated. This can be seen as an attempt by the addresser to enhance the degree of relevance of the turn's content for the addressee, who is now allowed or obliged to also take into consideration a more "normal" kind of tiredness. The *And* at the beginning of B's turn does not indicate a connection such as in "apples and oranges". It expresses the indignation of the whole turn, which with this marker becomes more subjective than a formal reproach.

Discourse markers have been studied in various ways to detect their usage and functions in different communication situations. In conversations, participants use discourse markers not only to express attitudes, but also to detect or to confirm which information is given and which is new (see Section 7.4 about given–new management). Discourse markers, in other words, also mark the presence or absence of common ground (see Section 3.3). This has been nicely demonstrated in a study by Jucker and Smith (1998). They asked their students to have conversations about topics like sports, travel, opera etc., and divided the group into pairs of students who were friends and pairs who were strangers. In total they transcribed three and a half hours of conversation by 15 participants. They counted and listed the discourse markers and found almost 3,000, which means one about every five seconds. Here is one passage from their transcriptions with the discourse markers italicized:

(19)   A: I play basketball
         B: *Oh yeah* what position (..) forward?
         A: yeah
         B: that's cool
         A: jus: (..) just playing with the friends *you know*

With the reaction "Oh yeah" B does not confirm the information that A gives, as the "yeah" in A's second turn does. B indicates that the information has been received and can be stored with other information available at that point in the conversation. The discourse marker "you know" does not remind B of knowledge already given, but presents more or less an invitation to make the right inferences for the assignment of relevance to an utterance, for example that person A is not a real top sportsman.

Jucker and Smith divided the discourse markers into markers that serve as indicators of information reception, like *yeah*, and markers that are used to present information, like *you know*. They counted these markers in the conversations between friends and strangers, and found some remarkable differences in their material (Table 1).

The most frequent reception marker is *yeah*. However, between friends it is significantly less frequent (every 18 seconds) than between strangers (every 13 seconds). This can be explained by the nature of the conversation. Between strangers it is more necessary to indicate that the information has been received than between friends, who have more common ground (see also Section 3.3) based on shared experiences.

Table 1.   Frequency of reception markers and presentation markers (average number of tokens per minute) in conversations between pairs of strangers and pairs of friends

Marker	Strangers	Friends
Reception markers		
yeah	4.5	3.4
oh	1.6	1.1
really	0.3	0.4
Presentation markers		
like	2.8	4.5
you know	1.0	1.4

The analysis of the conversations also indicated that there is a difference in information reception between *yeah, oh* and *really*. Compare the following examples.

(20) A: I like playing basketball
     B: Yeah, …

(21) A: I like playing basketball
     B: Oh, …

(22) A: I like playing basketball
     B: Really?

These three markers indicate a difference in the ease of integration of new information. *Yeah* indicates that the integration process is very easy, *oh* marks that some extra processing effort is needed, and *really* suggests that more information is needed before integration can be successful.

The presentation markers also showed a striking difference. Friends use them more often than strangers. This can be explained by the same factor of common ground. If there is more shared experience (between friends), there is a better basis for providing indicators about how to process information (for example, *you know* can be taken literally between friends). Hence, presentation markers like those mentioned above, and others like *well* and *I mean* are more frequent in conversations between friends than between strangers. With this study Jucker and Smith nicely show that discourse markers are not only indicators of attitude but also signposts for the exchange of information based on an important characteristic of communication: common ground.

Questions and assignments

Questions

9.1.1   In this chapter, two phenomena were mentioned that are ignored in transcription systems but are important for the course of a conversation. Name one other phenomenon.

9.2.1   Demonstrate that, besides the turn-taking model, there is a separate rule necessary for the closing of a conversation.

9.2.2   Give an example of a conversational excerpt in which a silence on the part of a participant must be interpreted as a turn, taking into account the fifth strategy for the execution of FTAS (see Section 2.6).

9.2.3   Indicate why back-channel behavior cannot be seen as a pre-turn.

9.3.1   Give examples of other types of adjacency pairs besides question-answer.

9.3.2   Explain why telephone conversations are often the focus of analysis of verbal interaction.

9.4.1   Provide examples of other discourse markers besides those given in Section 9.4.

9.4.2   Try to point out the difference in meaning in examples (17) and (18) when the discourse marker is not used.

9.4.3   In a conversation between strangers it is necessary to use indicators in order to enhance the processing of information. One would then expect presentation markers between strangers to occur more frequently. Explain why this does not show in, for example, the research done by Jucker and Smith.

Assignments

9.1.1   Make a tape recording of an everyday conversation between three people, for example, a conversation in a living room or a visit by friends. Try to transcribe two minutes of this conversation using dramaturgical notation.

9.2.1   A silence can be differentially assigned on the basis of the rules for turn-taking. Silence can be seen as either: 1. a gap before a subsequent application of rule 1b or 1c; 2. a lapse of the non-application of rule 1a, 1b or 1c; or 3. a significant silence of the next selected speaker after the application of rule 1a.

Try to find examples of each of these three types of silence in order to verify whether the tripartition works. Start, for example, by looking at the examples used in Jaworski (1997).

9.3.1   In the past attempts have been made to design computer programs that simulate human language behavior. In extreme cases, software "bots" were created to behave as if they were human interlocutors in interactive written discourse. Eliza, created in 1966 by Joseph Weizenbaum, is such a computer program. It reformulates operator answers in order to keep a conversation going and as such simulates psychoanalytical therapy.

Find an Eliza chatterbot on the Internet and start a conversation. Save the transcript of your conversation and try to point out the successful adjacency pairs and the more curious turns. Try to explain how Eliza works out how to respond to your turns. Which turns are the most difficult for Eliza and why would that be the case?

9.4.1   Find a corpus (500 to 1,000 words) of formal and informal conversation in your own language and count the number of discourse markers in it. Try to find differences in frequency between formal and informal conversation.

Bibliographical information

9.1   For more on the HIAT system, see Ehlich (1993), in which a more detailed system called HIAT II is suggested. See Jefferson (1978) for examples of dramaturgical notation. For an excellent introduction to conversation analysis see Ten Have (1999). See also Hutchby and Wooffitt (1998). This publication demonstrates the practical relevance of conversation analysis, for example, by discussing its merits in the analysis of human-computer interaction.

Edwards (2001) also provides a good overview of the various transcription methods and mentions their (dis)advantages. After an introductory work to conversation analysis (see Chapter 1) Eggins and Slade (1997) serves as a good further acquaintance. The founding father of conversation analysis is the sociologist Sacks, and his lectures were published by Jefferson; see Sacks, Jefferson and Schegloff (1992).

9.2   The turn-taking model was published in an article entitled *A Simplest Systematics for the Organization of Turn-taking for Conversation*; see Sacks, Schegloff and Jefferson (1974). See McLaughlin (1984) for criticism of this; example (6) was taken from this publication.

Instead of *turn*, the term *floor* is often used. This is a meeting term as in: "The floor is yours." There is as yet no clear definition. For the distinction between turn and position, see Levinson (1983). For further study see also Searle (1992), who criticizes the turn-taking model.

Jaworski (1997) is an excellent collection of papers on silence in, among other things, verbal interaction and narratives.

9.3   For the notion *adjacency pair*, see Schegloff (1977). For more on three-part sequences, see Edmondson (1981). See Ochs, Schegloff and Thompson (1996) for a collection of papers on interactional units and turn organization.

Conversation analysis has very specific roots in ethnomethodology. For a good introduction, see Nofsinger (1991).

9.4   Schiffrin's dissertation *Discourse Markers* is a landmark publication in this field of study, and was published as a book in 1987. Schiffrin takes discourse markers to be markers of four different types of communicative knowledge: cognitive, expressive, social and textual. In this book, only the expressive and textual types are discussed. Another good monograph is Brinton (1996). An excellent starting point for further research is the collection of articles by Jucker and Ziv (1998). The study by Jucker and Smith (1998) that is referred to in this section can also be found in this publication. The table in this section was taken from their article. Smith and Jucker also contributed an article to Fetzer and Meierkord (2002) in which they scrutinize the discourse marker *well*. For more on the discourse marker *okay*, see Heisler (1996).

For more information on the cognitive aspect of common ground that Jucker and Smith mention, see Clark's (1996) important publication on this subject, which was also mentioned earlier in this book.

10 Informative discourse

10.1 Readability in a formula

It is often said that discourse serves three main functions. In discourse the addresser wants to inform the addressee, or express his own opinions and feelings, and by doing so he wants to persuade the addressee to adopt a change in attitude or action, or both (see Section 4.1 about this tripartition in information, expression and argumentation). Chapter 11 focuses on narratives, the most suitable discourse mode for expression. Chapter 12 deals with argumentation and persuasion. This chapter is about informative discourse, which is mainly referred to as expository or explanatory discourse.

One of the oldest problems in research concerning discourse that is meant to inform the addressee is how to determine whether or not a discourse is comprehensible to a specific target group. In the last century researchers have tried to solve this problem by developing readability formulas. Some of these formulas are still popular in the field of education, where there is a great need for an efficient method of determining whether a textbook is suitable for a given scholastic level. The procedure for developing a readability formula consists of four steps.

1. The first step is to collect a number of texts that are known to have different levels of difficulty. This collection can consist of texts that have been used in school tests, and which have known score levels for each educational level. A text can then be assumed to be suitable for a certain level if pupils at that level get a given average score, for example, seven out of ten correct answers.
2. The texts can then be analyzed for all the possible characteristics which may have an influence on readability: the length of words, the percentage of abstract words, the number of subordinate clauses per sentence, the number of prepositions per hundred words, etc. (See, for example, the style analysis done by John Carroll discussed in Section 8.4.)
3. Statistical processing can then aid in determining to what extent the differences in difficulty (see step 1) can be ascribed to characteristics in the texts (see step 2).
4. On the basis of step 3, it can be determined which text characteristics contribute the most to the outcome of a reading comprehension test. Further statistical analysis can be done to determine how often these characteristics should or may occur in order for a text to be readable for a certain level.

The best-known formula is the Flesch formula, named after Rudolph Flesch. This formula contains two variables, word length and sentence length, and is therefore relatively easy to apply. Take a passage containing one hundred words. Count the number of syllables. Determine the average sentence length in words, whereby the last sentence boundary is the point that is closest to the hundredth word. The result will be two numbers: one for word length (wl), the total number of syllables in a hundred words, and one for the average sentence length (sl). These numbers have to be used in the following formula.

(1) Flesch's readability formula
     R.E. $= 206.84 - (0.85 \times wl) - (1.02 \times sl)$

R.E. stands for reading ease; the constants have been attained through statistical analysis. The number of syllables per hundred words must be multiplied by 0.85 and the average sentence length by 1.02. Both results must be subtracted from the beginning number. The result of this formula can be between 0 (very difficult to read) and 100 (very easy to read) and indicates which level of education is needed for comprehension of the text (Table 1).

To what extent do the results of this formula indicate differences in readability? As an illustration, two examples follow.

(2) Rocket
     A great black and yellow V-2 rocket forty-six feet long stood in a New Mexico desert. Empty, it weighed five tons. For fuel it carried eight tons of alcohol and liquid oxygen.
     Everything was ready. Scientists and generals withdrew to some distance and crouched behind earth mounds. Two red flares rose as a signal to fire the rocket. With a great roar and burst of flame the giant rocket rose slowly and then faster and faster. Behind it trailed sixty feet of yellow flame. Soon the flame looked like

Table 1.   Flesch formula, interpretation table

R.E.-result	Valuation	Level of education
0–30	very difficult	college
30–50	difficult	high school
50–60	fairly difficult	junior high school
60–70	standard	sixth grade
70–80	fairly easy	fifth grade
80–90	easy	fourth grade
90–100	very easy	third grade

a yellow star. In a few seconds it was too high to be seen, but radar tracked it as it sped upward to 3,000 miles per hour.

A few minutes after it was fired, the pilot of a watching plane saw it return at a speed of 2,400 miles per hour and plunge into earth forty miles from the starting point.

(3) Jimmie Cod

A long time ago the little fishes of the sea were at school down under the water, safe from dangerous animals. One pupil, Jimmie Cod, was not studying. He was looking at something dangling in front of him. He could not take his eyes off this shiny object. When the teacher of history asked him what he thought of the whale that swallowed Jonah, he replied: "It looks good enough to eat." Everyone was amused at Jimmie's strange answer and all turned to look at him. He was not thinking of school or history lessons, but he was getting hungrier every minute. Suddenly, while the teacher and pupils were looking, it happened. Jimmie took a quick bite and swallowed that shiny something which had been hanging just before his nose. Then like a flash he went up, up, out of sight. And no one in the class saw Jimmie Cod again.

The Flesch formula applied to the first hundred words of each example provides the following results:

(4) Rocket: R.E. 75
Jimmie Cod:R.E. 81

On the basis of these results, the conclusion can be drawn that text (3) is slightly easier than text (2) and that both texts are suitable for the same level of education. The value of this and other readability formulas is, however, questionable. In the literature on this topic, the following objections, among others, have been put forward.

1. A readability formula is based on a collection of school tests, but this does not mean that such a formula can be applied to other kinds of texts without adaptation.
2. Only those symptoms have been incorporated in the formula which best correspond to the results of text-comprehension tests. However, the variables in this case, word and sentence length, say little about the readability of a text.
3. The text-comprehension tests used as a bench model often have a somewhat dubious status.
4. The readability formulas developed so far have only made pronouncements about the characteristics of sentences. Flesch's formula would yield the same result even if the sentences of a text were arranged in a different order. Readability formulas are not sensitive to such important discourse characteristics as cohesion and coherence.

10.2   The measurement of understanding

Readability formulas have been developed to make it possible to measure the read-ability of a text without the assistance of a reader. All of the other methods of detecting whether the information has come through require proofreaders. With real readers one can gain insight into the process of understanding a text.

A widely used method is the cloze test. The word *cloze* is derived from the word *closure*, a term used in Gestalt psychology. This term describes the human tendency to observe a whole form (a Gestalt) even in situations where a part is missing. If, for example, observers are shown a drawing of a face in which the nose is missing, they will still see the drawing as one of a face. When applied to texts, this means that the reader can fill in a word that has been left out. If a number of words are left out of a text, the reader will be ... to indicate ... words should be ... in. The cloze test is used as a means of measuring understanding based on the following assumption: the more comprehensible a text is, the easier it is for a reader to fill in the missing words. One could, for example, block out every fifth word and assume that a text is suitable for a given group if subjects from that group can fill in 40 to 50 percent of the open spaces correctly.

However, research has shown that the test required some fine-tuning. The results proved to be dependent on what kind of word was left out. Compare the following examples.

(5) a.   ... 45 foot tall black ... yellow V-2 rocket stood ... the desert of New Mexico.
     b.   A 45 foot tall ... and yellow V-2 rocket ... in the desert of ...

In both sentences every fifth word has been left out; in (5a) this sequence starts with the first word and in (5b) with the fifth word. In (5a), however, there is much more chance of filling in a correct answer as in this case so-called function words have been left out: "A", "and", "in". There proved to be a big difference between function words, words belonging to parts of speech which are enumerable (articles, prepositions, con-junctions, numerals, etc.) and content words which are not enumerable: nouns, verbs, adjectives and adverbs. The function words can often be filled in on the basis of general knowledge of the language. At this point the cloze test is more a test of knowledge of language structures than a test of readability. In (5b), on the other hand, content words have been left out: "black", "stood", "New Mexico". Filling in content words requires knowledge of the topic of discourse. Readers who know nothing about the early days of rocketry will have much more trouble filling in the last word. Differences in the level of predictability of the various words of a text can only be nullified if so many versions of the text are created that each word is left out in one or another of the versions, for example, five versions if every fifth word is left out.

More important is the question whether or not a reader's ability to fill in missing words says anything about the comprehensibility of a text. If readers fill in the word *landed* instead of *stood*, can it be assumed that the sentence was more difficult for these readers than for those who filled in the correct answer? Proponents of the cloze test point out that the test can be useful in measuring understanding and discourse comprehension when the words to be left out are not chosen at random but are selected on the basis of their use as signposts of comprehension; these words can only be filled in if the text has been understood.

In addition to the cloze test, there are numerous other methods of determining the comprehensibility of a text for a specific group. Readers can be asked questions about the text, or can be asked to retell the text or write a summary of it. Readers can also be asked to judge the text on its comprehensibility, for example, by means of a think-aloud protocol or by indicating a text's strengths and weaknesses by putting pluses and minuses in the margin, the plus-minus method. Furthermore, readers can be asked to rank different versions of the text according to comprehensibility. Objections can be raised to each of these methods. Judging the quality of a summary is a subjective process. A reader's ability to reproduce a text does not automatically mean the text has been understood. Generating questions and judging the answers given can also be problematic. If a reader is asked whether a certain sentence occurred literally in the text, then what is, in fact, being tested is the reader's memory. And if an open-ended question is asked, then information that was contained in the text is almost always repeated in the question. This means that the level of understanding achieved directly after reading the text is no longer measurable. The shortcomings of the different methods are, however, not as serious when these methods are used for comparative research. The difference in comprehensibility between two texts can be determined by using any one of these methods, since the drawbacks would weigh equally heavily in both texts.

The methods mentioned are so-called "off-line" methods: they are all aimed at measuring the comprehension of a text after reading. In psychological research, methods have also been developed to examine the processes that occur during the reading of a text: "on-line" methods. The most important ones are the measurement of reading speed and the recording of eye movements during reading. To measure reading speed, a text is projected onto a screen sentence by sentence. The subjects are asked to press a button that stops a clock as soon as they understand the sentence. This method makes it possible to see, for example, if a sentence with only a vague reference to a previous sentence requires more processing time than a sentence with a clear reference. In addition, equipment has been developed which can measure precisely how long the reader's eye is fixed on a specific word. The assumption is that the length of a fixation is an indication of the complexity of the processes going on in the reader's mind. This method can be used to determine which elements in a text cause difficulties in processing.

Comprehensibility is just one of the aspects that determine the effectiveness of a text. For that matter, measuring a text's comprehensibility does not say everything about that text. In the next section two methods for evaluating the quality of a text are explained.

10.3   Judging discourse quality

One of the main causes of the failure to get information across to the reader is the lack of quality of a text. Hence, much attention has been paid to quality assessment, a topic that has been in focus for a long time in native-language teaching in which students have to write essays. Identifying the factors that determine the quality of text has proved to be very difficult. Research into discourse quality has been further hampered by the fact that judgments concerning discourse can vary greatly: quality judgments are not very reliable. They are as subjective as many stylistic labels; see Section 8.3.

In the 1960s Paul Diederich did some famous research. He constructed a judgment model with which it was possible to make reasonably reliable judgments of quality. He had 300 freshman essays judged by fifty readers from various levels and sectors of society: English teachers, lawyers, publishers, businessmen, managers, etc. There was a good deal of variation in the judgments. One-third of the essays were given every grade (grades ranged from 1 to 9) and no essay received less than five different grades.

It became clear, however, that there were trends in the manner in which judgments were made. Using statistical analysis, it was possible to distinguish five separate groups of judges. The largest group concentrated primarily on the content, the wealth of ideas, and the clarity and relevance for the topic and the audience. The second group focused primarily on errors in usage, sentence structure, punctuation, and spelling: this group consisted mostly of English teachers. The third group looked mainly at organization (there was a large number of businessmen in this group). The fourth group concentrated on vocabulary and the fifth on personal qualities (flavor, style); publishers and writers were well represented in the latter group.

All judgments (the fifty participants each read all 300 papers) could thus be reduced to five factors: ideas, mechanics, organization, wording, and flavor. These factors can also be found in Italian research that was done in the same period. In the Italian investigation a sixth factor was named; "handwriting, neatness". This was probably because they worked with original handwritten texts.

The data obtained in this investigation was used to see whether the differences between quality judgments – for example, that the same essay received an 8 from an

idea judge but only a 5 from an organization judge – could be explained by the different factors. This was only partially the case. In only 43 percent of the cases could the
differences be explained by the five factors. Nearly 60 percent of the variation must
therefore be attributed to highly personal criteria, free variation in judgment or errors
in judgment.

As a result of this investigation, a judgment model was constructed with which
teachers could achieve a reasonable level of consensus after only a short period of
training. In this model, factor II has been split into scholastically accepted elements
such as grammar and spelling. In addition, the category "handwriting" from the Italian
investigation has been added (Table 2).

A student who scores low across the board will receive ten points. The maximum
score is fifty points. The model provides indications of how to score in each category.
Here are two examples of instructions concerning the rather vague factor I, flavor
or style.

(6) (flavor, high)
     (...) The writer seems quite sincere and candid, and he writes about something
     he knows, often from personal experience. You could not mistake this writing
     for the writing of anyone else (...)

(7) (flavor, low)
     The writer reveals himself well enough but without meaning to. His thoughts
     and feelings are those of an uneducated person who does not realize how bad
     they sound (...)

Table 2.   Diederich's judgment model

	Low		Middle		High
I General Merit					
Ideas	2	4	6	8	10
Organization	2	4	6	8	10
Wording	1	2	3	4	5
Flavor, Style	1	2	3	4	5
II Mechanics					
Usage	1	2	3	4	5
Punctuation	1	2	3	4	5
Spelling	1	2	3	4	5
Handwriting	1	2	3	4	5

With this judgment model it is relatively easy to get a score of the judge's first impression, which can then be compared to that of another judge. When an essay receives different scores from different judges, the model also makes it possible to determine swiftly which factors are the cause of the difference.

So far, only pedagogical applications have been discussed. However, other applications have also been investigated. Most of the research has focused on informative texts. A good example is the following judgment model, which was developed on the basis of comments made by experts and lay people in discussions on discourse quality (Table 3).

The CCC model is based on three criteria: correspondence, consistency and correctness. It can be used to evaluate discourse quality. The first criterion, correspondence, is the most important one. By correspondence is meant that the quality of a text is only good if the sender achieves his goal and if the text fills a need on the part of the receiver. Therefore, the quality of a text is to a great extent based on the interplay – the correspondence – between sender goals and receiver needs. When searching for the balance between sender and receiver, there are various choices. This explains the second criterion: consistency. The quality of a text is greatly affected by the sender's ability to maintain the choices made (a principle of structure, a manner of wording, layout, etc.). The third criterion, correctness, requires the text to contain no mistakes, whether in content or in form; for example, the text should not contain any false information or an incorrect choice of words.

The three criteria are applied to the five levels that can be distinguished in discourse analysis: text type, content, structure, wording, and presentation. The CCC model thus contains fifteen evaluation points that can be used with any text type. The evaluation points have to be worked through from top to bottom and from left to right. This means, for example, that if a certain text type turns out not to be the

Table 3.   The CCC model for text evaluation

	Correspondence	Consistency	Correctness
A Text type	1 Appropriateness	2 Purity of genre	3 Application of genre rules
B Content	4 Sufficient information	5 Agreement between facts	6 Correctness of facts
C Structure	7 Sufficient coherence	8 Consistent structure	9 Correct linking words
D Wording	10 Appropriate wording	11 Unity of style	12 Correct syntax and choice of words
E Presentation	13 Appropriate layout	14 Layout adapted to text	15 Correct spelling and punctuation

appropriate means of communication, evaluation after the first point of evaluation under text type is hardly useful. And if the text is lacking in quality as far as content is concerned, then evaluation of the wording will have to be postponed until the content has been improved.

The CCC model can be used to obtain a clearly structured ordering of various reader comments. Moreover, the model and the fixed order of five times three evaluation points make a systematic and well-reasoned analysis possible. This is the most important gain over more subjective and unsystematic analyses, in which it is often unclear according to which criteria a discourse is being judged. However, it must be said that the model is not suitable for analyzing every type of discourse (for example, argumentative discourse). Moreover, the same holds true for this model as for the Diederich model: quality judgments can differ greatly.

The model is meant to facilitate the discussion of differences in judgment. Since it is a fairly abstract basic model, it needs to be concretized per text type. Moreover, the fifteen evaluation points can be subdivided. For example, "appropriate wording" (evaluation point 10) can be differentiated in comprehensibility, attractiveness, terseness and tone. The first two dimensions speak for themselves; the third has to do with "word economy", and the fourth with a wording that matches the content and the communication situation.

Negative comments on the choice of words pertain to a transgression towards the writer or the reader. For example, a text can fail on the comprehensibility dimension when a writer puts too little effort into adjusting to the reader's knowledge level; then it is too difficult. On the other hand, a writer can adjust too much as well. Then the text becomes too easy. The correspondence criterion means that one can make mistakes "towards both sides". In Table 4 the four dimensions are summed up in the middle column, with the effect of a transgression towards the writer on the left-hand side and towards the reader on the right-hand side.

Table 4.   Subdivision of evaluation point 10, appropriate wording

too close to the writer				too close to the reader
too difficult	<	comprehensibility	>	too easy
too boring	<	attractiveness	>	too familiar
too terse	<	terseness	>	too long-winded
too detached	<	tone	>	too informal

10.4 The improvement of documents

One of the most important problems confronting students of discourse studies is how to improve discourse that is not satisfactory. Or, to give a concrete example, how can discourse that is too difficult for the target group be simplified? The previous sections have shown that improving the comprehensibility of discourse involves more than simply shortening sentences. Examples of this are given in research done by Alice Davison and Robert Kantor (1982). They demonstrated that splitting a compound sentence may actually make discourse more complicated.

(8) a. If given a chance before another fire comes, the tree will heal its own wounds by growing new bark over the burned part.
     b. If given a chance before another fire comes, the tree will heal its own wounds. It will grow new bark over the burned part.

Example (8b) is a rewritten version of (8a); the subordinate clause has been converted into a full sentence. The effect of this conversion, however, is the removal of the discourse relation "means", thereby leaving it up to the reader to make the correct inference. In this case the rewritten version (8b) is more difficult than the original (8a).

An illustration of what discourse quality improvement entails can be found in Britt-Louise Gunnarsson (1984). Gunnarsson does not limit herself to the clarification of terminology or the simplification of sentences. Central to her approach is "functional comprehensibility", which means that discourse is only comprehensible to readers if it is possible for them to derive all of the information required. What is at issue here is not so much the semantic or syntactic characteristics of discourse (the terminology and the sentence structures) but the pragmatic factors. When simplifying discourse, one must ascertain in what way discourse functions for the reader. Readers using a legal discourse must be able to quickly find that part of the law that is applicable to their given circumstances, and furthermore be able to select the relevant articles of the law. Subsequently, they must be able to comprehend what those articles state and understand what the consequences are for their situation and any acts they may have committed.

When simplifying a legal discourse, one must take all these factors into consideration. Only then can semantic and syntactic simplifications have an effect. An example of a legal discourse is given below, followed by Gunnarsson's rewritten version.

(9) a. Before an employer decides on important alteration to his activity, he shall, on his own initiative, negotiate with an organization of employees in relation to which he is bound by collective agreement. The same shall be observed before an employer decides on important alteration of work or employment conditions for employees who belong to the organization.

If urgent reasons so necessitate, the employer may make and implement a decision before he has fulfilled his duty to negotiate under the first part of this section.

(9) b.   The employer's duty   *Where an employer is bound by a collective*
           to initiate negotiations   *agreement with an organization of employees and*
           before making   *where the employer plans*
           a decision   – *an important alteration to his operations, or*
                                        – *an important alteration to the working condi-*
                                            tions or conditions of employment of an em-
                                            ployee who is a member of the organization:
                                        The employer shall himself initiate negotiations
                                        on the planned alteration with the organization
                                        of employees and conclude these negotiations
                                        before making a decision on the alteration.
                                        If exceptional circumstances arise such that the
                                        employer cannot postpone making and implement-
                                        ing the decision:
                                        The employer may make and implement the
                                        decision before negotiating.

The typographical changes and the additions in (9b) were meant to simplify the search procedure. Readers can first read the situation description to see whether it is relevant to their own circumstances. It should be noted that the semantic and syntactic changes were kept to a minimum.

But is discourse, rewritten in this manner, also more comprehensible? Gunnarsson investigated this using three groups of subjects: employers, union officials and lawyers. Of, in total, more than 250 subjects, one half were given the original version and the other half the rewritten version. The comprehensibility was measured by asking questions about the text. The subjects given the rewritten version generally had more correct answers than those given the original one. The differences, however, were not great. On the other hand, it was observed that lawyers scored higher on both versions than union officials and that the latter did better than the employees. Evidently, the prior knowledge that subjects have of the topic at hand and the experience they have in reading this type of discourse are important factors in discourse comprehension. A reader with a good deal of prior knowledge can, on the basis of this, achieve a higher score on a discourse-comprehension test.

In many cases rewriting or restyling a document has only a slight positive effect on the comprehension of discourse. There are many factors in the discourse situation that are influential. Not only the addressees' prior knowledge and their motivation to obtain the information are important, but also the situation in which the message is conveyed. Then new questions arise, for example: "Is the message conveyed using the right discourse type at the right moment?" or "Is it really the case that readers have access to the information they consider important?" Questions like these form the basis for a more sociological approach to the analysis of information flow.

An important key to gaining insight into the discourse situation of informative documents is the communication audit, which is specifically used in the field of organizational communication. The communication audit is a questionnaire survey with which researchers can retrieve data on the communicative health of a company. The ICA, the International Communication Association, has developed a questionnaire that must be filled in by employees and that gives an overview of the type of information employees produce and receive. Below are some questions and statements that, in most cases, have to be answered or reacted to using a five-point Likert scale (1 = very little, and 5 = very great).

(10)   A selection from the ICA communication audit
  1a   What is the amount of information I receive now about how organization decisions are made that affect my job?
  1b   What is the amount of information I need to receive about how organization decisions are made that affect my job?
  2a   What is the amount of information I send now asking for clearer work instructions?
  2b   What is the amount of information I need to send asking clear work instructions?
  3   I have a say in decisions that affect my job.
  4   I am satisfied with my organization's overall communicative efforts.
  5   What is the amount of information I receive now by intranet?
  6   What is the amount of information I need to receive via bulletin boards?

Using such questions and data about the specific jobs in a company, the (lack or excess of) information can be mapped out in detail, especially if questions concerning specific topics on which information is needed are asked as well.

How can this communication audit research contribute to the improvement of information flow and to the function of informative discourse? To conclude this chapter, one example is given. Hargie, Tourish and Wilson (2002) report the results of a communication audit of a health services department with a staff of 4,000 people on different unconnected facilities. Senior management had received many complaints about the communication and the task performance, so employees were invited to analyze the communication climate and make suggestions for improving communication. They used a questionnaire with 77 items and selected a sample population that was representative of all subgroups in the organization. All answers showed that the staff expressed a significant need for more information. Therefore, it was recommended that the newsletter be revised and sent to all staff members' home addresses. Furthermore, it was suggested that the Chief Executive Officer should write a monthly letter (also sent to the staff's home addresses) stating key decisions made by the Trust Board, and that he should pay regular visits to all the subdepartments.

The recommendations mentioned above sparked a discussion on the widely held belief in communication studies that getting information prompts the need for more information. Is it perhaps the case that employees complain about a lack of information simply because they always want more? If this hypothesis were true, then the recommendations would not result in a more "satisfied" communication climate. Therefore, the communication audit was conducted again two years after implementation of the new initiatives. On the five-point scales employees indicated less need for information than they had two years earlier. So the findings did not support the "cumulating-information-need" hypothesis. The initial and the follow-up audit show that this research is a good example of how communication flows in a company can be improved and how hypotheses of information need can be tested. This approach, focusing on the discourse situation, is a useful completion of the trials to improve the discourse itself.

Questions and assignments

Questions

10.1.1   Apply Flesch's formula to two passages from this book and compare the results to your own intui-
tive judgment.

10.1.2   Name two elements that should be incorporated in readability formulas in order to make judgments on the cohesion between sentences possible.

10.2.1   Which objections can be raised against collecting readers' assessments as a method for the measurement of understanding?

10.2.2   Comment on the methods of measuring understanding mentioned in Section 10.2. Which
method would you prefer? Explain why.

10.3.1   Study the following comments and indicate under which evaluation points of the CCC model they
should be categorized. Give reasons for your answer. (If a comment can be categorized under
more than one evaluation point, choose the highest, i.e., the lowest in number.)
   a.   I think it is inappropriate to use the word "see" in a text for blind people.
   b.   I think something has been deleted in the transition to the next paragraph.
   c.   This paragraph speaks of "timely delivery". At the end of the text it says "delivery within two
        weeks".
   d.   I do not know the use of that figure is at this place in the text.
   e.   In my opinion, something like that should never be included in the minutes.
   f.   I think "Dear Sir" at the beginning of this letter is rather distant. And actually I think a letter
        is not appropriate at all.
   g.   Why does the writer refute this authoritative counterargument with only one sentence?
   h.   I think you should not refer to "waitresses" with "canteen staff".
   i.   The word "facultymeeting" does not exist; it has to be "faculty meeting".

10.4.1   Hargie, Tourish and Wilson (2002) found that employees with higher levels of training in communication skills also had higher reported levels of satisfaction with communication.

Assignments

10.2.1   Construct a text in which function words have been left out. Find subjects of various ages, and
have them fill in the missing words. Discuss and try to explain the possible differences in results
between younger and older people.

10.2.2 Have people apply the plus-minus method to a text of your choice and try to categorize their remarks on content, structure, formulation and presentation (spelling and punctuation marks).

10.3.1 Analyze a text of your choice with respect to the four aspects of appropriate wording in the CCC model (evaluation point 10). Try to prove that "attractiveness" and "tone" are sometimes difficult to distinguish.

10.4.1 Find a short text that, in your own opinion, is of poor quality and, using the knowledge you have gained from this chapter, attempt to improve it.

Bibliographical information

10.1   A good overview of readability formulas is provided by Duffy (1985) and Davison and Green (1988). The passages for which the readability formulas have been calculated are taken from Kintsch and Vipond (1979).

Despite all the objections raised against readability formulas, the popularity of the Flesch formula has remained quite high. In the State of Massachusetts, insurance contracts are required by law to score at least 50 on the Flesch scale (Massachusetts, General Laws Annotated 175, 1985, Section 26, supplement).

10.2   For more information on the cloze test, see Klein-Braley (1982). For an overview of various methods in the measurement of understanding, see De Jong and Schellens (1997). Schriver (1997) is a good publication on document design and it presents material for discussing the various methods measuring understanding. An overview of the research being done into discourse understanding is given in Britton and Black (1985).

10.3   For a further study of the quality of discourse, see Dillon (1981). A good collection of articles in this field is provided by Van Waes, Woudstra and Van den Hoven (1994). See also Lentz and Pander Maat (1997) for an overview of important questions concerning text quality. Yang (1989) is a nice example of some interesting research that can serve as a subject for an essay or thesis. See for the CCC model Renkema (2001).

10.4   Improving the quality of discourse involves more than simply applying readability formulas or shortening sentences. In research done by Davison and Kantor (1982) examples of this are given.

For more information on the ICA communication audit, see Downs and Goldhaber (1994), who give a concise review of the audit and list items of the survey questionnaire.

11 Narratives

11.1 The structure of fairy tales

In 1928, a study of magical fairy tales by the Russian scholar Vladimir Propp appeared. This publication, which only attracted attention after the appearance of a second English translation in 1968, became an important point of departure for research into narrative structures. Propp showed with his analysis that while fairy tales have varied motifs and topics, there is a consistency of structure underlying this variety. Propp's examples included the following taken from a set of one hundred fairy tales that he had studied.

(1) Variety of topics
1. A czar gives an eagle to a hero.
2. An old man gives Súĉenko a horse.
3. A sorcerer gives Ivan a little boat.
4. A princess gives Ivan a ring.

At first glance there would appear to be a great deal of variation, and yet all the stories are about something being given to a hero or to the story's protagonist. Only the names and the attributes are different. Propp stated that there are always seven characters that may appear in 31 functions or domains of activity. The seven characters are the following.

(2) The characters in fairy tales
1. Villain
2. Donor
3. Helper (magical agent)
4. Princess or person looked for
5. Dispatcher
6. Hero
7. False Hero

A function is defined by Propp as: "An act/deed on the part of a character, determined from the vantage point of the meaning of that act for the course of events." A function is actually the act plus the location of that act in the fairy tale. When, for example,

Ivan marries the czar's daughter at the end of the story, the act of "marriage" is equal to the marriage between the father of a princess and a widow located in the middle of another story. These two acts do, however, differ in meaning as they are located at different positions in the course of events. The function can only be determined by looking at the location of the act relative to the entire fairy tale.

It is not necessary to mention all 31 functions at this point. In the following overview a number of relevant functions are given.

(3) Functions in magical fairy tales according to Propp
1. *Absentation.* One of the members of a family absents himself from home.
2. *Interdiction.* An interdiction is addressed to the hero.
3. *Violation.* The interdiction is violated.
4. *Reconnaissance.* The villain makes an attempt at reconnaissance.
5. *Delivery.* The villain receives information about his victim.
6. *Trickery.* The villain attempts to deceive his victim in order to take possession of him or his belongings.
7. *Complicity.* The victim submits to deception and thereby unwittingly helps his enemy.
8. *Villainy.* The villain causes harm or injury to a member of a family.
8a. *Lack.* One member of a family either lacks something or desires to have something.
9. *Mediation, the connective incident.* Misfortune or lack is made known; the hero is approached with a request or command; he is allowed to go or he is dispatched.
10. *Beginning counteraction.* The seeker agrees to or decides upon counteraction.
11. *Departure.* The hero leaves home.
12. *The first function of the donor.* The hero is tested, interrogated, attacked, etc., which prepares the way for his receiving either a magical agent or helper.
13. *The hero's reaction.* The hero reacts to the actions of the future donor.
14. *Provision or receipt of a magical agent.* The hero acquires the use of a magical agent.
15. *Guidance.* The hero is transferred, delivered, or led to the whereabouts of an object of search.
(...)
30. *Punishment.* The villain is punished.
31. *Wedding.* The hero is married and ascends the throne.

The functions can be grouped as follows. First, there are preliminaries (1 through 7) after which follows a "complication" (8 through 11), then a "development" (from 12 on) in which a donor and a helper act. Finally, there is a "denouement", which can end with a marriage.

Propp's analysis can be criticized at certain points. Many fairy tales do not have a structure that consists of 31 functions in a fixed order. It has been stated that Propp was actually looking for the model of a fairy tale. This model fairy tale has as its theme a hero liberating a princess who is being held by a dragon. Because Propp was working towards this proto-tale in his analyses, he must have interpreted many phenomena in an unusual manner, or ignored them altogether. Despite this criticism, Propp's work formed the initiative towards a more formalized analysis of stories, which deals with the structures that form the foundation of the variety in topics and motifs.

11.2   The sociolinguistic approach

William Labov and Joshua Waletzky (1967) took an entirely different approach by asking the question "How do people tell each other stories in everyday life?" The purpose of this investigation was to find out if there were correlations between the social characteristics of storytellers and the structure of their stories. For this purpose, Labov and Waletzky collected stories from people belonging to different social classes. The issue of structural differences was not resolved. The investigation did, however, provide information on the structure of everyday narratives.

Labov and Waletzky elicited stories from 600 subjects by asking them if they had ever been in mortal danger. Here are two examples taken from the material they collected.

(4) A: Have you ever been in mortal danger?
     B: 1. yeh I was in the Boy Scouts at the time
         2. and we was doing the 50-yard dash
         3. racing
         4. but we was at the pier, marked off
         5. and so we was doing the 50-yard dash.
         6. there was about 8 or 9 of us, you know, going down, coming back
         7. and, going down the third time, I caught cramps
         8. and I started yelling: "Help!"
         9. but the fellows didn't believe me, you know,
        10. they thought I was just trying to catch up, because I was going on or slowing down
        11. so all of them kept going
        12. they leave me

13. and so I started going down
14. scoutmaster was up there
15. he was watching me
16. but he didn't pay me no attention either
17. and for no reason at all there was another guy, who had just walked up that minute ...
18. he just jumped over
19. and grabbed me.

(5) A: Have you ever been in mortal danger?
     B: Yes
     A: What happened?
     B: I'd rather not talk about it
     A: Could you tell me as much as possible?
     B: 1. Well this guy had been drinking too much
         2. and he attacked me
         3. and my friend came in
         4. and ended it.

In the analysis, a distinction was made between the story, the actual order of events, and the plot, the order of events as they occur in the story. The second story could also be told as follows.

(5) a. 3. My friend came in
         4. just in time to stop
         1. a guy who had too much to drink
         2. from attacking me.

This version is not a story but a report of events that took place in real order. By comparing the differences between real and narrative order, Labov and Waletzky arrived at a five-component general story structure.

(6) Labov and Waletzky's story structure
     1. Orientation
     2. Complication
     3. Evaluation
     4. Solution
     5. Coda

In the orientation information is given about the characters, the place, the time and the situation. See example (4), lines [1] to [7]. This orientation is not obligatory, as can be seen in example (5). Labov and Waletzky point out that this component is often left out of stories told by children and adults with limited verbal skills.

The complication is the main component of a story. In (4) this is [7] to [13]. This component usually ends with a result as in [3] in (5); it ends the complicating action of [1,2] in this example. Labov and Waletzky concede that it is often difficult to extract the result from a story. It is also necessary to look at the meaning of the sentences.

In order for a story to be complete, it must contain an evaluation. Story (4) would not be complete if it ended with [13]. It is in [14, 15, 16] that the storyteller makes it clear what the significance of the story is. It is also at this point that he can provide a solution to the tension that was created in the complication component. The evaluation can, for that matter, coincide with the solution to the complication. If a storyteller ends the complication component with a sentence such as "Well, I almost got killed", then this can be viewed as an evaluating statement.

After the evaluation comes the solution, as in the case of [17, 18, 19] in (4). Sometimes it coincides with the evaluation. If a story ends with "I almost got killed", then the solution is also being given, namely, that the first-person narrator is not dead. In some of the stories collected by Labov and Waletzky, they also encountered a number of closing sentences, the coda, with which the narrator returned, as it were, to the moment that the story began; for example: "Well, that's the way it happened."

Using this analytical model, Labov and Waletzky aimed to find out if there was a correlation between the narrator's social characteristics and the structure of his stories, but were not able to find one. Labov and Waletzky's story structure does provide a good general framework for the analysis of stories, but for a detailed analysis more precise distinctions are necessary. An attempt to make these distinctions has been made from the psycholinguistic perspective.

11.3   The psycholinguistic approach

In the psycholinguistic approach, rules similar in type to the phrase-structure rules used in generative grammar have been suggested for describing the structure of a story. The structure that forms the foundation of a story can then be rendered in a story grammar.

(7)   Story grammar rules
      story → setting, episode
      episode → beginning, development, ending
      development → complex reaction, goal path

A story consists of a setting plus an episode. The setting (see also Section 3.4) and the episode are in some respects similar to the orientation and the complication in Labov and Waletzky's analysis. The episode is divided into the beginning, the development, and the ending. The development consists of a complex reaction and a goal path. A classic example of a story grammar is given in a study by John Mandler and Nancy Johnson (1977) in which they analyzed the following story.

(8) Dog Story
1. It happened that a dog had got a piece of meat
2. and was carrying it home in his mouth.
3. Now on his way home he had to cross a plank lying across a stream.
4. As he crossed he looked down
5. and saw his own shadow reflected in the water beneath.
6. Thinking it was another dog with another piece of meat,
7. he made up his mind to have that also.
8. So he made a snap at the shadow,
9. but as he opened his mouth the piece of meat fell out,
10. dropped into the water,
11. and was never seen again.

(9) Structure of the Dog Story (8)

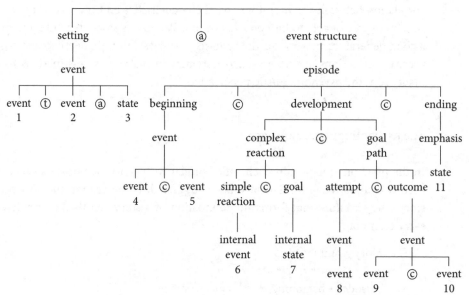

The complex reaction can be divided into a simple reaction and a goal. The goal path consists of an attempt and an outcome. The *a*, *c*, and *t* refer to the type of relationship between events: temporal if the events are sequential – the *and* (a) and *then* (t) relations – and causal if there is a causal connection between the events – the cause (c) relation. The final terms are always a state or an event. The numbers refer to the elements in the story itself.

Mandler and Johnson provide arguments to explain why some parts of a story are retained in memory better than other parts. They had subjects retell the story of the dog. This showed that the setting and the result, the elements [1, 2, 3 and 9, 10] in example (8), were easily retained. With other stories, it emerged that the best results in retelling were achieved when the following six components were stressed: setting, beginning, reaction, attempt, result, and ending. Mandler and Johnson concluded, on the basis of these results, that readers assume the existence of a structure consisting of these six elements.

Prompted by the psycholinguistic approach to narratives, the question of what constitutes a story has also been addressed. In the opinion of some researchers, Robert Wilensky (1983), for example, it is the occurrence of one or more "story-points". These are the aspects of a story that attract the interest of the reader. Wilensky provided the following examples.

(10) John was hungry. He went to a restaurant and ordered a hamburger. When the check came, he paid it and left.

(11) John loved Mary and he asked her to marry him. She agreed and they got married. Then one day John met another woman and fell in love with her. John didn't want to hurt Mary's feelings because he still felt a great deal for her and they got along well. But day after day he could think of nothing but his new love.

Text (10) is not a story as it has no "point", no element that attracts interest. Text (11), on the other hand, does contain such an element, and it is for this reason that it can be called a story. (10) could, of course, be converted into a story by stating that the hamburger was poisoned. This would, however, mean adding a point. Mandler and Johnson assumed that the goal element was an essential part of a story. In story (8) the goal element is: "He made up his mind to have that also." The goal criterion can, however, lead to difficulties. The two stories about the man in the bus given in Section 8.1 would then not qualify as stories; they do not have a goal.

In the literature on narratives, stories are defined in a number of different ways. One of the most important criteria is that a story must have characters or at least a main character or protagonist. This would, however, mean that the following text does not qualify as a story.

(12)   There was darkness and there was silence. Then, one day, the sun rose and the birds began to sing and the darkness and silence disappeared.

Research done by Nancy Stein and Margaret Policastro (1984) showed that it is impossible to compose a list of constant story characteristics. It has, however, become clear that subjects are apt to view a discourse as a story if it contains a protagonist or when events are presented in a causal relationship. Example (12) would then qualify as a story as it meets the second criterion: the rising of the sun makes the darkness disappear and the birds' singing ends the silence.

11.4   The organizational approach

Stories are studied from many different perspectives, including science of literature, rhetoric, linguistics, socio- and psycholinguistics, psychiatry and anthropology. A relatively new approach stems from a sociological framework, from the ethnography of communication, which is the study of discourse in relation to the social and cultural context. In this approach the term *narrative* is often used instead of *story*. In this view not only general verbal interaction but specifically narratives can tell us how people relate to each other and how they use narratives to position themselves as members of a group, a family, a religious communion, a school, a company or a nation. These narratives contain many values, beliefs and morals that are part of the culture of the group in question. Narratives are not only a resource for cultural and group-bound norms, they also serve as a creator of and an intermediary for those norms when they are told and told again.

It is important to note here that the stories under consideration are not personal stories (like the ones Labov and Waletsky collected; see Section 11.2), but stories that are told by fellow students about a school activity, or by members of a company about a narrow escape during a hostile take-over or narratives about the founder of a religious community. If one knows these narratives and can tell them to new members or is able to comment on the content during meetings, then that is seen as a proof of membership of that group.

Narratives are always heard from someone else; they are so-called non-participant narratives. The narrator of a non-participant narrative is neither a participant in the reported event nor a witness of what has happened. The narrator tells something that is stored in the collective memory of a group through rehearsed telling, just as stories about national history are stored in the memory of all fellow countrymen through history lessons. In doing so, the narrator establishes or confirms his social identity as a group member.

A field of research in which this view of stories has come up in recent decades is organizational or institutional studies. In every organization or corporation many stories are told. They serve as support in carrying out the work that has to be done (selling products, nursing patients, lecturing students, etc.), and they help to create the identity or the culture of an organization and its employees.

In this new field various research questions are dealt with. Two questions raised in research conducted by Linde (1993) are discussed here. Linde collected many life stories and narratives told in companies, for example, during a three-year ethnographic study at an American insurance company. She analyzed narratives in company training programs and staff meetings, etc. The examples below stem from Linde's material. The first question is: On the basis of what kind of discourse phenomena can we distinguish between a participant narrative and a non-participant narrative? Below are two narratives in which employees answered the question "How did you get this job?"

(13)   Uh, I started out in Renaissance studies, but I didn't like any of the people I was working with, and at first I thought I would just leave Y and go to another university, uh but a medievalist at Y university asked me to stay or at least reconsider whether I should leave or not, and um pointed out to me that I had done very well in the medieval course that I took with him and that I seemed to like it, and he was right. I did. And he suggested that I switch fields and stay at Y and that's how I got into medieval literature.

(14)   When this group started a couple of years – three years ago, the f- the five or six engineers who were already here felt that they wanted an interface person. They wanted somebody to take all those decisions off their hands. They didn't want to have to make them, they didn't feel qualified to make them, whatever. And so they actually pushed their manager who pushed his manager who was unwilling to spend money on an interface designer and they actually made this huge pitch to him that they wanted to have somebody there. And so that was when I was hired. And so they themselves made the decision that they wanted me to come here.

By using the notion of perspectivization (as defined in Section 7.3), and more specifically that of focalization, it is possible to determine whether examples (13) and (14) are non-participant narratives. In (13) the "I" is active from the start. In (14) the focus is on the events that took place prior to the point in time at which the "I" was hired. In (14) the narrator does not speak about himself, in (13) he does. The subject of focalization in (13) is the narrator, while in (14) this holds true for the narrator's colleagues.

Another question is: How can we detect whether or not the narrator establishes himself as a member of a group? Below are some passages from other stories.

(15) I don't know if it has – no I'm sure Robert wasn't involved. I'm sure Robert wasn't involved. I'm sure. I'm sure it was – what I imagine is a meeting with Nancy and Pete and Suzanne.

(16) Well it's because somebody's got a private agenda to have the back end be different and somebody else in the human interface group has got a – a private agenda to build the world's most complicated but funkiest looking front end.

In her analyses Linde used concepts like *evidentials* and *opacity*. With evidentials words or phrases are meant that indicate the extent to which the speaker believes that what he has said is proved, for example, *apparently* and *I guess*. Evidentials can be divided into evidentials of knowing (*I am sure*) and evidentials of not knowing (*I don't know*). Opacity denotes a critical representation of a person's action in a narrative, for example, "The boss, mean as he always was …" or "The head of my department who never understood what was going on …" Linde suggested that in narratives that function as member establishment, evidentials of not knowing and opacity seldom occur. That means that examples like (15) and (16) are most likely to be found in narratives of a speaker who is not a member of the group. This field of narrative analysis constitutes a special supplement to already existing research approaches, particularly because in this case the social function of the story is central.

Questions and assignments

Questions

11.1.1   Point out Propp's first seven functions in the fairy tale Little Red Riding Hood. What does it say about Propp's model that the functions given in (3) do not occur in the "correct" order in this particular fairy tale?

11.1.2   Below is a passage from a Russian fairy tale followed by a "Proppian" analysis, in simplified form.
Three brothers go for a walk in the garden and find an enormous stone. The strongest, Ivan the Cow's son, is able to lift the stone. A cellar is laid bare containing horses and suits of armor. The brothers go to their father and tell him that they are going on a journey with the horses. They meet Baba Yaga and tell her that they heard about a dragon which has been laying waste the land.

Analysis

11   Departure: The three brothers walking in the garden
12   First function of the donor; the hero is tested: The brothers find a stone and one of them tries to lift it.
13   The hero's reaction: Ivan succeeds in lifting the stone.
14   The reception of a magical tool: Ivan finds the horses and the suits of armor.
8   Villainy: The dragon destroys the land.

Do you agree with this analysis? If not, what would you change?

11.1.3   Does the analysis model developed by Propp refer to the macrostructure or superstructure (see Sections 5.3 and 5.4)?

11.2.1   Apply Labov and Waletzky's story structure to Little Red Riding Hood and indicate which parts are problematic.

11.2.2   Where are the evaluation and the solution in the story example given in (5)?

11.2.3   Analyze the dog story in Section 11.3 using Labov and Waletzky's story components.

11.3.1   Provide criticism of the term *story grammar* with reference to the remarks made in the answer to question 8.3.1.

11.4.1   Do evidentials and opacity phenomena occur in narrative (13)? What can you infer from your answer about the aspect of member establishment of this narrative?

Assignments

11.1.1 Just as Propp has done for fairy tales, try to construe a set of basic characters for another genre such as action movies. See, for example, Eco (1966) who analyzed James Bond stories and arrived at a number of basic characters and a standard story consisting of nine steps.

11.2.1 Collect ten stories from friends and colleagues with the question "Have you suffered grievous wrongs?", and analyze them according to Labov and Waletzky's five-component story structure.

11.3.1 Try to write a story that does not contain a protagonist or causal relationships. Point out the instances where (and explain why) it goes wrong.

11.4.1 Using Labov and Waletzky's story components, try to analyze one story that you must know in order to belong, for example, to your family or classmates/fellow students.

11.4.2 Write fragment (14) from the participant perspective.

Bibliographical information

11.1 The work done by Propp has been translated into English under the title *Morphology of the Folktale* (1968). This title is too broad. Propp analyzed Russian fairy tales, not folktales in general. In the translation the Russian word for *adversary* is translated as *villain*, but in view of the examples that Propp provides, a more general term should be used.

In 1946 Propp wrote on the proto-fairy tale in *The Historic Roots of the Magical Fairy Tale*. A portion of this monograph has been translated into English (Propp, 1984). In this last publication, the much-maligned 31 set functions are no longer mentioned.

11.2 The study done by Labov and Waletzky appeared in 1967. For further study of the sociological viewpoint see the Ehlich anthology (1980). See Bamberg (1997) for an overview of thirty years of narrative analysis.

11.3 A good starting point for further study of the psycholinguistic approach to narratives is Vorderer et al. (1996). For a good example of research in this area, see Van den Broek et al. (2000). The last example in this section is from Prince (1981).

11.4 For more information on anthropological analysis of narratives in organizations, Orr (1996) serves as a good introduction. For further study of functions of stories and narrative identity, see Briggs (1996), Kyratzis (1999) and Schiffrin (1997).

12 Argumentation and persuasion

12.1　The structure of argumentation

In narrative discourse, discussed in the previous chapter, the expressive function is of primary importance. Speakers or writers wish to express what is going on in their minds. Using the terminology of the Organon model (see Section 2.1), this is the "symptom" aspect of language. In this chapter on argumentative discourse, the "appeal" function of language is central. Listeners or readers must be convinced of something. In the Organon model, this is the "signal" aspect.

A significant stimulus for contemporary argumentation research was the publication by the English philosopher Stephen Toulmin (1958) of a model that can be used for the analysis of argumentation in everyday language. In Toulmin's approach, the main issue is not the logical form of an argument but the question of how an argument is structured. Below is a representation of the model.

(1)　Toulmin's model

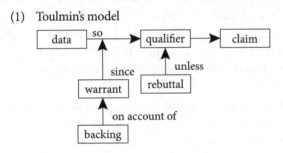

In this model, arguments are viewed as the motivation of a statement (the claim) by way of another statement (the data). The argumentative relationship between these two statements is called the warrant. See the following example.

(2)　Pete's door sign says "in". This means that he is at the university.

The claim that Pete is at the university is motivated by the fact that his sign says "in". In explicit argumentation, the data and the claim must be stated. The warrant and any possible backing can remain implicit. In the example above, they can be formulated as follows.

(3)   In general, anybody who is present makes sure his or her sign is in the "in" position (warrant).

(4)   Pete told me that this is always the first thing he does when he arrives (backing).

If the warrant does not provide a clear and definite link between the data and the claim, then a rebuttal can be made. Thus, a rebuttal can be expressed in a qualifier, which provides a measure of certainty:

(5)   Pete is here, unless he forgot to switch his door sign to "out" last night (rebuttal).

(6)   So Pete is probably here (qualifier).

Toulmin did not intend the model to serve as a general argumentation model. Nevertheless, it is included in many textbooks on argumentation because it is a good starting point for the analysis of argumentative discourse.

Toulmin's model has been subjected to criticism from many sides. One important objection was aimed at the artificiality of the distinctions between some elements in the model, for example, between the data and the warrant. An attack on the warrant can lead to new data and a new warrant in place of the old one that then serves as a new claim. In addition, the model does not distinguish between different types of data and warrants.

In argumentation analysis, a distinction is often made between three data types: data of the first, second and third order. First-order data are the convictions of the receiver; second-order data are claims by the source, and third-order data are the opinions of others as cited by the source. First-order data offer the best possibilities for convincing argumentation: the receiver is, after all, convinced of the data. Second-order data are dangerous when the credibility of the source is low; in that case third-order data must be resorted to.

Toulmin's model can be fine-tuned by distinguishing between the following warrant types: a. the motivational warrant; b. the authoritative warrant; c. the substantive warrant. To understand these different types of warrants, compare the statements after *as* in the following examples:

(7)   Every woman should have the right to decide for herself whether she wants an abortion. Therefore this abortion law, which conflicts with this right, cannot be ratified, as no law should infringe on the rights of the individual.

(8)   The Defense Department has announced that hostilities will soon cease. Peace is at hand. It is safe to draw this conclusion as the Defense Department is a reliable source.

Motivational warrants such as those in (7) link claim and data by expressing the benefit of the claim for the receiver. Authoritative warrants such as in (8) use the credibility of an authority to make the claim stick. There are several subtypes of substantive warrants, all based on systematic relationships between concepts in the external world, for example: "We are allowed to smoke here, because there is an ashtray on the table." A good example of a substantive warrant is a generalization such as in (9).

(9)   America's Vietnam policy has not brought world peace any closer. So America must remain neutral concerning internal conflicts in other countries. What proved true in Southeast Asia holds true for future conflicts.

It is likely that the type of warrant has an influence on the acceptability of the effect of an argument. If, for example, an individual is of the opinion that it is all right for laws to infringe on personal freedoms, then the argumentation in (7) will not be effective.

Using the fine-tuned version of Toulmin's model, it is possible to determine if the argumentation is sound. One of the characteristics of sound argumentation is that data and claim are linked by a warrant or possibly by backing. Sound argumentation makes it more likely that readers or listeners will think about the topic being discussed.

12.2   The pragma-dialectical approach

The structure of argumentation has been studied from a logical perspective. In this approach the focus is on the validity of arguments in reasoning from premises to a conclusion, as in syllogisms such as the famous example "All humans are mortal. Socrates is human. Therefore Socrates is mortal". Argumentation has also been studied from a rhetorical perspective. Then the focus is on argumentation techniques and their effectiveness for a certain audience. An example is the question whether, in defending a viewpoint, first the arguments of the opponent have to be disproved and then your own arguments presented or the other way round.

An approach that emerged in the last decades of the previous century is the "pragma-dialectical" perspective by Frans van Eemeren and Rob Grootendorst (1994). They based their work on notions taken from the fields of pragmatics and speech act theory (see Section 2.2). In their approach argumentation is viewed as part of a discussion in which the participants, the protagonist and the antagonist of a standpoint, exchange speech acts, the "moves" in a discussion; hence the notion *pragma* in this approach. The term *dialectic* stems from *dialectica*, in classical Greek, the art of reasoning with premises that though not incontrovertibly true, are generally accepted, such as "Exercise benefits your health". The antagonist then tries to ask questions that make the protagonist contradict his previous answers. The addition *dialectic* further indicates that argumentation is viewed as part of a critical discussion with rules that specify which moves contribute to eliminate a difference of opinion. Van Eemeren and Grootendorst introduced a code of conduct, a set of rules, for parties who want to act reasonably. Below are some examples from their set of ten rules.

(10) Some pragma-dialectic rules (Van Eemeren and Grootendorst)
  1. Parties must not prevent each other from advancing or casting doubt on standpoints.
  2. Whoever advances a standpoint is obliged to defend it if asked to do so.
  3. A person can be held to the premises he leaves implicit.
  4. A standpoint must be regarded as conclusively defended if the defence takes place by means of arguments in which a commonly accepted scheme of argumentation is correctly applied.

How do rules like these work out in debates? The next example is related to the third rule on implicit premises.

(11) John cannot do the dishes, because he has to vacuum the floor.

This argument is incomplete. If someone were to counter with the argument that John could first do the dishes and then vacuum the floor, the speaker would have to give another argument in order to support his original statement by stating a premise, for example, that John is only required to do one household chore. A listener could, however, deduce this implicit premise, this unspoken argument, from (11). This leaves the following questions: 1. How does a listener know that an argument has been left out? and 2. How can a listener know what that argument is?

These questions can be answered by assuming that the speaker is acting according to the cooperative principle and the accompanying maxims (see Section 2.4). A statement like (11) would seem to conflict with the cooperative principle. After all, owing to its incompleteness, statement (11) is invalid as an argument. Using the cooperative principle, the listener can deduce that the speaker meant to make a valid statement. In the opinion of Van Eemeren and Grootendorst, this is a conversational implicature (see again Section 2.4). The listener can, on the basis of the cooperative principle, know that an argument has been left out. Using the accompanying maxims, the missing argument can be searched for. This argument must not only be sufficiently informative (the maxim of quantity), but must also be a statement that, keeping the original statement in mind, can be defended (the maxim of quality). Of course, the additional argument must make the original statement valid; otherwise the original argument will not be a relevant contribution to the conversation (the maxim of relevance). On the basis of these maxims, listeners can now fill in an unspoken argument such as: "And he is only required to do one household chore." This is the premise a person can be held to following the third pragma-dialectal rule in (10).

The pragma-dialectical approach also offers a valuable contribution to the classical logical approach to argumentation, especially the research into the (ab)use of fallacies. Look at the following example.

> (12) In the long run there will not be enough food for the penguins at the South Pole, according to a study done by Greenpeace.

From the logical perspective, this is viewed as a fallacy. The truth of a statement is not after all linked to the fact that the source of the statement is an authority. Yet, it is a fallacy that is frequently accepted in everyday language. In Van Eemeren and Grootendorst's pragma-dialectical view, the conditions under which this fallacy is acceptable are accounted for. In their approach, the authority argument can be used if both discussion partners accept it as a proper argument. If an addressee rejects this type of argument, then the last discussion rule in (10) is violated. One example of a scheme of argumentation mentioned in this rule is the *argument ad verecundiam*. It may occur that an authority argument is accepted but that the addressee is of the opinion that the given authority is insufficiently qualified. In this situation, the last discussion rule in (10) has been transgressed: the scheme of argumentation is not applied correctly. Therefore, the fallacious appeal to authority can only be acceptable and, therefore, also convincing if the correct authority is cited and both conversational partners accept the authority argument. If one conversational participant states, for example, that Greenpeace is not an authority with respect to the South Pole, then the defender of the given viewpoint will be obliged to cite a more adequate authority or use another argument scheme.

12.3   The social-psychological approach

The clearest examples of argumentative discourse are discussions, advertisements and information pamphlets. The purpose of these forms of discourse is persuasion of the audience in thinking, feeling and acting. Since classical rhetoric (see Section 8.1) three main factors have been distinguished in persuading an audience: *logos, ethos* and *pathos*. The logos is the argumentation itself (the structure and the rules), as explained in the preceding sections of this chapter. The ethos (literally meaning *character*) is the personality of the orator, the image and all the other aspects that can have the function of enhancing the credibility of the orator, such as reputation and social status. Basically, it is everything about the speaker that influences the hearer's attitude towards the message. The pathos refers to all the emotions that an orator has to evoke in his audience in order to persuade.

Persuasive discourse research on attitudes and attitude changes is part of the body of research being done in the field of social psychology. Attitude, originally meaning *bodily position* or *physical orientation*, is used here as *mental posture*. A popular definition of attitude is: an evaluation a person holds with regard to himself, other people, objects, and issues. Within this broad concept different aspects can be distinguished, including, opinion, belief, preference, feeling and hope. Many researches use a threefold division into cognitive, affective and conative attitude. This division corresponds with thinking, feeling and planned action.

Attitudes are believed to be an important determiner of behavior. By changing attitudes, communicators hope to change the behavior of the recipients. In advertising, for example, the aim is to create a more positive evaluation of the product. This change in evaluation should result in a behavioral change: the purchase of the product.

The following example should make it clear which factors are important in this area of research. Suppose the following: opponents of abortion are to be convinced that abortion must be legalized in certain cases. In this case, as in any other persuasion process, four main factors are crucial in research into the effect of communication. These are the first four elements in the well-known research approach to communication of Harold Lasswell (1948): "Who? Says what? In which channel? To whom? To what effect?"

The first is the source (who?). The demands made on the source have to do with the credibility and what is called the likeability (sympathy/antipathy, like/dislike) the source evokes. A reputable hospital chaplain will convince people more effectively than a young woman who has just left an abortion clinic (credibility). If, however, the chaplain scores low on the likeability scale, this will have a negative effect on his or her persuasive abilities. A listener's attitude toward the source of communication has a good deal of influence on the likelihood of a shift in attitude concerning a specific issue.

The second major factor is the message (what?). Which arguments should be chosen? Should the con arguments be refuted or left out? In which order should the arguments be presented: the strong ones first, in the middle, or last? Which style would be most effective? And what kind of emotions does the message have to evoke: negative ones by way of scare tactics or fear appeals (for example, the medical dangers of non-legalized abortion), or more positive emotions (for example, that legalization diminishes medical dangers).

The third factor is the channel (in which channel?). Will opponents of abortion be more easily convinced when they read the persuasive message at their own pace or when they watch a television message with more nonverbal cues?

The fourth factor is the audience (to whom?). How much background knowledge does the receiver have about abortion, and what is the initial attitude? How involved is the reader or listener with the topic? Does he have the opportunity to inform himself? Does he have the ability and the motivation? And can he think critically about the pros and cons, or in other words, what is the degree of his need for cognition? Is the receiver male or female, old or young, educated or uneducated? After all, the same message can have an entirely different effect (which is the fifth factor) on young educated women than it does on older, less educated men, especially in the case of abortion.

In the discourse approach, the second major factor, the message, or more precisely the possible persuasive function of the form of the message, is the focus of attention. The research framework can be sketched using two models, the first one concerning the role of attitude in changing behavior, and the second one concerning the ways in which people change their attitudes.

Of course, attitude is not the only factor in the process of persuasion. The following model of planned behavior, designed by Icek Ajzen (1991), presents the relative function of attitude.

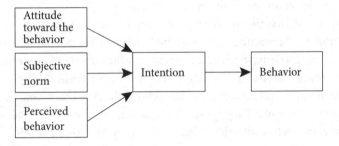

Figure 1. Ajzen's theory of planned behavior

Ajzen claims that attitude is one of the three determinants of behavior. Our behavior is also influenced by what is called a subjective norm (our belief about what others think we should do), and by the perceived behavior control (whether we think we could actually engage in a specific behavior). So, if someone tries to persuade you to study abroad for a half year, then not only is your attitude important, but also what your family and friends advise you to do (the subjective norm) and whether you think you will be able to organize it and feel happy at a foreign university (perceived behavior control). Very important is the distinction in this model between intention and behavior. Just having the intention to go abroad or to buy a new product is no guarantee for behavior. Hence, this is not a model about actual behavior but about planned behavior.

Ajzen's model of the role of attitude in changing behavior discussed above must be kept in mind when reading research on attitude change. The most widely used research model for attitude change by communication is the Elaboration Likelihood Model developed by Richard Petty and John Cacioppo (1986). Their model (see Figure 2) is based on the following idea: The variation in persuasive power is influenced by the likelihood that receivers will become preoccupied with the elaboration of the information presented. Elaboration in this case means the thought given to the topic.

The point of departure for the model is the idea that people are motivated to have correct attitudes. However, the amount of effort they are willing to put into evaluating the arguments of a persuasive message varies with individual and situational factors, in particular ability and motivation. If ability and motivation are high, people will devote a good deal of time and energy to scrutinizing the arguments. In this situation, they can only be persuaded by the force and quality of the arguments. However, motivation and ability are not sufficient. People must already have favorable or unfavorable thoughts on the topic of communication. Moreover, people must also adopt the newly acquired knowledge. If all of this is the case, a change in attitude occurs, which is said to have been reached through the "central route". This attitude change can be positive as well as negative, but either way it is relatively enduring and it is a good predictor of the behavior resulting from the attitude change.

When ability and motivation are low, people will not devote much energy to scrutinizing the arguments. The same holds true for people who are halfway on the central route, but have neutral thoughts on the subject of communication or do not adopt newly acquired knowledge. They can, nevertheless, be persuaded. Stimuli in the persuasion context can affect attitudes without necessitating the processing of the message arguments. They do so by triggering relatively primitive affective states that become associated with the object of the attitude. These stimuli, a pleasant style, for example, or the citing of expert sources or famous people, are called peripheral cues. If a change in attitude occurs, it is said to have been reached through the "peripheral route". When ability or motivation to scrutinize the arguments decreases, the chances of "peripheral cues" influencing the attitude increase. However, if no peripheral cues are present, the initial attitude is retained or regained.

The routes described here are prototypical. In reality, they do not occur in their pure form. Peripheral elements play a role in the central route. In the peripheral route, there is also a certain amount of elaboration. The routes are, however, complementary. As the likelihood of elaboration diminishes, the peripheral elements will have a more profound influence on the attitude change. Furthermore, the same persuasive message can have different effects on different people. Consider a persuasive message urging people to use public transportation, where the message contains strong arguments, but is poorly written. People who are not motivated or are unable to scrutinize the arguments will probably be negatively influenced by the clumsiness of the presentation, whereas people who are motivated and able to scrutinize the arguments could be positively influenced by the force of the arguments.

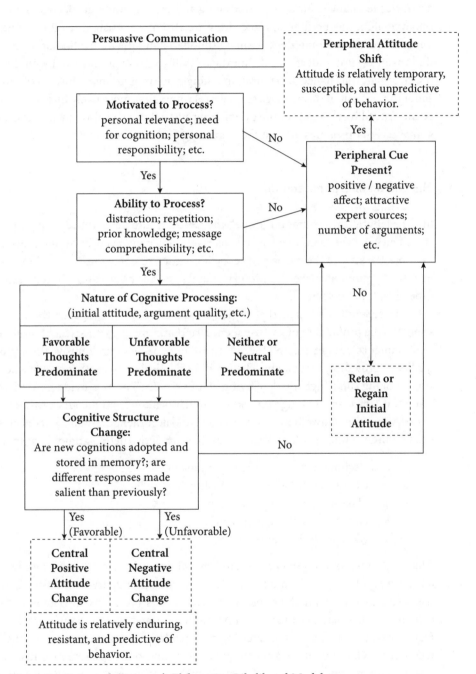

Figure 2. Petty and Cacioppo's Elaboration Likelihood Model

Attitude changes brought about along the central route go deeper than those achieved along the peripheral route. They are also more resistant to other influences. The level of elaboration is dependent on the ability and the motivation of the receiver. If receivers do not understand the message (ability) or are not involved with the topic (motivation), the chance of elaboration taking place is quite small. Instead of thinking about the content of the message (the central route), it is more likely that receivers will be influenced by elements of the peripheral route. This route also includes the factors *source* and *channel,* presented at the beginning of this section.

12.4   The quality of argumentation

In the Elaboration Likelihood Model, the central route deals with the quality of the arguments. In the peripheral route, receivers are convinced by other aspects, for example, the style of the message. The focus of much research into persuasion is on the quality of arguments in relation to peripheral cues. In this section two representative experiments are discussed.

It is generally assumed that argument quality has two aspects: the argument strength (the probability of a consequence) and argument valence (the desirability of a consequence). So, in arguing for or against an issue, one can improve the argument quality by providing a probability claim ("It is statistically proved that people who don't stop smoking run a higher risk of dying of lung cancer.") or by providing a desirability claim ("If you stop smoking you will feel much healthier."). Of course, this does not say anything about how to find or construct good arguments. If we look at debates and discussions, we find that four main techniques for constructing arguments emerge.

(13)   Four techniques for constructing arguments
1.   Give a reason, cause or explanation;
2.   Make a comparison, an analogy;
3.   Give an example or an instance;
4.   Name an authoritative source.

Along this line, four arguments for quitting smoking could be: 1. Your family seems quite susceptible to lung cancer since two of your grandparents died of it; 2. You tried hard to lower your cholesterol and succeeded, so you must also manage to quit smoking; 3. Use your brother as a role model; he managed to stop as well; 4. The Heart Foundation advises it. Interesting research has been done concerning the third technique. What would be more convincing: giving one representative instance or giving many instances? One would expect that many examples, presented as statistical evidence, would be more convincing than just one example that can only serve as anecdotal evidence. However, in many experiments researchers had to conclude that anecdotal evidence was more convincing than statistical evidence. In Baesler and Burgoon (1994) this result is explained by referring to an aspect of the peripheral route: the style. Anecdotal information is usually more concrete and vivid than statistical information. However, Baesler and Burgoon also found that vivid statistical evidence is more convincing than anecdotal evidence. So, vividness seems to be more important than the type of evidence.

Nonetheless, there is more at stake here, as was nicely demonstrated in an experiment by Hoeken (2001). Not only the vividness of the evidence, but also the type of claim may influence the persuasiveness of the evidence. As mentioned above, two types of claims can be distinguished: probability claims and desirability claims. A probability claim would be, for example, about the chances of juvenile delinquents growing up to be adult criminal offenders. A desirability claim would pertain, for example, to envisioning the undesirability of rheumatism.

Baesler and Burgoon already proved that, for a probability claim, the number of examples, hence statistical evidence, would be more convincing. But would the same hold true for a desirability claim? Hoeken chose as a topic a debate on raising local taxes so that more money could be spent on burglary prevention by putting extra streetlights on the sidewalks. He designed texts with different claims and different types of evidence. The two types of claims are given in (14). In (15) abbreviated examples are given of the two types of evidence (alike in vividness).

(14)   Two types of claims
  1.   *Probability claim*:
       Extra streetlights on the sidewalks will result in a sharp decrease in the
       number of burglaries.
  2.   *Desirability claim*:
       Burglaries have very undesirable consequences for the victims.

(15)   Two types of evidence
  1.   *Statistical*:
       (…) a survey by the Dutch Center for Mental Health (DCMH). In October
       last year the DCMH presented the results of a study conducted among 2,087
       victims of burglary. The study reported that burglars turn the house upside
       down, steal television sets and microwave ovens, and jewelry (which usually
       has a high sentimental value); 48% of the victims still need sleeping pills,
       65% repeatedly wake up suddenly, believing there is a burglar in the house,
       and even 21% of those who had a burglar alarm installed continue to be
       afraid of a new burglary.

2. *Anecdotal*:
   (…) the experiences of 62-year-old Mrs. Smith. In October last year burglars turned her house upside down while she was at her grandson's birthday party. Her microwave oven, television set, and jewelry (among which the wedding ring of her recently deceased husband) were stolen. Ever since, she has needed sleeping pills, but nevertheless she often awakes suddenly and feels certain there is a burglar in the house. Even the installation of a burglar alarm could not take away her fear of another burglary.

Different versions of a newspaper article were written, varying in claim and evidence, and were presented to subjects, who after reading had to answer on a seven-point scale such questions as "Raising taxes seems to me not sensible at all/very sensible". In this experiment it was found that in support of a desirability claim statistical evidence was more convincing than anecdotal evidence. For the probability claim there was no difference between the statistical and anecdotal evidence. In other words, giving more instances, statistical evidence, is more convincing, unless the claim itself has something statistical (probability claim). In that case one instance and many instances are equally convincing. So, persuasion is best served with statistical evidence in a vivid, concrete style.

The interaction between the central and the peripheral route, the content and the form, the argument quality and aspects of style, was also the focus of an experiment done by Hosman, Huebner and Siltanen (2002). They combined different styles with levels of argument quality. They chose a stylistic phenomenon that can indicate uncertainty about a standpoint, like "Uhm, it seems to me that this is not true" instead of "This is not true." This phenomenon is called hedging, meaning that the message is toned down. The texts were designed with a persuasive message supporting an increase in yearly parking fees at a university. Strong and weak arguments were selected and tested, and combined with a powerful style (without hedging) and a powerless style (with hedging). Below are two of the four possible examples (the hedgings are in italics).

(16) Low argument quality / powerful style
      A need exists to raise parking fees to $ 100 per year. Accordingly, the evidence suggests that there are valid reasons in support of such an increase. Initially, the money can be used to increase the number of existing university faculty members. (…) Likewise, in a poll conducted 3 years ago, the majority of faculty members indicated that they believed the university needed to hire more teachers.

(17) High argument quality / powerless style
A need exists to raise parking fees to $100 per year. Accordingly, the evidence *sort of* suggests that there are valid reasons in support of such an increase. *Uh* … initially, as reported in the Campus issues, Dr. James Carnahan, observed that, "in some cases there was a significant correlation between parking fee and condition of parking facilities." (…) Simply, an increase in parking fees is necessary … *um* … because it *might* enable existing facilities to be paved and repaired.

In this experiment one of the questions was whether style really functioned as a peripheral cue. From this experiment it was concluded that the style had no overall direct effect on persuasion. So, only the arguments matter: content goes before form. But, interestingly, the researchers found that a powerless style had a negative influence when a message contained weak arguments. This negative influence concerns not only the thoughts on the arguments but also the attitude toward the source. So, though style may be peripheral, it seems to be powerful as a technique in neutralizing a weak content. The form of a message does matter when in the process of argumentation and persuasion the content is problematic.

Questions and assignments

Questions

12.1.1 Analyze the following passage using Toulmin's model. Indicate the specific types of data and warrants.
The crops have failed again in Africa. There is danger of famine as the homegrown crops are the sole source of food. Africa is, after all, too poor to import food. Only swift help from the wealthy nations can avert a disaster.

12.1.2 Indicate the element in the Toulmin model under which A's utterances in the following fragment of conversation can be assigned.
A: The light bulb is burned out.
B: How do you know that?
A: The light isn't working.
B: So?
A: If the light doesn't work, it's because the light bulb is burned out.
B: But there could be other causes, couldn't there?
A: Yes, the electricity could be out. It would have been better to have said: The light bulb is probably burned out.
B: Why is your first assumption that it is the light bulb?
A: Light bulb filaments have a very limited life span as opposed to the other parts of a lamp and blackouts are rare.

12.2.1 What is the unspoken argument in the following argumentation?
He's home because his car is in the driveway.
Using the cooperative principle, explain why it is not necessary to state the unspoken argument.

12.2.2 If a literature professor takes part in a discussion of environmental issues by sending a letter to the editor and signing it as "Dr. So-and-so", which rule for the use of the authority argument is being broken?

12.3.1 Indicate which of the following terms belong to cognitive, affective or conative attitude: knowledge, intention to buy a product, sympathy, pleasure, belief.

12.3.2 Using your own examples, illustrate how the factors *source* and *channel* can influence attitude change.

12.3.3 Verify how the sixteen factors given in Hymes's SPEAKING model (see Section 3.4) can be classed using the four main factors in persuasive communication.

12.4.1 What would you advise a speaker or writer who has to convince someone and who has the choice between using statistical evidence and using anecdotal evidence? In which cases can that person use hedges?

Assignments

12.3.1 How would you incorporate logos, ethos and pathos in the Organon model (see Section 2.1)?

12.3.2 In their research into the Elaboration Likelihood Model, Petty and Cacioppo used a text that argued in favor of a senior comprehensive exam. They used versions of the text with arguments that had been determined to be strong or weak in previous investigations. Here are two examples of these arguments.

> *Senior comprehensive exam: Strong argument*
> The National Achievement Board recently revealed the results of a five-year study conducted on the effectiveness of comprehensive exams at Duke University. The results of the study showed that since the comprehensive exam has been introduced at Duke, the grade-point average of undergraduates has increased by 31%. At comparable schools without the exams, grades increased by only 8% over the same period. The prospect of a comprehensive exam clearly seems to be effective in challenging students to work harder and faculty to teach more effectively. It is likely that the benefits observed at Duke University could also be observed at other universities that adopt the exam policy.
>
> *Senior comprehensive exam: Weak argument*
> The National Achievement Board recently revealed the results of a study they conducted on the effectiveness of comprehensive exams at Duke University. One major finding was that student anxiety had increased by 31%. At comparable schools without the exam, anxiety increased by only 8%. The Board reasoned that anxiety over the exams, or fear of failure, would motivate students to study more in their courses while they were taking them. It is likely that this increase in anxiety observed at Duke University would also be observed and be of benefit at other universities that adopt the exam policy.

Give a detailed description of the stylistic and content differences and verify whether the stylistic differences also have an effect on the persuasive power. Rewrite the texts, concentrating on the factors of language intensity and the rhetorical question mentioned in Section 8.4.

12.4.1 A possible criticism of the research done by Hosman et al. is that the hedgings in text (17) such as "uh" and "uhm" do not occur in normal written texts. Therefore it should not be remarkable that a powerless style has a negative influence when the message contains weak arguments. Provide arguments in defense of the investigation and point out in which ways the research can be improved.

12.4.2 In much socio-psychological research the assumption is that by changing attitudes we can change behavior. However, there is also support for a statement the other way round: behavior changes attitude. The socio-psychologist Leo Festinger (1957) became famous for his cognitive dissonance theory. This theory, very simply stated, claims that all people have a desire for consistency between attitude and behavior. For example, if you had traveled a long time to attend a concert by a famous band, and if you unexpectedly had to wait many hours before you could enter the music hall, what would be your attitude if that concert were disappointing? The cognitive dissonance theory predicts that you would have a more positive evaluation of the concert, because of all the trouble it took you to get to see the concert. (In fact, this theory should be called the cognitive *consonance* theory.)

Try to use the cognitive dissonance theory as an argument in a discussion about the value of attitude research as a predictor for behavior.

Bibliographical information

12.1   The three types of data in this section are from McCroskey (1986). For a good introduction to argumentation theory in a historical and contemporary perspective, see Van Eemeren, Grootendorst and Snoeck Henkemans (1996). The publication includes extensive references that form a starting point for specific further readings.

12.2   For further study in the field of pragma-dialectics, see the collection of articles by Van Eemeren, Grootendorst, Blair and Willard (1999). Van Eemeren (2002) provides a good overview of the latest developments in pragma-dialectics. For a closer study of fallacies, see Walton (1987).

12.3   Ajzen (1991) based his work on the theory of reasoned action, which he extended into his model. An overview of the research into message effects is given in Burgoon (1989). A good starting point is the collection of articles by Bradac (1989).

12.4   An excellent introductory textbook on persuasion theory is O'Keefe (2002).

A good collection of articles on argumentation and persuasion in business communication is Ehlich and Wagner (1995).

PART IV

Special interests

13 Discourse and cognition

13.1   Modeling discourse production

This chapter deals with one of the three main research areas in discourse studies, the study of the question: what goes on in our minds in producing and understanding discourse? See the following chapters for the two other main areas in discourse studies: the sociological and the critical approach. In the psychological approach the cognitive capacities of the human being are in focus, hence the restriction *cognitive* as a subdomain of the much broader psychological approach already mentioned in the previous chapter. Within discourse studies *cognition* is normally used as a cover term for perception, attention, memory and concept formation.

In the cognitive approach to discourse much attention has been paid to discourse processing (see Section 13.3 and further), but cognitive aspects can also be studied from the production perspective. What goes on in the mind of the writer when he plans his content, formulates his message and revises his drafts? Characteristic of the research in this domain is the focus on modeling the writing process.

In the pioneering work done by Carl Bereiter and Marlene Scardamalia (1987), two models are presented. Bereiter and Scardamalia developed their models on the basis of the following observations. Young or inexperienced writers are successful in completing a text using only a minimum of planning. Twelve-year-old children are able to write about a day at the zoo or something scary that happened to them without a great amount of trouble. More experienced writers view the writing process quite differently. They say that writing is hard and often grueling work. They do, however, often note that by writing they have gained new insights into the subject they were writing about. New thoughts occur during writing; writing is experienced as a creative process.

On the basis of these observations, Bereiter and Scardamalia developed two models: one for the writing process of inexperienced writers, the knowledge-telling model, and one for experienced writers, the knowledge-transforming model. Experienced writers can use the knowledge-telling model or the knowledge-transforming model, depending on the writing task at hand, whereas inexperienced writers only have the knowledge-telling model at their disposal.

Bereiter and Scardamalia explained this model using the following writing exercise: an essay was to be written on the question of whether or not boys and girls should

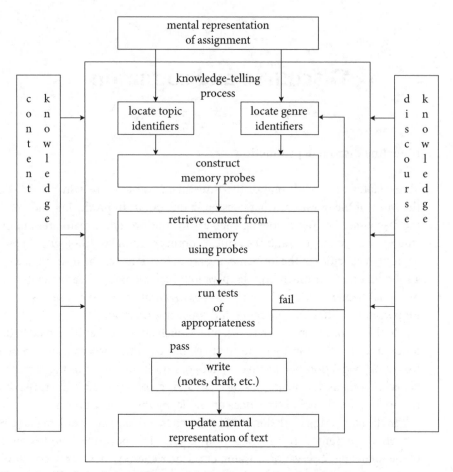

Figure 1. The knowledge-telling model (Bereiter and Scardamalia, 1987)

be allowed to play in the same sports teams. The following topic identifiers could be derived: boys, girls, and sports. More experienced writers could, however, probably also identify such topics as amateur sports and sexual equality. These identifiers are used to search in the writer's memory and the results are stored. A similar process takes place in the case of genre identifiers. The writing assignment implies that the text required is an opinion essay. Depending on the writer's level of proficiency, this could be anything from a simple data-claim (see Section 12.1) structure to a more complex structure of argument patterns and anticipations of counterarguments. The results of the searches are tested for their appropriateness, for example, to see if an item that might be included is sufficiently relevant to a given argument. If the test leads to a negative result, then the process starts again. If the result is positive, then the text

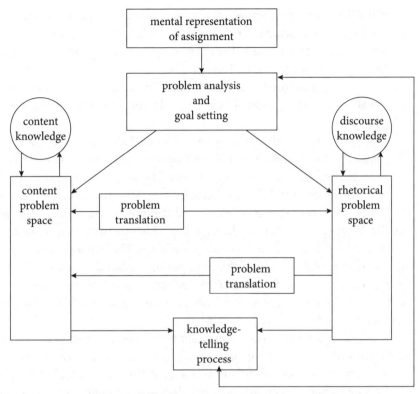

Figure 2. The knowledge-transforming model (Bereiter and Scardamalia, 1987)

segment is written down and the process starts again on the basis of what is already on paper, until the searches no longer result in new items.

In the knowledge-transforming model a more complex writing process is mapped out, namely, the process in which writers remain creative and gain insights or change their views while writing.

In this model the knowledge-telling model is embedded in a problem-solving process. The problems involve two domains, the content domain and the rhetorical domain. In the content domain, questions such as "What shall I write?" and "Is this a fact, an opinion or a suspicion?" are dealt with. In the rhetorical domain, the questions are of the order of "How do I present this to a given group of readers?" and "Is this argument convincing?" While writing, writers go back and forth between these two domains. When writers ask themselves whether or not a certain concept is clear enough to the reader (rhetorical domain), then this question can lead to the concept's being more clearly defined (content domain) and a more detailed definition can lead to the necessity of an introductory sentence in the previous paragraph (rhetorical domain). The interaction between the content domain and the rhetorical domain is the motor for the transformation of knowledge. This knowledge eventually shows up in the knowledge-telling process. The arrow starting at that point and pointing upwards in the diagram indicates the revision process.

The most general model for the writing process is developed by Hayes (1996), and is an elaboration of his 1980 model. It is called the individuo-environmental model (Figure 3).

The task of writing always takes place in a social and physical environment. Hence, the component *task environment*. This component refers to all the external, social and physical factors that can influence a writer. The social environment consists of two factors: the audience and the collaborators. Normally, the audience one is writing for influences the writing process. We write differently to friends and to an anonymous public. Writing also differs to the extent to which the writer has to collaborate with others, as, for example, in bureaucratic documents. The physical environment contains the factor "the text so far" and "the composing medium". Especially the last factor is given much attention in research into electronic discourse (see Section 4.4): To what extent do writing on the screen and writing on paper have a different influence on the writing process?

Central to the individual component is the working memory. Three aspects are distinguished here. The phonological memory refers to the writer's inner voice that continually repeats information to be retained. The visio/spatial sketchpad refers to visually or spatially coded information. The semantic memory refers to the formulation of the content of the discourse. This working memory is directly linked with the motivation subcomponent and cognition subcomponent. And these two subcomponents are also linked, which means that motivation and cognitive activities can directly influence each other. Four factors play a role in the motivation subcomponent: the communicative goals, the writer's predisposition (i.e., whether the writer can manage the writing task), the beliefs and attitudes relating to the task, and the estimation in terms of profitability. The cognitive component consists of three activities. During the *text interpretation* the writer (re)reads the text so far and continues with a coherent content, or makes revisions in content and formulation. During *reflection* the writer elaborates on the content of the text. During *text production* the writer elaborates on the text; this activity is the linguistic product of reflection. The fourth subcomponent in the individual component is long-term memory, in which knowledge about relevant aspects is stored: the text type, the language and the rules for writing, the addressee(s), the content and the procedures to control the realization of text.

With this framework Hayes has presented a general comprehensive description of the writing process in which all the relevant aspects are situated. The following points make his approach attractive. First, the social environment is considered to be just as

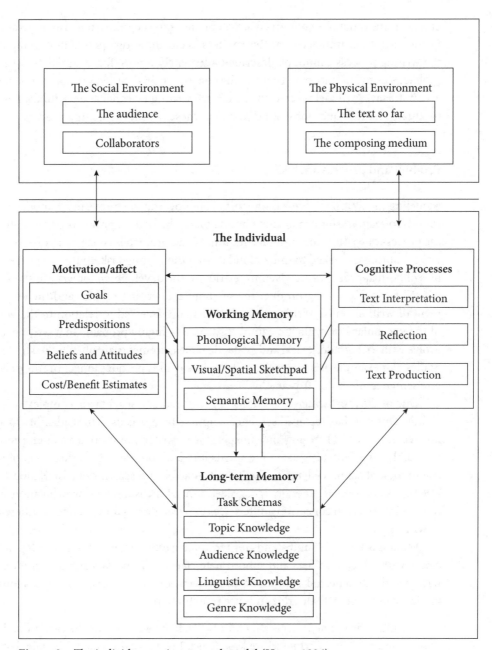

Figure 3. The individuo-environmental model (Hayes, 1996)

crucial as the other five components. Second, not only cognitive but also motivational factors are taken into account. Researchers deem these two points important since the writing process cannot be described adequately unless, for example, the specific problems of collaborative writing and the consequences of writer's block are taken into account. Hayes's model is referred to in much writing research as a useful framework to situate research questions and to test hypotheses about the writing process.

13.2   Product and process analysis

Modeling the writing process is one thing, but how can one prove that a model corresponds to reality? This can be done by analyzing the written products or by analyzing the process of writing, for example, in think-aloud protocols, collected in experiments where subjects are asked to think aloud during the writing task. In this section examples of both approaches are given in relation to the development of writing skills.

What does a writing product reveal about the writing process and the development of writing skills? Writing skills are normally assessed in relation to the wealth of the vocabulary or syntactic complexity. As it is highly probable that writing skills evolve with each grade, lexical and syntactical measurements are often linked to school grades. For example, it is conceivable that 14-year-olds produce longer or more elaborate sentences than do 10-year-olds.

One of the most widely used units of measurement of syntactic complexity is the T-unit. This unit has replaced sentence length, which was used in readability formulas (see Section 10.1). Young and inexperienced writers, in particular, often produce incredibly long sentences using the words *and* and *and then*. It is, therefore, of little use to look at sentence length. The T-unit, thanks to research done by Kellog Hunt (1970), has become a generally recognized unit of measurement, which can provide reliable information concerning differences between grades and, therefore, differences in writing skills.

What is a T-unit? T-unit stands for *terminable unit*, that is, a main or independent clause with all its modifiers and subordinate clauses. Grammatically, a T-unit can be terminated with a period or other terminal mark. Below is an example from a fourth-grader who, coincidentally, does not use punctuation.

(1)   I like the movie we saw about Moby Dick the white whale the captain said if you can kill the white whale Moby Dick I will give this gold to the one that can do it and it is worth sixteen dollars they tried and tried but while they were trying they killed a whale and used the oil for the lamps they almost caught the white whale.

This passage consists of the following T-units.

(2) 1. I like the movie we saw about Moby Dick the white whale.
2. the captain said if you can kill the white whale Moby Dick I will give this gold to the one that can do it.
3. and it is worth sixteen dollars.
4. they tried and tried.
5. but while they were trying they killed a whale and used the oil for the lamps.
6. they almost caught the white whale.

Hunt investigated the relationship between grades in school and the average length of the T-unit. The average length of a T-unit can be ascertained by dividing the number of words by the number of T-units. The average T-unit length for text (1) is 11.3 (68 words divided by 6 units). Hunt had students in different grades and adults rewrite the following discourse.

(3) 1. Aluminum is a metal.
2. It is abundant.
3. It has many uses.
4. It comes from bauxite.
5. Bauxite is an ore.
6. Bauxite looks like clay.

Below are two texts written by students at different levels and one by a skilled adult.

(4) (fourth-grader)
Aluminum is a metal and it is abundant. It has many uses and it comes from bauxite. Bauxite is an ore and looks like clay.

(5) (eighth-grader)
Aluminum is an abundant metal, has many uses, and comes from bauxite. Bauxite is an ore that looks like clay.

(6) (skilled adult)
Aluminum, an abundant metal with many uses, comes from bauxite, a clay-like ore.

The differences are striking. The fourth-grader made hardly any changes, only the coordination of the T-units and the predicates. The eighth-grader did much more: among other things, the transformation of a sentence into a preposed adjective ("abundant") and using a relative clause to link two thoughts ("that looks like clay"). The skilled adult made the most changes: all of the information has been compressed into one sentence. The differences between the texts can be expressed in average

Table 1.   Average T-unit length in relation to school grade

	grade					
	4	6	8	10	12	(skilled adults)
average T-unit length	5.4	6.8	9.8	10.7	11.3	(14.8)

T-unit length. The fourth-grader's score is 5, the eighth-grader's 10 and the skilled adult's 13. These scores mirror the trend that Hunt discovered in an investigation involving 300 subjects.

Hunt's approach gives insight into the writing process by investigating the end-product of that process. However, it can also be studied by analyzing what writers do or think during writing. Bereiter and Scardamalia offer some evidence to back up the knowledge-telling model, explained in Section 13.1, in giving data about the writing process. They asked inexperienced writers to think aloud during writing. These think-aloud protocols show that very little attention is given to the rhetorical aspects of texts. There is also, according to the model, little attention given to planning or revision. On the basis of these findings Bereiter and Scardamalia did research to ascertain whether planning is a factor in the development of writing skills. They had a number of pupils, aged 10, 12, and 14, write an essay on the topic: "Should children be able to choose the subjects they study in school?" The participants were asked to plan out loud and make notes for as long as possible before actually starting to write. Below are two representative examples of notes and written text.

(7)   *Notes*
      I don't like language and art is a bore
      I don't like novel study
      And I think 4s and 3s should be split up
      I think we should do math
      I don't think we should do diary
      I think we should do French
      Text
      I think children should be able to choose what subjects they want in school.
      I don't think we should have to do language, and art is a bore a lot. I don't think
      we should do novel study every week. I really think 4s and 3s should be split up
      for gym. I think we should do a lot of math. I don't think we should do diary. I
      think we should do French.

(8) *Notes*
     –   opinion (mine)
     –   responsibility of the children – their goal in life
     –   parents – their understanding of their children
     –   what will happen with what they take
     –   examples
     –   what rights do they have
     –   what I think about it
     –   the grade (if they choose) should be 7 and up
     –   school subjects should be made more interesting
     –   how future will be
     Text
     I personally think that students should be able to choose which subjects they
     want to study in school. In grade 9 students are allowed to choose certain
     subjects which they want to but even then the students aren't sure. Many don't
     know because they don't know what they want to be when they get older. If
     they choose the subjects they wanted most students would of course pick easier
     subjects such as art, gym, music, etc. I think that this doing is partly the schools
     fault. If the school made math classes more interesting students would more
     likely pick that (...)

Text (7) was written by a 10-year-old and text (8), an excerpt, was written by a 14-year-old. The notes from the planning phase do not directly say anything about the planning process, but one thing is quite striking. The 10-year-old's notes show a far greater resemblance to the final text than the 14-year-old's notes. The 10-year-old seemingly equates planning with writing. Experienced writers differentiate between the two activities. The investigation showed, therefore, that planning can in fact be a factor in the development of writing skills.

13.3 Processing and prior knowledge

Where Section 13.1 and 13.2 dealt with production, the following sections deal with perception. In discourse processing there is much more at stake than only perceiving verbal material, as already explained in the comments on the sender-message-receiver model in Section 3.3. Especially important is the knowledge the participants already have about the topic of communication or the situation in which the communication takes place; this is also called prior knowledge. The first researcher who focused on this phenomenon was the psychologist Frederic Bartlett. In 1932 he published a book in which an experiment on the retention of the following story was reported on.

The reader of this book can easily repeat this experiment. Read the following story carefully. Afterwards read the newspaper for approximately fifteen minutes. Then try to write down what you remember of the story.

(9)   The war of the ghosts
One night two young men from Egulac went down to the river to hunt seals, and while they were there it became foggy and calm. Then they heard war-cries, and they thought: "Maybe this is a war-party." They escaped to the shore and hid behind a log. Now canoes came up, and they heard the noise of paddles, and saw one canoe coming up to them. There were five men in the canoe, and they said: "What do you think? We wish to take you along. We are going up the river to make war on the people."
One of the young men said: "I have no arrows."
"Arrows are in the canoe," they said.
"I will not go along. I might be killed. My relatives do not know where I have gone. But you," he said, turning to the other, "may go with them."
So one of the young men went, but the other returned home.
And the warriors went on up the river to a town on the other side of Kalama. The people came down to the water, and they began to fight, and many were killed. But presently the young man heard one of the warriors say: "Quick, let us go home: that Indian has been hit." Now he thought: "Oh, they are ghosts." He did not feel sick, but they said he had been shot.
So the canoes went back to Egulac, and the young man went ashore to his house, and made a fire. And he told everybody and said: "Behold I accompanied the ghosts, and we went to fight. Many of our fellows were killed, and many of those who attacked us were killed. They said I was hit, and I did not feel sick."
He told it all, and then he became quiet. When the sun rose he fell down. Something black came out of his mouth. His face became contorted. The people jumped up and cried.
He was dead.

Bartlett asked many people to retell this story. One of the subjects rendered the story as follows.

(10)   The war of the ghosts (a rendition)
Two young men from Egulac went fishing. While thus engaged they heard a noise in the distance. "That sounds like a war-cry", said one, "there is going to be some fighting." Presently there appeared some warriors who invited them to join an expedition up the river.

One of the young men excused himself on the ground of family ties. "I cannot come", he said, "as I might get killed." So he returned home. The other man, however, joined the party, and they proceeded on canoes up the river. While landing on the banks the enemy appeared and were running down to meet them. Soon someone was wounded, and the party discovered that they were fighting against ghosts. The young man and his companion returned to the boats, and went back to their homes.

The next morning at dawn he was describing his adventures to his friends, who had gathered round him. Suddenly something black issued from his mouth, and he fell down uttering a cry. His friends closed around him, but found that he was dead.

The differences are striking. Many details from the original have disappeared in this version. In the story the men from Egulac hide behind a log and hear the noise of paddles. This information cannot, however, be found in the rendition. The phrasing has become more modern, for example, "on the ground of family ties". In the original, a war-party is going to wage war against the people; in the latter rendition, it is an expedition. In the original, the protagonist is shot; in the retelling, it is simply "someone".

How can these and the many other differences be explained? Bartlett argued that the retention of stories is influenced by the recipient's mental framework. By this he meant that prior knowledge is used to process new information. This mental framework ensures that new facts are integrated into the already existing body of knowledge (in the case of the story above, knowledge concerning Indians). It is, however, also the mental framework that contributes to the distortion of new facts. Reading this story, western subjects will adapt the information to their own knowledge of the world. The "seal hunt" in the original will be replaced with the more familiar "fishing", "war-cry" will become "yell" and "warriors" will become "enemies".

To describe this mental framework, Bartlett introduced the schema concept. A schema (plural: *schemata*; *schemas* are diagrammatic representations, outlines or models) is a set of organized knowledge about a specific element in the world. By *knowledge* is meant the stereotypical knowledge that is more or less the same for all language users in a particular culture. Every language user associates different things with the word *house*, for example, but the stereotypical or encyclopedic knowledge is the same for everyone: a house has rooms, a kitchen, a front door; a roof can be leaky; a house can be bought or rented, etc.

A schema contains standard elements and has "slots". An often-used example is the schema "face". A standard element here is the oval shape. Such a standard element serves as a framework for filling in slots: eyes, mouth, nose, etc. The schema "train" also contains slots for station, conductor, etc. As soon as the word *face* or *train* appears in discourse, references to those slots can be expected. The opposite also holds: if in discourse the word *nose* or *conductor* is used, then references to other elements of the schemata "face" and "train", for example, "skin color" or "station", can be expected.

If no separate information is given about the slots, then the so-called default value can be assumed. This is the modal value, i.e., the value that has the highest frequency. The schema "operation" has "surgeon" as a standard element. The slots deal with the type of surgery, the type of hospital, the surgeon's sex, age, etc. If nothing in particular is said about the surgeon, then in western cultures it is automatically assumed that the slot "sex" receives the value "man", as in westerns cultures there are more male than female surgeons.

How does a schema function in understanding discourse? Below is an example.

(11)   Late for school
       Karen had overslept. If she hurried, she might still make it. Quick, but she'd have
       to skip breakfast. Run! Almost! She saw the hands of the clock over the entrance
       move to the penultimate minute and started to run. There were no more seats
       left. Gasping, she leaned against the swinging door and thought: I hope I don't
       get caught.

The title makes it clear that two schemata are applicable here: "being late" and "school". These schemata direct the reader through discourse. "School" determines the interpretation of discourse that follows. The "seats" are classroom seats and among the people who could "catch" Karen are hall monitors.

But what would happen if the title of this story had been "The angry conductor"? This schema would drastically alter the interpretation. The swinging door, for example, would then be the door between two train cars, and "getting caught" would refer to the fact that Karen did not have a ticket. The text lacks information on this. The remark concerning the penultimate minute could have been followed by:

(12)   No time to buy a ticket, she thought, and started to run.

This information is not, however, necessary for the interpretation of "being caught". On the basis of the schemata "coming in late" and "train trip", readers can infer the missing information.

Schemata are of great importance in the reading and listening process as they serve the following four functions:

1.   They provide an interpretational framework. If readers cannot place a given passage, then the information cannot be processed. See for another illustration the passage about laundry in Section 3.6 (example 13).

2. They direct the interpretation. This can be seen in the subject's rendition of "The war of the ghosts" and the story with the two different titles: "Late for school" and "The angry conductor".

3. They indicate what is important and what is not in a given discourse. If example (11) had been given the title "Young people don't eat right", then the sentence about skipping breakfast would be much more important than it was in "Late for school". In other words, schemata indicate how to construct macropropositions of a discourse (see Section 5.3).

4. They make inferences possible (see Section 7.6). Based on the schema "train trip", in example (11) the inference "no ticket" can be made from "caught".

13.4 Aspects of processing

In understanding, listeners or readers have to engage in many different activities. They have to combine the signals (sounds, characters) into words and sentences, they have to analyze the structure of utterances or sentences, assign meanings to the words and distill the message, in order to mentally make what is called a discourse representation. What goes on in our minds in making a discourse representation is in fact guesswork. But there are reasonable and less reasonable guesses. In research of the past decades the results of experiments have prompted four premises that are fairly generally supported in different theories on discourse and cognition.

a. *Three levels of representation*
In discourse processing three different levels have to be distinguished. First, there is the surface representation. This is the representation of the formulation. In experiments from the 1970s evidence was found for the relative importance of this level. In an experiment by Jarvella (1971) subjects had to recall sentences like the following:

(13)   The confidence of Kofach was not unfounded. To stack the meeting for McDonald, the union had even brought in outsiders.

(14)   Kofach had been persuaded by the international to stack the meeting for McDonald. The union had even brought in outsiders.

The syntactic surface structure was of influence here. Subjects had a better recall of "to stack the meeting for McDonald" after (13), where it is at the beginning of the second sentence, than after (14) where it is at the end of the first sentence. But the influence of surface phenomena is not great. In an experiment by Fillenbaum (1974) subjects were asked to paraphrase sentences with solecisms (language errors), like the following:

(15)   John finished and wrote the article on the weekend.

In the majority of the paraphrases the illogical order was normalized, and even if subjects were asked to look again, about half of them did not see the solecism. In research nowadays it is commonly assumed that the level of surface representation has some short-duration influence on the process of understanding, but that the two following levels are of much more importance.

The second level is the propositional representation, the meaning of the discourse expressed in a network of propositions (see Section 5.1 for the propositional analysis). This level is also called the *text base*. In many experiments the existence of this level has been proved. Here is one experiment by Goetz, Anderson and Schallert (1981). They asked subjects to recall sentences with unfamiliar content, so that it was difficult to create a mental picture of the facts reported on. Here are two examples with a propositional analysis.

(16)   The comedian supplied glassware to the convicts
       a.   to supply ((comedian)$_{subject}$(glassware)$_{object}$(convicts)$_{indirect\ object}$)
(17)   The bedraggled, intelligent model sang
       a.   1. (sing, model)
             2. (model, bedraggled)
             3. (model, intelligent)

Almost every sentence with one proposition, like (16), was recalled completely. But sentences with additional propositions, like (17), were often recalled partially, e.g., "the model sang" or "the model was intelligent". That is why it is always important in research into discourse processing to work with a propositional representation of a text.

The third level is the situational representation, also called the mental model of the discourse. Evidence for this level is presented in many experiments, including that of Bransford, Barclay and Franks (1972). Subjects were asked to memorize spoken sentences like the following:

(18)   Three turtles rested *on* a floating log and a fish swam beneath *them*.
(19)   Three turtles rested *beside* a floating log and a fish swam beneath *them*.

On a later recognition task, participants who had heard sentence (18) often reported erroneously that they had heard sentence (20a). Participants who had heard sentence (19), however, did not report hearing sentence (20b).

(20)   a.   Three turtles rested *on* a floating log and a fish swam beneath *it*.
       b.   Three turtles rested *beside* a floating log and a fish swam beneath *it*.

The fact that during the recognition task readers of sentence (18) wrongly reported that they had heard sentence (20a) whereas readers of sentence (19) did not recognize (20b) means that subjects not only make a propositional representation; they also make a mental map of the situation. This roughly means that they create a picture in their heads, representing the discourse they have heard or read. One "mental picture" can represent both (18) and (20a), hence the possibility of confusing them, whereas (19) and (20b) are represented by two different mental pictures and as a result confusion is unlikely. This third level of representation, the mental model, receives the most attention in discourse processing research.

b. *The cyclical processing of propositions*
The assumption of an independent level of propositional representation suggests that listeners and readers have to link these propositions in order to extract the message from discourse. In discourse processing propositions have to be linked to macro-propositions (see Section 5.3) in order to give a summary or an interpretation of what the discourse is about. What goes on in our minds when we do this?

It seems reasonable to assume that the linking of propositions is a cyclical process. This assumption is derived from a generally accepted distinction made in the study of human memory, namely, the difference between long-term and short-term memory. Long-term memory makes it possible for a person to retell a text even after several days. This type of memory has, in principle, unlimited capacity. Short-term memory has limited capacity. In computer terms, short-time memory is working memory. Because this working memory is limited, readers cannot process all of the propositions in a text at once, but take in small groups of propositions at a time in a repetitive process until the entire text has been read. Obviously, the different cycles are not independent of each other. Information from the first cycle must be linked to the propositions from the second cycle, and so on.

The reading process can now be described as follows. If the assumption is made that a text is read sentence by sentence, then the first cycle must provide the propositions of the first sentence, for example, eleven propositions. It is likely that just a few propositions can be carried over into the next cycle since working memory has a limited capacity and there are also new propositions that have to be incorporated. The precise number can only be guessed at. A defensible assumption is that this number is about seven. But which seven? Another defensible assumption is that the most central or the last incoming propositions, or both will be transferred to the next cycle as a kind of buffer. This buffer of about seven propositions functions as a kind of coat hanger or anchor point for the propositions of the next sentence. If the next sentence has, for example, fourteen propositions, then out of the twenty-one propositions so far a new buffer of about seven has to be chosen, which functions as the input for the following sentence, etc.

It must be emphasized that the generally accepted assumption of cyclical processing is only a very rough sketch of what is going on in discourse processing. There are at least three factors for which dependent assumptions have to be made: the size of the cycle, the size of the buffer and the way in which the propositions that remain in the buffer are chosen. In this example it is assumed that the cycles mostly consist of one sentence, that the buffer can contain about seven propositions, and that the most important propositions and the propositions entered last are transferred into the buffer. Of course, the size of the cycle, the buffer, and the choice of propositions can differ from reader to reader or between groups of readers.

c. *Frames, scripts and scenarios as different knowledge systems*

In processing discourse, "something in the discourse" (the text base) interacts with "something in our minds", the knowledge we have about a topic or about a situation, such as the schemata introduced in Section 13.1. In cognitive discourse research it is generally assumed that the stereotypical knowledge stored in schemata plays an important role in understanding. But how this knowledge is organized is still under investigation. Three terms have been coined to describe different aspects of our knowledge systems: frame, script and scenario.

The term *frame* refers to our knowledge about concepts, like "wedding party", "student" or "bird". A frame is not to be thought of as a window frame, but as a skeleton or the frame of a bicycle. It can be visualized as a hierarchical structure with nodes and relations. For example, a part of the frame of a bird, let's say, the seagull, can be presented as shown in Figure 4.

The nodes consist of two parts: a constant part (●) and a variable part (□). One of the nodes is the color of the seagull. The constant part of this node pertains to the fact that seagulls have a color, while the variable part pertains to the various colors (gray-white, brown) a seagull can have. So, the variable part can have different values.

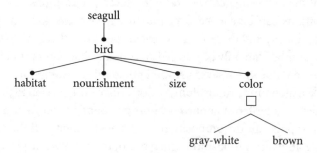

Figure 4. Partial frame of a "seagull"

The value it most often has is called the default value, "gray-white" in this example (see Section 13.3). A story about a seagull can, without the colors being mentioned in the text, end with, for example: "A gray-white bird flew away over the sea", and it will be clear to anyone that a seagull is meant. When the default value does not apply, however, the variable value must first be mentioned in the text in order to make the following sentence clear: "A brown bird flew away over the sea."

The term *script* refers to our knowledge about the roles people have in a specific situation. An often-used example is the restaurant script. This script contains information about the acts that participants in such a situation are supposed to perform: the guest orders the food, eats it and pays for it, while the waiter takes the order, brings the food and receives the payment, and the chef does the cooking, etc. Because of our knowledge of this restaurant script we can anticipate expected behavior. For example, it comes as no surprise if after dinner the cook shows up at your table and asks whether you have enjoyed your meal. Contrary to frames and schemata, a script pertains to our knowledge of role behavior of participants in stereotypical situations. In a script structure these role-bound acts are the nodes, while the participants and the objects are the variable parts.

The term *scenario* refers to our knowledge about the ordering of activities. An example is the scenario of a children's party: first come the gifts, then the cake and then the games, etc. Our knowledge of specific scenarios also explains why, for example, in the restaurant script it would strike us if paying the bill preceded eating the food. We know that the scenario in a restaurant does not follow this order.

Of course, the knowledge about concepts (frames) and roles (scripts) can be embedded in ordered activities (scenarios), resulting in very complicated knowledge systems. Presenting just parts of this system only serves as a tool in explaining how aspects of discourse processing can be clarified.

d. *The interplay between semantics and pragmatics*
In laymen's terms "understanding discourse" is to get the meaning out of the discourse, with "meaning" in the sense of what a dictionary says about words. This semantic narrowing of understanding, however, does not do justice to reality. The psycholinguist Herbert Clark, already mentioned in Section 3.3 his approach regarding to communication as joint action, wrote a seminal paper (1997) in which he refuted several dogmas in research on discourse processing. He used a famous example from Grice (which was also mentioned in Section 2.4) to emphasize the impact of pragmatic factors in understanding discourse. In this example speaker A is standing beside a car near the road.

(21) A: I am out of petrol.
      B: There is a garage round the corner.

Following Grice, speaker B uses conventional meanings of the words "garage", "corner", etc., in order to implicate that the garage may be open. So semantics precedes pragmatics (what is meant with the words when they are used in a specific situation). But Clark argues that one cannot recover the meaning of words without considering the situation in which these words are used: there is no semantics without pragmatics. The short exchange in example (21) prompts at least two questions concerning understanding. The first is: How does B know that the pronoun "I" refers to a car? If A had been standing beside a lawn mower then the word *I* would have had another reference, and a plausible reaction could then have been "I have a full jerry can in my barn" with the implicature "You can have some gasoline from me." The second question is: How does A know that the word "garage" here means a gas station and not a parking building, as in:

(22)   A: I think I am parked in an illegal zone.
       B: There is a garage around the corner.

The answer to the two questions is that understanding is directly influenced by the situation in which the words are used. So, in discourse processing pragmatic factors play a role at the same time as semantic factors do. How this interplay actually takes place in our mind, is difficult to imagine. But this fourth premise and the other three have led to attempts to sketch models of what happens during discourse processing.

13.5   Modeling discourse processing

A number of different models have been developed to chart the processes that take place during reading. The most influential model is that of Kintsch (1988), which is an extension of an earlier model by Kintsch and Van Dijk (1978), and was elaborated on in 1998. The model can best be explained with an example of a simple sentence and then some different contexts:

(23)   Lucy persuaded Mary to bake a cake.
(24)   Lucy persuaded Mary to bake a cake. But she did not know that the thermal insulation of the oven was damaged.
(25)   Mary could never decide what to prepare for dinner. So, Lucy persuaded Mary to bake a cake.
(26)   Lucy always succeeded in letting other people work for her. Now Lucy persuaded Mary to bake a cake!

A reader or listener processing a piece of discourse, say (23), in whatever context has to connect new elements in a mental model, among other things that Mary bakes a cake, with elements that are already in his mind, e.g., that a cake can be baked. Or to put it in more general words, in processing discourse one has to construct what is meant, and integrate that meaning in already existing knowledge. Therefore, Kintsch's model consists of two components: a construction component and an integration component; hence the name "construction-integration model".

In the construction component it is assumed that a network of propositions (see Section 5.1), a text base, is constructed on the basis of the input. This procedure is rather unstructured, since all kinds of associations take place, even contradictory ones, and bottom-up, in the sense that words from the discourse activate concepts in the mind. If we want to simulate this phase in understanding, then it is plausible to assume that there are four construction rules.

(27)   Four rules in the construction component (Kintsch, 1998)
  1.   rules for the construction of propositions
  2.   rules for interconnecting the propositions in a network
  3.   rules for the activation of knowledge
  4.   rules for constructing inferences

How can the result of this construction component be presented? Figure 5 shows only a part of the outcome of the rules under 1 and 2 applied to just one word in example sentence (23), the verb *to bake*.

Central to this representation is the proposition concerning *to bake*, containing the knowledge that the object of *to bake* can be a cake, and that the *agens* (*Ag*) or subject has to be a person. So Mary can only be the *agens* after it has been verified in the knowledge system that Mary is a person. Of course, in processing the input *to bake* other propositions can be constructed (rules under 1) as well, for example, that one can bake other objects (*Obj*) such as squash or bricks, or that a rock can lie baking in the sun, with the sun being an instrument (*Ins*). Virtually nothing prevents other propositions, for example, that the cake has to be put in the oven (the location, or *Loc* in Figure 5) in order to be baked, or that the result will be a hot cake.

Following the construction of propositions the rules for interconnecting them (rules under 2) have to be applied. The propositions can be related strongly or weakly, and even negatively. In this presentation the strongly related propositions are represented by black arrows (the weakly related ones are not presented), and the negatively related ones by lines with bullets: one cannot bake a cake and at the same time bake bricks. Subsequently, the rules under 3 activate knowledge that already exists in the memory, for example, that you can burn your fingers while cooking (example (24)), or that it is sometimes difficult to decide what to eat (example (25)), or that Lucy always knows how to get people to work for her (example (26)). Then, using the rules under

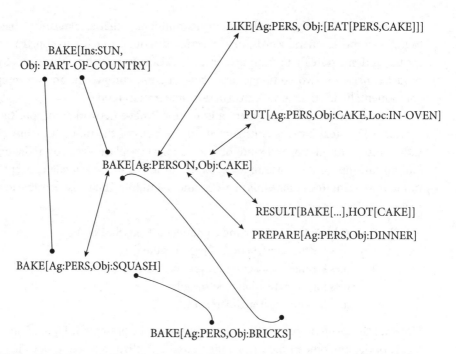

Figure 5. Representation of a fragment of the construction component for *to bake* (Kintsch, 1988)

4 inferences can be made, like the conclusion that Mary is easy to persuade, or that the cake was for dinner, or that Lucy is a mean girl, etc.

It is important to note here that Kintsch's model does not describe how exactly the text base, the propositional network, is built up. The model only claims that procedures such as the four described here take place in the first component, and that the outcome can be conceived of as a propositional network, with propositions that are linked more or less strongly, like Figure 5.

How does the reader or listener arrive at the correct interpretation of this incoming propositional network when some of the propositions are irrelevant, for example, that Mary likes the cake, or even contradictory, for example, baking in the sun? The interpretation of the result of the construction component takes place in the integration component, and the procedure by which that happens can be conceived of as spreading of activation. It means, simply formulated, that propositions spread their activation to other propositions in a process in which propositions that are irrelevant or contradictory are given lesser values and disappear at the end of the process. Kintsch (1998) presented a simple and abstract example in order to help us gain insight into this intriguing process. Below is a small part of a possible propositional network. For the sake of clarity letters are used and not real content such as the baking of a cake.

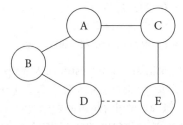

Figure 6. An abstract representation of a part of a propositional network (Kintsch, 1998)

In this network propositions A and D are directly connected to proposition B and to each other. C is directly connected to E, but only indirectly to B and D via A. E is contradictory-connected with D: if E is true then D cannot be true. The relations can be presented numerically in a so-called connectivity matrix. For convenience, in the matrix below the strength of each connection is set to 1, or –1 for the contradictory connection, and to 0 for no direct connection.

(28)   The connectivity matrix of the propositional network in Figure 6

	A	B	C	D	E
A	1	1	1	1	0
B	1	1	0	1	0
C	1	0	1	0	1
D	1	1	0	1	-1
E	0	0	1	-1	1

In this matrix a proposition, say A, is presented as a vector in this case, as a node with values for each of the connections to the other propositions. Proposition A has a *1* representing the direct nodes (including itself) four times and one *0* for the non-existent connection with E. The integration process is assumed to start with activation values of *1*. So, if proposition A first comes in as A(1), then in vector notation, A has the initial notation: A(1) = (1, 1, 1, 1, 1). The integration process now consists of multiplying each of these initial values by the respective values in the columns of the matrix. The integration process repeats itself until the outcome of the multiplication is stable, which means that the outcome of a value differs no more than .001 from the preceding multiplication. Then the final activation value of each of the propositions is established. This means we can see which proposition became stronger and which disappeared. Below are some steps in this multiplication series.

(29) Some steps in the multiplication process
1. A(1)   = (1, 1, 1, 1, 1)
2. A(2)   = (4, 3, 3, 2, 1)
3. A(2a)   = (1.00, .75, .75, .50, .25)
4. A(9)   = (1.00, .85, .46, .85, .00)

A(1) is the proposition in starting position. Multiplying the numbers 1 by the columns in the connectivity matrix gives: 4, 3, 3, 2, 1 in A(2). This can be presented as 1.00 down to .25 in A(2a). Multiplication is repeated till the values are stable (nine times). At the end, the activation value of proposition E, which is connected to C, is completely repressed (.00). The value of C (.46) is much lower than those of B and D. As such, the process sketched out above simulates how in the actual reading process propositions and concepts that are activated to various extents ultimately become stronger or disappear.

Kintsch's model is an attempt to map out what goes on in our minds during the processing of discourse, of incoming propositions. At the moment it is also the most-used model. However, as is the case with many other models, this one prompts questions, too. For example, does a (piece of) discourse have only one propositional representation? In Section 5.1 we already saw that the construction of a text base involves many subjective decisions. First, how can we, in a representation such as Figure 5, control the number of possible neighboring nodes? For example, the proposition that a location for baking a cake is the kitchen does not necessarily have to be activated, but it may be if later in the discourse a kitchen window is mentioned. And second, how can we represent the making of inferences, for example, that Lucy has a stronger character than Mary? Although many questions are still unanswered, the principles of this construction-integration model are now generally taken as a basis for further research.

13.6   The metaphor in cognitive research

Propositions and knowledge are pivotal in cognitive discourse studies, but there is another phenomenon that attracts much attention: what does language reveal about how we see or understand something in reality? Central to answering this question is an ancient literary concept: the metaphor (see Section 8.3). A new impulse to the long literary and stylistic research tradition in metaphors was given when George Lakoff and Mark Johnson published their *Metaphors We Live By* (1980). They demonstrated that much of what we call literal or non-metaphorical language is in fact metaphorical. They did not mean the so-called dead or petrified metaphors in isolated cases, like *the leg of a table*, but the hidden ones that are still alive, the metaphors we live by, such as the following ones:

(30)   It is easy to punch holes in his arguments.

(31)   That cost me a lot of time.

(32)   The refrigerator is acting up again.

(33)   He's not hitting on all eight cylinders.

Since criticism of an argument is often seen as being destructive to the argument, the expression "punch holes" in (30) can be seen as an argument-is-war metaphor. As time is often viewed as an economic factor, the time-is-money metaphor is not illogical in (31). Assigning human traits to machines is also not uncommon; (32) is a personification. Nor is it strange for humans to be described in terms from the world of machines as in (33), the man-is-a-machine metaphor.

Lakoff and Johnson viewed a metaphor as a cognitive device for understanding or experiencing one kind of thing or experience in terms of another. We need such a device because we have concepts that are not grounded in experience, say "abstract concepts", about which we want to communicate. Therefore, our imaginative capacity projects or maps one (mostly concrete) domain, e.g., "money", onto a more abstract domain, e.g., "time", so that the second domain is understood in terms of elements from the first one. The donor domain, the source, functions as a vehicle for some elements to the target, the recipient domain, also called the tenor. Below are some examples with the tenor "idea" and different "vehicles" to communicate about ideas:

(34)   1.   That idea has been fermenting for years. (food)

2.   His ideas will live on forever. (people)

3.   His ideas have finally come to fruition. (plant)

4.   We're really turning out new ideas. (product)

5.   That idea just won't sell. (commodity)

6.   He ran out of ideas. (resource)

7.   That's an incisive idea. (cutting instrument)

This cognitive approach to metaphors has received much attention because it gives more than the precise propositional approach in understanding what the "literal reality" is; it also provides a method for studying our less clear imaginative mechanisms. How should this mapping from one domain onto another be understood? To what extent must these different domains have something in common? Which roles do these mappings play in communication? Below are two examples of research.

The cognitive study of metaphors is based on analysis of ordinary language. A good example of the omnipresence of metaphors in our communication is provided by Ponterotto (2003). In this study the focus is on how participants in a conversation that seems to consist of incoherent and incomplete segments succeed in making themselves understood. Why is there no conversation clash? One of the keys in an answer to this question can be the use of metaphors. Below is a fragment from a conversation between two friends about intimate relationships. Try to find the metaphorical expressions in this text taken from Ponterotto (2003).

(35) B: And Mhmm, I don't know ... even though we had a big relationship I can't see the sense of getting married.

   A: Oh!

   B: Sometimes you go through life and you're really serious about someone but ... you just don't keep going and you have things to do.

   A: Six months ago ... I met him, six months later ... he moved to Australia and a month, two months later he got accepted to university.

   B: Yeah!

   A: So he took off thinking "Yeah we see each other in six months back in a month for another two months"

   B: [Yeah.

   A: so I said, "OK, I'll see you in a couple of months." So three times ... it happened, that separation

   B: Mmmm.

   A: and it's the fourth time in a month.

   B: It's just so hard to maintain a long distance

   A: [Six months ago he used to talk about it

   B: relationship. Yeah, it's very very difficult.

   A: Mhmmm, when you can't work things out but six months ago we used to talk about marriage.

   B: Yeah.

   A: It was really serious, but now it's like, mhmm, weaving out of it. But it's easier to hang on rather than let go ... and that's why I came here ...

In her analysis, as shown in Table 2 below, Ponterotto pointed out nine metaphors.

Ponterotto argues that speakers A and B together construct the thematic structure of the text: they negotiate the metaphorical overlap. Speaker B moves from *understanding is seeing* to *life is a journey* to *love is a journey* and finally to *love is hard work*, which is then picked up by speaker A, who repeats *love is hard work*, subsequently implying that as a result *love is a collaborative work of art*, which then triggers the concept of danger: *love is a precipice*. The conceptual representations of both speakers meet at the point *love is hard work*, which becomes the negotiated agreement of the problem announced at the beginning of the conversation. This cognitive metaphor seems to bind the conceptual perspectives of both speakers. According to Ponterotto the metaphor thus plays a role in the planning, execution and monitoring of discourse

Table 2.   The nine metaphors in (35)

	Conversation fragment	Metaphor	Speaker
1.	I don't *see the sense* of getting married.	UNDERSTANDING IS SEEING.	B
2.	Even though we had *a big relationship*.	SIGNIFICANT IS BIG.	B
3.	Sometimes you *go through life*.	LIFE IS A JOURNEY.	B
4.	You just don't *keep going*.	LOVE IS A JOURNEY.	B
5.	*It's so hard*.	LOVE IS HARD WORK.	A, B
6.	To maintain *a long distance relationship*.	LOVE IS CLOSENESS.	B
7.	You can't *work things out*.	LOVE IS WORK.	B
8.	Now it's sort of like, mhmm, *weaving out of it*.	LOVE IS A COLLABORATIVE WORK OF ART (knitting or quilt making).	A
9.	But it's easier *to hang on* then *to let go*.	LOVE IS A PRECIPICE.	A

production. On the one hand, it holds everything in place, on the other, it permits constant re-elaboration.

A very different cognitive approach to metaphors can be seen in research into the question of understanding metaphors. Is metaphorical language a special use of language that has to be reduced to its literal meaning before it can be understood? If this is true, metaphorical expressions require more cognitive effort in understanding than literal expressions, or they activate different processes in our mind. Compare the following examples that are used in a study by Kintsch (1998):

(36) John was in for a surprise when he visited his former professor after many years. The old rock had become brittle with age.

(37) John was in for a surprise when he touched the wall of the monastery tower. The old rock had become brittle with age.

In order to understand (36) the reader has to project something from the domain of "rock" onto the domain of "human being". This is not the case in the literal meaning of (37). How can we recover the concepts that come up in our minds when processing the literal or metaphorical meaning? We have to know that before we can decide whether the metaphor in (36) is more difficult to process than the literal meaning in (37).

Kintsch used a special semantic analysis to gain insight into the activation of concepts during discourse processing. This analysis is called Latent Semantic Analysis (LSA). The technique was developed by Landauer and Dumais (1997). At the basis of their analysis lies the assumption that the meaning of a word, say *father*, can be determined by the words that co-occur with this word in all kinds of other discourse that we have already read (*mother, children, job, remote control*, etc.). In fact, they used the notion of collocation, dealt with in Section 6.1 where examples were given of the

Table 3.   Three strongly associated neighbors of three concepts in examples (36) and (37)

Concept	Latently present concepts
Former professor	University
	Emeritus
	Faculty
Wall of monastery tower	Vaulted
	Buttresses
	Masonry
Old rock	Old
	Monolith
	Volcanic

co-occurrence of *Red Cross* with *donor* or *blood bank*, or with *war*. If we read the word *father* in a new context, then all kinds of collocations (*married, coming home at five,* etc.) are already latently present and contribute to the semantic description of this concept (hence the name of this analysis).

Landauer and Dumais collected their data by automatic analysis of the first 2,000 characters (some 30 sentences) of about 30,000 articles in an electronic version of an encyclopedia. This resulted in a huge matrix with the articles on the horizontal axis and words (like *father* in our example) on the vertical axis. By computation about 300 basic dimensions were extracted from the 30,000 articles. Each word on the vertical axis could now be presented as a vector with values on these 300 dimensions (more or less like the vector notation in Section 13.5). Moreover, they computed the relationships between vectors, which gave insight into the extent to which various words scored similarly on the 300 dimensions. Words with very similar scores could be indicated as synonyms. To give an idea of the power of their approach: the LSA analysis by computer made decisions about synonymy for English as well as non-native speakers of English did.

This LSA approach was used by Kintsch to describe concepts which are already latently present when three concepts (*wall, professor* and *rock*) are processed in the sentences above. Below is an overview of the concepts that are strongly associated with these concepts (proper nouns like *Westminster Abbey* as a concept related to *monastery tower* have been omitted).

With these concepts Kintsch constructed a network linking the noun phrase *former professor* in (36) and *wall of monastery tower* in (37) with *old rock*, just like linking a new proposition to already existing activated propositions in the approach presented in Section 3.5. He found that features of *old rock* were transferred to *wall* as well as to *professor*. The concept *wall* had higher activation values for *old* and *monolith*, but perhaps contrary to expectations, so did the concept *professor*. These results indicate that there is no difference in processing metaphoric and literal language use. Of course, this was only one experiment. The results have to be correlated with more research in the cognitive study of metaphors.

Questions and assignments

Questions

13.1.1 Why did Bereiter and Scardamalia introduce two models of the writing process?

13.1.2 Which model of the writing process best fits the following statement by E.M. Forster: "How do I know what I think till I see what I say?"

13.1.3 According to the knowledge-telling model, what can an instructor do to convert a writer into a knowledge transformer?

13.2.1 Below is an excerpt from a think-aloud protocol (taken from Witte, 1987). An American student was asked to write an essay about the role of education in society. After reading the assignment and making some notes, she started as follows. Only the italicized segments are text, the rest are thoughts said aloud. The numbers denote thought units.

(1) Well okay ... let's do a ... (2) what's gonna be the thesis on this ... (3) how about the educational system? (4) ... the educational system in America has ... uh ... transformed itself from ... a ... (5) golly ... a ... a... (6) god that doesn't make any kind of sense ... (7) the educational system in America ... (8) no ... (9) during the past thirty years ... the American public education system has been influenced and ... a ... a ... changed in ... a ... myriad of ways ... a ... a number of ways ... a lotta ways ... (10) ... um ... okay ... (11) *During the past thirty years, the American education system has been influenced and changed ... a ... ways ... tremendously.* (12) ... um ... okay ... now that's what we are gonna be working off of ...

Which phases of the writing process can be seen in this protocol?

13.3.1 Read the following passage (taken from Schank and Lebowitz, 1980):

> The President of the United States flew to Moscow yesterday. He met at length with Russian leaders. They signed an agreement for new cultural exchanges. The President continued his European swing by flying on to Paris.

Texts are not only understood on the basis of prior knowledge. From the news story fragment above, data can be deduced that are not literally included in the text. However, the data are assumed to be known. Use the terms *schema* and *default value* in answering the following questions:

- Can you prove that the signing of the agreement took place in Moscow?
- Did only the Russian leaders sign?
- Why did the President get scared?

13.4.1 Present subjects with the following text and ask them how many times the letter *f* occurs in it.

> The federal fuses are the ultimate results of scientific investigation combined with the fruits of long experience.

Try to explain the possible mistakes in answers in terms of content and function words (see Section 10.2). What does this say about the surface level in relation to the other two levels mentioned in Section 13.4?

13.4.2 Consider the next fragment (also mentioned earlier in this chapter).

> Late for school
>
> Karen had overslept. If she hurried, she might still make it. Quick, but she'd have to skip breakfast. Run! Almost! She saw the hands of the clock over the entrance move to the penultimate minute and started to run. There were no more seats left. Gasping, she leaned against the swinging door and thought: I hope I don't get caught.

Give examples of the various types of prior knowledge (frame, script, scenario) that play a role when this short passage is read.

13.5.1 Explain the influence of schemata in the construction component of Kintsch's model.

13.5.2 Devise a few more propositions that could come up in the schema of *to bake* and accordingly prove that Figure 5 is only a part of the propositional environment of *to bake*.

13.6.1 Explain whether or not the term *metaphor* is a metaphor.

13.6.2 Prove that in a metaphor such as "time is money" not everything is projected or mapped from one domain onto the other.

13.6.3 Below is a fragment of conversation from the movie *Scent of a Woman* as cited in Ponterotto (2003). Name the italicized metaphors.

George:	What did he say?
Charles:	Nothing.
George:	What do you mean ... nothing?
Charles:	He said the same things he said to both of us, only he said them over to me.
George:	You know what he's doing? He's *good cop-bad copping us*. He knows I'm *old guard* and you're *fringe*. He's going to *bear down on me* and he's going to *soft soap you*. Did he soft soap you, did he?
Charles:	No.
George:	Chas, I detect a slight *panic pulse* from you. Are you panicking?
Charles:	Yeah, a little.
George:	Come on, you're on scholarship, right?
Charles:	Yeah.
George:	You're on scholarship from Oregon at Baird. You're a long way from home, Chas.
Charles:	What has that got to do with me being on scholarship?
George:	I don't know how it works out there. But how it works here ... we *stick together*. It's us against them, no matter what. We don't *cover our ass*. We don't tell our parents. *Stonewall everybody*. And above all ... never ... never ... never ... *leave any of us twisting in the wind* ... And that's it.

Assignments

13.1.1 Look up other models of the writing process (for example Van Wijk, 1999) and compare these with Hayes's model. Try to describe the differences in importance of the various components.

13.2.1 See question 13.2.1. Repeat this procedure with someone you know. Formulate a writing assignment, for example, an application letter in reaction to a job advertisement, have your subject read the ad and make some notes. Then ask him or her to think aloud while commencing the writing task and note the thoughts that he or she says aloud. After that, verify which phases of the writing process you can distinguish in the protocol.

13.3.1 Present the following story (from Bransford & Johnson, 1973) to a small group of subjects and ask them to write it down 30 minutes after reading it.

> The view was breathtaking. From the window one could see the crowd below. Everything looked extremely small from such a distance, but the colorful costumes could still be seen. Everyone seemed to be moving in one direction in an orderly fashion and there seemed to be little children as well as adults. The landing was gentle, and luckily the atmosphere was such that no special suits had to be worn. At first there was a great deal of activity. Later, when the

speeches started, the crowd quieted down. The man with the television camera took many shots of the setting and the crowd. Everyone was very friendly and seemed glad when the music started.

Use this story in three conditions: 1. without title; 2. titled "Watching a peace march from the 40th floor"; 3. titled "A space trip to an inhabited planet". Compare the summaries, focusing on the four functions of schemata.

13.4.1 Explain, using the notions of semantic and pragmatic knowledge, whether or not it will take readers an equal amount of time to determine the antecedent for sentences (a) and (b).

    a.   Steve blamed Frank because he spilled the coffee.

    b.   Jane blamed Bill because he spilled the coffee.

13.5.1 Take the concept *to bake*. Present it to five people and have each of them name three associations with this concept. Render the associations of these five people in a propositional representation such as Figure 5.

13.6.1 Analyze a sports report in the light of the metaphor "all game is war game".

Bibliographical information

13.1   Since in the research field of cognitive discourse studies most attention is paid to writing and reading, this chapter is confined to these two topics. Chafe (1994), however, focuses on speaking and writing, and presents, though a bit wide of the mainstream, a valuable study about language and mind. For an influential example of a model of speaking, see Levelt (1989). Field (2003) provides a good and practical introduction to writing, reading, listening and speaking with useful exercises.

In this section only the three best-known models are discussed. For an overview of other models up to the 1980s, see Hillocks (1986). In the study of written communication, more attention is paid to the rhetorical domain, as in Bereiter and Scardamalia's second model, and to the audience factor. See also Kirsch and Roen (1990). For an overview of models from the past two decades, see Alamargot and Chanquoy (2001). A good starting point for further research is the model by Van Wijk (1999), which is based on Levelt (1989).

13.2   For research into the writing process through product and process analysis, various approaches can be found in the collections of papers by Levy and Randell (1996), Kent (1999), and Torrance and Galbraith (1999).

13.3   The notion of schema in the study by Bartlett (1932) inspired much research into cognitive aspects of discourse comprehension in the 1970s and 1980s. A classic in this cognitive approach in discourse studies is the publication Mental Models by Johnson-Laird (1983). A good introduction to the field of discourse processing is offered by Singer (1990). Of the many collections of papers Balota, Flores d'Arcais and Rayner (1990) is still very valuable.

In this chapter only the cognitive approach to discourse is dealt with. However, in other related domains the cognitive turn has also become important. See for seminal studies in cognitive grammar and cognitive semantics Langacker (1999, 2002) and Fauconnier (1994, 1997) respectively. Cognitive stylistics is also gaining in importance; see the collection of papers by Semino and Culpeper (2002), which was already mentioned in Chapter 8. Good introductions to cognitive linguistics are Ungerer and Schmid (1996), and Lee (2001).

13.4   In this section on the levels of representation only the older, more or less classic experiments that are discussed in several handbooks are dealt with. A good overview is provided by Noordman and Vonk (1999). Gernsbacher (1990) is valuable.

In the old model by Kintsch en Van Dijk (1978) the cyclical process is well described with examples. The assumption that seven propositions can be transferred from one cycle to a new cycle was inspired by Miller's 1956 article on "the magical number seven".

For more on anthropological research into frames, see Goffman (1974). More information on scripts can be found in Schank and Abelson (1977), while Sanford and Garrod (1981) address the notion of scenario.

There are many good collections of papers that cover a great variety of research topics in discourse processing. A good one, with introductory papers written for graduate students, is Graesser, Gernsbacher and Goldman (2003). Others good examples are Weaver, Mannes and Fletcher (1995), Gernsbacher and Givón (1995), Britton and Graesser (1996), Liebert, Redeker and Waugh (1997), Koenig (1998), Ashwin and Moorman (1999), and Otero, León and Graesser (2002).

13.5   In this section Kintsch's model is discussed in a simplified form. For a complete overview of and for background information on his model, see Kintsch (1998). For a very valuable contribution to research on discourse representation and a simulation model of the access process, see Myers and O'Brien (1998).

13.6   This section only deals with the comprehensibility of metaphors and not with metaphors as a grammatical manifestation. Only a very informal explanation of some characteristics of lsa is given. For some critical remarks, see Glenberg and Robertson (2000). Since the concept of metaphor is one of the most studied subjects, a vast quantity of literature is available. A very stimulating publication in this respect is still Lakoff and Johnson (1980). See also the references mentioned in the bibliographical information of Section 8.3.

There is also more social-psychological research into metaphors and their persuasive effects. A good overview of the research in the past decades is given by Mac Cormac (1985), Gibbs and Steen (1999), Sopori and Dillard (2002) and Barcelona (2003).

14 Discourse and institution

14.1 The agent–client approach

In this introduction it is emphasized many times that the discourse situation plays an important role in discourse research (see especially Section 3.4). One aspect of the situation that has been given special attention is the institution in which the discourse takes place. This chapter contains some main issues in research done into the language of and within institutions. For a clear understanding of this research, it is necessary to understand the theoretical ramifications of the concept *institution*.

Institution as a concept originated in sociology; it is used to describe those activities by which individuals construct and maintain a society. These activities are aimed, for example, at the transmission of knowledge (the institution "education") or combating crime (the institution "justice"). Many of these aims have an ethical aspect; for example, the ideal of a just and safe society (justice). Owing to these lofty aims, institutions are imbued with a certain amount of moral authority.

Institutions can be viewed as the mediators between individuals and society as a whole, or as the means by which individuals can form a society. Illustrative of this view are the speculations concerning the origins of institutions. The American sociologist William Sumner (1906) explained these origins by examining the nature of humanity. All humans have the same basic needs (food, intimacy, etc.). In order to satisfy these needs, individuals develop certain habits. Groups of people develop customs for repetitive behaviors (eating, styles of living together, etc.) that are passed on from generation to generation. When the members of the group start to believe that these usages or customs are correct, these become the norm in the individual and societal conscience. In this way mores and morals develop. When mores and morals are linked to rules, rules that carry penalties if broken, institutions come into existence to serve as social channeling systems of human behavior. Three aspects of the concept *institution* are important in discourse studies. They are illustrated below using the example of education.

a. *Role behavior*
Institutions regulate individual behavior through a system of social roles that participants must fulfill. An institution objectifies individuals, making them players of

particular roles. In the institution "education", for example, there are roles for the school principal, the teacher, the student, the class president, etc. The roles determine the individuals' behavior and what each may expect of others in their roles. A good example is the rules governing interruption. It is acceptable for a teacher to interrupt a student, but less acceptable for the student to interrupt the teacher.

b. *Differentiation trends*
In less complex societies, people and their roles are not really very separate. However, as societies grow more complex, the accent shifts towards the role and away from the person. These days the personal life of a teacher or the role that such a person fulfills in other institutions, for example, as a member of the city council or as the treasurer of a local club, is of little importance to the institution of education. In simpler societies the differentiation into roles is less defined. Each institution also has its own set of norms. The language within the institution "research" must meet different requirements (such as precision) than language in education (comprehensibility).

The trend towards differentiation also means that institutions specify their areas more and more precisely. Education does not concern itself with psychological well-being; teachers are only responsible for the transfer of information. Differentiation also takes place within institutions. In higher education there are more ways of imparting information than there were in previous centuries: lectures, seminars, tutorials, one-on-one sessions, etc. Language behavior in these meetings varies from more formal to more informal.

c. *Institutional power*
Institutions regulate individual behavior through their systems of rules, and exercise power through them. The teacher's advice usually weighs more heavily than the intuitions or preferences of the students or the parents. The power aspect also includes the tendency towards domain enlargement. Schools often perceive it as their task to provide religious or sex education, traditionally tasks of church and family. Another example in this regard is the attention universities currently give to finding employment for recent graduates.

So far three important aspects of institutions have been illustrated with the education example. In research into institutional language within the framework of discourse studies, attempts are made to describe the role that participants fulfill in an institution by analyzing their language use. The power relation is specifically in focus, as it manifests itself in the interaction between the agents and the clients of an institution: teacher–student, attorney/defendant–witness, doctor/therapist–patient, civil servant–citizen, priest–parishioner.

Other research questions deal with institutionally determined acts and the differences between institutions, or the influence of systems of institutional rules on institutional discourse. In other words, this research deals with the question of how a specific form of language (a medical examination, a police interrogation, etc.) is related to a specific function (making a diagnosis, finding evidence for a conviction, etc.). In this chapter the five institutions that receive the most attention in discourse studies are reviewed.

14.2 Politics

The perhaps most remarkable characteristics of the language of politicians are related to the strategy of obeying the face-keeping principle (see Section 2.6). This principle also plays a role in non-institutional, everyday discourse, but in political discourse it is more salient. Especially in discussions to reach agreement about discrepancies which at first and even second sight are irreconcilable – the essence of political discourse – it is important to make subtle distinctions and modifications in opinions defended at an earlier stage in the public debate, without losing face. At the same time it is necessary to develop strong arguments to convince opponents who are indispensable in the implementation of any decisions made. These two forces, the need for modification and the need for persuasion, explain why some phenomena occur more frequently in political discourse than in everyday discourse.

a. The need for modification
As regards modification, in the literature on political discourse three phenomena have attained special attention: the hedging strategy (see also Section 12.4), euphemisms and strategic ambiguity. Under hedging we find phenomena that reveal the degree of uncertainty about a given proposition. Hedging can also be used as a strategy to avoid full responsibility for the proposition that is made in an utterance. Compare the following examples:

(1) a. My opponent based his viewpoints on misinterpreted data.
    b. It seems to me that my opponent based his viewpoint on, what I might call, data that are to some extent possibly misinterpreted.

The clear statement (1a) can be attacked directly, but with (1b) the speaker only gives his own "humble" opinion, and merely suggests the possibility of misinterpretation to a certain degree. On the other hand, if the opponent does not criticize this statement (1b), then the proposition (that some data may have been misinterpreted) has to be accepted without restrictions.

The use of euphemism is most criticized in political language. In applying mild or vague words for offensive or unpleasant things politicians try to "soften" the content. Here are thirteen examples for rephrasing the unpopular measure of economy during a recession:

(2) 1. restriction on spending, 2. saving austerity, 3. retrenchment, 4. adjustment of expenses, 5. revision of long-range plans, 6. proposals to limit anticipated expenses, 7. reclassification of financial priorities, 8. gearing expenses to societal needs, 9. balancing earnings and expenditures, 10. postponing expenses, 11. zero growth, 12. completion of a slimming operation, 13. stipulating more detailed boundary conditions for the spending space.

Critics of euphemisms seem to believe that using milder words will result in a milder attitude. Still, it has never been convincingly proved that, for example, hearing the word *disincentivate* for *penalize* will result in a more positive attitude towards measures for penalizing.

Without context many utterances are ambiguous. Normally, the context provides enough information on whether, for example, in the utterance "John saw the man with the binoculars", John had the binoculars or the man. But ambiguity can also be used deliberately, especially in discourse situations where it is important that different parties can interpret one formulation differently according to their own values. This is called strategic ambiguity. A famous example is a passage in UN resolution 242 of 1967 concerning the territories occupied by Israel.

(3) (…) Withdrawal of Israel armed forces from territories occupied in the recent conflict (…)

This formulation lacks the definite article *the* before "territories". Hence, two inter-pretations are possible: "all territories" or "some territories". The Arabs had insisted, without result, on adding *all*. After much discussion they voted for the resolution with the argument that the formulation as in (3) can be interpreted as "the territories". The opponents of the resolution also voted for it because they were able to interpret this formulation as "some territories".

b. *The need for persuasion*

The second force, the need for persuasion, has given rise to much criticism in line with Orwell's book *1984*, a book that in the days of the Cold War (after the Second World War) parodied communism. Politicians, as has been said, are eager to change mean-ings or illocutions in their manipulation of the content of a message. What follows is an example from a Dutch parliamentary debate. A Dutch shipyard had secured an order from Peru to renovate a navy ship. The order was important for the shipyard's future, as it had been denied any further governmental financial support. At that time Peru's economic situation was poor and if Peru had failed to pay the order, the Dutch government would have been obliged to support the shipyard nonetheless. It turned out that the Dutch Finance Minister had sent a secret coded message to the ambassador of Peru. Many Dutch members of parliament suspected the Dutch government of a lack of willingness to support the Dutch company and wanted to know whether the government had gone beyond its authority by perhaps advising the Peruvian government to cancel the order. Here is a passage from the Dutch Finance Minister's answer to a question from a member of parliament about whether the Dutch government really had requested or suggested cancellation of the order.

> (4) Never, at any time in our contacts with Peru a request has been made
>   concerning postponement or cancellation of this order. We only made a
>   formal announcement concerning the negative decision about governmental
>   financial support. (…) I will now address the question whether the Minister has
>   interfered in this order. It depends on how one would like to explain this. The
>   word "interfere" is not to be understood as "trying to influence". That was not
>   the case at all. It has to be understood as "to inform".

In the longwinded debate on this question no clear information about the case was given. In fact, the debate focused on whether "giving financial information" had to be accounted for as the illocution *announcement*, *request* or *suggestion*.

In research into political language many attempts have been made to describe the kinds of strategies politicians use in manipulation. A good framework to start with is the approach used by Shmelev (2001). He analyzed Russian political discourse in the 1990s and used not only categories like metaphors, euphemisms and words with negative or positive connotations (*terrorists* versus *freedom fighters*) but also the following three categories.

> (5) Some manipulation ploys (Shmelev, 2001)
>   1. hiding a presupposition
>   "It is common knowledge that these measures have a negative influence on
>   our economy."
>   2. using an implicature as suggestion
>   "The money did not reach the miners. But the coal-mining bosses have
>   luxurious mansions built for them."
>   3. *de re* interpretation
>   "The American president went on rousing Americans' pseudo-patriotic
>   state of opinion."

A strong manipulative device is the hidden presupposition as in "Do you still drink a lot?" If the addressee answers negatively then he admits that he was a heavy drinker (see Section 7.5). The same goes for the first example in (5). The presupposition is the information that is unaffected by a negation ("It is *not* common knowledge that …"). So, the opponent of this utterance has to accept that the measures have a negative influence, even if he does not agree with this utterance. Understanding sequences of utterances means that an utterance B is relevant after an utterance A (see Section 2.4 about the cooperative principle). How can a listener attribute relevance to the second utterance in the second example in (5)? The only way to do this is by adding an implicature after the first utterance, namely, that the bosses keep the money for their own benefit. This implicature, however, is a suggestion that has to be proved. The third manipulation ploy refers to an interpretation that is opposite to a *de dicto* interpretation. The latter case concerns an interpretation of the formulation (the dictum), for example, if the listener thinks that the speaker judges the Americans' state of opinion as being "pseudo-patriotic". However, the *de re* interpretation as is meant above concerns an interpretation of the facts. The speaker presents his own interpretation as factual. The American president would, of course, only rouse a "patriotic state of opinion". In applying categories like these, Shmelev argues that a thorough pragmatic analysis is needed in political discourse.

14.3   Law

Discourse concerning the administration of justice is often criticized in three ways. First, in judicial interaction, and especially in a judicial interrogation, the suspect or the defendant sometimes seems to be manipulated or deprived of a fair chance by the cross-examination techniques in the courtroom. Second, a layman citizen who, for example, wants to explore his rights in judicial documents is often confronted with the unreadable text of a law. A third criticism is that a conviction or ruling often depends on the way in which the law or the behavior that lead to the initial indictment is interpreted. In the study of judicial discourse these criticisms recur in the three approaches that have prevailed in the last decades. The first addresses the question to what extent verbal interaction in the courtroom differs from everyday interaction or interactions in other institutional settings like a classroom or a surgery. The second approach deals with the genre of law itself and examines the question as to what extent the language of law can be clarified so that a citizen can understand legal language. In the third approach an analysis is made of the topics that discourse specialists are consulted about by lawyers who ask for help in interpreting linguistic behavior or legal documents. In this section examples are given of each approach.

a. *Characteristics of judicial interaction*

A current approach to analyzing institutional forms of interaction, like the judicial one, is the analysis of illocutions (see Section 2.3), especially the patterns in a series of illocutions. The central questions are: Which institutional patterns of speech acts can be discerned? Which strategies can the participants use to realize these patterns? What do these patterns and strategies reveal about the roles of the clients?

Below is an example of this type of analysis done by the German linguist Ludger Hoffmann (1983). The following is an analysis of a fragment of a court hearing. In this court case it had to be decided whether or not a suspect had jumped onto the hood of a police car. After one witness had given an unsatisfactory response, the examination of this witness continued as follows, with A as the prosecutor and B the witness.

```
(6)  A:        Now how exactly did het get up there, could you explain more
     A:  ⌈     precisely how he –?
     B:  ⌊                  No, well uh, no I didn't because uh as
     B:  ⌈     I said I was just leaving, I wanted to go in the direction of the S. Docks
 5   A:  ⌊                                                   Yes
     B:        and uh – he – I only saw, the two officers got in the car, hit
     B:        the doors shut, at that moment I turned again and – you see it was also
     B:        that – at that moment a moving car, the people mumbled and
     B:        – and said: "Good that they cleaned it up", and
10   B:        then uh – he passed me from the side, and then I saw Mr. X
     B:        on top of the car, and the officers stopped too
     B:        instantly. He skidded – at that moment f- he ran away again,
     B:  ⌈     so -, I know uh, too uh, therefore in that direction of uh – G. just ran
     A:  ⌊                                              Oh – but
15   B:  ⌈     away – and the two officers were lying behind – Oh!
     A:  ⌊     not so – not so fast, this is going too fast for us. Oh –
     A:        you just said, in your first description, that he
     A:  ⌈     suddenly jumped on the hood.    He jumped
     B:  ⌊                                 Yes
20   A:  ⌈     on it?    And you just said, that you first
     B:  ⌊        Yes
     A:  ⌈     saw him, when he was already on it?
     B:  ⌊     Well uh, I mean uh – it all happened
     B:        so fast, I mean, I followed him one way or another for a short while.
25   B:        how he sat on it and rode with them for five or ten meters
     B:        made them stop the car, the two officers got out, then he skidded
     B:        somehow he got off and probably -
     A:        He simply said: "The police car hit me and that's how
     A:        I wound up on the hood – I didn't jump, they ran me down," said Mr. X.
```

The witness's first answer does not make it clear whether or not he claims to have seen the accused jump onto the hood of the car. His testimony that the car was moving and that he saw the suspect, Mr. X, sitting on the car, does not eliminate the possibility that he jumped on it. The interrogator at this point reframes the question in line 18 and again in line 20. These reformulations are answered in the affirmative. This makes it possible for the interrogator to question the link to the witness's first statement. The witness is now forced to qualify his first statement and, when he becomes repetitious, is interrupted by the interrogator, who quotes the suspect. Hoffmann put the strategy of this interrogation into the form of a model:

(7) Speech acts as parts of a strategy
     Issue: Has the suspect committed the crime he is accused of?
     Basic Question → attempt to draw out a detailed description → reformulate →
     dispute connection with initial statement → present a different statement.

This pattern, which Hoffmann states is the basis of interrogation, maps out the specific linguistic form of discourse in a court of law. This analysis also shows how the court's function, ascertaining the truth concerning the guilt or innocence of a suspect, influences its procedures and organization and, therefore, judicial discourse.

b. *Legal documents and generic integrity*
The texts that are most criticized are legal documents because of their inaccessibility and incomprehensibility to the layman. In many societies action groups like the *Plain English Movement* claim that every citizen has the right to understand any document concerning civic rights and duties. Such movements prompt the question whether it is possible to simplify legal documents. Proponents of plain language argue that, especially in legal documents, many unnecessary distinctions and restrictions are made in obscure discourse structures and complex syntax. Opponents, however, argue that the first function of laws and legal documents should be to provide waterproof and airtight formulations concerning rights and duties, which may be at odds with criteria for comprehensibility.

The study by Bhatia (1993) gives good examples in support of the opponents while discussing a solution to the problems set out by proponents of plain legalese. Bhatia argues that legal documents can be clarified by some "easification devices", just like the example presented in Section 10.4 about the organization of legislative statements. The authors of a law can give extra information in the text about the structure, the kernel information, the motivation to use a special formulation, or the legislative intention for adding a special section. These easification devices, however, require extra information. As soon as the easification bears on the formulation itself, the risk of losing the legal waterproof formulation is great. Below is a short example.

(8)   Child benefit shall not be payable in respect of a child over the age of 16 years (…)

One could argue that the complex preposition "in respect of" is needlessly formal, and can easily be replaced by *to* or *for*. But this is not true. A formulation with *to* suggests that the money which can be made payable to parents or guardians must be paid to the child. A formulation with *for* wrongly indicates that the money has to be used for the child.

Bhatia argues that plain language in laws is not always possible, because the essence of the law is to give unambiguous formulations that enable judges to make decisions about the rightness or wrongness of human behavior. If one tries to reformulate a law in order to communicate with a layman audience then the "generic integrity" of a law is violated, because the genre of laws or legal documents is a special form for a special occasion (see Section 4.5 for this genre approach). So, a law cannot be waterproof and communicative at the same time, or in other words, a genre cannot serve two masters.

Better than reformulating the law is the design of a companion text with about the same content but without the judicial strength of the law itself. Below is another example cited in Bhatia's study.

(9)   The debtor under a regulated contract may discharge his obligations under the contract by paying or tendering to the credit provider the net balance due to the credit provider at the time of payment or tender.

(10)   When is the debtor entitled to pay out the contract?
      The debtor may pay out the contract any time. The contract is then discharged.

The reformulation in (10) of the legal formulation in (9) only gives the key content in a format that is much more accessible to the layman, namely, the question–answer pattern. Of course, this "law explanation" cannot function as the law itself. In that case this specific genre's integrity would be violated.

c. *Forensic linguistics*

In judicial practice language plays an important role. Many decisions depend on interpretations of legal documents or verbal behavior of people who defend their cases in the courtroom. Therefore, it is no surprise that discourse specialists are consulted in legal matters. This consultancy has led to a new branch of linguistics: forensic linguistics. Below is a representative example of a problem with which the author of this book was confronted.

A taxpayer turned to a government complaints office, because in his opinion the Internal Revenue Service had wrongfully not approved of a deduction. The taxpayer had moved three years after a job change and was of the opinion that he could lay claim to deduction of removal expenses, on the basis of the following explanation in the tax form.

(11)   Removal
Removal expenses are only deductible if the removal was necessary for your job. You must make a reasonable case for this.
Beware! Removal expenses are definitely deductible if:
  –   Within two years after having changed jobs or having been relocated, you move to a home located less than 10 kilometers from your new place of work while the distance from your previous home was more than 10 kilometers;
  –   Because of the removal the travel distance between your home and your work has at least been halved and has been shortened by at least 10 kilometers.

"No," the Internal Revenue Service said, "you must comply with both conditions, and you have had that job for three years now." So in their opinion, the enumeration in (11) had to be read as a conjunctive. "No," the taxpayer said, "it says nowhere that I must comply with both conditions. I comply with the second condition, so I am right." On the basis of linguistic advice the ombudsman managed to convince the Internal Revenue Service that the explanation was open to two interpretations, and therefore had to be changed. An enumeration whereby two parts do not exclude each other can be read both conjunctively and disjunctively, unless the introductory part of the enumeration explicitly excludes one of the two readings.

The previous is just one example of the many kinds of problems for which linguists are consulted by lawyers and judges. Here are some other questions with which forensic discourse experts are confronted.

(12)   Some questions in forensic linguistics
  1.   Is the voice on this tape the voice of the suspect?
  2.   What kind of personal characteristics could be derived from this anonymous letter?
  3.   Can this utterance really be interpreted as a request or an order?
  4.   Can it be proved that the image of my client is damaged owing to this newspaper article?

It must be emphasized that discourse specialists can provide supporting evidence only. So, if there is a news report that, for example, the writer of letters containing a bullet was detected owing to specific words he used or typical aspects of typewriting, then there must have been other, non-linguistic clues as well. In that respect forensic linguistics is a "supporting science".

14.4   Bureaucracy

Verbal interaction can be perceived as being ruled by principles concerning cooperation, relevance and politeness (see Chapter 2). These principles can easily be detected
in symmetrical interaction in which the participants have the same rights and obligations. In the interaction between government and citizens, however, one of the most
prevailing characteristics is asymmetry. In spite of governmental campaigns in many
countries to address citizens as clients or even customers, the exchange of information
seems to be based not on coordination but on attempts to enhance the compliance
of citizens. The latter are, in many cases, overwhelmed by the irrelevance and lack of
politeness of governmental organizations.

Many research projects concerning bureaucratic discourse deal with the harmful
consequences of this asymmetric interaction for both government and citizens. The
government often does not succeed in obtaining the information necessary for solving
societal problems, and citizens often have too much difficulty in delivering the information in the right format. Many approaches in discourse studies focus on analyzing
this miscommunication and suggest improvements in document design in order to
tone down this asymmetry. Two research lines are more or less successful. The first
aims to develop and test more effective governmental documents. The second aims to
change the government's Big Brother image.

a. *Research on effective governmental documents*
The forms that governmental organizations use to obtain information are a text type
that pre-eminently indicates the asymmetry in the relation between government and
citizen. Among the form characteristics are:

(13)   Some characteristics of governmental forms
    1.   Obligation to provide information, without explication of relevance;
    2.   Questions concerning routine information (about address, etc.) that is
        already available at the organization;
    3.   Pre-sets of questions in which personal situations often do not fit;
    4.   Obligation to answer before a certain date without information about
        reaction time;
    5.   Lack of support and motivation to give the required information.

How do forms have to be designed in order to cope with such problems? A good example of research is presented in Jansen and Steehouder (2001). They analyzed what happened in the process of filling out a form by asking subjects to think aloud while they
were answering questions. Using this method they could, among many other things,
detect precisely where and why subjects had problems in understanding a question or

read more or less than was necessary to answer a question. One of the conclusions they drew was that readers are very economical in their strategy. They want to fill out a form as quickly as possible, and are very reluctant to spend much time reading explanations, without realizing that they actually need the instruction or more information. This reader's strategy was the cause of many mistakes, which in fact brings about the asymmetry between government and citizen, as the forms have to be returned to citizens, the latter then being obliged to fill them out again correctly.

In one of their experiments on improving form documents, Jansen and Steehouder designed different formats to test which design prompted subjects most effectively to read explanations when necessary. They placed the explanation at three different places: 1. on a separate sheet (as is customary in most governmental forms); 2. in the form to the left of the question; 3. in the form to the right of the question. Figures 1 and 2 give examples of designs 2 and 3.

Out of the target group of the form, 120 subjects were asked to fill out one of the three versions while thinking aloud. There proved to be a striking difference between the traditional form and the forms presented above. Of the subjects who filled in the traditional form with an explanation on a separate sheet, thirty percent did not examine the explanations, in contrast with ten percent of the subjects who were confronted

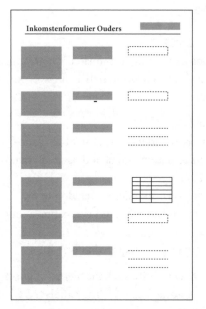

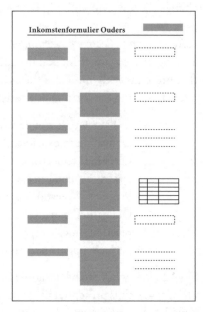

Figure 1. Three-column layout: explanations on the left, questions in the middle, answers on the right

Figure 2. Three-column layout: questions on the left, explanations in the middle, answers on the right

with the new forms. The researchers, however, found no difference between the "explanations-first" version in which the questions and answers were kept together, and the "questions-first" version which invited the reader to take notice of the explanation while going from question to answer. So, the issue of the best location for an explanation was not solved. However, in combination with optimizing other aspects, Jansen and Steehouder proved that the number of forms that had to be returned to citizens owing to mistakes dropped so remarkably that it was possible to recoup the expenses of this study within a year. In drawing this conclusion they underlined the societal relevance of the research.

b. *Research on government image*
Another approach in the study of bureaucratic discourse is research into the effect of image. Even if the government succeeds in high-standard document design, this is no guarantee that citizens will cooperate with "Big Brother". Hence, governmental institutions have spent much time and money on changing their image to that of a responsible firm that wants to serve its clients. In Sarangi and Slembrouck (1996) this issue is addressed with reference to the fact that tax authorities in European countries are trying to change their images by using a different register in their leaflets. Below are two examples from the UK Inland Revenue, from the 1980s and the 1990s.

(14) UK Inland Revenue Leaflet 1984 opening passage
      How to fill in your tax return
      These notes will tell you what I need to know about your income and capital gains and the allowances you may claim.
      Remember:
      – It is a serious offence to conceal any part of your income or chargeable gains.
      – Keep any vouchers, papers etc. that you use to fill in your tax return, in case I need to see them later.
      – (...)

(15) UK Inland Revenue Charter 1992 opening passage
      Filling in your tax return
      You are entitled to expect the Inland Revenue
      – To be fair
         – by settling your tax affairs impartially;
         – by expecting you to pay only what is due under the law;
         – by treating everyone with equal fairness.
      – To help you
         – to get your tax affairs right;
         – (...)

The differences in intended images are great. In version (14) the government restricts itself to factual information and addresses the citizen as someone who always evades paying taxes and is not capable of realizing himself that he must keep all evidence. This approach was considered unsuitable: citizens are, after all, self-confident and responsible members of society. The second version exudes the atmosphere of an invitation to enter into a contract in which both participants are obliged to cooperate. Nonetheless, Sarangi and Slembrouck criticized this approach, asking whether difference in style can really help reduce the asymmetry in societies where governmental institutions keep the power to impose fines if citizens refuse to follow the rules. Convincing evidence for either case still remains to be found, but it seems clear that the construction of citizens' clienthood is in fact a false construction; the asymmetry cannot be neutralized with the help of document design alone.

14.5   Media

The discourse approach to media can be seen as a special branch within the study of mass communication, the study of the continuous process of disseminating messages by professional communicators without restrictions on the number of audiences via public channels like press, television, radio and the Internet. Nowadays, important issues in mass communication studies are: How is it decided what is news? What is the quality of media content? Is there freedom of the press? What is the power of the media? Is journalistic objectivity possible?

The last question, the neutrality of the news, has been the stimulus for many discourse approaches to media, especially the written media. Theoretically speaking (and following Bühler, see Section 2.1) linguistic signs, and also discourse like a news story, are not only purely symbolic in referring to objects and states of affairs. A discourse is also a symptom of the intentions of a sender. When a journalist describes the events to be reported, he has to select from the many data the facts that fit the five journalistic *w*'s in "who, what, when, where and why". He cannot do otherwise than, by making choices, present the information from a perspective, containing a vision, a focalization and empathy (see Section 7.3). And moreover, when a journalist interviews people, he finds himself, as a receiver of the news, in the same position as the listeners to the Ghost Story of Bartlett in Section 13.1. The schemata he has will color his rendering of the news. The discourse approach to the debate on objectivity, that everything is always described from a certain perspective, can be summarized as "All news is views". In other words, objectivity is impossible. A journalist may come close to objectivity by hearing both sides of the argument, but even then he cannot be completely neutral.

The challenge of the media discourse approach is to prove from discourse analysis and research into production and perception to what extent news stories are biased, in what way this is caused by the opinions of the journalists and to what extent this influences readers or listeners. Discourse analysis of the media is an extended stylistic analysis. It includes the study of content (which topics are selected or excluded?), the structure (what is put in the lead of a story and what kind of information is located at important places, at the start of a paragraph?) and the wording: the structuring of the information and lexical choices. There are important stylistic differences between the two following formulations.

(16)   a.   The police killed ten protestors
       b.   Ten people died in riots.

Sentence structures can be analyzed according to the *w*'s in "who, what, when, where and why". In the so-called transitivity analysis the focus is on verbs, like the transitive *to kill*, which can be used in an active or passive form, and the intransitive verb *to die*, where there is no actor. In (16b) the actors are not mentioned. This could mean that the journalist does not think it is important to mention the actors. In analyzing lexical choices the focus is on connotations of words. Many words have a denotation, roughly speaking the factual meaning, and a connotation, a more emotive and evaluative meaning (see also Section 7.6). Compare the more factual *father* with the more emotive *daddy*, or the more neutral *to kill* with the more evaluative *to murder*. In this example there is a striking difference between the more positive "protest" and the more negative "riot", both presumably referring to "civil unrest".

a. *The production of news*
Of course, just giving one or two news-story examples is not enough to prove journalistic bias. Many attempts have been made to systematically analyze reports in different newspapers to detect differences in ideologies. A representative example of this kind of research is the analysis done by Fang (2001). He analyzed China's official newspaper and Taiwan's official newspaper in order to detect ideologically motivated differences. He chose "civil unrest" as a topic, as the controversy between government and demonstrators could provoke different ideologically motivated reports. He collected 153 articles from the two newspapers and compared their reports on demonstrations in South Africa and Argentina in the 1980s.

Since the white apartheid regime of the time had friendly relations with Taiwan but not with China, one would expect the Taiwanese newspaper to be more positive about the South African government and more negative about black demonstrators. For the Argentine case, however, one would expect no differences since Argentina had friendly relations with both China and Taiwan. In this research, all kinds of analysis were carried out, from theme analysis to lexical choices. Below are some examples from the analyses of headlines on "South African civil unrest".

(17) a. Some headlines from the Chinese newspaper
1. South African authorities have issued orders prohibiting mass rallies and dispatched police, who opened fire to suppress the demonstrating crowd.
2. Further demonstrations by the blacks in South Africa are again suppressed.
3. South African masses defy brute force to continue marching.

b. Some headlines from the Taiwanese newspaper
1. South African riots not over yet. Masses are still assembling in troubled townships.
2. South Africa continues to have riots. Many police and civilians injured or dead.
3. A series of riots in South Africa evolved into a political crisis.

In the Chinese newspaper the script of "racial struggle" seems to be dominant. The black demonstrators are reported on as victims and the white policemen as aggressors. In the Taiwanese newspaper the "law and order" script is more dominant. In mentioning the police and the civilians no reference is made to the racial background. Various analyses of the complete texts proved that the Taiwanese newspaper handled this unrest as a more or less normal civilian protest, while the Chinese newspaper supported the black demonstrators in their struggle against the white regime.

One could argue that the results based on just this one case are more or less coincidental. However, the strong point of this research is that the analysis was compared with that of another case: civil unrest in Argentina. Because both China and Taiwan had friendly relations with this country, it could be predicted that there would not be any differences in ideological stance between the two countries. And, indeed, thorough analysis of the Argentine case did not uncover important differences. Below are some headlines on "Argentine civil unrest".

(18) a. Some headlines from the Chinese newspaper
1. Argentina declares curfew for 30 days. People think riots related to worsening economic situation.
2. Argentine situation remains tense.

b. Some headlines from the Taiwanese newspaper
1. Argentina declares state of emergency. Inflation caused violent civilians to loot
2. In Argentina more troops sent to quell unrest.

There are stylistic differences in lexical choices, for example, "curfew" versus "state of emergency" and "riots" versus "looting" but these differences could not be related to different perspectives on the unrest.

This research demonstrated that one can do research on language and ideology based on independently formulated hypotheses based on ideological data outside the discourse. Let's now turn from the production aspect of the news to the perception aspect.

b. *The perception of news*

In the study of news perception, research into persuasion (see Section 12.4) plays an important role. The main question in this domain is: To what extent do differences in reporting influence the readers' attitude? This question led to an experiment concerning the influence of negative publicity (Renkema and Hoeken, 1998).

In mass communication studies, the power of the media is a much-debated issue. Are elections won through positive television exposure? Are the media just a serving hatch for the (lack of) power of the people reported on? Or are the media so powerful that they can create or break a reputation or an image? The following contribution to this debate stems from the context of the Dutch culture. In an experiment the question whether readers really change their attitude owing to the characteristics of a news story was addressed. An explanation of the news case follows first.

In several news stories in a regional daily, a company had become the topic as the main actor in a bribery scandal involving politicians. As a result of this publicity, the company's managing director had to move to another town and several job applicants turned down job offers when they found out about it. One of the leads that were used in the experiment was this version from the regional newspaper.

> (19)   The lead of the original newspaper article
>   *No taboo on bribery at Van der Grient*
>   Father Toon and son Hans Van der Grient have in recent years built up an
>   empire in West-Brabant from their head office in Krabbendijke in Zeeland. One
>   company after the other was set up or taken over. The company is active in the
>   areas of building contracting, road construction, and various related activities.
>   The tempestuous growth of the empire has gone hand in hand with the ever
>   more intimate contacts that father and son developed with administrators and
>   functionaries in West-Brabant. And indeed, Van der Grient has been a part of
>   many a shady business deal. There was no taboo on bribery within the company.

The company instituted legal proceedings against the newspaper, because in their opinion the news story was false or at least very biased. The company thought the following rendering of the case to be more objective.

(20) The lead of the rewritten version
Bribery investigated in public works contracts
The Public Prosecutor has begun an investigation into the acceptance of bribes by West-Brabant politicians and the possible involvement of the Van der Grient Construction Company. This company, headed by father Toon and son Hans van der Grient, is also active in West-Brabant in building contracting, road construction, and various related activities. Recently, a judicial inquiry has been underway to investigate the possible involvement of administrators and functionaries in the awarding of public work contracts. The conduct of Van der Grient is also being investigated in this regard. Earlier, an affiliated company was connected to a bribery scandal.

The company argued that even the information in the rewritten lead should not be reported. After all, the investigation had only just been started, and the mere mention of this information might cause people to react with the "no smoke without fire" attitude; the results for the company would then be just as negative. To test this hypothesis, purely factual information about the company was used in the experiment as well.

(21) The neutral information about the company
Van der Grient is a construction company that has its head office in Krabbendijke in Zeeland. In recent years, the company has also had operations in West-Brabant. There it is active in building contracting, road construction, and various related activities.

In order to avoid the interference of variables such as knowledge about the actual news case, the experiment was conducted in a different, comparable region of the Low Countries. The central question was: What is the effect of the manner of reporting on the corporate image of the company? Readers were asked to read three newspaper articles, including the original or the rewritten version of the report on the company. Subjects were not aware that the research concerned the image of this company. Other readers received only the neutral information. About 450 subjects participated. They were told that the study had to do with the way in which newspaper articles were read and they were asked to answer questions about the trustworthiness, the expertise, and the attractiveness of the company.

The results showed that subjects who had read the original or rewritten version gave the company a much lower score on each aspect of image, and that they were more likely to say that the company's growth was owed to bribes than were participants who had only read the neutral information. The manner of reporting was of influence, too. Reading the original version resulted in a harsher judgment of the company's trustworthiness than reading the other versions.

One could argue that image damage due to negative publicity is only temporary. Newspaper readers get so much information that they will forget the negative publicity after a few days. To test this view, readers of the original and rewritten versions were interviewed by telephone two weeks after the experiment (without knowing about this follow-up). They were asked a selection of the same questions. The results indicated that though the damage to the trustworthiness had slightly decreased it was still quite large, and that the damage to attractiveness had even increased. Therefore, the results of this experiment contradict the slogan "Today's headline is tomorrow's history." And even more important, using this approach to media studies it was shown how significant specific discourse characteristics can be in changing opinions.

14.6   Health care

One of the first discourse approaches to health care was a co-production of the socio-linguist Labov and the psychotherapist Fanshel (1977). They analyzed fifteen minutes of interaction between a therapist and a client suffering from anorexia nervosa. Their aim was to explain why sequences of utterances that are at first sight non-coherent do make sense to the participants. One of their examples is the following (T is the therapist, C is the client).

(22) T: And it never occurred to her to prepare dinner.
       C: No.
       T: She was home all afternoon.
       C: No, she doesn't know how.

What is remarkable here is the fact that the client indicates, by giving the reaction "No", that she understands a statement as a question. How can this uptake (see Section 2.3) be explained? Labov and Fanshel argued that such sequences can only be analyzed adequately if one takes into consideration the differences in "knowledge domains" between the agent and the client of an institution. In this example the therapist refers to facts or events that are only known by the client. And in other cases the therapist will refer to facts that are only known in medical handbooks, for example, the causes of anorexia. Using this approach Labov and Fanshel stimulated the analysis of institutional interaction in relation to the differences between agents and clients, especially differences that are related to knowledge and knowledge gaps.

In the past decades a variety of topics has been studied in the discourse approach to health care. The problems of knowledge gaps and differences in knowledge domain have been dealt with in the study of the medical register. What is the effect of using medical jargon, like *mamma carcinoma* instead of *breast cancer* or euphemisms like *seedlings* instead of *spread of cancer*? Also the metaphor in medical discourse has received attention. Does the use of metaphors contribute to the healing process or is it a hindrance? If we talk of a body as a machine with broken parts, does that enhance the power attributed to a doctor as a person who can fix bodies like cars, and is that positive or negative? Or if we talk of a medicine as declaring war on cancer cells, does that reflect the masculine medical culture and does that contribute to a depersonalization of the patient, who is not more than a battlefield on which soldiers are fighting? Medical narratives have been analyzed as well. There proves to be a difference between the narratives patients tell about their illnesses, and which are often disrupted not by conversational questions but by diagnostic questions from doctors, and the narratives that medical personnel write down in reports on the patient's disease.

In this section two other topics are chosen. The first can be considered a representative example of applied discourse studies: how can stylistic analysis help in solving problems of mental health care? The second topic deals with medical health care and addresses one of the central problems in institutional discourse: the power relation between agents and clients.

a. *Stylistic analysis of therapeutic discourse*

What kind of data does a therapist need to decide whether therapy can be successfully ended? This question is not only important for the therapist and the client, as it has managerial implications, too. If therapies take too much time, other clients are unnecessarily placed on a waiting list. If therapies end too early, clients may have to come back later to resume therapy, which is very inefficient.

The question of therapy success lies at the heart of a study by the social psychologist Baus and the linguist Sandig (1985). They started from the assumption that a therapy is successful to the extent that a client can talk coherently about feelings. Therefore, they stylistically examined the way clients talk about their feelings. Forty therapy sessions that dealt with a patient who had trouble with her role as a wife were analyzed. In this investigation an attempt was made to find out, among other things, if the patient's style changed in the process of the therapy, as that is seen as a sign of success. At the beginning of the therapy the patient stated that she was considering leaving her husband.

(23)   About a year ago I did consider whether I wouldn't prefer having to leave the house and living alone, and in part that was completely unthreatening to me.

This formulation contains contradictions. The words "prefer" and "having to leave" are contradictory, which is also true of the words "completely" and "in part". After being prompted by the therapist, the patient said the following:

(24) There is a contradiction. The thought of him having a traffic accident or something doesn't make me feel bad at all nor do I find myself feeling guilty. Although I do think that I should feel that way.

The therapist called this a discrepancy between feeling and thinking. Stylistic analysis showed that in the first sessions, formulations were given in which descriptions of feelings were choked off and words were chosen that were more rational.

Eighteen months later at the end of the therapy, the patient's language had changed dramatically. There were more expressions of observation such as *it struck me that, I sense*, and *I experienced*. The expressions of emotion were also more differentiated: for example, *I couldn't stand it, I was frozen*, as is clear from the following excerpts.

(25) Yesterday in the psychodrama group it struck me that I really managed not to look at the others during such a game.

(26) I believe that that truly surprised me.

These and other examples that showed that the patient was more in touch with her feelings proved to Baus and Sandig that their intriguing assumption was true; a correlation does exist between style change in patients' language and therapy success.

b. *Power relations in doctor–patient interaction*

In one of her studies Ruth Wodak (1996) addressed the power relation between doctors and patients as she tried to answer the question about the typical discourse patterns that can be identified in doctor–patient interaction. Wodak analyzed almost a hundred conversations in a Viennese hospital. In these analyses she focused, among other things, on speech acts, particles and ways of addressing. Here is an example from a conversation between a doctor (D) and an 87-year-old patient (P), presented in the HIAT notation (see Section 9.1) as explained in (28).

(27) 1. D: ⌈ Right we'll have to take off the gown too
          P: ⌊   (.........) don't

       2. D: Why not? – We *are* in the hospital you know. Right –
               now then

       3. D: ⌈ let's sit down here shall we?
          P: ⌊   /quietly/   (.........)

       4. D: ⌈ *Right* take off the gown please.
          P: ⌊   Gown – but I've

       5. D: ⌈   take it off please – the gown. We've
          P: ⌊ got nothing under the gown.

6. D: ⎡ got to do an ECG. Right   No one's
   P: ⎣   (.........) Gown

7. D: looking – – well – it's only the doctor

8. D: ⎡ – isn't it.   He's allowed
   P: ⎣   The doctor can look – but

9. D: to look isn't he – right let's sit down here

10. D: ⎡ shall we.   exactly
    P: ⎣   Sometimes he even has to look (.........)

11. D: Right – tell me, which was the broken arm?

(28) Transcription symbols (after HIAT)

[	line brackets to show that people are speaking at the same time
(.........)	inaudible passage
–	break in intonation
– –	short pause
/quietly/	non-verbal feature
are	word spoken with emphasis (example)
.	falling intonation
?	question intonation

The doctor tries to make it clear four times that the patient has to take off her gown. The first attempt has the form of an indirect speech act and addresses the patient in the so-called "pluralis hospitalis". The second attempt consists of a rationalization of the situation: "We are in the hospital." The third attempt is a polite request. And the fourth attempt is an imperative, motivated with a technical reference to the situation. It is only after being given the information that only the doctor will be looking, that the patient gives in. Obviously the doctor has difficulties in analyzing the patient's fears. Instead of asking why the patient refuses to take off her gown or explaining the question, the doctor keeps repeating the question, each time in a stronger form. Based on such analyses Wodak concluded, among many other things, that the doctor's behavior was a form of exercising power. And in this interaction we again see that the knowledge gap between the doctor and the patient who does not seem to know why she has to undress for an ECG is a main factor in explaining this behavior.

Questions and assignments

Questions

14.1.1   What is the difference between the concept of role and the concept of face in politeness theory (Section 2.6)?

14.1.2   Explain why *language* and *marriage* can also be seen as institutions.

14.2.1   The modification phenomena *hedges*, *euphemisms* and *strategic ambiguity* are not only used in political discourse. They also occur in everyday language use. For example, picture the following situation. Two people are having an argument on the stairwell at work. One of them wants to leave and says: "Perhaps we can discuss this matter another time." Point out the three modification phenomena in this utterance.

14.3.1   Consider the following utterance: "For God's sake, let this man stay silent forever." What extra information do you need in order to produce evidence for a judge or a jury whether this is a request or an order? See also the felicity conditions for requests in Section 2.3.

14.4.1   Verify with which of Grice's maxims (see Section 2.4) the characteristics of governmental forms, as given in (13), conflict.

14.5.1   Describe the precise differences between texts (19) and (20) about a bribery scandal involving politicians.

14.6.1   Which views of style (see Section 8.2) are presupposed in the stylistic analysis of therapeutic discourse?

Assignments

14.1.1   What is the similarity between the concept of institution used in Section 14.1 and the meaning of the word *institution* in *De Institutione Oratoria* by Quintilianus and Calvin's *Religionis Christianae Institutio*?

14.2.1   Analyze a political speech (by, for example, Martin Luther King, John F. Kennedy or a famous politician from your own country) in terms of phenomena concerning modification and manipulation mentioned in Section 14.2.

14.3.1 The following passage in the Crimes (Hijacking of Aircraft, Section 8.3) Act 1972, cited in Bhatia (1993), created many problems for the courts because of the simple plain language it is formulated in. The subsection provides,

"The punishment for an offense against this section is imprisonment for life."

Two interpretations of this provision are possible: 1. The provision imposes a mandatory life imprisonment, or 2. The courts have a discretion to impose a penalty less than life imprisonment. Make a proposal for the procedure to determine which of the two interpretations is correct?

14.4.1 Choose a governmental form and analyze it according to the characteristics of governmental forms mentioned in (13). Try to improve the form by using the politeness principle (see Section 2.6).

14.5.1 Collect articles from various newspapers on one topic in which the same people recur. Verify how the quotations are assigned to the various characters, taking into consideration the denomination (naming), the verb that leads in the quotation and the omissions in comparable quotations. Verify whether, apart from direct speech (e.g., *John said: "I will come tomorrow."*), the following ways of reporting speech occur: free indirect speech (e.g., *He would come tomorrow.*) and indirect speech (e.g., *John said he would come tomorrow.*).

14.6.1 See the following narrative fragment, in which A is a working-class man, taken from Wodak (1996:150). Try to do a stylistic analysis according to the approach of Baus and Sandig. Collect and analyze other stories from Wodak's publication as well and compare the various analyses.

A: Often I stand there and think I am being swallowed up by the earth, then I, then I can't see anything anymore, I am quite gone ... Yes, in private industry, I think you are really done for, because I am still free in a way. Not long ago I was up on the, up on the Ringturm, on the eighteenth floor, and I thought the whole, the whole – what do you call it, the thing you hold on to, you know –

B: Railing?

A: That's it, the railing would break; I got giddy again, and thought, should I jump, but then I went to the lift, went down, took a seat in the coffeehouse, and tried like mad to read. I ran round the block, but it didn't work, then I went again.

Bibliographical information

14.1   The concept of institution was developed during the French Revolution to describe culturally deep-rooted forms of relations within a society that guaranteed people potential freedom from oppressive legislation. For the characteristics of institutions, see Luhmann (1970 & 1975).

A good starting point for further study is Stubbs (1996), who analyzed how discourse both constitutes and is constituted by institutions. In this chapter only the institutions are dealt with that have long had a prominent place in research. Therefore, such institutions as Church and family are not mentioned here. The research on education is rising; see for further reading Cazden (1988), Green and Harker (1988), Hicks (1996) and Duszak (1997). For more on the institution of business, see Drew and Heritage (1992), Taylor (1993), Boden (1994), Ehlich (1995), and Bargiela-Chiappini and Harris (1997).

14.2   Example (4) stems from a Dutch parliamentary debate of January 24, 1984.

An evergreen on political language is Bolinger (1982). A good introduction is Geis (1987). Papers by some leading researchers in this field are collected in Chilton and Schäffner (2002).

14.3   Atkinson and Drew (1979) is still a good introduction to the analysis of courtroom interaction. An ideological approach can be found in Philips (1998). For the readability of laws, see also Gunnarson (1989).

There is much good literature on forensic linguistics; see McMenamin (1993), a publication that was already mentioned in Section 8.3. See further Shuy (1992), which gives intriguing examples of the (ab)use of language evidence in the courtroom, and Gibbons (1994) and (2003) about law as a linguistic institution itself and about problems of understanding.

14.4   For several studies of bureaucratic discourse from a document design approach, see the series of papers edited by Jansen and Neutelings (2001). The research examples mentioned there refer to the Dutch government, but are also applicable to bureaucracy in other cultures.

14.5   A good introduction to mass communications studies is the oft-reprinted handbook by Agee, Ault and Emery (1994). An easily readable overview of the key issues in this field is provided by Dennis and Merrill (1996).

One of the first researchers in discourse studies to investigate the discourse aspects of news was, again, Van Dijk (1988). A good start to the media approach in discourse studies is given by Bell (1991), who was also a journalist himself. A stimulating collection of papers is presented in Bell and Garret (1998).

14.6   A good introduction to the field of discourse and health care is given by Mishler (1984). A good starting point for further study is provided by the collection of papers in Raffler-Engel (1990) and Platt (1995). See for medical narratives Epstein (1995), Frank (1995) and Smith (1996), and for medical metaphors Van Rijn-Van Tongeren (1997). The different studies in Ainsworth-Vaughn (1998) form a good basis for further study.

15 Discourse and culture

15.1 The Sapir-Whorf hypothesis

In Chapter 13, Discourse and cognition, we have seen that the study of discourse lifts a corner of the veil over how the mind works. In Chapter 14, Discourse and institution, we have seen how the study of discourse can provide insight into the way people, in their roles of citizens, patients, etc., interact in a society. In this final chapter the view is broadened to a more general aspect of society that goes beyond specific roles of communicators: culture. Roughly speaking, culture can be defined as the deposit of knowledge, beliefs, values and attitudes a group of people share; examples are Chinese culture, pop culture, a company culture, etc. Three questions are of special importance in discourse studies: Can we detect cultural values from discourse? If so, what can discourse tell us about how people are influenced by culture? And, is it possible to change cultural values by changing discourse?

At the heart of the study of the relation between discourse and culture lies a well-known and often criticized hypothesis, which is named after two American researchers in the first half of the twentieth century. Edward Sapir, a linguist and anthropologist, studied the Indian cultures in America and found many differences between their languages and the English language. One can easily observe that some languages have many different words for *ship* and others for *sand*, or that in one language people refer to the base of a mountain as *backside* and others as *foot*, or that some languages have specific verb forms for *we both* (the *dualis*). Sapir found many striking differences between the "exotic" Indian languages and the Indo-European languages. In his view of language he was influenced by the German philosopher Wilhelm von Humboldt, who was also mentioned in the chapter on stylistics (Section 8.1), with his principle of a one-on-one relation between form and meaning. Von Humboldt was of the opinion that the way a human being "views his world" is determined by his language. So, if our language has only one word for *sand*, Von Humboldt assumed that we do not perceive different sorts of sand.

Sapir defended a more subtle relation between language and worldview. In his opinion, language is not only an instrument for communication but the language system also creates schemata (see Section 13.3) for analyzing our world. If, for example, a language has a dualis then the speakers of that language will probably more easily differentiate between groups of two and groups of more than two. One of Sapir's students who himself became famous was Benjamin Whorf, a chemical engineer who worked as a fire damage expert at an insurance company. He studied many different languages (among which Hebrew), and visited many Indian reserves. In his work activities he found many instances of the way language influences our worldview. One of his well-known examples is the following. In an inspection into the causes of a fire at a company, Whorf found that in a description of company belongings employees described gasoline drums as empty. However, these drums had caused the fire, as they had exploded after an employee had thrown a red-hot match into a drum. The employee had not realized that an "empty" drum still contains inflammable vapors. Had the drums been described as "full", then they would have been handled more cautiously. So, the description "empty" constructed a specific perception of the world.

The Sapir-Whorf hypothesis has raised many violent and sometimes chaotic discussions about the relation between language and worldview. At least three obscurities have to be clarified.

First, what is meant by language? The fact that languages vary in the number of different words for objects is not surprising. A society based on commerce by sea needs more words for different ships, but does that mean that speakers of languages with only one word for ship do not see the differences between a vessel and a coaster? And it has to be said that many examples of differences between lexicons are not evidence-based. The well-known example that Eskimos have so many words for snow (falling snow, melting snow, hard snow, snow on the ground, old snow, etc.) is not true. Linguistics have shown that the Eskimo language has only two different word stems for snow (*qanik* for "snow in the air" and *aput* for "snow on the ground"). Language phenomena that are more likely to produce evidence of the influence of language on worldview are the metaphor (like the foot or backside of a mountain), or grammatical characteristics. An example is that in the Navaho language an action is presented as something that happens to a person, like "Dancing is happening with White Eagle" instead of our way of saying "White Eagle is dancing". Of course, it has to be proved convincingly that this way of presenting reality influences the worldview of English- and Navaho-speaking people.

Second, it is not clear what is meant by worldview. Is it a way of thinking? Is it the perception of reality or is it the way something is memorized (as in the Bartlett example in Section 13.3)? Or is worldview something like attitude or beliefs, or perhaps behavior? Most proponents of the Sapir-Whorf hypothesis in discourse studies seem to restrict themselves to attitude. But even then the influence of discourse on attitude has to be proved.

Third, the term *relation* is rather vague. A relation can mean "influence", but there are many researchers who only admit that there is some kind of non-causal relation.

In this weak form the hypothesis gives only a kind of parallel between language structure and the structuring of the reality. In this mitigated formulation the Sapir-Whorf hypothesis is often called the "linguistic relativity principle", which means that linguistic descriptions of reality are always relative.

Up to now there has not been much evidence for the idea that our language system influences our cognition. One of the most cited experiments is that by Carroll and Casagrande (1958). They studied the effect of differences between the Indian Hopi language and the English language on perception and behavior. In the English language one does not say "Cover the door opening", but "Close the door". The verb *to close* is used when a top or a lid exactly "covers" an opening. The verb *to cover* is used when we hide an object or enshroud an opening. In the Hopi language other distinctions are made. The verb *'u'ta* refers to closing lids or placing covers on boxes, whereas the verb *nonoma* means "to protect an object". In an experiment an Anglo group and a Hopi group were asked which two out of the three pictures presented in Figure 1 belonged together. If the language system influences perception, then the Anglo group would choose pictures 2 and 3, whereas the Hopi would opt for 1 and 3.

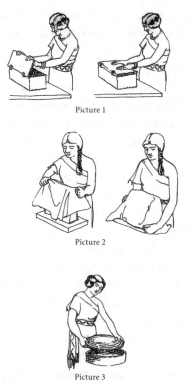

Picture 1

Picture 2

Picture 3

Figure 1. The pictures of Carroll and Casagrande's test

The results showed that there was only a slight tendency to choose the pictures in correspondence with the language system. However, in other experiments among Navaho and English people it was proved that white American children made more choices following the prediction for the Navaho than Navaho children themselves did. In discussions on linguistic relativity, evidence from experiments still does not fully convince the opponents of the Sapir-Whorf hypothesis, but the idea that language somehow reflects the way reality is looked upon has incited the study of the relation between discourse and culture.

15.2   Critical Discourse Analysis

The most prominent approach to discourse and culture is Critical Discourse Analysis, a method in which many central concepts in discourse studies play an important role. In this approach the aim of analysis is to detect societal problems, especially discrimination. In fact, discourse is studied from a Sapir-Whorf viewpoint, with reference not to differences between language systems, but to differences in language use within one language, while the broad concept of worldview is defined as an ideological perspective (see Section 7.3 on vision). Discourse is seen as a reflection of the power relations in society.

Critical Discourse Analysis is as old as discourse studies itself. In the first publication that contained the term *discourse* (Harris, 1954; see the bibliographical information in Section 1.1), an advertisement was analyzed with suggestions for two approaches: the internal cohesion relations and the correlation with society and culture. The last approach flourished in the socio-semiotic framework mentioned in Section 3.5, in which discourse is seen as a vehicle of meaning in a social context. Just as many sociologically oriented conversation analysts (see Chapter 9) analyze interactions in the hope of gaining insight into how people succeed in forming a community or society, the critical discourse analysts see discourse as an instrument to gain insight into societal problems.

The term *critical* in this approach means that an analysis cannot be neutral or free of values. Many researchers in this area regard pure sociological analyses as superficial and pure linguistic and stylistic analyses as low-informative. They draw consequences from the claim that discourse (in part) constitutes its context, and aim to prove by analysis that much discourse contains biased representations of reality. The aim of this kind of analysis is not only to detect manipulation and discrimination but also to understand the essence of these societal problems. In this critical view discourse analysis must have the aim of empowering powerless groups or minorities. In fact, discourse is seen as a form of social action or a political act that can be criticized.

Critical Discourse Analysis pays much attention to power relations and ideology, which are precipitated in discourse, and force the reader or listener to perceive reality in a specific, biased way. Put in the framework of speech act theory (see Section 2.2), the illocutionary force of utterances does not depend on the utterances themselves, as the philosopher Austin seemed to claim, but on the social position of the speaker or writer. Following Habermas's validity approach (see Section 2.3) the focus is on the legitimacy of the powerful to present reality as they do in discourse. Discourse is seen as a constitutive factor of social relations and belief systems. This view is based on the socio-semiotic approach (see Section 3.5), in which language performs not only the ideational function of representing the world and the textual function of relating discourse and context, but also the interpersonal function of enacting social identities and relations.

How does this critical analysis work? Most analytic work is inspired by stylistics (see Chapter 8) with the central question: Why is a given content formulated in the way it is and not in another possible form? Below are two short examples concerning racism.

(1)   Britain invaded by an army of illegals
      Britain is being swamped by a tide of illegal immigrants so desperate for a job
      that they will work for a pittance (…) slaving behind bars, cleaning hotel rooms
      and working in kitchens (…)

In Van Dijk (1996) such citations are used to demonstrate that certain newspapers are strongly racist. The war metaphor in the headline signals this explicitly. Why not "Britain gets support from foreigners" or "Many foreigners want to live in Britain"? And the phrase "work for a pittance" implies that immigrants want to take the jobs from native British workers. So, Critical Discourse Analysis indicates how this rendition of reality provides a negative image of poor foreigners.

(2)   (From a South African newspaper about a black student demonstration.)
      Exactly how and why a student protest became a killer riot may not be known
      until the conclusion of an elaborate inquiry that will be carried out by Justice
      Petrus Cillie, Judge President of the Transvaal.

In this passage, cited in Fairclough (1995), the key expression is "killer riot". The use of "riot" implies that the students themselves are responsible and "killer" suggests the involvement in the riot. Moreover, "killer", as in the collocation "killer whale" or "killer hurricane", normally indicates something whose nature it is to kill. Hence, the collocation "killer riot" implies that black South Africans are monstrous.

Especially in publications on critical discourse with a focus on fighting discrimination, such analyses are frequently found. Still, it has to be kept in mind that this approach, no matter how understandable in the light of social abuses, can be criticized itself. The following comments are from Widdowson (1998), who pleas for a more systematic and objective analysis, based on extensive corpus research and on reactions from real readers of discourse that has been analyzed as discriminatory or racist. The comment in (3) pertains to example (1) while the comment in (4) pertains to example (2).

(3)   1.   Why is the phrase "working for a pittance" not interpreted as a positive commiseration with the immigrants?
      2.   Why is "slaving" not linked to the colonial history of Britain, and analyzed as support for the poor workers, with the ambiguous "behind bars" (instead of "serving in bars") as reference to imprisonment?

(4)   1.   How should one evaluate a counterexample like "killer instinct" in the claim that "killer" is used in the indicated way?
      2.   Why not label "elaborate" as a key expression? This word normally has a negative connotation because it collocates with "too" and could therefore imply some skepticism on the position of authorities.

In Critical Discourse Analysis more and more attempts are being made to ground analyses and interpretations of power relations on systematic descriptions of discourse. A promising perspective was developed by the founding father of the socio-semiotic approach, who was already introduced in Section 3.5, Michael Halliday. In an introduction to functional grammar (Halliday, 1994) he proposed analyzing clauses in a discourse starting with the events or actions, and then making all the involved participants explicit. The following simple example can clarify this.

(5)   Many presents were given.

The verb *to give* has, as a syntactic pattern, so-called roles: There must be someone (the actor) to give something (the affected) to someone (the beneficiary). This phenomenon is usually referred to as *transitivity* (see also Section 14.5). Analyzing discourse in terms of actions and participants has the benefit that the analysis is independent of whether the participants are verbally mentioned. So, in (5) only the action and the affected are mentioned, which could mean that the writer thinks that it is of less importance to mention the actor and the beneficiary. In this transitivity analysis also the specific possible functions of passivization and nominalization can be clarified. Compare the following sentences:

(6)   The police arrested a lot of activists.
(7)   A lot of activists were arrested. (passivization)
(8)   There were a lot of arrests. (nominalization)

In this passivization the actor is left out, which in this case may be advantageous to the police. In the nominalization the affected is omitted while the action of the verb is sheltered in a noun. This might be less discriminatory than passivization. The results of a transitivity analysis of discourse can be the basis for experiments in which, for example, readers have to estimate to what extent participants in the event are discriminated against.

In another approach, started by Van Leeuwen (1996), not the events but the social actors themselves are in focus. On the basis of thorough discourse analysis he developed a model for doing research on how actors are presented. Here are three examples.

(9) An intake of some 54,000 skilled immigrants is expected this year.
(10) Australians feel they cannot voice legitimate fears about immigration.
(11) Australia is in danger of saddling itself up with a lot of unwanted problems.

Actors are not only presented as full constituents or simply skipped over as the subject of a clause. They can also be introduced in more subtle manners. In (9) one actor is skipped, the subject of "expected", but another actor is presented in a so-called possessivation "of some 54,000 skilled immigrants", and in this position is not foregrounded (see Section 7.2 on fore- and background information). In (10) there is one overt actor, "Australians", but also another nearly completely hidden actor; nearly, for a trace of its presence can be detected in the special kind of adjective, namely, an adjective in which a process is congealed: "legitimate". Who is the actor of legitimizing fear? In (11), which is also a sentence about "new immigrants", there is again one overt actor, "Australia", and one actor that has totally disappeared because it has been depersonalized as a problem. And the adjective "unwanted" leaves, as in (10), only a trace of the actor that does not want this problem. These relatively simple utterances show that an analysis of only actors who are mentioned in full constituents is not enough to answer questions about whether or not social actors have been presented in discourse.

In Critical Discourse Analysis many attempts have been made in the past decades to develop analysis models that can cope with discourse aspects in relation to discrimination. Two topics have received special attention. They are dealt with in the next two sections.

15.3 Gender

The study of gender and discourse has expanded enormously during the last decades. Many researchers try to analyze the difference between men and women in interaction or in representation in verbal material. Many other researchers try to find evidence for the dominance of men as a class over women, or to put it in a more nuanced fashion, that the relationship between men and women can result in dominance in conversation even if the individual man does not have the intention to dominate. The difference and the dominance theory have stimulated much research. Below are some examples concerning the difference between men and women.

How do we describe men and women? Can we put the possible differences in an ordered model? And, more important, do these differences really have anything to say about the way men and women differ? Here are two examples of texts about toys, presented in Caldas-Coulthard and Van Leeuwen (2002).

(12) Autumn Glory Barbie
       Autumn Glory Barbie doll from the Enchanted Seasons Collection is a stunning tribute to the wonders of fall. Her fitted, metallic appliquéd bodice transitions to a long, chiffon gown shimmering in hues of copper and auburn, adorned with fall leaves, and accented with hints of purple and gold. Her earrings are shaped like graceful golden leaves. Atop her long, auburn hair sits a dark, wine-colored hat, embellished with feather and leaves, adding the final touch to this wondrous autumn portrait.

(13) Action Man Bungee
       Action Man is the greatest hero of them all! Action Man leaps into the unknown with his fabulous bungee jumping kit, which includes a two-stage harness, grappling hook and super-cool sunglasses.

The differences are striking. Barbie is presented as static ("is", "wears"). The sentence structure contains long nominal groups referring to parts of her body ("face") or her clothes ("bodice", "earrings") with many evaluations from the aesthetic domain: "stunning", "shimmering", etc. The description suggests that she has had no influence on the way she looks; she has been dressed, styled and made up by other people, as is the case with, for example, a fashion model. The Action Man, on the contrary, is dynamic ("leaps") and controls his own actions, even "into the unknown". He is evaluated using terms belonging to social judgements, like "fabulous" and "super-cool". The Barbie text belongs to a genre that could be called "catwalk texts", which describe models to people interested in features and attributes. The Action Man text looks more like a television ad urging the audience to watch the next episode of a series.

In analyzing discourse it is not difficult to find such differences, for example that women use more mitigated discourse and back-channel elements (*hm, oh yeah*, etc.), and that men are not focused on verbalizing their feelings and that they often display macho behavior. Analyzing is one thing, but interpreting is another. In the literature on gender and discourse up to now there has been no strong support for the claim that such differences are only caused by gender. There are so many other psychological and sociological factors in the complex process of producing discourse, that it seems almost impossible to relate a phenomenon only to gender or to the dominant behavior of men.

Possibly, an important function of the study of discourse and gender is to check the so-called characteristics of female and male language in popular scientific literature. Here is one example. It is often assumed that women fill more verbal space in conversation and that they interrupt more frequently than men, not only in back-channel behavior but also in taking the floor. Deborah Tannen (1994) gives a nice personal example of a conversation in which she shows, at first sight, disturbing interrupting behavior. In this passage the author (A) is talking with a good male friend of hers (F), who is an interpreter of American Sign Language.

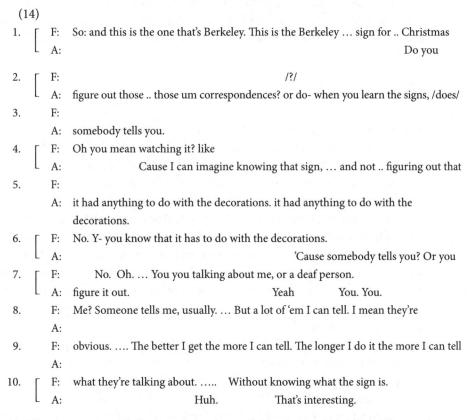

(14)

1. F: So: and this is the one that's Berkeley. This is the Berkeley ... sign for .. Christmas
    A: Do you

2. F: /?/
    A: figure out those .. those um correspondences? or do- when you learn the signs, /does/

3. F:
    A: somebody tells you.

4. F: Oh you mean watching it? like
    A: Cause I can imagine knowing that sign, ... and not .. figuring out that

5. F:
    A: it had anything to do with the decorations. it had anything to do with the
        decorations.

6. F: No. Y- you know that it has to do with the decorations.
    A: 'Cause somebody tells you? Or you

7. F: No. Oh. ... You you talking about me, or a deaf person.
    A: figure it out.   Yeah   You. You.

8. F: Me? Someone tells me, usually. ... But a lot of 'em I can tell. I mean they're
    A:

9. F: obvious. .... The better I get the more I can tell. The longer I do it the more I can tell
    A:

10. F: what they're talking about. ..... Without knowing what the sign is.
    A: Huh.   That's interesting.

In this conversation all the woman's turns overlap the man's, while of the man's turns only two overlap a prior turn of the woman. Moreover, the man makes an inaudible interruption in 2 and a "No" in 7; both can be seen as reactions to previous questions of the woman. In playbacks of the original tape one could see that the man was discomforted. In his comment on this passage the man said that he was irritated by the fast pace of all the questions. But the woman meant these overlapping questions as a display of interest, to encourage the speaker and not to take the floor. So, what can be seen as an interruption can also be seen as proof of involvement. If the same phenomenon can cause these various interpretations, then other factors must be of importance too. For example, it may be that an overlapping question only counts as an interruption in a conversation in which the participants differ in involvement or both have a low involvement.

In the last decades of the previous century much was published on gender and discourse studies; many intriguing phenomena were described in terms of difference and dominance. However, it is not yet definite whether these discourse phenomena are only gender-bound, and even if they are, it remains unclear how they should be interpreted. Of course, this does not say anything about the possible dominance of men. The results only show that this cannot be proved by discourse analysis alone.

15.4   Racism

As in research into gender and discourse, the starting point of the study of racism and discourse is that racism manifests and (re)produces itself in discourse. Racism is usually defined as a prejudice or stereotypical belief that discriminates against a minority group (however, not necessarily of another race) or a group with less status than the group in power. Racism is usually mixed with ethnicism and xenofobia. Discrimination can become manifest, as van Dijk (1984) says, in seven D's: dominance, differentiation, distance, diffusion, diversion, depersonalization and destruction. In analyzing discourse on racist phenomena, researchers aim to contribute to the fight against discrimination. Hence, research in this area has a strong societal drift. In Section 15.2 some early examples of analyses of racist discourse were cited to indicate the need for a more objective model of analysis. In this section two more systematic approaches are presented.

In research by Flowerdew, Li and Tran (2002), the most important studies of racism in discourse were analyzed in respect of discourse strategies that are believed to be proof of discrimination. They found that in the various schemes of analysis four main strategies of discrimination could be discerned. They collected a corpus of eighty newspaper articles from a leading Hong Kong Newspaper in 1999 and 2000 concerning the topic whether immigrants from mainland China have the right-of-abode. They succeeded in categorizing all the racist phenomena under the following headings.

(15)   Discriminatory discourse strategies (Flowerdew, Li and Tran, 2002)

1. Negative other presentation;
2. Scare tactics;
3. Blaming the victim;
4. Delegitimation.

In 1, the negative other presentation, the minority received negative attributions in a scheme of "positive us" and "negative them". Migrants were presented with negative metaphors such as a "mass influx" that imposes a "heavy burden" on society. In their corpus Flowerdew, Li and Tran found examples such as the following:

(16) Negative other presentation
      People are becoming less tolerant towards mainland immigrants and regard
      them as uneducated and unhygienic, according to a survey. (…) The survey
      found new arrivals were generally seen as uneducated, dirty and with little
      understanding of the rule of law.

By 2, scare tactics, is meant the extensive attention to the alleged threat by the minority to the privileges of the dominant group, such as in:

(17) Scare tactics
      The arrival of thousands of migrant children could have a "serious and adverse
      impact" on education for Hong Kong students.

Here the privilege of education is presented as being threatened by immigrants. In 3, blaming the victim, the most salient feature is scapegoating, mixed with a general strategy of accusing a minority group of causing bad developments, such as in the following example.

(18) Blaming the victim
      Government economist Tang Kwong-yiu said mass immigration would "pull
      down the standard of living, wage levels," push up unemployment and thin out
      resources for economic development and improvement of living conditions.

There may be other causes for the poor economy, but these are not mentioned here. In 4, delegitimation, a minority group is considered outlawed. The result can be that the minority is discredited and disempowered. In the following example this strategy can be found in a judicial context.

(19) "These immigrants have no right of abode in Hong Kong under the Basic Law.
      They have no right to enter Hong Kong illegally or to remain in Hong Kong in
      breach of the conditions of stay", Mr. Justice Yeung added.

Table 1.   Strategies for presenting social actors (Reisigl and Wodak, 2001)

Strategy	Question
1. referential strategies	How are persons named and referred to?
2. predicational strategies	Which characteristics and features are attributed to "them"?
3. argumentation strategies	What kind of argumentation schemes are used to discriminate between "us" and "them"?
4. perspectivization strategies	From which point of view are the nominations (1), attributions (2) and arguments (3) used?
5. intensifying strategies	How are the discriminating utterances formulated; overtly, intensified or mitigated?

Of course, it depends on the context whether these strategies really are racist. Example (16) is not discriminating if it is presented in a newspaper article in which the preceding context actually describes the immigrants positively and it is reported that these immigrants have to face, without reason, many negative attitudes from the majority. The benefit of Flowerdew, Li and Tran's scheme is that a discourse analysis based on these strategies is more systematic than a more or less impressionistic list of anecdotal or disputable examples.

Such schemes can be refined for more detailed research questions. The first strategy, on negative other-presentation (and positive self-presentation) as mentioned in (16), refers to the way social actors are dealt with (see also Section 15.2). These actors can be presented in different ways. In their study of the rhetoric of racism and anti-Semitism in Austria, Reisigl and Wodak (2001) developed a model for analyzing the presentation of social actors in a discourse. The model contains five strategies that are related to five questions with which discourse can be analyzed; see Table 1.

How does this scheme of analysis work? Below is one of the examples Reisigl and Wodak present. Some background information will help in understanding the gist of the passage. In Austria the head of the province of Carinthia, Karl-Heinz Grasser, has ordered that public building projects be carried out exclusively by Austrian workers. This measure elicited an intensive public debate on exclusionary practice, urging Grasser to give in. During this debate a journalist interviewed Grasser's party leader, who is known for his anti-foreigner attitude (Haider of the FPÖ).

   (20) Journalist: You will not recommend Karl-Heinz Grasser to give in?

            Haider: We never thought differently and will continue to do so. The indignation, of course, just comes from the side of those like the Carinthian guild master for construction, a socialist, who makes money out of cheap labor from Slovenia and Croatia. And if, today, one goes by one of Hans Peter Haselsteiner's "Illbau" building sites, and there, the foreigners, even down to black Africans, cut and carry bricks, then the Austrian construction worker really thinks something. Then one must understand, if there are emotions.

In this passage different techniques are used in referring to social actors (strategy 1). Compare, for example, the depersonalized actors in "cheap labor" and the individual mentioning of "the Austrian construction worker". The predications attributed to actors are also different (strategy 2). Compare the positive "we" who acts in harmony in public and the "socialist guild master" who is implicitly accused of being an unsocial, capitalist socialist in hiring cheap labor from abroad. In the argumentation (strategy 3) that leads to the last sentence "Then one must understand (…)" there is an unspoken argument (see Section 12.2), namely, that foreigners are robbing native Austrians of their jobs. It is this argument that has to be proved first. The perspective (strategy 4) is somewhat diffuse. An indefinable "man in the street" occurs two times ("if one goes", "one must"). Finally, in presenting the actors, intensification and mitigation are used (strategy 5). According to Reisigl and Wodak intensification can be seen in the addition of "black" to Africans. They argue that it emphasizes the "visual" difference between Austrians and "foreigners", and implies that they are "an even worse evil" than other "foreigners". Moreover, in the wording "emotions" the overt hostilities to foreigners are euphemistically toned down. This is an example of mitigation.

With this scheme of analysis Reisigl and Wodak's research aim was similar to that of Flowerdew, Li and Tran. This scheme is based on more general strategies, which makes it easier to compare data and to discuss analyses that are, inevitably, subjective to some extent.

15.5   Intercultural communication

The study of discourse in its social and cultural context conceivably leads to the study of communication patterns dependent on differences between cultures. In a world in which globalization and localization forces are getting stronger, it becomes more and more important to compare cultures in cross-cultural studies and to analyze in intercultural studies the impact of cultural differences when members of different cultures communicate. The concept *culture*, like many key concepts, has many different definitions. As mentioned in Section 5.1, in the discourse approach it is usually conceived of as the system of knowledge, values, attitudes and behavior shared by a group of people.

The most-cited author in this area is the Dutch engineer and social psychologist Geert Hofstede (2001). Mainly in the 1970s and 1980s, he collected as an employee of a big computer company a huge amount of data on cultural values in about 60 countries. He got the data by sending out about 100,000 questionnaires with more than a hundred items to the company's employees. He asked questions and gave statements like the following (some with multiple choice answers, others with a five-point scale):

(21) Some questions from the attitude survey by Hofstede
  1. How important is it to you to fully use your skills and abilities on the job?
  2. How satisfied are you at present with your fringe benefits?
  3. Competition among employees usually does more harm than good.
  4. How important is it to you to work in a department which is run efficiently?
  5. Even if an employee may feel he deserves a salary increase, he should not ask his manager for it.
  6. Most employees have an inherent dislike of work and will avoid it if they can.

On the basis of statistical analysis Hofstede found that the differences in answers could be explained by the assumption of four, and in later research five basic dimensions.

(22) The five basic cultural dimensions from Hofstede
  1. Power distance
  2. Uncertainty avoidance
  3. Individualism versus collectivism
  4. Masculinity versus femininity
  5. Long- versus short-term orientation

The first dimension, power distance, refers to inequality. It is defined as the extent to which the less powerful members of institutions and organizations accept and expect that power is distributed unequally. The power distance is greater to the extent that inequality is more accepted. In India, for example, the scores are much higher than in the Netherlands. In high power-distance countries subordinates expect to be told, and in low power-distance countries subordinates expect to be consulted.

The second dimension, uncertainty avoidance, refers to the extent to which members of a culture feel comfortable in unstructured situations. If uncertainty avoidance is high, as in Japan, then formal rules and procedures are highly estimated. If uncertainty avoidance is low, as in India, then people can tolerate more chaos and differences are welcomed.

The third dimension, individualism versus collectivism, refers to the extent to which individuals are supposed to look after themselves and the extent to which the behavior of an individual is influenced by others. In cultures with low individualism or high collectivism, there are, for example, many financial and ritual obligations to relatives or there is no obligation to start or continue a conversation when people are together. In cultures with high individualism the opposite is true. The data showed that the USA has the highest rank on individualism, or – as people from countries with a medium or low score as Japan and Indonesia would probably say – has the lowest rank on collectivism.

The fourth dimension, masculinity versus femininity, refers to gender roles in a culture. In more masculine cultures, values such as self-assertion, competition and success are important, with a clear distinction between the gender roles. In more feminine cultures, values like unpretentiousness, solidarity and orientation towards quality are important, with more diffusion between the gender roles. In low-masculine countries, like the Netherlands and Costa Rica, there is, for example, a preference for smaller companies and shorter working weeks. In high-masculine countries, like Austria and Jamaica, there is a preference for larger companies and higher pay.

The fifth dimension, long- versus short-term orientation, refers to the extent to which people esteem virtues oriented towards future awards, like perseverance and thrift. In a culture with a short-term orientation, values like respect for tradition and keeping face (see Section 2.6) are of high importance. Short-term orientation is seen as more eastern, more African, at least from the western point of view. China has a high rank on this dimension, and the USA and Canada have low rankings, but so do Nigeria and Pakistan.

Hofstede's study gave a strong impulse to research into cultural differences. In the last decade a discourse approach to intercultural communication has received more attention, especially miscommunication as a result of cultural differences. The most influential study is that by Scollon and Scollon (2001). They presented a framework for functional analysis of discourse between participants from different cultures. Their analyses are very insightful and go a step further than Hofstede's framework with its more general labels. Below is just one of their examples, a passage from a conversation between an American and a Chinese businessman (A and C).

(23) A: By the way, I'm Andrew Richardson. My friends call me Andy. This is my business card.
       C: I'm David Chu. Pleased to meet you, Mr. Richardson. This is my card.
       A: No, no. Call me Andy. I think we'll be doing a lot of business together.
       C: Yes, I hope so.
       A: (reading Mr. Chu's card) "Chu, Hon-fai." Hon-fai, I'll give you a call tomorrow as soon as I get settled at my hotel.
       C: (smiling) Yes, I'll expect your call.

In intercultural communication one can often see that partners try to be sensitive, but in doing so cause more problems. In this conversation the American and the Chinese are communicating with different politeness concepts (see Section 2.6). Americans in this situation normally act on the basis of solidarity politeness, insisting on communication based on first names. Chinese people normally act on the basis of respect politeness, based on *Mr.* and family names. Both seem to be aware of these differences, but both choose the wrong solution. The Chinese man knows that Americans feel comfortable on a first-name basis, and for this reason he adopted a western name, David. The American man knows that Chinese people want to be respected in their culture, and believes that using a western name is offensive, and chooses the Chinese first name. Moreover, the interpretation of the smile causes serious problems. In American culture a smile is clearly distinguished from a nervous laugh, but in Chinese culture a smile can also be an expression of feeling uncomfortable.

Using this and other examples Scollon and Scollon showed that there is much more at stake in intercultural communication than Hofstede's cross-cultural study could bring to light. In analyzing intercultural contact they incorporated not only the politeness principle but in fact many of the other concepts that were dealt with in this introduction to discourse studies.

Questions and assignments

Questions

15.1.1 Two people walk through fields of barley, rye, oats and wheat. One of them is a farmer's daughter who knows all the varieties of grain, the other is a boy from town who only knows the word grain. What would the linguistic relativity principle say about the differences in worldview between the girl and the boy?

15.2.1 Present a critical analysis of the following sentence (taken from Fairclough, 1995):
"Frightened and perhaps in real danger of their lives, the police simply leveled their carbines and Sten guns and fired at point-blank range."
Take into consideration that the following formulation also could have been used:
"Frightened and in real danger of their lives, the police fired at point-blank range."

15.3.1 In the following passage (taken from Caldas-Coulthard and Van Leeuwen (2002)) a male social actor is presented with elements found in descriptions of Barbie dolls. Indicate some of the elements in this description that can be considered "feminine".
"Stunning Californian man is as lovely as the State he represents in his shimmering black Caterpillar boots, felt-like crimson-hued designer pants and sensual cut-away vest, with silver and orange abstract design. The chest-hugging vest tapers dramatically to emphasize his narrow waist. His accessories include a gold diamond studded ring, wafer-thin gold watch with white gold strap, a solid shimmering gold necklace and an earring shaped like a graceful rose petal. His delicate painted face conveys the firmness of his personality. Atop his beautifully coiffured jet-black hair sits a dark wine-colored hat embellished with swan's tail feathers adding the final touch to the wondrous portrait of American manhood."

15.4.1 How many social actors (cf. the end of Section 15.2) are mentioned in the passage from the interview with Haider (see Section 15.4)? Is "one" in the last sentence also an actor?

15.5.1 Explain which type of knowledge is more important in overcoming intercultural miscommunication: semantic or pragmatic knowledge?

Assignments

15.1.1 Try to set up an experiment on the basis of news report research in Section 14.5, in order to prove the Sapir-Whorf hypothesis.

15.2.1 Collect newspaper articles about the same social actor from different newspapers, for example, a social or cultural minority or a politician in your country. Analyze the way in which this actor is presented, using the concepts passivization and nominalization.

15.2.2 Try to find arguments for or against a pejorative meaning or negative connotation of the word *elaborate* as an adjective and as a verb by exploring the Internet. Also consider the noun *elaboration* as used in Rhetorical Structure Theory (Section 6.4) and in the Elaboration Likelihood Model (Section 12.3).

15.3.1 Present the passage from question 15.3.1 to male and female proofreaders. Try to find out whether there are any differences in attitude by having subjects answer such questions as "How masculine do you find Californian man?" or "How pleasant do you find Californian man?". Try to design a dozen questions which subjects can answer with numerical judgments from 1 to 10 (from "very low" to "very high").

15.4.1 Collect texts that are, in your opinion, discriminatory (e.g., towards women, gays, cultural minorities). The texts do not necessarily have to be newspaper articles. Analyze the texts according to the discriminatory discourse strategies identified by Flowerdew, Li and Tran. Try to expand and refine their analysis scheme on the basis of your results.

15.5.1 Consult the appendices in Hofstede (2001) and present some of his questions concerning the attitude towards a manager to subjects. Try to find out whether there are differences in views of the concept of power distance between subjects older and younger than fifty.

Bibliographical information

15.1   Collections of selected writings by the researchers who gave their names to the Sapir-Whorf hypothesis have been issued that are still worth reading and that go much deeper than superficial speculations about language and worldview: Sapir (1949) and Whorf (1956). In the literature, Whorf is often portrayed as a dilettante who knew very little of linguistics, but this view is too negative; see, for example, Lakoff (1987). Though the Sapir-Whorf hypothesis was controversial for a long time, it nowadays forms a starting point for research again. For evidence of the influence of culture on language, see, for example, Wierzbicka (1986). A good point of departure for research is offered by Duranti (1997). See further the collections by Gumperz and Levinson (1996) and Niemeier and Dirven (2000).

15.2   Perhaps the best introduction to the fast-growing literature on Critical Discourse Analysis are the four volumes edited by Toolan (2002) with about seventy classic and modern articles on this kind of analysis. The following monographs provide a good insight into general aspects of critical analysis: Pêcheux (1969), Fowler, Hodge, Kress and Trew (1979) and Fairclough (1992 & 1995). Much research is reported on in the journal *Discourse and Society*.

    In Critical Discourse Analysis the concepts of power and ideology are central. The analysis of the power relation has been deeply influenced by the work on symbolic power of the French philosopher Bourdieu (1991). A good starting point for power analysis is Ng and Bradac (1993). For more on ideology, see Hodge and Kress (1993), and Van Dijk (1998).

15.3   The publication by Lakoff (1975) is seen as the starting point for the study of discourse and gender. The most influential researcher on this topic is Tannen, who also published for a broader audience. Tannen (1994) gives a good impression of her research methods. Of the numerous collections of papers available Wodak (1997), Coates (1998), Bucholtz, Liang and Sutton (1999), Litosseliti and Sunderland (2002), and Holmes and Meyerhoff (2003) are mentioned here. See further Goddard and Patterson (2000) and the three volumes edited by Hellinger and Bußmann (2003), in which data relating to gender are presented from 30 languages.

15.4   One of the first studies of discourse and racism is Van Dijk (1984). In Van Dijk (1993) this topic is elaborated and focuses on elite discourse. Roberts, Davies and Jupp (1992) is also insightful. Reisigl and Wodak (2001) provide detailed case studies of racism and anti-Semitism in the Austrian context.

15.5   Hofstede (2001) is an adapted and extended version of his 1980 publication. He has popularized his own work in Hofstede (1997).

    Classic works in this field of study are those by Gumperz (1982) and Lavendera (1988). Schirato and Yell (2000) is a good introduction. Scollon and Scollon (2001) is now the leading publication in intercultural communication.

Key to the questions

1.1.1 A definition of the concept *discourse studies* must contain at least the following elements:
- The focus is on all forms of oral and written communication.
- The topic of study is the relationship between form and function of utterances.
- The foundations of discourse studies lie within several disciplines such as psychology, sociology and philosophy.

1.1.2 The form of the first utterance "Could you pass the salt?" is a question. The addresser asks the addressee if the latter is capable of picking up the salt and passing it. The function of this utterance is a request to pass the salt to the "asker". The form of the utterance "Of course" is a confirmation of the question. However, because the second speaker subsequently does not pass the salt, he does not fulfill the request. The function of the first utterance is thus ignored.

1.1.3 In the first version, the suspicion of molesting is integrated as an independent main clause. As a result, it is emphasized. It is to be expected that the following text will focus on that suspicion. In the second version, the suspicion is embedded in a subordinate clause and, therefore, less emphasized. The subsequent text will probably address the question of who will take over the doctor's duty. By changing the form of the utterance, the importance of the various elements can shift.

Answers Chapter 2

2.1.1 According to the Organon model every utterance has a relation with three elements: the sender, the world and the receiver. All three relations have a different function. The utterance "This is quite an interesting model" is a linguistic sign with three functions. First, the utterance has a "symptom" function: the utterance says something about the sender. This utterance reflects the sender's opinion. Second, the utterance has a "symbol" function: it says something about the world, an object, in this case a certain model. Third, the utterance has a "signal" function: the receiver has to interpret the utterance or react to it.

2.2.1 The utterance "It's raining" can have various illocutions. It can be a very simple announcement, but also a warning, for example, to bring an umbrella when leaving the house. It can also be a way of emphasizing the mutual bond: by making conversation the silence is broken. Possible perlocutions of the utterance are that the person being addressed becomes aware of the fact that it is raining, or should bring an umbrella. If the utterance was meant just for making conversation, the perlocution could be that the person addressed reacts, mostly by approving, smiling or giving his opinion about the weather or something similar.

Possible illocutions of the utterance "Here comes a dog" are an announcement, for example, at the circus, or a warning, for example, if a dangerous dog that easily bites is involved. The perlocutions could be that the person addressed becomes aware of the fact that a dog will now appear (announcement) or that the person addressed runs away before the dog starts biting.

2.2.2   In this sentence a person other than the one who has to carry out the promised act makes the promise. This is a violation of the propositional content condition. However, a situation is conceivable in which a speaker promises something that he himself is not going to carry out. The sentence, for example, may be uttered by the operator of the electricity company, who promises that a mechanic will visit the addressee tomorrow. Therefore, the propositional content condition must not be taken too strictly.

2.2.3   Someone who flatters makes a remark with the purpose of making the addressee feel appreciated, as a result of which the latter becomes favorably disposed towards the speaker and is more inclined to do something for the speaker. The remark is prompted by self-interest. If the addressee sees through the flattery, the positive comments will more likely result in the addressee gaining a rather negative impression of the flatterer. If the addressee recognizes the illocution of the flattery, the speech act has not been successful.

A lie is not successful if the addressee finds out that the speaker is not telling the truth. The illocution of lying presents inaccurate information as accurate information. If the addressee realizes that the information is inaccurate, the illocution has failed.

2.2.4   This is a possible classification; try to come up with other defensible classifications yourself.

invite: regulative	describe: constative
presume: constative	acquit: regulative
defy: regulative	guarantee: expressivee
offer condolences: expressive	order: regulative
request: regulative	

2.3.1   According to the preparatory condition a promise always implies a positive result for the addressee. In this case the speaker promises some negative consequences: a whipping. The preparatory condition is thus violated. According to the cooperative principle, language users only violate conditions if there is a reason for it. The addressee can thus assume the violation is deliberate and that because of this a threat and not a promise is implied.

2.3.2 "The door is wide open!"
- – Order: Close the door!
- – Request: Could you close the door please?
- – Warning: Burglars can walk in just like that.
- – Complaint: It's draughty here.

2.3.3 In (a) the word "warning" explicitly expresses the illocution. In (b) the word "bull" indicates that the addressee is being warned. Mostly, bulls are depicted as dangerous and aggressive animals.

2.4.1 B's utterance conveys more than just the literal meaning of the utterance. Let's assume that B is cooperative and that his answer is thus relevant to the question what time it is. B's answer is only relevant when both A and B know at what time the mail usually arrives. From this conversation, prior knowledge of A and B, and the cooperative principle, A can deduce the conversational implicature that B says that it is later than the time at which the mail arrives (but not too much later either, otherwise the utterance would not be precise enough).

2.4.2 Not all maxims are equally important. In practice, some maxims have to be sacrificed to the benefit of others, depending on the goal of the utterance. If person A wants to warn person B of a speeding car approaching, the fourth maxim (of manner) is very important. For example, it may be that strictly speaking the utterance ("Look out!") is not (locally) relevant (for example, because the current conversation is brutally interrupted), and does not provide enough information (what does A have to look out for?). Often speakers choose to provide more information than is necessary, for example, repeating a message, because they want to make sure they get the message across. The purpose and the context of an utterance thus also determine which maxims are (less) important.

2.4.3 Leech's reasoning is not correct. When speakers believe something, this does not necessarily mean that they can also prove it. Therefore, maxim 2 is not a predictable extension of maxim 1. There are more grounds on which a position can be taken or adopted than mere concrete, demonstrable evidence. When speakers say something which they believe to be true, this can also be based on religion, intuition, experience or a (reasoned) gamble. Actually, the second submaxim of quality is violated so often in practice that its existence is disputable. After all, people say so much more than they can actually prove.

2.4.4 In dialogue (a) also the maxim of relevance is violated. After B's answer, one would expect a positive reaction, since dinner will be served shortly. A's answer, a remark about the sudden loss of appetite, does not seem relevant in this dialogue. On the basis of the cooperative principle we have to assume that the remark is directly linked with the previous utterance. Thus we have to deduce the conversational implicature that A does not like liver and that he does not care when dinner is served.

In dialogue (a) the maxim of quality is violated. Probably A has not lost his appetite, but he just does not like liver. We can deduce this conversational implicature because appetite is not normally something that is lost all of a sudden.

In dialogue (b) the relevance maxim is violated as well. Contrary to expectations, A's remark is not followed by a reaction to this remark, but by a totally different statement. On the basis of the cooperative principle we have to assume that B does not utter his reaction for no reason. Why does B not go into A's remark? Several conversational implicatures can be deduced: perhaps Mrs. Johnson is present or B finds it inappropriate to gossip about Mrs. Johnson.

2.4.5 Deliberate violations of the cooperative principle can only bear meaning when the sender intends the reader to perceive them as such. If the receiver does not perceive them as such or if he does not realize that the violations are deliberate, then the utterances are perceived as, for example, lies, and the communication becomes confusing or fails altogether. Examples (a) and (b) are not literally true, but most people will recognize them as figures of speech, in this case sarcasm and hyperbole, instead of lies. In using these deliberate floutings it is important for the sender to correctly assess the receiver's knowledge. They only work if the receiver has enough knowledge to know that singing out of key is not pleasant to listen to and that the average cell phone does not run dead very often. Children or foreign language learners sometimes take these figures of speech literally. Owing to the wrong assessment of their knowledge by the sender, the sarcasm in (a) is not recognized ("Thanks for the compliment, dad!") and the hyperbole in (b) is perceived as a lie.

2.5.1 No, this is not a counter-example. The customer's utterance can be relevant as well, for example, if we deduce the conversational implicature that when everyone drinks, this customer will want something to drink too.

2.5.2 The locution can bear the meaning that you *must* carry a dog whenever you want to make use of the escalator, but no one will interpret the notice like that. Almost everyone will understand that this message is only relevant if you have a dog with you, partially on the basis of the knowledge that a dog's paws are small enough to become trapped in slots and moving parts of the escalator. To prevent this from happening, carrying the dog is advised (and not ordered).

2.6.1 B assumes that A wants to protect both A and B's face by using face work techniques, in this case the off-record strategy. B thinks that A in fact wants the chairs, but that he is using a pre-request in order to check the chances of a positive answer to the actual request. However, A does not want the chairs. The question is not a pre-request, but simply a request for information.

2.6.2 This is a matter of positive politeness. A wants to feel appreciated and B takes this into account. B does not say that the dress is ugly, but uses a more abstract and ambiguous description. In the case of negative politeness a speaker makes use of strategies that prevent a receiver from feeling forced into a certain position or action.

2.6.3 d.   with redressive action: negative politeness;
a.   with redressive action: positive politeness;
b.   off record;
c.   without redressive action, baldly.

2.6.4 B assumes that A wants to protect both A and B's face and, therefore, uses a pre-request in order to check the chances of a positive answer to the actual request. Since the answer to the pre-request is affirmative, B immediately reacts to the actual request ("Can I have an ice cream?"), by making a proposal. In this way, B prevents A from having to ask the question and thereby possibly taking up a vulnerable position. (After all, the answer can be negative, resulting in A losing face.)

Answers Chapter 3

3.1.1 Leech claims that communication by definition is problem-solving. He assumes that a speaker always has a certain goal. The speaker's problem is that he has to choose the most suitable utterance for achieving this goal. Leech emphasizes the choice of the speaker, who has to choose a certain form. However, the approach described in the first section of Chapter 3 also takes the context into account. The context influences the interpretation, and the way in which an utterance is interpreted determines the effect. Furthermore, Leech seems to imply that the choice of a linguistic form is always a conscious one, while scientists of the ordinary language philosophy were concerned with spontaneously produced utterances. There is a similarity as well: the scientists of the ordinary language philosophy assumed that language can provide insight into philosophical matters. Language is then seen as a symptom of deeper underlying principles. Leech also assumes that an utterance is a result of a deeper underlying reason.

3.2.1 A grammatical rule can be both descriptive and prescriptive. A grammatical rule is descriptive when it describes how people actually talk. An example would be the rule that (in English) the subject precedes the verb and that the object follows the verb. This is a descriptive rule because it has not been agreed on by people, but simply describes the way in which people use language (first there was language, which was later "written down" in grammar). A grammatical rule is prescriptive when it says how people ought to talk and write. An example would be the rule that one should not end a sentence with a preposition. This is a prescriptive rule, because it is advised, for example, by language teachers. Prescriptive rules are based on opinions about good and bad language use or on what the majority says or on how highly esteemed novelists use language, etc.

3.3.1   The question whether or not a graffiti text consisting of one sentence is a text can be answered mathematically. A sequence or a set of sentences can consist of one element. A text can, therefore, be made up of just one utterance. Because of that, a one-word notice such as "Closed" on a shop door can also qualify as a text. Given the situational factors it functions as an independent statement, a text.

3.3.2   To a certain extent the words *text* and *texture* meet the same criteria:

    a.   A text and textile both consist of several elements (sentences or threads) that are connected. Both a text and textile are cohesive.

    b.   A text and textile are coherent on the basis of something outside the text or textile; in both cases this is often knowledge of the world. Knowledge of a text's topic is needed in order to understand the text. The reader has to know which elements are associated with the topic. The same applies for a piece of textile: the textile's shape or form can only be explained if one knows which type of garment is involved. In that respect both a text and textile are coherent.

    c.   A text and textile serve a purpose. This purpose determines and explains the way in which the elements of a text or a piece of fabric are connected.

3.3.3   A message can be incomprehensible owing to causes in each of the components of the model:

    –   Information source: a message can be incomprehensible if, for example, the speaker has a very poor command of communicative skills, does not know what he wants to say or is distracted by other matters.

    –   Transmitter: a message can be incomprehensible if, for example, a telephone line is interrupted or if a text is poorly copied.

    –   Receiver: a message can be incomprehensible if, for example, someone who receives a letter is partially sighted or if the fax toner is running out.

    –   Destination: a message can be incomprehensible if the receiver cannot concentrate, is confused or speaks a different language than the one the message is written in.

3.4.1   The discourse in this situation has a strong institutional character, since it is about a lawsuit. This has consequences for the status of the various participants. Hierarchically speaking, the judge is positioned higher than the suspect is. In the quoted utterances, however, the suspect treats the judge with little respect. The suspect does not comply with the hierarchic rules that go with the institution "lawsuit". Also with respect to the content, the suspect does not seem to understand what is expected of him. In a lawsuit the discourse is always started with a formal identification of the suspect.

The objective of the discourse is to determine whether or not the suspect is guilty of the facts he is charged with. The suspect will have to convince the judge of the fact that he is innocent. Therefore, the objective of the discourse is persuasion.

3.4.2   The doctor and the nurse find themselves in two different *Settings*: for example, in an operating room and at a local bar. The *Scene* is different owing to the different roles that the participants assume: the doctor–nurse conversation at the hospital will be more formal than that in a bar in the sense that work-related matters are discussed in a professional setting (e.g., when the doctor operates and the nurse assists).

The two conversations also serve different *Ends*. At the hospital the purpose is to diagnose or obtain information about a patient's medical status, whereas at the bar the goal is to relax or get to know each other better.

The *Norms* differ as well, as during an operation the doctor is in charge and can "command" or ask the nurse for instruments, whereas in the bar both participants are at a more equal level.

The doctor-nurse conversation at the hospital will also be of a different *Genre* than the conversation between them at the bar: at work they may discuss, for example, the medical status of a patient, whereas at the bar they may talk about what they did during the past weekend.

3.5.1   The ideational meaning refers to the content, to the topic of discourse. So the words "movie", "tonight" and "study" in (1) are good examples of words that contain ideational meaning.

The interpersonal meaning refers to the participants, their attitudes and the social relation. So, words like "Actually" and "Well" and a phrase like "Yes, I am sorry" are good examples of formulations that contain interpersonal meaning.

The textual meaning refers to the way a topic is dealt with, to the organization of the text and the way sentences are combined. So, the fact that an invitation is put in a statement about a movie is a good example of textual meaning. Also the fact that a statement of regret, "Too bad", is answered with "Yes, I'm sorry" is an example of textual meaning.

3.6.1   Determining the correct meaning of the word "run" depends on the coherence of the text. After all, the exact meaning of the words cannot be established purely on the basis of the information in the text: knowledge of the text's topic is needed. The topic of the first text is "clocks". The reader or listener knows that clocks are inanimate objects, devices that work and that break down. "Run" is then interpreted as "working" or "functioning". In the second example the topic is "elections". Knowledge of elections includes elements such as "come up for elections" or "stand for election", which directs the interpretation here.

3.6.2   The coherence criterion is not valid in this example. Coherence involves a link or connection on the basis of something outside the text: the receiver's or addressee's knowledge. However, knowledge of buildings does not include the fact that buildings can blossom like flowers.

3.6.3   Participants in a dialogue assume that all speakers are cooperative and that their contributions are relevant. So even an utterance that ostensibly does not provide new information has to have a reason for existence: the utterance must be a relevant contribution to the dialogue.

New information can even be deduced from apparently non-informative utterances, on the basis of additional knowledge that both speaker and listener have. Depending on the situation, the speaker who utters the sentence "John is sleeping" may mean that John must have had a hard day, that the situation in which A, B and John find themselves is quite tedious or that A and B can now finally discuss a certain topic. The utterance is then informative.

Answers Chapter 4

4.1.1 In an informative conversation the following basic forms can occur:
1. Descriptive: a description of, for example, the parts of a computer.
2. Explanatory: an explanation of, for example, philosophical principles.
3. Instructive: an enumeration of, for example, house rules.

4.1.2
- Sermon: one speaker, unequal rank, theme predetermined, argumentative. Therefore, a sermon should be placed in category 1, presentation.
- Radio news bulletin: one speaker, unequal rank, theme predetermined, descriptive. Therefore, a news bulletin should be placed in category 3, report.
- Oral exam: multiple speakers, unequal rank, theme predetermined, argumentative. Therefore, an oral exam should be placed in category 6, interview.

4.2.1 The differences that Chafe mentioned are indeed present. The newspaper article contains more complete, well-constructed sentences. They are more complex as well: they contain more embedded constructions. Language use is more formal ("would provide incriminating evidence") and clear without any further context. Conversely, the dialogue is rather incomprehensible without further context. The sentences run on, are fragmented and often not finished. The dialogue contains explicit references to the other participant (for example, "Listen" and "believe me") and the tone is more subjective and informal.

4.3.1 According to Jakobson the poetic function projects the principle of equivalence from the axis of selection onto the axis of combination. If one wants to say something like "Is getting a master's" degree a condition for a good career?", then one can just write this sentence on a banner. If one wants to be more poetic, then the word choice depends on other things. Let's start with "master's" at the end. One could then, on the horizontal axis of combination, question whether life without a master's degree will be a failure, a fiasco or a flop, to mention only three words beginning with an f. But in poetics the choice of the words does depends not only on possibilities of horizontal combination. On the axis of selection, the vertical axis, which can be conveyed as a column of words that are to some extent equivalent, for example, synonyms, one can choose a word that has something in common with that other word on the axis of combination, in this case a word with some similar sound characteristics. This is called the projection of the vertical axis onto the horizontal axis.

4.4.1 In a conversation you are expected or obliged to take the turn, otherwise the communication will break down (especially in a one-on-one conversation). In a text, such as a hypertext (where there is no direct interaction) or in a chat group (where there are multiple participants) this obligation does not apply. Interaction can be seen as a controlled action from the sender. He has built in some possibilities for the reader. The reader can only choose from the given possibilities and cannot undertake new initiatives.

4.4.2 Internet lurkers typically log on to chat groups, discussion forums and e-mail lists with little or no intention of sending messages. They prefer to read the communication of others. An eavesdropper in face-to-face conversation secretly listens to the private conversation of others. Eavesdropping is considered rude behavior, and lurking in chat and news groups for a long period is also perceived as impolite. The difference, however, is that lurking is more acceptable because members of a chat group normally know that lurking is possible. Moreover, they may have been lurkers themselves before deciding to join in. In the situation of eavesdropping the participants are not aware of being listened to. That makes eavesdropping much more objectionable than lurking.

4.4.3 Contributions to chat groups are usually more informal and more personal than, for example, contributions to discussions in newspapers. This explains why verbs expressing personal experiences occur more frequently in e-discourse than in written discourse.
Personal pronouns are more frequent in electronic discourse than in writing; see Table 4 in Section 4.4. In this respect e-discourse resembles speech in which participants are salient. This presence of the participants is in line with the frequency of private verbs, since these verbs especially increase the use of pronouns: I think, I feel, you know. These verbs are rather seldom used in a passive form like It is known that.

4.5.1 In the definition of genre as a class of communicative events with shared recognizable communicative purposes the following aspects of social rules are important in genre rules.
Like social rules, genre rules have to be acquired (characteristic 1). This can be seen in examples (9) and (10) of the PhD student. The recognizability of the communicative purposes presupposes that genre rules must be communal (characteristic 3). The fact that these purposes as a consequence have constraints on content and form refers to characteristic 4 of the social rules: they are a framework for understanding and judging an illocution. On the basis of this characteristic the same sentence in a newspaper or in a novel can be interpreted differently. The addition "exploitable" before "constraints" in Swales's definition refers to characteristics 5 and 6: genre rules can be violated as well and they are liable to change. So, only characteristic 2 does not seem to be relevant. Genre rules are usually applied consciously and not unconsciously, as are social rules.

4.6.1   Among the numerous additions are the following: 1. The text adds reflection ("if ...then") and argumentation ("since ... insulated"); 2. The text adds possible problems, for example, "the break in the
middle of a wire"; 3. The text adds general knowledge such as the fact that the electricity flow must
be steady or that the human voice does not carry that far.

Answers Chapter 5

5.1.1   A possible propositional analysis, proposed by Kintsch and Van Dijk (1978) is the following:

1.	(GREAT, ROCKET)	17.	(AND, ALCOHOL, OXYGEN)
2.	(BLACK, ROCKET)	18.	(LIQUID, OXYGEN)
3.	(YELLOW, ROCKET)	19.	(READY, EVERYTHING)
4.	(V-2, ROCKET)	20.	(AND, SCIENTIST, GENERAL)
5.	(LONG, ROCKET)	21.	(WITHDRAW, 20, DISTANCE)
6.	(FORTY-SIX FEET, 5)	22.	(SOME, DISTANCE)
7.	(STAND, ROCKET)	23.	(CROUCH, 20)
8.	(IN, 7, DESERT)	24.	(BEHIND, 23, MOUND)
9.	(NEW MEXICO, DESERT)	25.	(EARTH, MOUND)
10.	(EMPTY, ROCKET)	26.	(TWO, FLARE)
11.	(WEIGH, 10)	27.	(RED, FLARE)
12.	(FIVE TON, 11)	28.	(RISE, FLARE)
13.	(FOR, 14, FUEL)	29.	(REFERENCE, FLARE, SIGNAL)
14.	(CARRY, ROCKET, 17)	30.	(PURPOSE, 28, 31)
15.	(EIGHT TON, 16)	31.	(FIRE, ROCKET)

5.1.2   A possible analysis of the first four sentences from discourse fragment (26) is:

1.   (TALL, BLONDE)
2.   (SLIM, BLONDE)
3.   (IN, BLONDE, FROCK)
4.   (WHITE, FROCK)
5.   (SUMMER, FROCK)
6.   (WALK, BLONDE, AHEAD OF KEN HOLLAND)
7.   (CATCH, BLONDE, EYE)
8.   (KEN HOLLAND, EYE)
9.   (STUDY, KEN HOLLAND, BLONDE)
10.   (WATCH, KEN HOLLAND, UNDULATIONS)
11.   (BLONDE, UNDULATIONS)
12.   (GENTLE, INDULATIONS)
13.   (WALK, BLONDE)
14.   (AS, 10, 13)

15. (SHIFT, EYES)
16. (KEN HOLLAND, EYES)
17. (QUICK, SHIFT)
18. (LOOK AT, KEN HOLLAND, WOMAN)
19. (LOOK AT, LIKE 10)
20. (NOT 18, SINCE 21)
21. (MEET, KEN HOLLAND, ANN)
22. (FIRST, 21)

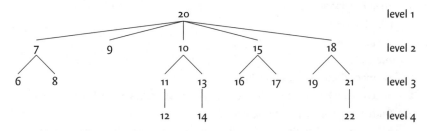

5.2.1 A starts the interaction with the topic "the movie (that is playing tonight)". B's comment is indirect. B tells A what he is occupied with that evening: studying. This implies that B has not got the time to go to the movies. The topic of the complete fragment is "(whether or not to) go to the movies tonight". Between the sentences a topic shift takes place. In A's first sentence the specific movie is the topic. After B has made it clear that he cannot join A, the topic shifts to the fact that B cannot come along. The movie itself is no longer a topic in the conversation.
A topic does not always have to be given. An example is the sentence: "See that radio there, I have always wanted to buy such a model!" The radio is the topic, and is new information. The fact that the speaker has always wanted to buy such a model is the comment.

5.2.2 The topic does not have to be definite: "A stereo set nowadays also has to include a CD player" (topic is indefinite).
The topic does not have to be the subject: "Have you already bought that stereo set you were talking about recently?" (topic is object).
The topic does not have to be a pronoun: "Cycling is good for your health" (topic is a verb).
The topic does not have to precede the comment: "Black is the color of the stereo set that I have bought" (topic, the stereo set, follows the comment, the fact that the set is black).

5.2.3   A possible arrangement is:

    8   Whenever [...] ice.

    10   Motorists [...] road.

    2   Road [...] surfaces.

    7   Such [...] snowfalls.

    5   Its [...] tires.

    9   In [...] tires.

    6   These tires [...] snow.

    4   Their [...] disastrous.

    1   In [...] melted.

    3   We [...] evils.

The topics are:

1.   Sentence 8: country roads in England.
2.   Sentence 10: motorists coming suddenly upon stretches of black ice.
3.   Sentence 2: the danger of skidding.
4.   Sentences 7 and 5: the measure (of scattering sand upon the road surfaces).
5.   Sentence 9: the law of Norway.
6.   Sentences 6, 4 and 1: (special steel spiked) tires.
4.   Sentence 3: the measure (of scattering sand upon the road surfaces).

This analysis makes it clear that the text contains six different topics. Some topics extend over more than one sentence while others extend to just one. After every topic a topic shift takes place at the sentence level.

At the paragraph level, two topics can be distinguished: the road safety measures that are taken when snow is falling in England versus those taken in Norway. In sentence 9 the situation in England is alternated with the situation in Norway. Subsequently, the situation in England is reverted to in sentence 1.

At the text level, one topic can be distinguished: the road safety measures that have to be taken when snow is falling.

5.3.1   In the process of converting text (a) into text (b) the deletion and generalization rules were applied. Doing the dishes and vacuum cleaning are generalized into cleaning the house. Who carries out which task and the fact that mother sings while carrying out her task are deleted.

5.4.1   Most texts can be characterized by a superstructure, since a text derives its quality not only from the content, but also for a great part from its structure. The superstructure makes it possible to structure the texts of various people who write about the same topic or in the same text type in a similar manner. Because of this a text can be made more insightful. However, many texts lack these conventional schemas that provide this roughly sketched form or superstructure. Think, for example, of literature and reports. For these text types a superstructure is not a necessary condition.

5.4.2   The table of contents of a book can also be seen as an advance organizer. When readers read the table of contents, they get an impression of what the text is about in advance. These advance organizers not only list the various topics that will be dealt with, but they also show in which order these topics will occur (the table of contents in particular). Because of this, a reader can often see beforehand how much importance is attached to the various elements. In a way, the table of contents points out in which mental container the upcoming information should be placed. It organizes the reading process and facilitates the processing of information.

Answers Chapter 6

6.1.1   With substitution and ellipsis the anaphor can be identified by observing the grammatical functions of possible referents. An example of ellipsis:
    "I grabbed him and pulled his hair."
In the second part of the sentence, the subject is missing. This subject can be identified by looking at the subject in the first part of the sentence: "I".
With reference the anaphor can be identified by observing the semantic properties of possible referents.
    "Mary gave John a kiss. Then he yelled at her."
Who is yelling at who becomes clear by looking at the semantic properties of the referents. Since Mary is a female name and "her" refers to a feminine referent, and since John is a masculine name and "he" refers to a masculine referent, it can be established that John yelled at Mary.

6.1.2   If *and* is used for an additive relation, a certain element is simply added to another element. In this case the connected clauses can just as well be placed in a different order: "Mary washed the car and Sue mowed the lawn" means exactly the same as "Sue mowed the lawn and Mary washed the car". However, in some cases *and* expresses more than just an additive relation:
    "I pressed the button and the door opened."
This example contains a causal relation: pressing the button causes the door to open. Changing the order of the parts results in a completely different meaning.
    "I ate a candy bar and brushed my teeth."
In this example, *and* expresses a temporal relation. The eating of the candy bar precedes the brushing of the teeth.

6.1.3   The following cohesion phenomena are contained in the excerpt: substitution, ellipsis, reference, conjunction, repetition, synonymy, hyponymy, metonymy, antonymy and collocation.

(1)   the last word (substitution)

(2)   she (reference), who (reference), herself (reference), wool (collocation)

(3)   Alice (repetition), her eyes (meronymy), and (conjunction), (Alice) looked (ellipsis),

(4)   she (reference)

(5)   she (reference)

(6)   and (conjunction), that (reference), it (reference), sheep (repetition), counter (collocation)

(7)   rub (repetition), she (reference), she (reference), it (reference)

6.2.1   (1) anaphor; (2) cataphor; (3) anaphor; (4) anaphor; (5) cataphor; (6) anaphor; (7) anaphor; (8) anaphor; (9) cataphor; (10) anaphor; (11) cataphor; (12) anaphor; (13)   cataphor; (14) anaphor.

6.2.2   When a new referent (a discourse topic, an individual, an object) is introduced in the text, this is normally done the first time in such a way that it is clear to the reader which referent in reality is referred to. If further on in the discourse this referent is reverted to, usually a short reference is used (and not a detailed introduction all over again). Anaphors, so to speak, are the short references used to refer to the already introduced referent. Cataphors on the other hand are short references that still have to be introduced. The reader then has to memorize all the information about the referent still to be introduced, until a more elaborate introduction has taken place. The cataphor thus forms a bigger load on the working memory than the anaphor, and is therefore used less often.

6.2.3   The anaphor "he" is more difficult to interpret in sentence (a). In (a) "quit" can refer back to both John and Pete, while in (b) "complaining" can practically only refer back to Pete. In (a) John can tell Pete that John has been forced to quit smoking (for example, when he has been fired) or John can tell Pete that Pete has to stop smoking. In (b) John can ask Pete to quit complaining, but John cannot tell Pete that John himself has to stop complaining. Because (a) is ambiguous, this sentence is more difficult to interpret than (b).

6.3.1   Additional examples are:
   - While I was on sentry duty, I saw the enemy approaching. But I beat off the attack, because I opened fire.
   - I saw the enemy approaching, because I was on sentry duty. So I beat off the attack by opening fire.
   - I opened fire when I was on sentry duty. That was because I saw the enemy approaching and therefore had to beat off the attack.
   - Since I was on sentry duty, and I saw the enemy approaching, I opened fire and I beat off the attack.

– I beat off the attack. First I saw the enemy approaching, then I opened fire. By the way, I was on sentry duty.

6.3.2　a.　motivation
b.　concession
c.　cause
d.　conclusion, evidence
e.　elaboration (no meaning-bearing relationship)
f.　means

6.3.3　(38) John bought a present for his mother, (but) he forgot to take it with him.
(if *but* is included in the sentence) explicit, 2 nuclei
John forgot to take it with him, but he did buy a present for his mother.
(39) John did not go to school. He was sick.
implicit, 1st part nucleus
John was sick. (Therefore) he did not go to school.
(40) John did not come with us. He hates parties.
implicit, 1st part nucleus
John hates parties. (That's why) he did not come with us.
(41) Would you mind opening the door? Here is the key.
implicit, 1st part nucleus
Here is the key. Would you mind opening the door?
(42) John is sick. He is not going to school.
implicit, 2nd part nucleus
John is not going to school. He is sick.
(43) The instructions should be printed in capital letters. It is hoped that in this way, difficulties in reading them will be avoided.
explicit, 1st part nucleus
It is hoped that, when the instructions are printed in capital letters, difficulties in reading will be avoided.
(44) You can get a job this summer. But first you have to pass your exams.
explicit, 1st part nucleus
If you pass your exams, you can get a job this summer.
(45) He was rich. Yet he never gave anything to charity.
explicit, 2nd part nucleus
He never gave anything to charity, although he was rich.
(56) Pete is corporate president. You should take this to him.
implicit, 2nd part nucleus
You should take this to Pete. He is corporate president.

6.4.1

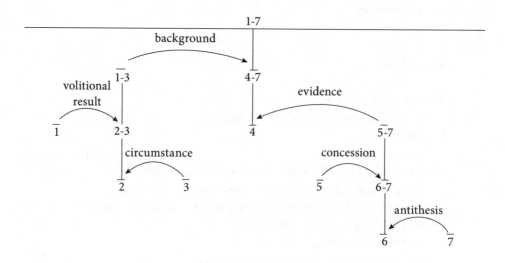

6.5.1   Semantic relations refer to the reality that can be perceived by the participants in the interaction. Pragmatic relations refer to the purpose with which the relation is used (see Section 3.1). Or in other words (see Section 6.3), semantic relations connect locutions whereas pragmatic relations connect illocutions. Based on this distinction and the definitions given in Section 6.5 the following division can be made:

Semantic relations: subject matter, informational.

Pragmatic relations: epistemic, speech act, presentational, intentional, metalinguistic.

6.5.2   Example (a) contains a cause-consequence relation. The basic operation is *causal*, marked by the connective *Because*. The relation is *semantic*, since the two segments in this utterance are related because of their propositional content: it is part of our knowledge that (the location of) a low-pressure area influences the weather type somewhere else. The order is *basic*, as the antecedent (the cause, in this case the low-pressure area) is to the left of the consequence (in this case the bad weather that is coming). The relation is *positive*, because the two text segments are connected as given.

Example (b) contains an argument-claim relation. The basic operation is *causal*, the relation is *pragmatic*, the order is *basic*, and the relation is *positive*, because the connection is as given in the example, and not based on the content of one segment and the negated content of the other.

Example (c) contains a concession relation. The three primitives are (order of the segments does not apply to additive relations): additive, pragmatic, negative.

6.5.3 In the original text fragment, either clause (a), the result, or (b), the volitional cause, can be the nucleus in the volitional cause relation. Which clause is the nucleus depends on the writer or speaker's goal. A context sentence can provide that goal. Note that adding a context sentence has led to changes in the pronouns in the original clause (a); otherwise the texts would come across as unnatural. In the examples below the context sentences are italicized.

(1) *Mary is an attentive woman.*
      a.   She buys her husband flowers every week
      b.   because he cooks so deliciously for her.

(2) *John is an ideal husband.*
      a.   His wife buys him flowers every week
      b.   because he cooks so deliciously for her.

When context sentence (1) is provided, (a) is the nucleus in the relation between (a) and (b), as Mary buying flowers says more about her being attentive than does her husband's cooking. When context (2) is provided, (b) is the nucleus in the relation between (a) and (b), as John cooking deliciously says more about him being an ideal husband than does the fact that his wife buys him flowers every week.

Answers Chapter 7

7.1.1 – I am the man who knocked on your door. (cataphor)
    – That man in the picture is me. (anaphor)
    – You, the most talented basketball player of the past fifty years, you have always been my idol. (cataphor)
    – My dearest Joanna, you have been our neighbor for ten years now. (anaphor)

7.1.2 Note that deixis is constrained by time, place and person deixis. Of course, the phone in (a) is a different phone than Mary's phone, but the meaning of *phone* remains more or less constant. The same goes for "garden" in (d). Of course, Pete's garden is a different one than John's, but again the meaning is rather constant.
In all the examples, except for (c), the verb contains temporal deixis, because the time reference of the verb depends on the time at which the utterance is made. In (c) the verb is a so-called existential verb with no special time reference: the meaning is not influenced by the time of speaking. In (b) "I" and "them" are examples of person deixis (also with "them" referring to things and not to persons). In (c) "there" is not an example of place deixis, because the meaning of "there" is not influenced by the place in which "there" is used. It is a so-called existential "there". Example (d) only has time deixis.

7.1.3 He could refer to himself and to his wife by using their first names, for example: "Would Julia perhaps make breakfast for Tom?"

7.2.1   Look at the following example: "It is said that Mr. Smith has died after a long period of disease." This sentence starts with a main clause and ends with a subordinate clause. But the main clause is a kind of shell that only contains background information (unless, of course, the word "said" is stressed, meaning "It is only *said* that …"). It is most likely that the discourse will continue with a sentence related to Mr. Smith's death. Therefore, the subordinate clause contains the foreground information.

7.3.1   In the example both an external and a character-bound focalizer can apply. In the case of the external focalizer the narrator is also inside the bar and sees how a man is sitting at the bar and how the door opens and a woman and child enter. In this situation the described persons are probably the (main) characters in the story.
A character-bound focalizer can be in the bar as well, observing the events as described. However, he himself plays an important part in the story as well. (For example, one would expect him to start a conversation with the woman who just came in or with the man who is sitting at the bar.) In the case of a character-bound narrator, you see the world from this character's viewpoint. This means that this character does not know the man at the bar and the woman with the child entering the bar, otherwise he would have used names rather than indefinite articles. The people observed do not necessarily have to take part in the rest of the story.

7.3.2   Since "His brother" is in subject position, this should be the person with whom the author can identify most. But the second characteristic of the person with whom the author identifies is the way in which this person is described: with the first name or in relation to someone else? "His brother" is defined in relation to someone else (John, or a third person), as a result of which the extent to which the author identifies with this person decreases. These two characteristics are in contrast and that is why this sentence is flawed.

7.4.1   In sentence (a) the car in which the speaker sits begins to weave. In sentence (b) it is a car in the speaker's vicinity that begins to weave. Since a definite article is used in sentence (a), "car" must be given information. The reader infers the car because of the fact that the speaker is driving down a highway. In sentence (b) an indefinite article is used, which makes it clear to the reader that this should be interpreted as new information. Therefore, it is incorrect if in sentence (b) "a car" refers to the speaker's car.
According to Prince's given–new taxonomy in (a) "the car" is inferable, as it can be derived from the fact that the "I" is driving down a highway. In (b) "a car" is unused, as one knows that there is more than one car on a highway. In this last case it is tenable to say that "a car" is a brand new object, for it is possible for a reader to imagine a deserted highway.

7.4.2   Substitution is textually evoked, because a dummy word in the text substitutes a word that occurred earlier on in the text. Ellipsis is textually evoked for the same reason, but in this case a previously occurring word is omitted. Reference is also textually evoked, because this phenomenon always contains two elements: an antecedent and a referent, for example, *a man* and *he* or *the* in *the man*. Conjunction is textually evoked when the relation is explicit (e.g., marked with a connective). When it is implicit, it is inferable, as the reader has to infer the relation between sentences on the basis of knowledge of the world. Of lexical cohesion, repetition and synonymy are textually evoked, because with these types of cohesion the concept is repeated literally. Hyponomy, meronymy, antonymy and collocation are inferable, because with these types of cohesion the reader needs knowledge of the world.

7.5.1 In order to determine if an inference is a presupposition the negation test can be used:
"It *didn't* take John seven years to complete his studies."
Inferences (36a) and (36b) still hold: there is a person named John and he is a student. Whether or not he is a brilliant student (36c) cannot be concluded from the sentence. That depends on the average length of the studies that John took up. Therefore, inferences (36a) and (36b) are presuppositions.

7.5.2 The fact that the speaker has had enough of that racket from next door is the claim. The fact that the neighbors are making noise is the presupposition, as this information is still true after the utterance has been negated:
"I *haven't* had enough of that racket from next door."
In the first example, B answers the claim, by saying that A must do something about what he has had enough of. In the second example B answers the presupposition, as he reacts to something which is implicit information: that that racket from next door is noise made by the neighbors.

7.5.3 In the first example, B reacts to the presupposition in A's utterance. B tackles the presupposition, as a result of which A's utterance is no longer true. After all, the presupposition has to tally with the situation in reality.
In the second example, in B1, B reacts to the claim in A's utterance. B denies the claim, but this does not affect the correctness or truth of A's utterance. In B2 the presupposition in A's utterance is tackled, making this utterance no longer concur with the truth.
The course of the interaction is influenced when the presupposition of the question is tackled in an answer. The situation in the world must match the presupposition, because the information in the presupposition is a condition for the rest of the claim.

7.6.1 In (a) there is a necessary, backward inference: in general the speaker thinks conservative people are less sympathetic. The inference is necessary because otherwise you would not understand the words "[...] but all in all [...]". These words make it clear to the reader that the speaker thinks there is a relationship between someone's conservative views and how sympathetic that person is. Furthermore, the text becomes inconsistent if the inference is denied. The inference is backwards because the relation is not obvious to everyone. Only after reading the words "but all in all" does this relation become clear to the reader. The reader needs knowledge of the beliefs and characteristics of conservatives in order to make the inference.

In (b) there is a necessary inference: The neighbors' parties are usually rather noisy. Because of the noise, I cannot sleep well. The inference is necessary because otherwise you would not understand the cause of this poor night's rest. It is necessary in order to make the connection between the two sentences. Denying the inference makes the utterance inconsistent. Whether the inference is backward or forward depends on the reader's knowledge and experiences. If the reader has had the same experiences of neighbors' parties as the writer, then the inference may be forward. If the reader has never experienced neighbors' noisy parties, then a backward inference is more probable. The image that the reader has of the object *house* also determines the moment at which the inference takes place. If the reader thinks of apartments while reading the first sentence, then the inference may be forward. If the reader thinks of detached houses in a woody environment, then a backward inference is more probable. Furthermore, the inference can take place at a different moment for, on the one hand, readers with an often-disturbed night's rest and, on the other hand, readers who have no problems at all. However, in general in western societies the image has arisen of parties that are a nuisance to neighbors. Even though the reader may never have had this experience, he knows from movies and other media how these parties can be. That is why most people will probably make a forward inference.

In (c) there is a necessary, backward inference: S. Mehlam is a woman. The inference is necessary because otherwise the reader does not know who "her" refers to in the second sentence. Furthermore, denying the inference makes the utterances inconsistent. The inference is backward because the name does not reveal the gender. When reading "her", the reader looks for the person that is referred to and finds the name "S. Mehlam". The fact that an experiment includes a hypothesis can also be seen as an inference. However, in this case a type of coherence is involved (see Section 6.1). "Experiment" and "hypothesis" are in a "part versus whole" relation: metonymy.

In (d) the reader does not have to infer information. There is no implicit information.

7.6.2   For text (a) the reading time will be longer, since the average reader will make the forward inference that John is a student. However, later on it turns out that he is a teacher. In order to process this and to make the inference, the reader needs more time. The fact that John is seen as a student and not as a teacher may have several causes. For example, the fact that John is only called by his first name and that he takes the bus to go to school. The reading time for text (b) will be shorter, since it is immediately clear that the text is about a teacher, and therefore the reader will not make the wrong inference.

Answers Chapter 8

8.1.1   Especially the fourth maxim (manner) is of importance to stylistic research. After all, this maxim pertains to the form that is chosen for a specific content. According to the third definition of style

(style is a deviation from a certain expectation), all maxims can be formulated from a stylistic perspective. For example, someone can provide more information than the receiver expects (maxim of quantity), say a lot of things that are not true (maxim of quality) or constantly say things that ostensibly are not true (maxim of relevance). These types of (seeming) violations determine, according to the third definition, the sender's style as well.

8.1.2   In an emotional style the "keys" factor is most important, since the tone of voice is especially characteristic of this type of language use.

When a formal style is used, the scene is the most important factor. Hymes indicates here that in using formal language participants change the scene into a formal setting. However, the keys factor is of importance as well.

In legalese the act sequences are the most important factor, as the topic of the conversation is crucial: laws.

In officialese the participants are of importance, if not crucial: a civil servant and a citizen. Moreover, the act sequences are important, since the topic of conversation is crucial: government regulations.

In social workers' jargon the participants are important, because the person leading the conversation adopts the role of advising, comforting and helping his audience. The act sequences are of importance too, as the topic of conversation is crucial: emotional, social or psychological problems.

In stock exchange language the setting is important, because the place of the conversation is crucial: the stock market. But also the act sequences are a factor, since the topic of the conversation is crucial: stock exchange quotations.

The important factor in persuasive language is the ends, since the aim of the conversation is crucial: to convince or persuade someone.

8.2.1   Uttering sentence (4a) would be appropriate in a situation where the speaker has not got much power over the hearer and where the social distance is relatively great, e.g., a student asking his professor. However, it would not be strange either if the same professor asked the student the question in this way. Having power over the hearer does not necessarily mean that one can be blunt or direct. Thus, it would not be appropriate for a professor to utter sentence (b) to a student in the aforementioned situation, just because he has got power over the student. The appropriateness of uttering (b) depends on the social distance. Uttering (b) is only appropriate when the social distance is small, for example, if you are talking to a friend or a family member; and even then the language use is not really polite.

8.2.2   Basically, the illocutionary tenor of the sentence is the same content: a request to shut the window.

8.3.1   The term *text grammar* is a metaphor in which the object *text* is understood in terms of the object *sentence*. This metaphor suggests that a text can, at least in part, be described in the same manner as a sentence. As in a generative sentence grammar, constituents can be formed into sentences using phrase structure rules. Just as the symbol S can be taken as a starting point in a sentence grammar (S 6 NP + VP, etc.), in a text grammar, using the symbol T as a point of departure, a text could be generated by applying a limited number of rules to combine sentences (T 6 S1, S2, etc.) It is, however, highly improbable that a limited set of rules can describe the connections between sentences in a text. The possibilities for combining sentences are endlessly more varied than those for combining constituents within a sentence (topic, direct object, etc.). See, for example, Section 3.6 on cohesion phenomena. The possibilities of lexical cohesion alone are myriad, while the phrase structure rules are extremely limited in number. Thus, a text cannot really be described as a sentence.

8.3.2   The type-token ratio of the first three sentences of Chapter 8 is 0.76 (28 different words divided by 37 words in total).

8.4.1   It depends on whether the arguments are strong. It is likely that you only want your audience to think about your arguments if the arguments are strong. If that is the case, it is best to use a rhetorical question after the argument(s), because otherwise the audience's judgment will not be based on the arguments, but on an appeal to emotions prompted by the rhetorical question.

8.4.2   Using intensifiers can have a positive effect on attitude change. However, this effect is indirect. Moreover, a positive effect will only take place if the source is seen as reliable. If you want your audience to think about your arguments, it is best to use intensifiers only if you have strong arguments and if it is likely that you will be seen as a reliable source. Otherwise you would only highlight weak arguments.

Answers Chapter 9

9.1.1   In this book posture and mimicry are mentioned as examples of parts of a conversation that are ignored in transcription. More in general, it can be noted that most nonverbal communication is left out of the transcription system. A laugh or a sigh can be put in parentheses, but how should a grin, a certain expression or looking away be indicated?

9.2.1   The turn-taking model consists of two components: the *turn-construction component* and the *turn-taking component*. A turn consists of a number of *turn-constructional units* (TCUs). The first point at which the assignment of a turn can take place is at the end of such a unit. This point is called the *transition-relevance place* (TRP). As soon as a TRP is reached, a *turn-taking component* is applicable. Several turn-taking rules come into force then. This set of rules is recursive, which means that it comes into force again at every subsequent TRP. However, this would mean that in every conversation the turn-taking keeps going on. But conversations come to an end at some point, which means that an extra rule is needed in order to prevent the turn-taking from continuing endlessly.

9.2.2   The fifth strategy for carrying out a Face Threatening Act is "Don't do the FTA". This strategy can be identified in a conversation as a silence. It is an example of a meaningful silence, which sometimes says more than words. It is a silence that should be interpreted as a turn in a conversation. An example is a situation in which person A asks person B what the latter thinks of A's new hairdo. If there is no answer, the silence and the nonverbal communication usually suffice. However, a silence does not always have to be preceded by a question in order to be meaningful. A silence after someone has received a present can also be significant. It remains unclear, however, how the silence should be interpreted: is the person who received the present impressed and does he lack the words, or does he not want to give a negative opinion?

9.2.3   The idea that back-channel behavior is a pre-turn means that an interlocutor, by using these short utterances, indicates that he wants to say something, that he wants the speaker to give him the opportunity to take the next turn. However, this view, like the idea that back-channel behavior is not a pre-turn, is too simplistic.
A general description of back-channel behavior would be the short moments at which the listener gives feedback on what the speaker says. However, a distinction has to be made between the several types of back-channel behavior: 1. There are utterances with which a listener indicates that he is still listening carefully ("Mhm ..."); 2. There are utterances with which the listener indicates that he agrees with the speaker ("Yes, yes ..."); 3. There are utterances with which the listener tries to tone down what the speaker is saying ("Well, ..."); 4. There are utterances with which the listener indicates that he wants to react to a certain topic (tone and intonation are of special importance). Whether or not a pre-turn is involved has to be established for each specific situation. It all depends on the interlocutors and their intentions.
In general, however, a pre-turn is not involved in the first two types of back-channel behavior, since the listener encourages the speaker, which would not be favorable in the process of trying to "win" a turn. Most of the time these minimal utterances are verbalized simultaneously with what the speaker says, which means that the latter can continue to speak. The third type, on the other hand, can be a pre-turn, since the listener clearly expresses that he holds a different opinion concerning the topic. If a listener does not agree with something, chances are that he wants to express and found his opinion. The fourth type of back-channel behavior can also be a pre-turn, since the listener makes it clear by using intonation and nonverbal communication that he wants to react to something.
The fact that back-channel behavior can be expressed without the speaker being interrupted is the main reason for saying that it cannot be seen as a pre-turn. Since these minimal utterances can fulfill various functions it would also be too simplistic to call all these utterances pre-turns.

9.3.1   Adjacency pairs are pairs of utterances that often occur in each other's vicinity. Besides the question–answer pair there are more examples, such as a compliment followed by a word of thanks or acceptance; an offer followed by an acceptance or rejection; a request followed by an answer in the form of a agreement or refusal; a threat followed by an attempt at self-defense (oral).

9.3.2   Telephone conversations lack an important aspect of communication that can obstruct the analysis of verbal interaction: nonverbal communication. In default of this information, interlocutors have to express themselves more explicitly, which results in more information for researchers about the development of conversations.

9.4.1   Other discourse markers might include *because, moreover, oh, in any case* and *I mean*.

9.4.2   When the markers in (17) and (18) are omitted the conversations come across as rather impersonal, as staccato, as if the two participants are not really listening to each other. But more specifically, discourse markers indicate the attitude of a speaker. The omission of markers in (17) makes it less clear how to interpret the intentions that the speakers have with their utterances. The omission of markers in (18) makes A's utterance less malicious and B's utterance less indifferent.

9.4.3   When the speaker has more assumptions about the current state of knowledge of the interlocutor, i.e., in conversations between friends, the speaker will have a better basis for providing advice on how to process the information, which will increase the likelihood of the occurrence of presentation markers. This can explain why *like* and *you know* show higher frequencies in conversations between friends than in those between strangers.

Answers Chapter 10

10.1.1   Text 1 (page 221: "Bereiter and Scardamalia ... required is an") contains one hundred words, 171 syllables and six sentences. The word length (wl) is 171, the sentence length (sl) is 16.7.

$$R.E. = 206.84 - (0.85 \times wl) - (1.02 \times sl)$$
$$= 206.84 - (0.85 \times 171) - (1.02 \times 16.7)$$
$$= 206.84 - 145.35 - 17.03$$
$$= 44.46$$

Text 2 (page 2: "This book ... a general") contains one hundred words, 158 syllables and seven sentences. The word length (wl) is 158, the sentence length (sl) is 14.3.

$$R.E. = 206.84 - (0.85 \times wl) - (1.02 \times sl)$$
$$= 206.84 - (0.85 \times 158) - (1.02 \times 14.3)$$
$$= 206.84 - 134.30 - 14.59$$
$$= 57.95$$

The outcome of the formula for the first text can be interpreted as "difficult". The text would be appropriate for high-school level. The second text is somewhat easier, but still fairly difficult. In general one would expect that the reading ease of this textbook would lie between 0 and 30, as it is used at college level. According to Flesh's readability formula, the book has been written more readably than strictly would have been necessary. The small difference in readability between the two texts is expected, because the second text is part of the introduction, whereas the first text delves more deeply into a specific topic in this textbook.

10.1.2　There are various ways to measure cohesion within a discourse. A readability formula should, for example, incorporate the number of words that occur more than once: the more overlap, the more cohesive a discourse is. A second possibility is to include the number of reference words in a text. A problem with these variables is that quantity is not always an indicator of quality. A discourse with a lot of overlap is not necessarily better than a text with less overlap; too much overlap can even have the opposite effect. A formula only considers quantity. Therefore, the cohesion of a discourse is better measured in a qualitative way.

10.2.1　A reader's opinion on a text or a text's topic may say something about the extent to which the reader has understood the text. Does the reader address relevant issues or insignificant details, and has he understood the writer's viewpoint? However, the reader's judgment does not always indicate the level of understanding. For one, it is possible to have an opinion on a topic without having read a text about it. Or a reader can have an opinion about a text's quality without having read it, based on prejudice about the writer or the text type. Another disadvantage of this manner of judging a text in terms of readability is the fact that it is quite subjective and perhaps such a judgment says as much about the judge as about the text.

10.2.2　There are various methods for measuring a text's readability. An initial possibility is to ask readers about their judgment of readability; this is fairly subjective, however. Another method is to apply a readability formula. However, these are restricted in their application and they only address word and sentence length. A third possibility is the cloze test. This method, however, is only suited when the words that are left out are chosen on the basis of their function as signal words. Another disadvantage is the rather unnatural reading situation that is created: the reader will scrutinize the text, reading it word for word. A fourth option is to have the reader summarize or retell the text. However, in this method factors other than comprehensibility come into play as well, such as personal preferences. After all, what someone includes in a summary also depends on the type of information that this person regards as important. It may also be that the person summarizing the text forgets to include certain information that he did understand.
A better method is to ask questions about the content of the text. The answers are more suited to prove the comprehensibility of the text since questions can be attuned to the measurement of a certain level of understanding. For example, the questions can specifically address a text's stumbling-blocks or the difficulty of the questions can be varied. Another useful method is measuring reading speed and recording eye fixation. Using these on-line methods it can be determined which parts of a text are difficult for a reader in terms of information processing. A combination

of asking questions and measuring reading time and recording eye movement would be the best method to determine a text's comprehensibility: on- and off-line methods are combined and, in addition to questions concerning the content, an objective method is applied.

10.3.1   a.   10
         b.   7
         c.   5
         d.   14
         e.   1
         f.   10 and 1
         g.   4
         h.   10
         i.   15

10.4.1   The authors themselves give only the following explanation (2002:431) and indicate that further research is needed: "It may be that such training improves people's sensitivity to the overall communication climate, and in particular, to both the constraints on management on this issue and their own communicative responsibilities."

Answers Chapter 11

11.1.1   1.   Absentation: Little Red Riding Hood sets out for her grandmother.
         2.   Interdiction: Her mother forbids her to run off the path.
         4.   Reconnaisance: The wolf scouts out.
         5.   Delivery: The wolf sees Little Red Riding Hood.
         6.   Trickery: The wolf tempts Little Red Riding Hood to run off the path and pick some flowers. Little Red Riding Hood will now take more time to reach grandmother's house, so that the wolf can take a shortcut and arrive there earlier.
         3.   Violation: Little Red Riding Hood violates her mother's prohibition: she runs off the path to pick some flowers.
         7.   Complicity: Little Red Riding Hood adopts the wolf's advice. Without knowing it, she helps the wolf carry out his plan.

In *Little Red Riding Hood* Propp's functions are clearly present. However, they are not all in the correct order. The violation, for example, only takes place after the wolf has been introduced.

Propp's theory of a fairytale's structure assumes the prototype of a fairytale. He claims that there is a fixed order of succession. A fairytale must meet certain basic conditions, but it cannot be that a "model structure" is the only one possible. His theory might be more descriptive and less prescriptive: the correct order for a "correct" fairytale cannot be dictated. The order of functions as Propp appoints it in his theory is not as restricted as is put forward. Variations of this order do not necessarily make a "less correct" fairytale. An example of this is *Little Red Riding Hood*.

11.1.2 First of all, the denomination of the functions is disputable. In this analysis, the walk in the garden (sentence 1) is called "Departure". The function "Departure" however, is not a regular departure such as a walk, but more a departure with a specific goal, a journey. The function "Departure" has to conclude the complication (functions 8 through 11). However, there is no complication prior to the walk. Function 8 ("Villainy") is fulfilled by the sentence in which the dragon (the villain) that destroys the country is introduced. This sentence forms the beginning of the complication as well. The journey the brothers are about to commence forms the "Departure" (sentence 4).

The events that take place before the brothers decide to undertake a journey are of an introductory nature. The garden walk is an (unconscious) exploration, for which function 4 ("Reconnaissance") would be a suitable analysis. However, because this function is appointed to the bandit it is not the correct analysis.

Furthermore, small parts of the story are omitted: the moment at which they tell their father that they have decided to undertake a journey and the moment that they meet Baba Yaga and tell her that they have heard that there is a dragon. This analysis leaves no room for details and nuances:
- that the *strongest* son tries to lift the stone;
- that there is a hidden *cellar* underneath and that the horses and suits of armor are hidden there;
- that they have *heard* that there is a dragon that is destroying the country.

An analysis in terms of heroes and villains proves to be oversimplified.

11.1.3 A macrostructure represents the core of the content of discourse. It is a kind of summary that results from rules for deleting less important information, and rules for generalization and construction in order to get the gist of the discourse (see Section 5.3). A superstructure is a prefab structure that exists independently of a piece of discourse, hence the term *superstructure*. It is best compared with a "skeleton" for content (see Section 5.4). In short, macrostructures refer to the content while superstructures refer to the form.

Propp's analysis model does not refer to the content, but to the structure in form. The elements *absentation, punishment*, etc., are filled in with different contents depending on the fairytale in question. Of course, the elements themselves contain some content, the meaning of the concept *absentation*, etc., but we also see this aspect in other superstructures, like the superstructure of a scientific article presented in Section 5.4 in which elements as *hypothesis* and *results* have a meaning as concepts. The real content of these elements, however, varies depending on the experiment reported on in the article.

11.2.1 1. *Orientation*: This is the introduction to the fairytale ("Once upon a time there was ...") in which the characters are introduced and the setting and time in which the story takes place are given. The fairytale is about Little Red Riding Hood, who is going to bring her sick grandmother some food and drink. Her mother forbidding her to run off the path is also part of the orientation.

2. *Complication*: The complication takes up the biggest part of the fairytale. The complication starts with the wolf's appearance (when he sees Little Red Riding Hood walking through the woods) and does not end until the huntsman approaches grandmother's house.

3. *Evaluation*: The importance of the story emerges at various moments. For example, the fact that the wolf snores very loudly and, therefore, attracts the huntsman's attention can be seen as an evaluative element: what would have happened had the wolf not been snoring and had the huntsman not come to see what was wrong?

4. *Solution*: The huntsman who saves Little Red Riding Hood and her grandmother from the wolf's stomach presents the solution. After that he punishes the wolf by stuffing his stomach with large stones, making the wolf collapse and die as soon as he wakes up and tries to flee.

5. *Coda*: The end of the fairytale forms the coda of Little Red Riding Hood. The huntsman skins the wolf and goes home, grandmother eats and drinks and revives and Little Red Riding Hood has learned never to leave the path again.

11.2.2 The solution of story example (5) is that a friend ended the attack by intervening (sentence 4). The evaluation is an utterance with which the storyteller points out the importance of the event. There are four possibilities for analyzing the evaluation in this example. The third possibility is the best.

1. The sentence "I'd rather not talk about it" has a strong evaluative character. This sentence indicates what the storyteller thinks of the story. However, this sentence is less suitable since it is not part of the text to be analyzed.

2. Sentence 3, "and my friend came in", could be the evaluation since the reader can ask himself "What would have happened had that friend not intervened?" This sentence thus indicates how dangerous the storyteller's situation was. However, since this sentence is the result of the complication, this is not the best analysis.

3. The evaluation can also coincide with the solution (sentence 4). This is the most probable analysis. Either way, the fragment "and ended it" is both solution and evaluation.

4. A fourth possibility would be to give no evaluation. The speaker reluctantly gives a brief report of the events that have occurred. In a rather objective manner he points out what has actually happened. However, it is this objectivity that "colors" the story. Clearly, the storyteller is still bitter, an evaluation that can be read "between the lines".

11.2.3 Labov and Waletsky distinguish five components in a story structure. These components emerge in the analysis of the "dog story" in Section 11.3. The story starts with an *orientation* (sentences 1 and 2): an introductory text fragment that provides information on the characters, the setting, the time and the situation. Then comes the *complication* (sentences 3 through 10) with a result (sentence 10: "dropped into the water"). This *evaluation* can be localized in sentence 11 ("and was never seen again"), which at the same time is the story's *solution*. A *coda* is missing in this story.

11.3.1 The term *story grammar* is a metaphor in which the object *story* is understood in terms of the object *sentence*. *Story grammar* implies that stories, just as sentences, are constructed from a restricted set of constituents. However, as shown in the answer to question 8.3.1, the structure of a text, and certainly of a story, is less restricted than the structure of a sentence. A sentence is ungrammatical if it does not meet the possible sentence structures. A text, however, can vary endlessly in sentence and section order.

Labov and Waletsky, for example, distinguish between the story (the actual order in which the events have taken place) and the plot (the order in which the events are presented in the story). Analyzing a story in relation to the actual order in which the events have taken place can become problematic when several events take place at the same time. Simultaneity is more difficult to point out in the actual order. In a plot the manner in which the simultaneity is communicated can influence the suspense and curiosity that the reader experiences. In a plot certain parts of events can be omitted, which has a certain effect on a reader. If the actual order has to be determined, it may well be the case that these "gaps" cannot be filled using information from the plot.

In a story it is possible to make temporal leaps; most stories are not told chronologically. The storyteller can even begin with the end (a murder, for example) and subsequently reconstruct the preceding events step by step (e.g., who are the suspects, who has an alibi?).

In Mandler and Johnson's psycholinguistic approach to narratives, the term *story grammar* is used. However, when looking at the rules that underpin such a grammar, it is quickly established that these rules can be applied more freely than those for constructing sentences can. It is pointed out how certain components of a story can be constructed from other parts, but the order in which the components should be told is not bound by rules.

11.4.1 In (13) there are no evidentials, expressions indicating to what extent the narrator believes that his story is proved, like "I am not quite sure, but ...". One can doubt the occurrence of opacity phenomena. Are there any critical presentations of persons' actions? The only phrase that, to some extent, fits into this definition is "I didn't like any of the people I was working with." But this statement says more about the narrator than about other people.

So, the answer must be negative. This means that this narrative presents the narrator as a member of the group, as can be also deduced from the content of the story. The protagonist is telling how she got a job at a university and that she stayed there.

Answers Chapter 12

12.1.1

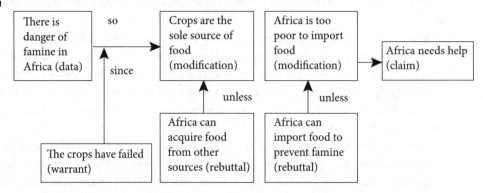

More analyses are possible. For example, the fact that crops have failed may also be seen as *data* and the famine as a *warrant*. This illustrates that data and warrants are often confused. Also the fact that crops are the sole source of food in Africa could be a *backing* for the fact that there is danger of famine. In this analysis the interpretation was chosen that two possible counterarguments are rebutted (*rebuttal → modification*): namely, Africa could make use of other sources of food and Africa could import food. This analysis lacks a *backing*. The *claim* is that Africa needs help.

Most data from this example are second-order data. The source tells us about the situation in Africa. First-order data do not occur explicitly. However, if the receiver agrees with the information and argumentation, there may be first-order data. Third-order data, opinions of others, are not explicitly used. Nonetheless, there is an implicit reference to information of others: "Africa is, *after all*, too poor to import food." "After all" suggests that this is known, generally "accepted" information.

The argumentation in this text includes a substantive warrant. If crops do not produce food, this usually results in danger of famine in poor countries. This is a generalization.

12.1.2

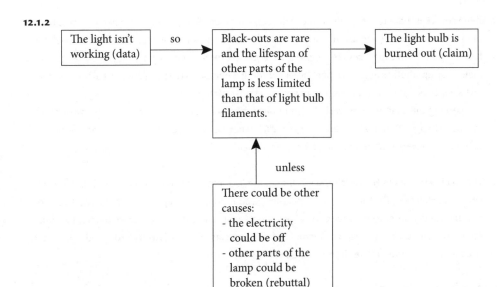

In this analysis we see that the *warrant* may be absent as well. In this conversation two counterarguments are rebutted (*rebuttal → modification*). In doing so the speaker makes it clear that the fact that the light bulb is burned out is most likely explained by the fact that the light is not working.

12.2.1 The unspoken argument is: "When he leaves, he usually takes the car." But since the conversation partners follow the cooperative principle (see Section 2.4) it is not necessary to make this argument explicit. The receiver can retrieve the omitted information on the basis of the four maxims (quantity, quality, relevance and manner). The receiver assumes that the speaker provides sufficient, true, relevant and clear information and subsequently derives the most obvious interpretation.

12.2.2 Signing the letter as "Dr." may leave the impression that the professor is an authority on environmental issues. Though he can have an opinion on environmental issues, he is not a professor in this field; he is a literature professor. He presents himself as a "false" authority.

12.3.1 knowledge: cognitive
intention: conative
sympathy: affective
pleasure: affective
belief: cognitive

12.3.2 If the source is a doctor who tells you to take certain medicines, you are more likely to take them than when your aunt (who is not a doctor) tells you that certain medicines worked really well for her. A doctor is an expert source, whose advice you are more likely to act on than your aunt's, who may be sympathetic but is no expert. In persuading a person to take a certain medicine, someone's expertise is more important than someone's sympathy.

Concerning the channel, non-verbal communication can have a big influence on the process of attitude change. That is why there is a great difference between convincing someone during a telephone conversation or during a face-to-face meeting.

12.3.2 The sixteen factors in Hymes's SPEAKING model are formulated from an interactive conversational situation. However, the four factors of persuasive communication apply to both interactive and non-interactive situations. Since textual persuasive communication is concerned here, the non-interactive situation has been chosen in the following classification. Afterwards, both the interactive and the non-interactive situation are dealt with.

Source

Speaker, Addressor, [Purpose – goals], [Scene], [Setting], [Norms of interaction], [Norms of interpretation]

Message

Form, Content, [Keys], Form of speech

Channel

Channel, [Norms of interaction], [Norms of interpretation]

Receiver

Hearer, Addressee, [Norms of interaction], [Norms of interpretation]

In an interactive situation participants are alternately sender and receiver. In such a situation all participants influence the *Scene*. However, in a non-interactive situation the receiver has no influence on the *Scene* (for example, when watching a commercial or reading a brochure).

The *Setting* of persuasive communication can be manipulated by the sender (especially time and place of communication: a commercial is aired after a certain television program, a pleasant atmosphere is created during important business negotiations, etc.). In an interactive situation the receiver can influence this *Setting* too. But there are also situations in which neither conversation partner can influence the communication situation. Thus, the *Setting* is partly outside the situation in which communication takes place (the weather condition when someone sees a billboard, disturbing influences while reading a newspaper, etc.) and it can partly be influenced by the sender.

In an interactive situation each conversation partner (both sender and receiver) strives towards a certain goal (*purpose/goals*). However, this is different in non-interactive communication. Here the message is designed in accordance with the goal that the sender has. The receiver's goal while reading the information is unrelated to the message; it is, however, related to the final result.

The *Keys*, the tone of the conversation, is influenced by each conversation partner. It is true that in a commercial or advertisement the tone is geared to the target group, but the sender has the final say in this. The tone is an aspect of the message.

In textual persuasive communication the sender determines the message. All factors that are classed under "message" can, therefore, be seen as sender factors. The form, the contents, the tone and the style of the message are determined by the sender.

Norms of interaction and *Norms of interpretation* are for a great part embedded in the culture that we are part of and for some part there are universal norms for interaction and interpretation. These norms are different for each communication situation and are determined by the sender, the receiver and the channel. The result of a communication situation depends on the norms that the participants in a conversation or the writer and the reader of a letter or a brochure employ. The channel also influences the norms that are applied: telephone conversations, personal contact, chatting on the Internet and writing a letter all require different norms.

12.4.1 The research reported on in Section 12.4 suggests the following. It depends on the type of claim that is used. If the claim is a desirability claim, like "The future would be very gloomy for this person if he does not get any help", then statistical evidence is more convincing than anecdotal evidence. If the claim is a probability claim, like "A little help will make the future less gloomy for this person", it does not matter whether the evidence is statistical or anecdotal. If the claim is of another type, then the vividness of the formulation in the evidence is of more importance than the type of evidence.

The research on the effect of hedges suggests that they have a negative influence when the arguments are weak. So the advice depends on the argument quality. Only with strong evidence should hedges be used.

Answers Chapter 13

13.1.1 Bereiter and Scardamalia introduced two models for the writing process, since there are various types of writing processes. The process depends on the extent to which someone is an experienced writer and on the purpose of the writing task. Inexperienced writers hardly plan the writing process. They start without having prepared themselves properly. Without much effort they write down an entire story off the top of their heads. This is called "knowledge-telling". Experienced writers plan more and gain new insights and ideas while writing. They regard the writing process as a creative process that consists of "knowledge-transforming". Experienced writers can choose between the knowledge-telling and the knowledge-transforming model. Inexperienced writers do not have this opportunity. In order to describe the differences between the various writing processes, Bereiter and Scardamalia introduced these two models.

13.1.2   This quote illustrates how a writer forms his thoughts about the topics during the writing process. Only after the writer *sees* what he *says* does he know what he thinks. In making explicit one's thoughts one can order them and gain insight. This best fits the knowledge-transforming model.

13.1.3   The most important difference between "knowledge-telling" and "knowledge-transforming" is the fact that the first model does not incorporate the planning phase. An instructor can teach a writer to plan the writing task and to be aware of the purpose, the intended audience and the genre. The writer can learn how to make a writing plan. Furthermore, the "knowledge-teller" must become conscious of possible structures and approaches to the topic. An instructor can also provide hints and tips on the way in which the writer can gain more knowledge about the text's topic.
Training in correct formulation or applying grammar rules is useful to all writers, but it cannot change a "knowledge-teller" into a "knowledge-transformer". It is important that the writer gains insight into his own writing process and that he learns how to evaluate his own text and reflect on the topic.

13.2.1   In the think-aloud protocol three phases of the writing process can be seen. First is the planning phase. The writer searches for the exact position she wants to adopt and she selects a topic that she wants to discuss ("*the educational system*"). Other possible topics have not explicitly come up for consideration. The ordering of the information, a part of the planning phase, is not part of the protocol.
In the protocol the formulation phase is most clearly present. This is the phase in which the sentences are generated. The writer tries to find the right words ("*transformed itself from …*" → "*has been influenced by …*", "*a myriad of ways*" → "*a number of ways*" → "*a lotta ways*" → "*tremendously*"). The evaluation phase also recurs a few times. When the writer tries to find the right words, she evaluates these and decides whether or not the formulation is good. Examples are: "*god that doesn't make any kind of sense*", "*no*", "*okay*" and "*now that's where we are gonna be working off of*".

13.3.1   No, one cannot prove that the signing of the agreement took place in Moscow. But it can be inferred (the fourth function of a schema) on the basis of common knowledge about agreements that are signed at the location where the partners meet each other.
By default pronouns such as *they* refer to the nearest antecedent, in this case "Russian leaders". But the schema of signing an agreement is already active, and this prompts the reader to interpret "they" as both parties.
Of course, "flying" also has the meaning of "withdraw with fear", but the already activated schematic knowledge that presidents travel by airplane prohibits this interpretation.

13.4.1   The letter *f* occurs six times in this passage. Many subjects will miss the *f* in the word "of", which occurs twice in this passage. They probably pay less attention to these functions words. These often short words (mainly articles, prepositions and conjunctions) serve to link the words that are more important for the content: nouns, verbs, adjectives and adverbs. The f in the content words is less often overlooked.

From this experiment it can be concluded that the surface level is less important than the other levels of representation: the propositional and situational representation. It is not necessary to fully process the surface representation before trying to process the propositional and situational content. Thus, the results with mistakes in noting the frequency of the letter f support the experiment by Fillenbaum on overlooking solecisms.

13.4.2 A frame refers to stereotypical knowledge about concepts. The concept *school*, for example, contains elements such as classrooms, a hall, teachers and fixed schedules. These and other elements are activated by the title and play a role in the interpretation: on the basis of this concept the seats, for example, are interpreted as seats in a classroom or an auditorium, and not as seats in a coach or a train.

A script refers to stereotypical knowledge about roles. Most readers attribute the student role to Karen. In fact, Karen could have been a teacher until the sentence "There were no more seats left." But because schools have more students than teachers the default role for a person in a school frame is that of a student. Based on this script knowledge the word "caught" can be interpreted as "spotted by a superintendent" and not as, for example, "overtaken by a rapist".

A scenario refers to the stereotypical knowledge about the order of activities, for example, first wake up, then have breakfast, then go to school. On the basis of this knowledge the sentence about skipping breakfast makes sense. No reader will think "Well, she can have breakfast after arriving at school."

13.5.1 The notion of schemata is incorporated in the third type of rules in the construction component concerning the activation of knowledge. These rules refer to all kinds of associations that can come up with a concept or an activity. So, the notion of schemata has a very high place in Kintsch's model, directly after the processing of the propositions in discourse. This position is necessary to explain the variety of inferences that can be made during discourse processing. It is only after these processing activities that the process of correct interpretation can start in the integration component.

13.5.2 Among the numerous propositions that could come up with *to bake* the following ones are possible:

1. INGREDIENTS[FLOUR, OIL]
2. NECESSITIES[HEAT SOURCE, BAKING TIN]
3. BAKE[Ag:PERS,obj:POTTERY]

Propositions 1 and 2 have to be linked to the object of *to bake*: cake. Proposition 3 refers to another meaning of *to bake* and has to be negatively related to the baking of a cake. In fact all stereotypical or encyclopedic knowledge about the concept *to bake* could be of relevance when this verb occurs in discourse. So, Figure 5 contains only some statements in the form of a predicate and some arguments. Also see Section 5.1 about another notation of the propositions.

13.6.1   The term *metaphor* literally means that something is carried over (in Greek, *meta + ferein* means *over + carry*). So, something of the meaning of a concept is carried over onto another concept. In a metaphor such as "a sea of troubles" the meaning of the concept *sea* is associated with the concept *troubles*. In this case the associations would be "unpredictable", "turbulent", "vast" and "something that hard to tackle". Of course, the action of "carrying over" is not meant literally, associations are rather evoked and connected, but not literally transferred, So, the term *metaphor* in itself is a metaphorical term as well, since it doesn't transfer but rather evokes associations.

13.6.2   In the metaphor "time is money", the concept *money* is the donor, the source domain that serves as a vehicle for some aspects to attach to the tenor, or the target or the recipient domain *time*. The most important aspect that is transferred is the aspect *expensive*. But many other aspects are not transferred, e.g., that if you lend someone some time you can get it back, or that time should also be subject to inflation.

13.6.3   Ponterotto (2003) suggests the following metaphors:
1.   *Good cop-bad cop*: persuasion is policing
2.   *Old guard*: Solidarity is militancy
3.   *Fringe*: Non-solidarity is marginality
4.   *Bear down on me*: Persuasion is threatening
5.   *Soft soap you*: Persuasion is seducing
6.   *Panic pulse*: Fear is a fast heartbeat
7.   *Stick together*: Solidarity is closeness
8.   *Cover our ass*: Non-solidarity is self-protection
9.   *Stonewall everybody*: Solidarity is resistance
10.   *Leave twisting in the wind*: Non-solidarity is solitude

Answers Chapter 14

14.1.1   The sociological concept of role can be defined as the function in societal life with respect to an institutional context, for example, the role of student, teacher, priest, doctor, patient, etc. Roles are the social characteristics of agents in institutions. The psycho-sociological concept of face is more general and more basic. It is the image that a person projects in his social contacts with others, independent of the institutional role. The concept of face is defined by the need to be appreciated (positive face) and the need to not be interfered with (negative face).

However, there is some overlap regarding face threatening acts (FTAs). The face of an institutional agent can be threatened even more dramatically when the role of the agent comes under attack, for example, when a teacher accuses a student of not being curious enough, or when a student criticizes a teacher for a vague explanation.

14.1.2   An institution serves as a mediator between individuals and society. In that respect language is an institution as well. Language is an important tool for individuals to form a group or a society. In using the same jargon or dialect, individuals can prove that they belong to the same group. An institution serves as a means by which individuals can form a society or a group. In that respect marriage is an institution as well, as it is an official confirmation of the bond between two people, involving duties and rights. Marriage also has its ethical aspects and institutional power. The agents of a marriage, the husband and wife, also exhibit certain role behavior. Note that differentiation trends can also be distinguished in "marriage of convenience", "modern marriage" (with roles as equal as possible) and "cohabitation contract" (toning down certain ethical aspects).

14.2.1   "Perhaps" is a hedge. It reveals a degree of uncertainty. The speaker says that it is not definite whether the possibility of discussion will still exist later on. "Discuss" is rather euphemistic considering the situation in which the participants have an argument. The phrasing "another time" is ambiguous. It can mean "the following day", but it leaves open the possibility of postponing the discussion until some day in the future.

14.3.1   A request must meet felicity conditions such as the preparatory condition, i.e., that the addressee is capable of executing the act (see Section 2.3, example (16)). So, if it is evident from the context that the addressee was not capable of performing the act, then the utterance cannot count as a request. But even if the four conditions listed in Section 2.6 are met, the interpretation "order" is still possible. If, for example, a supervisor utters this formulation to a subordinate, then the locution can count as the illocution *order*. Thus, you need information about the roles of the participants in the interaction and their power relation.

14.4.1   The maxim of quantity is flouted in the second characteristic (the information is already available) and in the fourth characteristic (information is lacking). The maxim of relevance is flouted in the first characteristic. The maxim of manner is flouted in the third and fifth characteristics. If the questions were formulated in another manner and if the formulation were stimulating, then the form would be more appropriate to the situation. The third and the fifth characteristics can also be seen as a flouting of the maxim of quantity if, for example, the answer segments to questions do not provide enough options or space for respondents to fill in all the necessary information concerning the personal situation or if motivational content is missing.

14.5.1   The original article (19) is one-sided and unambiguous in accusing the company. The accusation is based on three items: (1) the Public Prosecutor's charges against the company; (2) the company's conviction the previous year on a similar charge; (3) the company's alleged involvement in a corruption affair concerning a soccer club. The rewritten version (20) is more ambiguous and vague about the accusation. The perspective has been changed: at issue is the possible conduct of administrators in awarding public works contracts. In addition, the focus is not on a single actor;

the construction industry as a whole is at issue. Further, the scope of each of the three items on which the accusation is based is restricted: (1) the Public Prosecutor does not suspect the company as a whole but only one of its directors; (2) the conviction against the company the previous year is reduced to an indictment against the director of an affiliated company in which a settlement is reached which includes a denial of guilt on the part of the director; (3) in the company's alleged involvement in a bribery scandal involving a professional soccer club, the Public Prosecutor finds no grounds for prosecution.

14.6.1   In Section 8.2 three views are dealt with: (a) style as a possible form for a content; (b) style as the choice of specific patterns: (c) style as a deviation from expectations.
Baus and Sandig explored stylistic phenomena based on the assumption that patients have reduced possibilities in choosing their wording at the beginning of therapy, and that in the end the possibilities are enriched. So, the second view is the best candidate. The first view is also tenable here. One could argue that the content at the beginning of therapy is incoherent and that the formulation mirrors the content. The same goes for the end of therapy. The third view of style is not relevant here. Patients are expected to formulate in the way patients are presented in this chapter.

Answers Chapter 15

15.1.1   The linguistic relativity principle says that there is a parallel between language structure and the structuring of reality. If lexical characteristics like hyponyms are seen as belonging to the language structure, then one could say that the fact that the boy has only one word for grain parallels his view of reality: he only sees grain, whereas the girl sees all the different types of grain. But that does not mean that knowing only the hyperonym *grain* will prevent the boy from seeing the differences between barley, oats, etc. Even a person who does not know the names of different automobiles can see the differences between various cars.
However, linguistic relativists would state that it is reasonable to suppose that the boy has more difficulty in detecting and storing the differences when he does not know the different names. The different names will probably be helpful in the perception and storage of the differences. So, there is no causal relation between knowing one word *grain* and seeing only grain, but knowing the different words will provide support in learning the differences in reality.

15.2.1   In adding the adverb *perhaps* the author states that the police were not sure about that. Another possibility is that the author is trying to give an explanation for the police's behavior. However, this is less likely because the word *simply* before "leveled their carbines" does not fit into this explanation mode. The word *simply* probably hides a judgment about shooting at short distance: why not act differently? The situation of endangered life could after all have prompted other reactions such as shooting in the air or drawing back. The naming of the weapons (carbines and Sten guns) is not necessary in this message. However, it colors the scenic description and can have the effect of focusing on the contested police behavior. From the point of view of critical discourse analysis, the police are presented as brute actors in this sentence.

15.3.1 The description is static. Instead of action verbs, only verbs that describe a situation are used, such as "is", "tapers", "include", "conveys" and "sits". The focus is on the clothes and not on mental qualities except for the reference by the "painted face" to the "firmness of his personality". Through the use of adjectives many esthetic aspects are highlighted: "shimmering", "sensual", "delicate" and "wondrous".

15.4.1 In this passage eight social actors are mentioned: (1) "we" referring to Karl-Heinz Grasser and Haider; (2) the "guild master" already present in the word "indignation", which must have an actor; (3) "the cheap labor from Slovenia and Croatia" referring to laborers from those countries; (4) "Hans Peter Haselsteiner", probably a building contractor; (5) "foreigners"; (6) "black Africans"; (7) "the Austrian construction worker"; (8) "one", mentioned twice in "one goes" and "one must". "One", which refers to the man in the street, is also an (anonymous) social actor because this "one" performs actions like walking and understanding.

15.5.1 Pragmatic knowledge, the knowledge of how words are used, is more important than semantic knowledge referring to the meaning of a word as described in a dictionary. In fact this can already be seen in example (23) about the use of first names in a business contact. More important than knowing the first names is knowing when to use them. Another, frequently cited, example is the "Arab rule", which says that it is impolite to say "no". If an Arabic interlocutor answers a question with "yes", then different pragmatic knowledge is needed in order to interpret this answer as an affirmation or as a polite refusal.

References

Agee, W., Ault, P., & Emery, E. (1994). *Introduction to mass communications* (11th ed.). New York: Harper Collins. [14.5]

Ainsworth-Vaughn, N. (1998). *Claiming power in doctor–patient talk.* New York: Oxford University Press. [14.6]

Ajzen, I. (1991). The theory of planned behavior. *Organizational Behavior and Human Decision Processes,* 179–211. [12.3]

Alamargot, D., & Chanquoy, L. (2001). *Through the models of writing.* Dordrecht: Kluwer Academic Publishers. [13.1]

Atkinson, J.M., & Drew, P. (1979). *Order in court: The organisation of verbal interaction in judicial settings.* Atlantic Highlands, NJ: Humanity Press. [14.3]

Auer, P., & Luzio, A. di (Eds.). (1992). *The contextualization of language.* Amsterdam: Benjamins. [3.4]

Austin, J.L., Urmson, J.O., & Sbisà, M. (1976). *How to do things with words* (2nd ed.). Oxford: Oxford University Press. [2.2]

Ausubel, D. (1960). The use of advance organizers in the learning and retention of meaningful verbal material. *Journal of Educational Psychology, 51,* 267–272. [5.4]

Baesler, J., & Burgoon, J. (1994). The temporal effects of story and statistical evidence on belief change. *Communication Research, 21,* 582–602. [12.4]

Bakhtin, M. (1981). *The dialogic imagination: Four essays* (M. Holquist, Ed., C. Emerson & M. Holquist, Trans.). Austin: University of Texas Press. [4.2]

Bal, M. (1985). *Narratology: Introduction to the theory of narrative.* Toronto: University of Toronto Press. [7.3]

Balota, D.A., Flores d'Arcais, G.B., & Rayner, K. (Eds.). (1990). *Comprehension processes in reading.* Hillsdale, NJ: Erlbaum. [13.3]

Bamberg, M. (Ed.). (1997). *Oral versions of personal experience: Three decades of narrative analysis.* Mahwah, NJ: Erlbaum. [11.2]

Barcelona, A. (Ed.). (2003). *Metaphor and metonymy at the crossroads: A cognitive perspective.* Berlin: Mouton de Gruyter. [13.6]

Bar-Hillel, Y. (1954). Indexical expressions. *Mind, 63,* 359–379. [7.1]

Bargiela-Chiappini, F., & Harris, S. (1997). *Managing language: The discourse of corporate meetings.* Amsterdam: Benjamins. [14.1]

Bartlett, F.C. (1932). *Remembering.* Cambridge: Cambridge University Press. [13.3]

Bartsch, R. (1987). *Norms of language: Theoretical and practical issues.* London: Longman. [3.2]

Baten, L. (1981). *Text comprehension. The parameters of difficulty in narrative and expository prose texts: A redefinition of readability.* Doctoral dissertation, University of Illinois, Urbana. [5.1]

Baus, M., & Sandig, B. (1985). *Gesprächspsychotherapie und weibliches Selbstkonzept: Sozialpsychologische und linguistische Analyse am Beispiel eines Falles* [Conversational psychotherapy and female self-concept: Socio-psychological and linguistic analysis of a case example]. Hildesheim: Olms. [14.6]

Beaugrande, R.A. de, & Dressler, W.U. (1981). *Introduction to text linguistics*. London: Longman. [1, 3.6]

Bell, A. (1991). *The language of news media*. Oxford: Blackwell. [14.5]

Bell, A., & Garrett, P. (Eds.). (1998). *Approaches to media discourse*. Oxford: Blackwell. [14.5]

Bereiter, C., & Scardamalia, M. (1987). *The psychology of written composition*. Hillsdale, NJ: Erlbaum. [13.1]

Bhatia, V.K. (1993). *Analyzing genre: Language use in professional settings*. London: Longman. [4.5, 14.3]

Biber, D. (1989). A typology of English texts. *Linguistics, 27*, 3–43. [4.1]

Biber, D., & Conrad, S. (2001). Register variation: A corpus approach. In D. Tannen, D. Schiffrin, & H. Hamilton (Eds.), *The handbook of discourse analysis* (pp. 175–196). Oxford: Blackwell. [8.1]

Blakemore, D.L. (1992). *Understanding utterances*. Oxford: Blackwell. [2.5]

Boden, D. (1994). *The business of talk: Organizations in action*. Cambridge: Polity. [14.1]

Bolinger, D. (1982). *Language, the loaded weapon: The use and abuse of language today*. London: Longman. [14.2]

Bosch, P. (1983). *Agreement and anaphora: A study in the role of pronouns in syntax and discourse*. London: Academic Press. [6.2]

Bourdieu, P. (1991). *Language and symbolic power*. Cambridge: Polity. [15.5]

Bradac, J. (Ed.). (1989). *Message effects in communication science*. London: Sage. [12.3]

Bransford, J., Barclay, J., & Franks, J. (1972). Sentence memory: A constructive versus interpretative approach. *Cognitive Psychology, 3*, 193–209. [13.4]

Bransford, J., & Johnson, M. (1973). Considerations of some problems of comprehension. In W.G. Chase (Ed.), *Visual information processing* (pp. 383–438). London: Academic Press. [3.6, 4.6, 13.3]

Briggs, C. (Ed.). (1996). *Disorderly discourse, narrative conflict and inequality*. Oxford: Oxford University Press. [11.4]

Brinton, L. (1996). *Pragmatic markers in English: Grammaticalization and discourse functions*. Berlin: Mouton de Gruyter. [9.4]

Britton, B.K., & Black, J.B. (Eds.). (1985). *Understanding expository text: A theoretical and practical handbook for analyzing explanatory text*. Hillsdale, NJ: Erlbaum. [10.2]

Britton, B.K., & Graesser, A.C. (Eds.). (1996). *Models of understanding text*. Mahwah, NJ: Erlbaum. [13.4]

Broek, P. van den, Linzie, B., Fletcher, C., & Marsolek, C. (2000). The role of causal discourse structure in narrative writing. *Memory and Cognition, 28*, 711–721. [11.3]

Brown, P., & Levinson, S.C. (1990). *Politeness: Some universals in language usage*. Cambridge: Cambridge University Press. [2.6]

Brown, G., & Yule, G. (1983). *Discourse analysis*. Cambridge: Cambridge University Press. [1, 3.4, 3.6, 5.2, 7.2, 7.4]

Bruthiaux, P. (1996). *The discourse of classified advertising*. New York: Oxford University Press. [14.1]

Bucholtz, M., Liang, A., & Sutton, L. (Eds.). (1999). *Reinventing identities: The gendered self in discourse*. Oxford: Oxford University Press. [15.3]

Bühler, K. (1990). *Theory of language: The representational function of language* (D.F. Goodwin, Trans.). Amsterdam: Benjamins. (Original work published 1934) [2.1, 6.2, 7.1]

Burgoon, M. (1989). Messages and persuasive effects. In J.J. Bradac (Ed.), *Message effects in communication science* (pp. 129–164). London: Sage. [12.3]

Caldas-Coulthard, C., & Leeuwen, T. van (2002). Stunning, shimmering, iridescent: Toys as the representation of gendered social actors. In L. Litosseliti & J. Sunderland (Eds.), *Gender identity and discourse analysis* (pp. 91–108). Amsterdam: Benjamins. [15.3]

Carroll, J., & Casagrande, J. (1958). The function of language classifications in behavior. In E. Maccoby, T. Newcomb & E. Hartley (Eds.), *Readings in social psychology* (pp. 18–31). New York: Henry Holt. [15.1]

Carroll, J. (1960). Vectors of prose style. In T.A. Sebeok (Ed.), *Style in language* (pp. 283–292). Cambridge, MA: MIT Press. [8.4]

Carston, R. (2002). *Thoughts and utterances: The pragmatics of explicit communication.* Malden, MA: Blackwell. [2.5]

Cazden, C. (1988). *Classroom discourse: The language of teaching and learning.* Portsmouth, NH: Heinemann. [14.1]

Chafe, W.L. (1976). Givenness, contrastiveness, definiteness, subjects, topics and point of view. In C.N. Li (Ed.), *Subject and topic* (pp. 25–55). New York: Academic Press. [7.4]

Chafe, W.L. (1982). Integration and involvement in speaking, writing and oral literature. In D. Tannen (Ed.), *Spoken and written language: Exploring orality and literacy* (pp. 35–53). Norwood, NJ: Ablex. [4.2]

Chafe, W.L. (1994). *Discourse, consciousness, and time: The flow and displacement of conscious experience in speaking and writing.* Chicago: University of Chicago Press. [13.1]

Cherny, L. (1999). *Conversation and community: Chat in a virtual world.* Stanford, CA: CSLI Publications. [4.4]

Chiaro, D. (1992). *The language of jokes: Analyzing verbal play.* London: Routledge. [2 of 4]

Chilton, P., & Schäffner, C. (Eds.). (2002). *Politics as text and talk: Analytical approaches to political discourse.* Amsterdam: Benjamins. [14.2]

Clark, H.H. (1996). *Using language.* Cambridge: Cambridge University Press. [2.4, 3.3, 9.4]

Clark, H.H. (1997). Dogmas of understanding. *Discourse Processes, 23*, 567–598. [13.4]

Clark, H.H., & Haviland, S.E. (1977). Comprehension and the given–new contract. In R.O. Freedle (Ed.), *Discourse production and comprehension* (pp. 1–40). Norwood, NJ: Ablex. [7.4]

Clark, U. (1996). *An introduction to stylistics.* Cheltenham: Stanley Thornes. [8.1]

Coates, J. (Ed.). (1998). *Language and gender: A reader.* Oxford: Blackwell. [15.3]

Cook, G. (1989). *Discourse.* Oxford: Oxford University Press. [1]

Coseriu, E. (1980). *Textlinguistik: Eine Einführung* [Text linguistics: An introduction]. Tübingen: Narr. [1]

Coulthard, M. (1985). *An introduction to discourse analysis.* London: Longman. [1]

Couper-Kuhlen, E., & Kortmann, B. (Eds.). (2000). *Cause, condition, concession, contrast: Cognitive and discourse perspectives.* Berlin: Mouton de Gruyter. [6.3]

Crystal, D. (2001). *Language and the Internet.* Cambridge: Cambridge University Press. [4.4]

Crystal, D., & Davy, D. (1969). *Investigating English style.* London: Longman. [8.3]

Cutting, J. (2002). *Pragmatics and discourse: A resource book for students.* London: Routledge. [3.1]

Davis, B., & Brewer, J. (1997). *Electronic discourse: Linguistic individuals in virtual space.* Albany, NY: State University of New York Press. [4.4]

Davison, A., & Green, A.M. (Eds.). (1988). *Linguistic complexity and text comprehension: Readability issues reconsidered.* Hillsdale, NJ: Erlbaum. [10.1]

Davison, A., & Kantor, R. (1982). On the failure of readability formulas to define readable texts: A case study from adaptations. *Reading Research Quarterly, 17,* 187–209. [10.4]

Delin, J., & Bateman, J. (2002). Describing and critiquing multimodal documents. *Document Design, 3,* 141–155. [4.6]

Dennis, E., & Merrill, J. (1996). *Media debates: Issues in mass communication.* White Plains, NY: Longman. [14.5]

Di Blas, N., & Paolini, P. (2003). There and back again: What happens to phoric elements in a 'web dialogue'. *Document Design, 4,* 194–206. [6.2]

Dijk, T.A. van (1977). *Text and context: Explorations in the semantics and pragmatics of discourse.* London: Longman. [3.4]

Dijk, T.A. van (1980). *Macrostructures: An interdisciplinary study of global structures in discourse, interaction and cognition.* Hillsdale, NJ: Erlbaum. [5.3, 5.4]

Dijk, T.A. van (1984). *Prejudice in discourse: An analysis of ethnic prejudice in cognition and conversation.* Amsterdam: Benjamins. [15.4]

Dijk, T.A. van (Ed.). (1985). *Handbook of discourse analysis* (4 vols.). London: Academic Press. [1]

Dijk, T.A. van (1988). *News analysis: Case studies of international and national news in the press.* Hillsdale, NJ: Erlbaum. [14.5]

Dijk, T.A. van (1993). *Elite discourse and racism.* Newbury Park, CA: Sage. [15.4]

Dijk, T.A. van (1996). Discourse, power and access. In C. Caldas-Coulthard & M. Coulthard (Eds.), *Texts and practices: Readings in Critical Discourse Analysis* (pp. 84–104). London: Routledge. [15.2]

Dijk, T.A. van (Ed.). (1997). *Discourse studies: A multidisciplinary introduction* (2 vols.). London: Sage. [1]

Dijk, T.A. van (1998). *Ideology.* London: Sage. [15.2]

Dillon, G.L. (1981). *Constructing texts: Elements of a theory of composition and style.* Bloomington: Indiana University Press. [10.3]

Dimter, M. (1981). *Textklassenkonzepte heutiger Alltagssprache: Kommunikationssituation, Textfunktion und Textinhalt als Kategorien alltagssprachlicher Textklassifikation* [Text classification concepts of current colloquial language: Communication situation, text function and text content as categories for text classification of colloquial language]. Tübingen: Niemeyer. [4.1]

Downs, C., & Goldhaber. G. (1994). International Communication Association audit. In R. Rubin, P. Palmgreen & H. Sypher (Eds.), *Communication research measures: A sourcebook* (pp. 193–205). New York: Guilford. [10.4]

Drew, P., & Heritage, J. (Eds.). (1992). *Talk at work: Interaction in institutional settings.* Cambridge: Cambridge University Press. [14.1]

Duchan, J.F., Bruder, G.A., & Hewitt, L.E. (Eds.). (1995). *Deixis in narrative: A cognitive science perspective.* Hillsdale, NJ: Erlbaum. [7.1]

Duffy, T. (1985). Readability formulas: What's the use? In T. Duffy & R. Waller (Eds.), *Designing usable texts* (pp. 113–143). Orlando, FL: Academic Press. [10.1]

Duranti, A. (1997). *Linguistic anthropology.* New York: Cambridge University Press. [15.1]

Duranti, A., & Goodwin, C. (Eds.). (1992). *Rethinking context: Language as an interactive phenomenon.* Cambridge: Cambridge University Press. [3.4]

Duszak, A. (Ed.). (1997). *Culture and styles of academic discourse.* Berlin: Mouton de Gruyter. [14.1]

Eco, U. (1966). The narrative structure in Fleming. In U. Eco & O. Del Buono (Eds.), *The Bond affair.* London: McDonald. [11.1]

Edmondson, W.J. (1981). *Spoken discourse: A model for analysis.* London: Longman. [1, 9.3]

Edwards, J. (2001). Transcription in discourse. In D. Tannen, D. Schiffrin, & H. Hamilton (Eds.), *The handbook of discourse analysis* (pp. 321–348). Oxford: Blackwell. [9.1]

Eemeren, F. H. van (Ed.). (2002). *Advances in pragma-dialectics.* Amsterdam: Sic Sat. [12.2]

Eemeren, F.H. van, & Grootendorst, R. (1994). *Studies in pragma-dialectics.* Amsterdam: Sic Sat. [12.2]

Eemeren, F.H. van, Grootendorst, R., Blair, J.A., & Willard, C.A. (Eds.). (1999). *Proceedings of the 4th international conference of the International Society for the Study of Argumentation.* Amsterdam: Sic Sat. [12.2]

Eemeren, F. H. van, Grootendorst, R., & Snoeck Henkemans, F. (1996). *Fundamentals of argumentation theory: A handbook of historical backgrounds and contemporary developments.* Mahwah, NJ: Erlbaum. [12.1]

Eggins, S., & Slade, D. (1997). *Analyzing casual conversation.* London: Cassell. [9.1]

Ehlich, K. (Ed.). (1980). *Erzählen im Alltag* [Narrating in everyday life]. Frankfurt am Main: Suhrkamp. [11.2]

Ehlich, K. (1993). HIAT: A transcription system for discourse data. In J. Edwards & M. Lampert (Eds.), *Talking data: Transcription and coding in discourse research* (pp. 123–148). Hillsdale, NJ: Erlbaum. [9.1]

Ehlich, K. (1995). *The discourse of business negotiation.* Berlin: Mouton de Gruyter. [14.1]

Ehlich, K., & Wagner, J. (Eds.). (1995). *The discourse of business communication.* Berlin: Mouton de Gruyter. [12.4]

Ehrlich, S. (1980). Comprehension of pronouns. *The Quarterly Journal of Experimental Psychology, 32,* 247–255. [6.2]

Enkvist, N.E. (1973). *Linguistic stylistics.* The Hague: Mouton. [8.2]

Epstein, J. (1995). *Altered conditions: Disease, medicine, and storytelling.* New York: Routledge. [14.6]

Fairclough, N. (1992). *Language and power.* London: Longman. [3.6, 15.2]

Fairclough, N. (1995). *Critical discourse analysis: The critical study of language.* London: Longman. [15.2]

Fang, Y.-J. (2001). Reporting the same events? A critical analysis of Chinese print news media texts. *Discourse & Society, 12,* 585–613. [14.5]

Fauconnier, G. (1994). *Mental spaces: Aspects of meaning construction in natural language* (New ed.). Cambridge: Cambridge University Press. [13.3]

Fauconnier, G. (1997). *Mappings in thought and language.* Cambridge: Cambridge University Press. [13.3]

Festinger, L. (1957). *A theory of cognitive dissonance.* Stanford, CA: Stanford University Press. [12.4]

Fetzer, A., & Meierkord, C. (Eds.). (2002). *Rethinking sequentiality: Linguistics meets conversational interaction.* Amsterdam: Benjamins. [9.4]

Field, J. (2003). *Psycholinguistics: A resource book for students.* London: Routledge. [13.1]

Fillenbaum, S. (1974). Pragmatic normalization: Further results for some conjunctive and disjunctive sentences. *Journal of Experimental Psychology, 87,* 93–98. [13.4]

Firbas, J. (1992). *Functional sentence perspective in written and spoken communication.* Cambridge: Cambridge University Press. [5.2]

Flowerdew, J., Li, D, & Tran, S. (2002). Discriminatory news discourse: Some Hong Kong data. *Discourse & Society, 13,* 319–345. [15.4]

Ford, C. (1986). Overlapping relations in text structure. In S. DeLancey & R. Tomlin (Eds.), *Proceedings of the second annual meeting of the Pacific Linguistics Conference* (pp. 107–123). Oregon: University of Oregon. [6.5]

Ford, C. (1993). *Grammar in interaction: Adverbial clauses in American English conversations.* Cambridge: Cambridge University Press. [6.3]

Fowler, H.N. (1977). *Plato in twelve volumes: Vol. 4. Cratilus, Parmenides, Greater Hippias, Lesser Hippias.* London: Heinemann. [2.1]

Fowler, R. (1991). *Language in the news: Discourse and ideology in the press.* London: Routledge. [7.3]

Fowler, R., Hodge, R., Kress, G., & Trew, T. (1979). *Language and control.* London: Routledge & Kegan Paul. [15.2]

Fox, B.A. (1987). *Discourse structure and anaphora: Written and conversational English.* Cambridge: Cambridge University Press. [6.2]

Frank, A.W. (1995). *The wounded storyteller: Body, illness, and ethics.* Chicago: University of Chicago Press. [14.6]

Gardiner, A. (1969). *The theory of speech and language* (2nd ed.). Oxford: Oxford University Press. [2.1]

Gee, J.P. (1999). *An introduction to discourse analysis: Theory and method.* London: Routledge. [1]

Geis, M. (1987). *The language of politics.* New York: Springer Verlag. [14.2]

Georgakopoulou, A., & Goutsos, D. (1997). *Discourse analysis: An introduction.* Edinburgh: Edinburgh University Press. [1]

Gernsbacher, M.A. (1990). *Language comprehension as structure building.* Hillsdale, NJ: Erlbaum. [13.4]

Gernsbacher. M.A., & Givón, T. (Eds.). (1995). *Coherence in spontaneous text.* Amsterdam: Benjamins. [13.4]

Ghadessy, M. (Ed.). (1993). *Register analysis: Theory and practice.* London: Pinter. [8.1]

Gibbons, J. (Ed.). (1994). *Language and the law.* London: Longman. [14.3]

Gibbons, J. (2003). *Forensic linguistics: An introduction to language in the justice system.* Malden, MA: Blackwell. [14.3]

Gibbs, R., & Steen, G. (Eds.). (1999). *Metaphor in cognitive linguistics.* Amsterdam: John Benjamins. [13.6]

Glenberg, A.M. (2002). The indexical hypothesis: Meaning from language, world, and image. In N. Allen (Ed.), *Working with words and images: New steps in an old dance* (pp. 27–42). Westport, CT: Ablex. [4.6]

Glenberg, A.M., & Robertson, D.A. (2000). Symbol grounding and meaning: A comparison of high-dimensional and embodied theories of meaning. *Journal of Memory and Language, 43,* 379–401. [13.6]

Goatly, A. (2000). *Critical reading and writing: An introductory coursebook.* London: Routledge. [1]

Goddard, A., & Patterson, L. (2000). *Language and gender.* London: Routledge. [15.3]

Goetz, E., Anderson, R., & Schallert, D. (1981). The representation of sentences in memory. *Journal of Verbal Learning and Verbal Behavior, 20,* 369–385. [13.4]

Goffman, E. (1956). *The presentation of self in every day life.* Edinburgh: University of Edinburgh Press. [2.6]

Goffman, E. (1967). On face-work: An analysis of ritual elements in social interaction. In E. Goffman (Ed.), *Interaction ritual: Essays in face-to face behavior* (pp. 5–45). Chicago: Aldine. [2.6]

Goffman, E. (1974). *Frame analysis: An essay on the organization of experience.* New York: Harper & Row. [13.4]

Goffman, E. (1981). *Forms of talk.* Oxford: Blackwell. [2.6]

Goodwin, C. (1981). *Conversational organization: Interaction between speakers and hearers.* New York: Academic Press. [9.3]

Graesser, A.C., & Bower, G.H. (Eds.). (1990). *Inferences and text comprehension.* New York: Academic Press. [7.6]

Graesser, A.C., Gernsbacher, M.A., & Goldman, S.R. (Eds.). (2003). *Handbook of discourse processes.* Mahwah, NJ: Erlbaum. [13.4]

Graumann, C.F., & Kallmeyer, W. (Eds.). (2002). *Perspective and perspectivation in discourse.* Amsterdam: Benjamins. [7.3]

Grice, H.P. (1975). Logic and conversation. In P. Cole & J.L. Morgan (Eds.), *Syntax and semantics: Vol. 3. Speech acts* (pp. 41–58). New York: Academic Press. [2.4]

Grimes, J.E. (1975). *The thread of discourse.* The Hague: Mouton. [6.3]

Green, G.M. (1989). *Pragmatics and natural language understanding.* Hillsdale, NJ: Erlbaum. [3.1]

Green, J.L., & Harker, J.O. (Eds.). (1988). *Multiple perspective analyses of classroom discourse.* Norwood, NJ: Ablex. [14.1]

Grootendorst, R. (1987). Some fallacies about fallacies. In F. van Eemeren, R. Grootendorst, J. Blair & C. Willard (Eds.), *Argumentation: Across the lines of discipline* (pp. 331–342). Dordrecht: Foris. [12.2]

Grosz, B., & Sidner, C. (1986). Attention, intention and the structure of discourse. *Computational Linguistics, 12,* 175–204. [6.5]

Grundy, P. (2000). *Doing pragmatics* (2nd ed.). London: Arnold. [2.5, 3.1]

Gumperz, J. (1982). *Discourse strategies.* Cambridge: Cambridge University Press. [15.5]

Gumperz, J., & Levinson, S.C. (Eds.). (1996). *Rethinking linguistic relativity.* Cambridge: Cambridge University Press. [15.1]

Gunnarsson, B.L. (1984). Functional comprehensibility of legislative texts: Experiments with a Swedish act of parliament. *Text, 4,* 71–105. [10.4]

Gunnarsson, B.L. (1989). Text comprehensibility and the writing process: The case of law and lawmaking. *Written Communication, 6,* 86–107. [14.3]

Habermas, J. (1981). *Theorie des Kommunikativen Handeln: Bd. 1. Handelungsrationalität und gesellschaftliche Rationalisierung* [The theory of communicative action: Vol. 1. Reason and the rationalization of society]. Frankfurt am Main: Suhrkamp. [2.2]

Haiman, J., & Thompson, S. (Eds.). (1988). *Clause combining in grammar and discourse.* Amsterdam: Benjamins. [6.3]

Hall, K., & Bucholtz, M. (Eds.). (1995). *Gender articulated: Language and the socially constructed self.* London: Routledge. [15.3]

Halliday, M.A.K. (1978). *Language as social semiotic: The social interpretation of language and meaning.* London: Arnold. [3.5]

Halliday, M.A.K. (1994). *An introduction to functional grammar* (2nd edition). London: Arnold. [3.5]

Halliday, M.A.K., & Hasan, R. (1976). *Cohesion in English.* London: Longman. [6.1, 6.2]

Halliday, M.A.K., & Hasan, R. (1985). *Language, context, and text: Aspects of language in a social-semiotic perspective.* Victoria: Deakin University. [3.5]

Hamilton, M., Hunter, J., & Burgoon, M. (1990). An empirical test of an axiomatic model of the relationship between language intensity and persuasion. *Journal of Language and Social Psychology, 9,* 235–255. [8.4]

Hargie, O., Tourish, D., & Wilson, N. (2002). Communication audits and the effects of increased information: A follow-up study. *Journal of Business Communication, 39,* 414–436. [10.4]

Harris, Z. (1952). Discourse analysis. *Language, 28,* 1–30. [1]

Hayes, J.R. (1996). A new framework for understanding cognition and affect in writing. In C.M. Levy & S. Ransdell (Eds.), *The science of writing: Theories, methods, individual differences, and applications* (pp. 1–27). Mahwah, NJ: Erlbaum. [13.1]

Have, P. ten (1999). *Doing conversation analysis: A practical guide.* London: Sage. [9.1]

Haviland, S.E., & Clark, H.H. (1974). What's new? Acquiring new information as a process in comprehension. *Journal of Learning and Verbal Behavior, 13,* 512–521. [7.6]

Heisler, T. (1996). OK, a dynamic discourse marker in Montreal French. In J. Arnold, R. Blake, B. Davidson, S. Schwenter & J. Solomon (Eds.), *Sociolinguistic variation: Data, theory and Analysis* (pp. 293–312). Stanford, CA: CSLI Publications. [9.4]

Hellinger, M., & Bußmann, H. (Eds.). (2003). *Gender across languages: The linguistic representation of women and men* (3 vols.). Amsterdam: Benjamins. [15.3]

Henne, H., & Rehbock, H. (1982). *Einführung in die Gesprächsanalyse* [Introduction to conversation analysis]. Berlin: De Gruyter. [1]

Herring, S. (1996). *Computer-mediated communication: Linguistic, social, and cross-cultural perspectives.* Amsterdam: Benjamins. [4.4]

Hicks, D. (Ed.). (1996). *Discourse, learning, and schooling.* Cambridge: Cambridge University Press. [14.1]

Hillocks, G. (1986). *Research on written composition: New directions for teaching.* New York: NCRE. [13.1]

Hodge, R., & Kress, G. (1993). *Language as ideology* (2nd ed.). London: Routledge. [15.2]

Hoeken, H. (2001). Convincing citizens: The role of argument quality. In D. Janssen & R. Neutelings (Eds.), *Reading and writing public documents* (pp. 147–169). Amsterdam: Benjamins. [12.4]

Hoey, M. (1983). *On the surface of discourse.* London: Allen & Unwin. [6.1]

Hoey, M. (2001). *Textual interaction: An introduction to written discourse analysis.* London: Routledge. [1]

Hoffmann, L. (1983). *Kommunikation vor Gericht* [Communication before the court]. Tübingen: Narr. [14.3]

Hofstede, G. (1997). *Cultures and organizations: Software of the mind* (Rev. ed.). [15.5]

Hofstede, G. (2001). *Culture's consequences: Comparing values, bahaviors, institutions, and organizations across nations* (2nd ed.). London: Sage. [15.5]

Holmes, J., & Meyerhoff, M. (Eds.). (2003). *The handbook of language and gender.* Malden, MA: Blackwell. [15.3]

Hosman, L., Huebner, T., & Siltanen, S. (2002). The impact of power-of-speech style, argument strength, and need for cognition on impression formation, cognitive responses, and persuasion. *Journal of Language and Social Psychology, 21*, 361–379. [12.4]

Hovy, E., & Scott, D. (Eds.). (1996). *Computational and conversational discourse: Burning issues: An interdisciplinary account.* Berlin: Springer. [6.5]

Howard, D. (1990). Rhetorical question effects on message processing and persuasion: The role of information availability and the elicitation of judgment. *Journal of Experimental Social Psychology, 26*, 217–239. [8.4]

Humboldt, W. von (1836). *Uber die Verschiedenheit des menslichen Sprachbaues und ihren Einfluss auf die geistige Entwicklung des Menschengeschlechts* (Bd. 7) [On the variety of human language construction and its influence on the mental development of mankind (Vol. 7)]. Berlin: Königliche Akademie der Wissenschaften. [8.1, 15.1]

Hunt, K.W. (1970). Syntactic maturity in schoolchildren and adults. *Monographs of the society for research in child development, 35*, 1–67. [13.2]

Hutchby, I., & Wooffitt, R. (1998). *Conversation analysis: Principles, practices and applications.* Cambridge: Polity Press. [9.1]

Hymes, D. (1972). Models of the interaction of language and social life. In J.J. Gumperz & D. Hymes (Eds.), *Directions in sociolinguistics: The etnography of communication* (pp. 35–71). New York: Holt, Rinehart and Winston. [3.4]

Jakobson, R. (1960). Closing statement: Linguistics and poetics. In T.A. Sebeok (Ed.), *Style in language* (pp. 350–377). Cambridge, MA: MIT Press. [4.1, 4.3]

Jansen, C., & Steehouder, M. (2001). How research can lead to better government forms. In D. Janssen & R. Neutelings (Eds.), *Reading and writing public documents* (pp. 12–36). Amsterdam: Benjamins. [14.4]

Janssen, D., & Neutelings, R. (Eds.). (2001). *Reading and writing public documents.* Amsterdam: Benjamins. [14.4]

Jarvella, R. (1971). Syntactic processing of connected speech. *Journal of Verbal Learning and Verbal Behavior, 10*, 409–416. [13.4]

Jaworski, A. (Ed.). (1997). *Silence: Interdisciplinary perspectives.* Berlin: Mouton de Gruyter. [9.2]

Jaworski, A., & Coupland, N. (1999). *The discourse reader.* London: Routledge. [1]

Jefferson, G. (1978). Sequential aspects of storytelling in conversation. In J. Schenkein (Ed.), *Studies in the organization of conversational interaction* (pp. 219–248). New York: Academic Press. [9.1]

Jespersen, O. (1924). *The philosophy of grammar.* London: Allen & Unwin. [2.1]

Johnson-Laird, P.N. (1983). *Mental models: Towards a cognitive science of language, inference, and consciousness.* Cambridge: Cambridge University Press. [13.3]

Johnstone, B. (2002). *Discourse analysis.* Oxford: Blackwell. [1]

Jonassen, D. (1982). Advance organizers in text. In D. Jonassen (Ed.), *The technology of text* (pp. 253–275). Englewood Cliffs, NJ: Educational Technology. [5.4]

Jones, S. (Ed.). (1995). *Cybersociety: Computer-mediated communication and community.* Thousand Oaks, CA: Sage. [4.4]

Jong, M. de, & Schellens, P. (1997). Reader-focused text-evaluation: An overview of goals and methods. *Journal of Business and Technical Communication, 11*, 402–432. [10.2]

Jucker, A., & Smith, S. (1998). And people just you know like 'wow': Discourse markers as negotiating strategies. In A. Jucker & Y. Ziv (Eds.), *Discourse markers: Descriptions and theory.* Amsterdam: Benjamins. [9.4]

Jurafsky, D., & Martin, J. (2000). *Speech and language processing: An introduction to natural language processing, computational linguistics and speech recognition.* Up Saddle River, NJ: Prentice Hall. [6.2]

Kallmeyer, W., et al. (1980). *Lekturekolleg zur Textlinguistik: Bd. 1. Einführung* [Lecture on text linguistics: Vol. 1. Introduction]. Königstein: Athenäum. [6.2]

Kalverkämper, H. (1981). *Orientierung zur Textlinguistik* [Orientation towards text linguistics]. Tübingen: Niemeyer. [1]

Kennedy, G.A. (1994). *A new history of classical rhetoric.* Princeton, NJ: Princeton University Press. [8.1]

Kent, T. (Ed.). (1999). *Post-process theory: Behind the writing-process paradigm.* Carbondale, IL: Southern Illinois University Press. [13.2]

Kintsch, W. (1988). The role of knowledge in discourse comprehension: A construction- integration model. *Psychological Review, 95,*163–182. [13.5]

Kintsch, W. (1998). *Comprehension: A paradigm for cognition.* Cambridge: Cambridge University Press. [5.1, 13.5, 13.6]

Kintsch, W., & Dijk, T.A. van (1978). Toward a model of text comprehension and production. *Psychological review, 85,* 363–394. [13.4, 13.5]

Kintsch, W., & Vipond, D. (1979). Reading comprehension and readability in educational practice and psychological theory. In L.G. Nilsson (Ed.), *Perspectives on memory research* (pp. 329–365). Hillsdale, NJ: Erlbaum. [10.1]

Kirsch, G., & Roen, D.H. (1990). *A sense of audience in written communication.* Newbury Park, CA: Sage. [13.1]

Klein-Braley, C. (1982). On the suitability of cloze tests as measures of reading comprehension. *Toegepaste Taalwetenschap in Artikelen,* 13, 49–61. [10.2]

Knott, A. (1993). Using cue phrases to determine a set of rhetorical relations. In O. Rambow (Ed.), *Intentionality and structure in discourse relations: Proceedings of the ACL SIGGEN Workshop* (pp. 48–51). Columbus: Ohio State University. [6.5]

Knott, A. & Sanders, T. (1998). The classification of coherence relations and their linguistic markers: An exploration of two languages. *Journal of Pragmatics, 30,* 135–175. [6.5]

Koenig, J.-P. (Ed.). (1998). *Discourse and cognition: Bridging the gap.* Stanford, CA: CSLI. [13.4]

Kress, G. (1989). *Linguistic processes in sociocultural practice.* Oxford: Oxford University Press. [3.5]

Kress, G., & Leeuwen, T. van (2001). *Multimodal discourse: The modes and media of contemporary communication.* London: Arnold. [4.6]

Kuno, S. (1987). *Functional syntax: Anaphora, discourse and empathy.* Chicago: University of Chicago Press. [7.3]

Kuppevelt, J. van (1995). Discourse structure, topicality and questioning. *Journal of Linguistics, 31,* 109–147. [4.2]

Kyratzis, A. (1999). Narrative identity: Preschoolers' self-construction through narrative in friendship group dramatic play. *Narrative Inquiry, 9,* 427–455. [11.4]

Labov, W., & Fanshel, D. (1977). *Therapeutic discourse.* New York: Academic Press. [14.6]

Labov, W., & Waletzky, J. (1967). Narrative analysis: Oral versions of personal experience. In J. Helm (Ed.), *Essays on the verbal and visual arts* (pp. 12–44). Seattle: University of Washington Press. [11.2]

Lakoff, G. (1987). *Women, fire and dangerous things: What categories tell us about the nature of thought*. Chicago: University of Chicago Press. [15.1]

Lakoff, G. (1990). *Talking power: The politics of language in our lives*. New York: Basic Books. [15.5]

Lakoff, G., & Johnson, M. (1980). *Metaphors we live by*. Chicago: University of Chicago Press. [13.6]

Lakoff, R. (1975). *Language and woman's place*. New York: Harper and Row. [15.3]

Landauer, T., & Dumais, S. (1997). A solution to Plato's problem: The Latent Semantic Analysis theory of acquisition, induction and representation of knowledge. *Psychological Review, 104*, 211–240. [13.6]

Langacker, R.W. (1999). *Grammar and conceptualization*. Berlin: Mouton de Gruyter. [13.3]

Langacker, R.W. (2002). *Concept, image, and symbol: The cognitive basis of grammar* (2nd ed.). Berlin: Mouton de Gruyter. [13.3]

Lanham, R.A. (1991). *A handlist of rhetorical terms* (2nd ed.). Berkeley: University of California Press. [8.1]

Lasswell, H. (1948). The structure and function of communication in society. In L. Bryson (Ed.), *The communication of ideas*. New York: Harper and Row. [12.3]

Lavendera, B. (1988). The study of language in its socio-culural context. In F.J. Newmeyer (Ed.), *Linguistics: The Cambridge Survey: Vol. 4. Language: The socio-cultural context* (pp. 1–13). Cambridge: Cambridge University Press. [15.5]

Lee, D. (2001). *Cognitive linguistics: An introduction*. Melbourne: Oxford University Press. [13.3]

Leech, G.N. (1983). *Principles of pragmatics*. London: Longman. [2.5, 2.6]

Leeuwen, T. van (1996). The representation of social actors. In C. Caldas-Coulthard & M. Coulthard (Eds.), *Texts and practices: Readings in Critical Discourse Analysis* (pp. 32–70). [15.2]

Lentz, L., & Pander Maat, H. (Eds.). (1997). *Discourse analysis and evaluation: Functional approaches*. Amsterdam: Rodopi. [10.3]

Levelt, W.J.M. (1982). Cognitive styles in the use of spatial direction terms. In R.J. Jarvella & W. Klein (Eds.), *Speech, place and action: Studies in deixis and related topics* (pp. 251–268). Chichester: Wiley. [7.1]

Levelt, W.J.M. (1989). *Speaking: From intention to articulation*. Cambridge, MA: MIT Press. [4.2, 7.1, 13.1]

Levinson, S.C. (1983). *Pragmatics*. Cambridge: Cambridge University Press. [2.6, 3.1, 7.1, 7.5, 9.2]

Levy, M., & Randell, S. (Eds.). (1996). *The science of writing: Theories, methods, individual differences, and applications*. Hillsdale, NJ: Erlbaum. [13.2]

Liebert, W.-A., Redeker, G., & Waugh, L. (Eds.). (1997). *Discourse and perspective in cognitive linguistics*. Amsterdam: Benjamins. [13.4]

Linde, C. (1993). *Life stories: The creation of coherence*. Oxford: Oxford University Press. [11.4]

Litosseliti, L., & Sunderland, J. (Eds.). (2002). *Gender identity and discourse analysis*. Amsterdam: Benjamins. [15.3]

Longacre, R.E. (1996). *The grammar of discourse* (2nd ed.). New York: Plenum Press. [6.3]

Louwerse, M., & Peer, W. van der (Eds.). (2002). *Thematics: Interdisciplinary studies*. Amsterdam: Benjamins. [5.2]

Luhmann, N. (1970 & 1975). *Soziologische Aufklärung* (Bd. 1 & 2) [Sociological clarification (Vols. 1 & 2)]. Opladen: Westdeutscher Verlag. [14.1]

Mac Cormac, E. (1985). *A cognitive theory of metaphor.* Cambridge, MA: MIT Press. [13.6]

Macdonell, D. (1986). *Theories of discourse: An introduction.* Oxford: Blackwell. [3.6]

Malinowski, B. (1930). The problem of meaning in primitive languages. In C.K. Ogden & I.A. Richards (Eds.), *The meaning of meaning* (pp. 296–336). London: Routledge and Kegan Paul. [4.1]

Mandler, J.M., & Johnson, N.S. (1977). Remembrance of things parsed: Story structure and recall. *Cognitive Psychology, 9,* 111–151. [11.3]

Mann, W.C., & Thompson, S.A. (1988). Rhetorical Structure Theory: Toward a functional theory of text organisation. *Text, 8,* 243–281. [6.4]

Mann, W.C., & Thompson, S.A. (Eds.). (1992). *Discourse description: Diverse linguistic analyses of a fund-raising text.* Amsterdam: Benjamins. [1]

Mann, W.C., & Thompson, S.A. (2001). Deux perspectives sur la théorie de la structure Rhétorique [Two views of Rhetorical Structure Theory]. *Verbum, 23,* 9–30. [6.4]

Martin, J. (1992). *English text: System and structure.* Amsterdam: Benjamins. [3.5]

Martin, J., & Rose, D. (2002). *Working with discourse: Meaning beyond the clause.* London: Continuum. [3.5]

Mayer, R. (1979). Twenty years of research on advance organizers: Assimilation theory is still the best predictor of results. *Instructional Science, 8,* 133–167. [5.4]

McCarthy, M. (1991). *Discourse analysis for language teachers.* Cambridge: Cambridge University Press. [1]

McCroskey, J.C. (1986). An introduction to rhetorical communication (5th ed.). Englewood Cliffs, NJ: Prentice-Hall. [12.1]

McLaughlin, M.L. (1984). *Conversation: How talk is organized.* Beverly Hills, CA: Sage. [1, 9.2]

McMenamin, G. (1993). *Forensic stylistics.* Amsterdam: Elsevier. [8.3, 14.3]

Mey, J. (2001). *Pragmatics: An introduction* (2nd ed.). Malden, MA: Blackwell. [3.1]

Miller, G. (1956). The magical number seven, plus or minus two: Some limits on our capacity for processing information. *Psychological Review, 63,* 81–97. [13.4]

Mishler, E. (1984). *The discourse of medicine.* Norwoord, NJ: Ablex. [14.6]

Moore, J., & Pollack, M. (1992). A problem for RST: The need for multi-level discourse analysis. *Computational Linguistics, 18,* 537–544. [6.5]

Morris, C. (1938). *Foundations of the theory of signs.* Chicago: University of Chicago Press. [3.1]

Morris, P. (Ed.). (1994). *The Bakhtin reader: Selected writings of Bakhtin, Medvedev and Voloshinov.* London: Arnold. [4.2]

Moser, M., & Moore, J. (1996). Toward a synthesis of two accounts of discourse structure. *Computational Linguistics, 22,* 409–419. [6.5]

Myers, J. L., & O'Brien, E. J. (1998). Accessing the discourse representation during reading. *Discourse Processes, 26,* 131–157. [13.5]

Ng, S.H., & Bradac, J.J. (1993). *Power in language: Verbal communication and social influence.* Newbury Park, CA: Sage. [15.2]

Nielsen, J. (1999). *Designing web usability: The practice of simplicity.* Indianapolis, IN: New Riders Press. [4.4]

Niemeier, S., & Dirven, R. (Eds.). (2000). *Evidence for linguistic relativity.* Amsterdam: Benjamins. [15.1]

Nofsinger, R.E. (1991). *Everyday conversation.* London: Sage. [1, 9.3]

Noordman, L., & Vonk, W. (1992). Reader's knowledge and the control of inferences in reading. *Language and Cognitive Processes, 7,* 373–391. [7.6]

Noordman, L., & Vonk, W. (1999). Discourse comprehension. In A. Friederici (Ed.), *Language comprehension: A biological perspective* (pp. 229–263). [13.4]

Nunan, D. (1987). *Introducing discourse analysis.* London: Penguin. [1]

Nystrand, M. (1986). *The structure of written communication: Studies in reciprocity between writers and readers.* Orlando, FL: Academic Press. [4.2]

Ochs, E., Schegloff, E.A., & Thompson, S.A. (Eds.). (1996). *Interaction and grammar.* Cambridge: Cambridge University Press. [9.3]

O'Keefe, D. (2002). Persuasion: Theory and research (2nd ed.). Thousand Oaks, CA: Sage. [12.4]

Orr, J. (1996). *Talking about machines: An etnography of a modern job.* London: Cornell University Press. [11.4]

Ortony, A. (Ed.). (1993). *Metaphor and thought* (2nd ed.). Cambridge: Cambridge University Press. [8.3]

Osgood, C. (1971). Where do sentences come from? In D. Steinberg & L. Jakobovits (Eds.), *Semantics: An interdisciplinary reader in philosophy, linguistics and psychology* (497–529). Cambridge: Cambridge University Press. [7.4]

Otero, J., León, J.A., & Graesser, A.C. (Eds.). (2002). *The psychology of science text comprehension.* Mahwah, NJ: Erlbaum. [13.4]

Peccei, J. Stilwell (1999). *Pragmatics.* London: Routledge. [3.1]

Pêcheux, M. (1969). *Analyse automatique du discours* [Automatic discourse analysis]. Paris: Dunod. [15.2]

Pemberton, L., & Shurville, S. (Eds.). (2000). *Words on the web: Computer-mediated communication.* Exeter: Intellect. [4.4]

Petty, R.E., & Cacioppo, J.T. (1986). *Communication and persuasion: Central and peripheral routes to attitude change.* New York: Springer. [12.3]

Philips, S. (1998). *Ideology in the language of judges: How judges practice law, politics and courtroom control.* Oxford: Oxford University Press. [14.3]

Platt, F.W. (Ed.). (1995). *Conversation repair: Case studies in doctor–patient communication.* Boston: Little, Brown. [14.6]

Polanyi, L., & Berg, M.H. van den (1996). Discourse structure and discourse contexts. In P. Dekker & M. Stokhof (Eds.), *Proceedings of the 10th Amsterdam Colloquium* (pp.113–131). Amsterdam: University of Amsterdam. [5.4]

Ponterotto, D. (2003). The cohesive role of cognitive metaphor in discourse and conversation. In A. Barcelona (Ed.), *Metaphor and metonymy at the crossroads: A cognitive perspective* (pp. 283–298). Berlin: Mouton de Gruyter. [13.6]

Price, J, & Price, L. (2002). *Hot text: Web writing that works.* Indianapolis, IN: New Riders Press. [4.4]

Prince, E.F. (1981). Toward a taxonomy of given–new information. In P. Cole (Ed.), *Radical pragmatics* (pp. 223–255). New York: Academic Press. [7.4]

Prince, E.F. (1997). On the functions of left-dislocation in English discourse. In A. Kamio (Ed.), *Directions in functional linguistics* (pp. 117–143). Amsterdam: Benjamins. [7.4]

Propp, V.J. (1968). *Morphology of the folktale* (2nd edition). (S. Pírková-Jakobsonová, Ed., L. Scott, Trans.). Bloomington: Indiana University. (Original work published 1928) [11.1]

Propp, V.J. (1984). *Theory and history of folklore* (A. Liberman, Ed., A. Martin & P. Martin, Trans.). Manchester: Manchester University Press. (Original work published 1946) [11.1]

Queneau, R. (1981). *Exercises in style* (B. Wright, Trans.). New York: New Directions. (Original work published 1947) [8.1]

Raffler-Engel, W. von (Ed.). (1990). *Doctor–patient interaction.* Amsterdam: Benjamins. [14.6]

Rambow, O. (Ed.). (1993). *Intentionality and structure in discourse relations: Proceedings of the ACL SIGGEN Workshop.* Columbus: Ohio State University. [6.5]

Reid, T.B.W (1956). Linguistics, structuralism and philology. *Archivum Linguisticum, 8,* 28–37. [8.1]

Reisigl, M., & Wodak, R. (2001). *Discourse and discrimination: Rhetorics of racism and antisemitism.* London: Routledge and Keagan Paul. [15.4]

Renkema, J. (1984). Text linguistics and media: An experimental inquiry into coloured news reporting. In W. van Peer & J. Renkema (Eds.), *Pragmatics and stylistics* (pp. 317–371). Leuven: Acco. [7.3]

Renkema, J. (2001). Undercover research into text quality as a tool for communication management: The case of the Dutch tax department. In D. Janssen & R. Neutelings (Eds.), *Reading and writing public documents* (pp. 37–57). Amsterdam: Benjamins. [10.3]

Renkema, J., & Hoeken, H. (1998). The influence of negative newspaper publicity on corporate image in the Netherlands. *Journal of Business Communication, 35,* 521–535. [14.5]

Rijn-van Tongeren, G. van (1997). *Metaphors in medical texts.* Amsterdam: Rodopi. [14.6]

Roberts, C., Davies, E., & Jupp, T. (1992). *Language and discrimination: A study of communication in multi-ethnic workplaces.* London: Longman. [15.4]

Rouet, J.-F., Levonen, J., & Dillon, A. (Eds.). (1996). *Hypertext and cognition.* Mahwah, NJ: Erlbaum. [4.4]

Roulet, E. (1984). Speech acts, discourse structure, and pragmatic connectives. *Journal of Pragmatics, 8,* 31–47. [4.2]

Sacks, H., Jefferson, G., & Schegloff, E.A. (1992). Lectures on conversation (2 vols.). Oxford: Blackwell. [9.1]

Sacks, H., Schlegloff, E.A., & Jefferson, G. (1974). A simplest systematics for the organization of turn-taking for conversation. *Language, 50,* 696–735. [9.2]

Salkie, R. (1995). *Text and discourse analysis.* London: Routledge. [1]

Sandell, R. (1977). Linguistic style and persuasion. London: Academic Press. [8.4]

Sanders, T., Schilperoord, J., & Spooren, W. (Eds.). (2001). Text representation: Linguistic and psycholinguistic aspects. Amsterdam: Benjamins. [6.5]

Sanders, T., & Spooren, W. (1999). Communicative intentions and coherence relations. In W. Bublitz, U. Lenk & E. Ventola (Eds.), *Coherence in spoken and written discourse* (pp. 235–250). Amsterdam: Benjamins. [6.5]

Sanders, T., Spooren, W., & Noordman, L. (1992). Towards a taxonomy of coherence relations. *Discourse Processes, 15,* 1–36. [6.5]

Sanford, A.J. (1990). On the nature of text-driven inference. In D.A. Balota, G.B. Flores d'Arcais & K. Rayner (Eds.), *Comprehension processes in reading* (pp. 515–535). Hillsdale, NJ: Erlbaum. [7.6]

Sanford, A.J., & Garrod, S.C. (1981). *Understanding written language: Explorations of comprehension beyond the sentence.* Chicester: Wiley. [6.2, 13.4]

Sapir, E. (1949). Selected writings of Edward Sapir in language, culture, and personality. Berkeley: University of California Press. [15.1]

Sarangi, S., & Slembrouck, S. (1996). *Language, bureaucracy & social control.* London: Longman. [14.4]

Schank, R.C., & Abelson, R.P. (1977). *Scripts, plans, goals and understanding: An inquiry into human knowledge structures.* Hillsdale, NJ: Erlbaum. [13.4]

Schank, R.C., & Lebowitz, M. (1980). Levels of understanding in computers and people. *Poetics, 9,* 251–273. [13.3]

Schegloff, E.A., & Sacks, H. (1973). Opening up closings. *Semiotica, 8,* 289–327. [9.3]

Schegloff, E.A. (1977). On some questions and ambiguities in conversation. In W. Dressler (Ed.), *Current trends in textlinguistics* (pp. 81–102). Berlin: De Gruyter. [9.3]

Scherner, M. (1984). *Sprache als Text* [Language as text]. Tübingen: Niemeyer. [1]

Schiffrin, D. (1987). *Discourse markers.* Cambridge: Cambridge University Press. [9.4]

Schiffrin, D. (1994). *Approaches to discourse.* Cambridge: Blackwell. [1]

Schiffrin, D. (1997). Stories in answer to questions in research interviews. *Journal of Narrative and Life History, 7,* 129–137. [11.4]

Schiffrin, D., Tannen, D., & Hamilton, H. (Eds.). (2001). *The handbook of discourse analysis.* Oxford: Blackwell. [1]

Schirato, T., & Yell, S. (2000). *Communication and culture: An introduction.* London: Sage. [15.5]

Schriver, K. (1997). *Dynamics in document design: Creating text for readers.* New York: Wiley [10.2]

Scollon, R., & Scollon, S. (2001). *Intercultural communication* (2nd ed.). Oxford: Blackwell. [15.5]

Searle, J.R. (1969). *Speech acts: An essay in the philosophy of language.* Cambridge: Cambridge University Press. [2.2]

Searle, J.R. (1979). *Expression and meaning: Studies in the theory of speech acts.* Cambridge: Cambridge University Press. [2.3]

Searle, J.R., et al. (1992). *(On) Searle on conversation.* Amsterdam: Benjamins. [9.2]

Semino, E., & Culpeper, J. (Eds.). (2002). *Cognitive stylistics: Language and cognition in text analysis.* Amsterdam: Benjamins. [8.4, 13.3]

Shannon, C.E., & Weaver, W. (1949). *The mathematical theory of communication.* Urbana: University of Illinois Press. [3.3]

Shmelev, A. (2001). Manipulation in Russian political journalism. *Studies in Communication Sciences, 1,* 101–116. [14.2]

Shuy, R.W. (1992). *Language crimes: The use and abuse of language evidence in the court room.* Oxford: Blackwell. [14.3]

Singer, M. (1990). *Psychology of language: An introduction to sentence and discourse processes.* Hillsdale, NJ: Erlbaum. [13.3]

Smith, N., & Wilson, D. (1979). *Modern linguistics: The results of Chomsky's revolution.* Brighton: Harvester Press. [2.5]

Smith, R.C. (1996). *The patient's story: Integrated patient-doctor interviewing.* Boston: Little, Brown. [14.6]

Sopory, P., & Dillard, J. (2002). The persuasive effects of metaphor: A meta-analysis. *Human Communication Research, 28,* 382–419. [13.6]

Sowinski, B. (1983). *Textlinguistik: Eine Einführung* [Text linguistics: An introduction]. Stuttgart: Kohlhammer. [1]

Sperber, D., & Wilson, D. (1995). *Relevance, communication and cognition* (2nd ed.). Oxford: Blackwell. [2.5]

Steger, H. et al. (1974). Redekonstellation, Redekonstellationstyp, Textexemplar, Textsorte im Rahmen eines Sprachverhaltenmodells: Begründung einer Forschungshypothese. [A paper about the principles of discourse classification.] In H. Moser (Ed.), *Jahrbuch Gesprochene Sprache* (pp. 39–97). Düsseldorf: Schwann. [4.1]

Stein, N.L., & Policastro, M. (1984). The concept of a story: A comparison between children's and teachers' viewpoints. In H. Mandl, N.L. Stein & T. Trabasso (Eds.), *Comprehension of text* (pp. 113–155). Hillsdale, NJ: Erlbaum. [11.3]

Strunk, W., & White, E. (2000). *The elements of style* (4th ed.). Boston: Ellyn and Bacon. [8.3]

Stubbs, M.W. (1983). *Discourse analysis: The sociolinguistic analysis of natural language.* Oxford: Blackwell. [1, 3.6]

Stubbs, M.W. (1996). *Text and corpus analysis: Computer-assisted studies of language and culture.* Oxford: Blackwell. [14.1]

Sumner, W.G. (1906). *Folkways.* New York: Dover Publications. (Original work published 1906) [14.1]

Swales, J. (1990). *Genre analysis: English in academic and research settings.* Cambridge: Cambridge University Press. [4.5]

Sweetser, E. (1990). *From etymology to pragmatics.* Cambridge: Cambridge University Press. [6.3]

Tannen, D. (1988). *Linguistics in context: Connecting observation and understanding.* Norwood, NJ: Ablex. [3.6]

Tannen, D. (1994). *Gender and discourse.* Oxford: Oxford University Press. [15.3]

Taylor, J.R. (1993). *Rethinking the theory of organizational communication: How to read an organization.* Norwood, NJ: Ablex. [14.1]

Tejera, V. (1988). *Semiotics from Peirce to Barthes: A conceptual introduction to the study of communication, interpretation and expression.* Leiden: Brill. [3.1]

Toolan, M. (2001). *Narrative: A critical linguistic introduction* (2nd ed.). London: Routledge and Keagan Paul. [1]

Toolan, M. (Ed.). (2002). *Critical discourse analysis: Critical concepts in linguistics* (4 vols.). London: Routledge. [15.2]

Torrance, M., & Galbraith, D. (Eds.). (1999). *Knowing what to write: Cognitive perspectives on conceptual processes in text production.* Amsterdam: Amsterdam University Press. [13.2]

Toulmin, S.E. (1958). *The uses of argument.* Cambridge: Cambridge University Press. [12.1]

Tufte, V. (1971). *Grammar as style.* New York: Holt, Rinehart and Winston. [8.3]

Ungerer, F., & Schmid, H.-J. (1996). *An introduction to cognitive linguistics.* London: Longman. [13.3]

Uyl, M. den (1983). A cognitive perspective on text coherence. In K. Ehlich & H. van Riemsdijk (Eds.), *Connectedness in sentence, discourse and text* (pp. 259–283). Tilburg: Tilburg University. [3.6]

Vanderveken, D., & Kubo, S. (Eds.). (2001). *Essays in speech act theory.* Amsterdam: Benjamins. [2.3]

Vanneste, A. (1980). *Unité et multiplicité dans la langue: Essai d'introduction à la problématique de la norme et de la variabilité* [Unity and multiplicity in language: Introduction to the problems of norm and variability](3 vols.). Brussel: Vrije Universiteit. [3.2]

Ventola, E., Charles, C., & Kaltenbacher, M. (Eds.). (2004). *Perspectives on multimodal discourse.* Amsterdam: Benjamins. [4.6]

Verschueren, J., Östman, J.O., & Blommaert, J. (Eds.). (1995). *Handbook of pragmatics*. Amsterdam: Benjamins. [3.1]

Verschueren, J. (1999). *Understanding pragmatics*. Amsterdam: Benjamins. [3.1]

Vonk, W., & Noordman, L. (1990). On the control of inferences in text understanding. In D. Balota, G. Flores d'Arcais & K. Rayner (Eds.), *Comprehension processes in reading* (pp. 447–464). Hillsdale, NJ: Erlbaum. [7.6]

Vorderer, P., Wulff, H., & Friedrichsen M. (Eds.). (1996). *Suspense: Conceptualizations, theoretical analyses, and empirical explorations*. Mahwah, NJ: Erlbaum. [11.3]

Waes, L. van, Woudstra, E., & Hoven, P. van den (Eds.). (1994). *Functional communication quality*. Amsterdam: Rodopi. [10.3]

Wales, K. (1988). Back to the future: Bakhtin, stylistics and discourse. In W. van Peer (Ed.), *The taming of the text* (pp. 176–192). London: Routledge. [4.2]

Walton, D. (1987). *Informal fallacies: Towards a theory of argument criticisms*. Amsterdam: Benjamins. [12.2]

Watzlawick, P., Beavin, J., & Jackson, D. (1967). *Pragmatics of human communication: A study of interactional patterns, pathologies, and paradoxes*. New York: Norton. [3.1]

Weaver, C.A., Mannes, S., & Fletcher, C.R. (Eds.). (1995). *Discourse comprehension: Essays in honor of Walter Kintsch*. Hillsdale, NJ: Erlbaum. [13.4]

Weber, J.J. (Ed.). (1996). *The stylistics reader: From Roman Jakobson to the present*. London: Arnold. [8.4]

Wegener, Ph. (1885). *Untersuchungen über die Grundfragen des Sprachlebens* [Inquiries into the fundamental questions of language survival]. Halle: Niemeyer. [2.1]

Werlich, E. (1982). *A text grammar of English*. Heidelberg: Quelle and Meyer. [4.1]

Werth, P. (1976). Roman Jakobson's verbal analysis of poetry. *Journal of Linguistics, 12*, 21–73. [4.3]

Whorf, B.L. (1956). *Language, thought, and reality: Selected writings of Benjamin Lee Whorf*. New York: Wiley. [15.1]

Widdowson, H. (1998). The theory and practice of Critical Discourse Analysis. *Applied Linguistics, 19*, 136–151. [15.2]

Wierzbicka, A. (1986). Does language reflect culture? Evidence from Australian English. *Language in Society, 15*, 349–374. [15.1]

Wijk, C. van (1999). Conceptual processes in argumentation: A developmental perspective. In M. Torrance & D. Galbraith (Eds.), *Knowing what to write: Conceptual processes in text production* (pp. 31–50). Amsterdam: Amsterdam University Press. [13.1]

Wilson, D. (1975). *Presuppositions and non-truth-conditional semantics*. London: Academic Press. [7.5]

Winter, E. (1976). *Fundamentals of information structure: Pilot manual for further development according to student need* (Mimeograph). Hatfield: Hatfield Polytechnic. [5.2]

Witte, S. P. (1987). Pre-text and composing. *College Composition and Communication, 38*, 397–425. [13.2]

Wodak, R. (1996). *Disorders of discourse*. London: Longman. [14.6]

Wodak, R. (Ed.). (1997). *Gender and discourse*. London: Sage. [15.3]

Yang, A. (1989). Cohesive chains and writing quality. *Word, 40*, 235–254. [10.3]

Yates, S. (1996). Oral and written linguistics aspects of computer conferencing: A corpus based study. In S. Herring (Ed.), *Computer-mediated communication: Linguistic, social and cross-cultural perspectives* (pp. 28–46). Amsterdam: Benjamins. [4.4]

Index